DATE DUE

APR 21 1997	
MAR 26 1999	
NOV 15 2000	
NOV 25 2000	
OCT - 9 2001	
NOV 21 2001	
NOV 1 2003	
NOV 24 2003	
DEC - 9 2003	

BRODART   Cat. No. 23-221

GOVERNOR HENRY ELLIS
AND THE TRANSFORMATION OF
BRITISH NORTH AMERICA

GOVERNOR
HENRY ELLIS

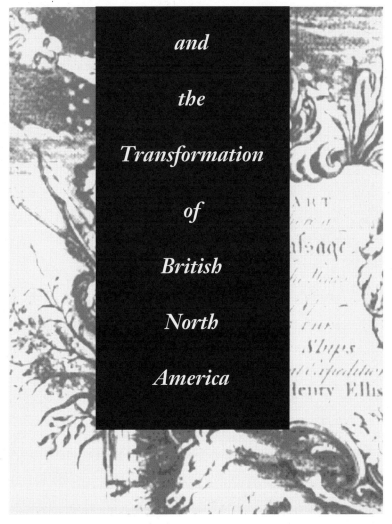

and

the

Transformation

of

British

North

America

EDWARD J. CASHIN

The University of Georgia Press   *Athens and London*

© 1994 by the University of Georgia Press
Athens, Georgia 30602
All rights reserved
Designed by Mary Mendell
Set in Janson Text by Tseng Information Systems, Inc.
Printed and bound by Thomson-Shore, Inc.
The paper in this book meets the guidelines for permanence and
durability of the Committee on Production Guidelines for Book
Longevity of the Council on Library Resources.
Printed in the United States of America

98 97 96 95 94 C 5 4 3 2 1

Library of Congress Cataloging in Publication Data
Cashin, Edward J., 1927–
Governor Henry Ellis and the transformation of British North
America / Edward J. Cashin.
p. cm.
Includes bibliographical references and index.
ISBN 0–8203–1582–6 (alk. paper)
1. Ellis, Henry, 1721–1806. 2. Governors—Georgia—Biography.
3. Georgia—History—Colonial period, ca. 1600–1775. 4. Great
Britain—Colonies—North America—History. I. Title.
F289.E45C37 1994
975.8'03—dc20 93–15730 CIP
British Library Cataloging in Publication Data available

To my son, Ed,
my daughter, Milette,
and to the future

Contents

Maps

Preface

W HETHER IT IS because of the way the original records are filed, or our libraries organized, or our curricula divided, or the tendency of the Western mind to categorize, our histories usually focus on one segment of the past. Colonial histories, for example, are confined within colonial boundaries. South Carolina historians deal with South Carolina and Georgians with Georgia.

The people who actually inhabited colonial America and who made its history were not so restricted. They did not realize that they were traveling from English history to New York history when they took passage from Bristol to New York. People traveled about in the eighteenth century as they do in ours; it just took longer to get from place to place. One attempt to portray the American colonial world authentically is Bernard Bailyn's godlike view of "worlds in motion," great cultural migrations, encounters, and conflicts.

Another way is simpler and easier to manage, and that is to follow an individual about and view his world through his eyes. Henry Ellis is an ideal person to provide us with such a tour. He permits us to visit the Ireland of the English transplantations, to discover what life was like aboard a sailing ship, to go exploring for a northwest passage, to join him in the fellowship of the Royal Society, and to convey a cargo of slaves from Africa to Jamaica. We meet Lord Halifax, the "father of colonies" and begin to see the empire as a whole and Henry Ellis's special mission as governor of Georgia. Ellis's highly successful stay in Georgia was important not only because he taught Georgians how to govern themselves but because it provided him with lessons in the management of the entire British system.

When Ellis left Georgia, far from being consigned to oblivion as Georgia histories suggest by their silence, he became the expert on American affairs to ministers who knew too little about America, and that at a crucial moment in history, the culmination of the Great War for the Empire. Ellis leads us into the labyrinthine world of British politics at the court of George III. The key decisions that were made by the great lords of state were based on the advice of a very few individuals, Henry Ellis prominent among them.

Finally, we accompany him in his genteel retirement as a celebrity and absentee Irish landlord. Like his favored contemporaries, he followed the sun to southern France and to Italy. He was one of the British colony at Naples and a friend of Sir William Hamilton when Lord Nelson came to call on Emma, Lady Hamilton. Nelson's victory at Trafalgar ensured the continuation of the British maritime supremacy which Ellis had promoted and helped to establish.

Hence the career of Henry Ellis can reveal much about the British colonial empire. His years as governor of Georgia and adviser to the secretaries of state witnessed a profound change in British North America. France was eliminated from the contest for the continent; Spain was relegated to New Orleans and west of the Mississippi; new provinces were established; an Indian reserve was created; and new regulations were imposed on old provinces. The massive changes led to another transformation, the separation of the thirteen colonies from the mother country. In short, Henry Ellis was largely responsible for the transformation of Georgia, and the lessons he learned were instrumental in the transformation of British North America.

Like many Georgians, I had known since childhood that Ellis was the middle one of Georgia's three colonial governors. There is an Ellis Square in Savannah, and one of Augusta's oldest streets is Ellis Street. I first became aware that Ellis was a cut above the typical colonial governor by reading William W. Abbot's *Royal Governors of Georgia*. I was convinced that he was exceptional when I perused his letters to William Henry Lyttelton at the William L. Clements Library in Ann Arbor. The letters revealed an intelligent, well-educated, sensitive, and sensible man. John Shy, whom I met at the Clements, encouraged me to take a close look at Ellis's career.

The search was an interesting one. It began with a visit to Monaghan County, Ireland. I want to thank Martha and Ger O'Grady for making me feel at home at Glynch House, Monaghan County. Theo

McMahon was a source of information on the history of Monaghan. Canon Terence Golding of Scotshouse near the border of Northern Ireland gave me a night's lodging and a lesson in current history. We stopped to invite one of his Church of Ireland parishioners to go with us to a community Christmas dinner. "I'll rot in hell before I eat with Papists," he said. In Ireland, the past still sears the souls of these border people.

Jim Derriman helped me find documents in the Public Record Office at Chancery Lane and introduced me to a well-kept secret eatery, "Briefs" in Lincoln's Inn. The American researcher should be warned that the Public Record Office moves very deliberately. The reader is told that it will take forty minutes to deliver an order, but it may be twice that. The person in charge of photocopying is frequently away, at lunch or tea, so the windows of opportunity for doing business are narrow.

Mary Ann and I were grateful that Lord and Lady Cobham let us use their private library at Hagley Hall containing some of the Lyttelton papers and for the secretary, Stanley Hodkinson, who showed us where things were and had tea sent up. The American researcher is advised to write ahead to every place to be visited; a second letter confirming your original request is recommended, as well as a letter of introduction indicating that you really are who you say you are.

I owe a grateful acknowledgment to the staffs of the Linnean Society Library, Burlington House; the library of the Royal Society of Arts; the Wren Library, Trinity College, Cambridge; the West Sussex and Staffordshire Public Record Offices; and the Public Archives in Halifax, Nova Scotia.

W. W. Abbot was both thorough and gracious in his editorial comments. Finally, I must thank my colleague Charles Saggus for his comments on the manuscript, Linda Jones for correcting my punctuation, and Kaye Keel for her good-natured and efficient work in typing. For the third time, I owe thanks to Trudie Calvert for her expert scrutiny of the text. An Augusta College research grant helped defray the travel costs. My wife, Mary Ann, has stood the severest tests of marriage. She accompanied me on most expeditions, was forced to listen to extended passages of the story, and did the indexing. She knows how much I owe her.

GOVERNOR HENRY ELLIS

AND THE TRANSFORMATION OF

BRITISH NORTH AMERICA

CHAPTER ONE

A Monaghan Lad

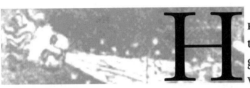ENRY ELLIS was born in the town and county of Monaghan, Ireland, but he never would be of the town and county of Monaghan. He was a third-generation stranger on his native soil. That fact of birth and heritage was both an advantage and a disadvantage in his career. He could never disassociate himself from Monaghan, but neither would he remain there for long. He was fated to be an expatriate, a citizen of the world.

The problem was not in a lack of kindred. His grandfather had provided him with uncles, aunts, and cousins enough. This grandfather was named Thomas; he was the son of John Ellis and the grandson of Sir Thomas Ellis of Wyham, England.[1] That he was descended from gentry was an important element in Henry Ellis's search for identity, perhaps more significant than the place of his birth. He would be a displaced person and a gentleman.

Thomas Ellis, the grandfather, came to Ireland as a settler during the reign of Charles II. The word *settler* had a special connotation in post-Cromwellian Ireland. Monaghan was part of the Ulster Plantation of 1609, a project that coincided with the establishment of the Virginia colony. The two "transplantations" were similar in that the natives in both were to be eliminated to the extent possible to make way for a proper English colony. Similar, too, was the way some of the Irish chiefs fought with the English against other Irish chiefs, just as some native American tribes welcomed the English as allies against ancient enemies. Because the MacMahons and MacHughs of Monaghan had helped the English, they were allowed to retain their traditional lands.

All the rest of the county was given to English planters. Lord Edward Blayney established Monaghan as his garrison town.[2] Blayney was the only true planter in that he brought over English settlers as tenants for his estate.

The landlords, Irish and English alike, were supposed to collect rent from their tenants and in turn pay the government annual fees. This business of renting was entirely foreign to the Irish; the idea of paying the English for lands that they had always owned was intolerable. In 1641 the Ulster Irish rebelled against the system, venting their frustrations on the Ulster Protestants. After the distraction of the English Civil War, Cromwell turned his grim attention to the Irish rebels. By 1650 the rebellion was suppressed and Heber MacMahon's head was spiked to the walls of Enniskillen castle. Cromwellian soldiers pillaged everything of value in Monaghan County. The Irish have long memories of the atrocities committed in those days. "Cromwell still lives," said a perceptive Church of Ireland clergyman in 1990.[3]

The Cromwellian settlement meant simply that all the lands formerly held by the Irish were confiscated. The new owners were English soldiers and speculators. But there were never enough English to displace the native Irish, except in pockets such as Monaghan town. The reason for this incomplete colonization of Monaghan County was the land itself. The Irish inhabitants of Monaghan today admit that their soil is poor and blame the prehistoric glacier for pushing the topsoil further south. The glacier did more than that; it sculpted the terrain in a curious manner, unique to Monaghan. All Irish counties have nicknames, and Monaghan's is "a basket of eggs."[4] The landscape bulges with little rounded hills or "drums," as they are called. The fertile Irish imagination visualizes a collection of gigantic green eggs, green even in the moderate cold of December. A reader of Tolkien might wonder if this were not the shire of the Hobbits. Those pleasant wee folk would be comfortable among the small green mountains. Because the moist air from the Gulf Stream becomes mist over Monaghan, the valleys are cut by clear-flowing streams, or else they are boglands that defy the plow. The Irish loved their little hills and vales and love them today, but at the time of the Cromwellian settlement the landlords could not persuade English or Scottish farmers to migrate there. So the native Irish remained as tenants.

It was during the reign of King Charles II that Thomas Ellis acquired property in Monaghan. Other settlers were the Maxwells, Dawsons, Harpers, Dobbs, and Thompsons. They had hardly established their residences when King James II ascended the throne. The Catholic tenants hoped that James would restore their property and promptly ceased paying their rents. The hope seemed a reality when James consented to an Act of Attainder, which provided for the confiscation of the estates of those who refused to swear loyalty to him before the end of 1689. Thus 153 landlords in Monaghan were proscribed, among them Thomas Ellis, Gentleman.[5]

The Battle of the Boyne on July 1, 1690 (July 12 new style), restored Ellis's title to his property and guaranteed the Protestant ascendancy. Ireland assumed the character that endured for two centuries. Henceforth, to be a Catholic meant that one belonged to a defeated race, spoke a despised language, and clung to an outlawed religion. The penal laws banished all bishops, deans, and priests in religious orders. Only parish priests were allowed to remain in Ireland, and without bishops, no new priests could be ordained. Catholics were excluded from the bench, bar, and grand juries. They could not serve as constables, gameskeepers, or in the army. Their churches were taken over by the government and reopened as Protestant churches for the support of which Catholics were taxed. The eighteenth century held the prospect of poverty, ignorance, and oppression for the native Irish, but they clung stubbornly to the land, paid their rents, attended mass in the fields, taught their children to read, and somehow endured.[6]

Gradually the inhabitants of Ireland sorted out into classes. At the top were the Irish nobility who owned vast estates; then there were the gentry, the smaller landowners, like Thomas Ellis. Next there was a growing middle class of merchants in the towns. Many of them were Presbyterians from other Ulster counties, but as the century wore on, Catholics moved into Monaghan, Clones, Castleblayney, and other towns and with money acquired middle-class respectability. In the countryside were the tenants, mostly native Irish. They in turn subleased small parcels of their holdings to cottiers who worked for them. Below the cottiers were the laborers who had no fixed abode and wandered about looking for work.[7]

The identity of the transplanted Irish became clear after the Boyne. They were Protestant, mainly Church of Ireland, but there were some Scottish Presbyterians in the towns. They were privileged persons, able to own land and participate in government. The rallying cry of the Orange Lodges as they paraded on July 12, 1990, in celebration of the victory at the Boyne was "the perpetuation of Protestant liberties." The slogan means less today than it did in the eighteenth century, but it is as fervently felt by those who utter it. To be Protestant and privileged also meant to be a stranger on the land, an oppressor. Above all, it meant being a non-Gael, a person of alien roots, folkways, language, and culture.[8]

Thomas Ellis established his residence in Monaghan town and gathered properties in the countryside. His town holdings included a dwelling house, stables, outhouses, and gardens. He also owned "parks" in Monaghan, probably fields open to the public. An old map of Monaghan shows a section called Ellis Fields. If so, then Thomas set an example of public benefaction that was followed by his son Francis and his grandson Henry.[9]

Presumably, he had a commodious house because he had a large family. By his first wife, whose name is not known, he had seven sons and one daughter. There were Robert, Francis, Richard, William, John, Thomas, and Henry. The daughter, Elizabeth, married a man named Spear. Thomas's second wife was Elizabeth, daughter of John Harper and widow of a man named White. Four more children followed: Usher, Edward, Samuel, and Rebecca. Another child was expected when Thomas made his will. He left instructions for his wife to bury him in the church in Monaghan, and he provided for "all necessarys of meat, drink, washing, lodging and schooling" for young John, Thomas, Henry, Usher, Edward, Samuel, Rebecca, and the unborn child. Robert, Francis, William, and Elizabeth were old enough to fend for themselves in 1714, the year of Thomas's death. Thus Thomas had succeeded in planting his family in Ireland and in providing Henry Ellis an abundance of relatives.

Henry's father, Francis, was born in 1683, soon after Thomas's arrival in Ireland. Francis married Joan Maxwell in 1715, the year after his father's death, when he was thirty-two.[10] If the family historian can be believed, Francis and Joan were extraordinarily unfortunate in their efforts to raise a family. The first child, Lucas, was born and died in 1716; the second, Robert, died at birth in 1717; another Robert died before he was a year old in 1722, twin girls, Maria and Sarah, died shortly after birth in 1727, and Francis, born in 1729, lived only five years. The children who gained maturity were James, born in 1718, who died unmarried, Henry, born in 1721 and also died unmarried in 1806, and Joanna, who was born in 1723 and whose death date is not known. The family history is incomplete in several instances. From other sources, it is known that James ran away to Kilkenny, where he fathered a son and two daughters without the formality of marriage. His father, who was as stern as he was unforgiving, disinherited James and had no more to do with him.[11] In addition to the two children named Robert who died in infancy, there was a third Robert, born in 1726, who grew to manhood, married a charming girl named Penelope Leslie, and by her produced four sons and four daughters. They followed Henry to England and set up house in Lansdowne Crescent, Bath, a fashionable neighborhood. Robert's oldest son, Francis, was chosen by Henry to be heir to his extensive property.[12]

Each Church of Ireland rector was required to establish a parish school. Henry Ellis's education was so clearly superior to that he might have received at a parish school that it is likely his father sent him to the classical school across the county at Carrickmacross. The school was established in 1711 by Thomas Thynne, later Viscount Weymouth, who specified the conditions that governed it. The headmaster had to be a Trinity College graduate, a man of good morals, and he had to reside on the premises. It went without saying that he must belong to the Church of Ireland. The curriculum included religion, Latin, Greek, Hebrew, oratory, poetry, arithmetic, geography, surveying, writing, antiquaries, and, to cap it all, "virtue." Presumably "virtue" was not the same as "religion." Henry Ellis probably liked all these studies, but geography and antiquaries fascinated him. During Henry Ellis's boyhood new worlds as well as old were being discovered. William Stulkeley's *Itinerarium Curiosum*, printed in 1724, excited interest in the study of ancient ruins. Stulkeley investigated Stonehenge and other prehistoric ruins and was the first to speculate about a druidic civilization before the Romans.[13]

Schooling was a serious business. Classes began at 6 A.M. and lasted until 11 A.M. After a break for lunch, work resumed at 1 P.M. and continued until 5 P.M. The students were not through yet. There was a study period from 6 P.M. until 8 P.M. Required prayer services were held each morning and evening, leaving time for very little else.[14] Survivors of the grueling schedule were broadly educated and could feel comfortable in polite society.

Another powerful influence on the young Ellis was the remarkable Philip Skelton, curate of the established church in Monaghan. The Reverend Mr. Skelton was a giant of a man who did not hesitate to use physical suasion if the occasion demanded. Once when he reproved a tinker for cursing, the tinker and his friends assaulted him. The tinkers got the worst of it, and Skelton was only slightly late for his appointment. On another occasion he cautioned an arrogant army major against using bad language in the presence of ladies. The major made the mistake of challenging Skelton to fisticuffs and ended by begging for mercy.[15]

Skelton was a Trinity graduate, and his sermons were carefully crafted. His writings attracted attention, and his pamphlet *Deism Revealed*, a defense of orthodox religion against the laxities of modernism, was noticed in London. When his works were later collected and published, they filled six volumes.[16] Skelton would have challenged the mind and inspired the soul of Ellis. If the Church of Ireland canonized its servants, Skelton would be a candidate. His charities during his eighteen years at Monaghan were extraordinary and were extended to the Catholic as well as Protestant needy. His example may well have been the cause of Francis Ellis's generous support of worthy causes. The latter's best-remembered benefaction was his £4,000 bequest for a hospital in Monaghan. The building, constructed in 1768, was still standing in 1968. In that year an architectural survey remarked about the infirmary, the town's oldest structure: "Perhaps the building has deteriorated beyond redemption, but if a new use could be found for it, it might still make a notable contribution to the town."[17] No use was found, and the memorial to Francis Ellis's charity was torn down.

Another local lad whose life was changed by Philip Skelton's example was William Knox of a Presbyterian family in nearby Clones. If young Knox was not already deeply religious, he certainly became so. He remained in contact with Skelton until the latter's death in 1786. Knox sent Skelton books from London, and even though he was never a wealthy man, he contributed to the support of Skelton's charitable causes.[18] Knox knew Henry Ellis, but their ten-year age difference caused a gulf that was not bridged until adulthood. Then they became fast friends and remained so.

The curate Skelton was a friend of the Pringle family, as was Henry Ellis. Ellis later stood as godfather for William Henry Pringle, son of General William Pringle, constable of Monaghan. Henry Ellis formed lasting relationships during his formative years in Monaghan.[19] There was a hint that Henry formed a relationship like the one that caused his father to disinherit his brother James. A Monaghan woman claimed that Henry was the father of her illegitimate child. That was an accusation a man of honor had to face up to in the Ireland of the eighteenth century as well as today. Henry Ellis denied that he was the child's father, but the little girl grew up believing that he was. Ellis blamed the mother rather than the daughter for the allegation and in his will remembered the woman who bore his name.[20]

There were light moments in the life of young people of Monaghan. Athletic contests were common; foot-racing and ball-throwing were standard features of such events. Parties and celebrations were as frequent then as now, at least in the houses of the gentry. Traveling musicians entertained on these occasions. Fiddlers, pipers, and flutists were numerous in Ireland. The favorite form of dancing, in the drawing rooms of the wealthy as in the farmer's kitchen, was step-dancing, which featured rapid foot movement, marked by tapping, bouncing, and leg swinging. The contrast between the mobility of the lower body and the stoic rigidity of the upper is striking. Eighteenth-century visitors admired the carriage and gait of Irish girls and credited step-dancing as the reason. Others said the erect posture and graceful stride came from the custom of carrying pitchers of milk and buckets of water on the head.[21]

There was much that was quaint and appealing in eighteenth-century Monaghan. The friendliness and essential dignity of even the very poor was noted by travelers. The Irish gift for storytelling was legendary. With education limited to Protestant schools and books a rarity, oral history and ballads were means of perpetuating ancient traditions. A belief in fairies and wee folk enlivened the imagination. Although the gulf between gentry and peasantry was all but impassable, there was a more informal relationship between classes than was the case in England of the same period. The climate was pleasant, the landscape as varied and interesting as it is today.[22]

When Henry Ellis reached maturity, however, only blind patriotic faith would have made Monaghan seem to be a desirable place in which to live out one's life. A visitor described Monaghan streets as cluttered with evil-smelling refuse, pigs wallowing in the gutters, drunken men and women lolling about, and out on Gallows Hill eleven bodies swinging from the gibbets.[23] It is likely that the aggravating miseries of the time prompted Henry Ellis to seek his fortune outside Monaghan.

The years 1740–41 were ones of famine and disease. An anonymous pamphlet entitled *The Groans of Ireland* described how the roads were littered with dead bodies and entire villages were depopulated. The good and generous Philip Skelton wrote that the dead in Monaghan were being eaten by dogs for want of people to bury them.[24] Skelton is said to have told his people, "If you don't have food, beg it. If you cannot get it by begging, steal."[25] Another option was to quit Ireland, and thousands of Ulstermen went to America. Aside from other reasons—youth, ambition, restlessness, the call of adventure—that might have motivated a nineteen-year-old, the need to escape a desperately poor, fever-wracked country was cause enough for Henry Ellis's decision to leave home in search of a better life. And so, at about the age of twenty, Henry Ellis went to sea.

It was not the only reason, however. Francis Ellis was a strict parent; he alienated his eldest son, James, and the two were never reconciled. Henry was a high-spirited youth. Later in life he admitted that he occasionally gave way to a "juvenile wildness." Henry was proud, intelligent, and headstrong, and so was his father. The immediate occasion for Henry's abrupt departure from Monaghan was the "ill-judged severity" of his parent. During Henry's long absence, Francis had ample opportunity to soften his attitude. A forgiving Francis made it a point to advance Henry's career every way he could and eventually left him his fortune.[26]

Dundalk was the port town nearest Monaghan. Most of the ships sailing from Dundalk were coasters, plying their trade along both sides of the Irish Sea. All new sailors, regardless of age, were called "boy" and treated as the lowest form of human life on shipboard. They were immediately initiated by a dramatic test of nerve by being sent aloft to learn how to work the rigging. Anyone who was afraid of heights or physically unfit was quickly exposed. The climb up the mainmast was through the "lubber-hold," through which the shrouds of the lower rigging passed. The experienced sailors scorned this easy route and climbed out and over the futtock shrouds of the royal yardarm. The ascent required strong muscles and good coordination. At the topgallant masthead, the sailor had to accustom himself to the slight corkscrew roll of the ship that swept him in a wide circle, up, forward, sideways, and down. From this height, a hundred feet and more above the deck, the deckhands looked curiously foreshortened. This was no place for someone with vertigo.[27]

The reason for the early introduction to the study of the ship's rigging was that loosing and furling the sails were tasks that required the services of every hand. If the new sailor was lucky, he could practice climbing about the high rigging in fair weather. Inevitably, however, the storms came and, with them, gale winds and heavy seas. Then negotiating a yardarm and tying down a sail was a life-threatening adventure. There was no way Henry Ellis could have avoided this duty. Nor could he have escaped the other routine chores of the new boy, slushing down the masts, swabbing the decks, coiling all loose ropes, standing his watch, learning the proper use of ropes and knots, and running errands of all sorts.

The next grade in the career of a sailor was that of ordinary seaman. The tests were the ability to gauge the wind, to read a compass, to loosen and furl light sails, and to steer under the instructions of an officer. An ordinary seaman was expected to do everything aboard ship except the truly menial chores reserved for the boys. After two years as an ordinary seaman, the sailor was ready for promotion to able-bodied seaman. The test included his ability to handle a marlin spike on a piece of rigging, make a long and short splice in a rope, lower riggings, and do clever ropework. In addition, he had the prestigious privilege of steering the ship.[28] It was impossible to fake the claim to able-bodied status. The sailor had to perform the tasks expected of him when given orders. In the rare case when a pretender was discovered, the unfortunate man was assigned the most humiliating jobs possible.

The ship was a school of social relationships. The slow progress from boy to able-bodied seaman was under the eye of a mate, and on British ships in the eighteenth century, mates were petty tyrants. The captains were absolute tyrants who seldom condescended to speak to common sailors. The captain would give orders to the mate, who would shout at one or all of the hands. The apprenticeship of a sailor was a long exercise in humility, obedience, and discipline. The cramped and confined quarters of a forecastle provided another learning experience. It was no place for the weak or timid. Any assumption of airs of superiority would be an open invitation to a thrashing. Perhaps surprisingly, education was an advantage rather than otherwise. Sailors were curious people and liked to listen to those who had something to say. Many were eager to learn to read; a willing teacher could make friends that way.

A different lesson in life was provided in port cities such as Liverpool. The behavior of the hard types who infested the dockside dives shocked a clean-living lad from Ireland. Painted women would take a sailor's money, drug his drink, and hand him over to a press gang. The man might wake up as a crewman aboard a strange vessel. The squalor of Liverpool's dockside or London's Whitechapel district made Monaghan's poverty seem insignificant.[29]

A smart youth like Ellis might learn seamanship by finding an officer willing to teach the practical mathematics of navigation, which was not part of the classical school curriculum. Ellis would have mastered the rudiments of geometry and trigonometry so as to plot a course, keep a record of the ship's movements, compute the distance traveled each day, figure in the effect of wind and tides, and decide where the ship was in relation to where it should be.

As Ellis moved from the constrained coasting trade to deep-sea sailing, a new educational experience opened to him. The Mediterranean ports such as Marseilles and Naples offered a climate and culture that intrigued Ellis and influenced him to return to those places in later life. Ellis was a keen observer wherever he went. Twenty years later he could advise British ministers on the geography of the Canary Islands and of the Greater and Lesser Antilles in the West Indies. He could describe the climate and natural resources of Cuba and Jamaica. He understood the wind and ocean currents of the Caribbean. In his own words, he "frequented Guinea and the West Indies not inattentively."[30] Henry Ellis's adventures on the sea were partly a lesson in geography and partly an introduction to the heady game of empire building. England was at war with Spain and France while Ellis sailed the high seas, and English ships had to know which harbors were safe and which were not.

Along the coast of Africa, the Royal African Company had trading posts in Gambia, the Gold Coast, and the Bight of Benin. The lonely island of St. Helena in the South Atlantic, to the west of Africa, was a property of the East India Company, governed by the same Robert Jenkins whose severed ear provoked the war between England and Spain in 1739.[31] The war grew into a general European conflict, the War of the Austrian Succession, with Spain and France pitted against England.

In the West Indies the British flag flew over the Bermuda Islands, the Bahamas, Jamaica, the Leeward Islands, and Barbados. The Windward Islands (St. Lucia, Tobago, St. Vincent, Dominica, and Grenada) were called the Neutral Islands, but both England and France had designs on them. British lumberjacks had begun cutting timber along the coast of Honduras, and the custom was at the point of becoming a right.[32]

Spain controlled all of South America except Brazil, French Guiana, and Dutch Surinam. The Spanish empire extended along the west coast of North America and included Florida. There on the Florida borders, Spain's claims clashed with England's. General James Oglethorpe annoyed the Spaniards by planting the colony of Georgia in an area Spain considered the northern reaches of Florida. The War of Jenkins's Ear was about Florida as well as English smuggling. Most of the military activity of this war was conducted on this southern frontier. Oglethorpe besieged St. Augustine unsuccessfully in 1740. He beat off a Spanish counterattack near Frederica on St. Simons Island in 1742, and he failed again to take St. Augustine in 1743. Those engagements, together with Admiral Edward Vernon's costly attack on Cartagena in 1742, constituted the main events of the war in the South.[33]

In his voyages to Jamaica, Ellis would have learned the strategic importance of Havana, Cuba, or "the Havannah," as it was usually called, situated on the passage from the Spanish Main to Europe. That knowledge would enable him, in the next war, to advise the British ministry to attack and take possession of the Havannah and thereby control the principal trade routes.

The impressionable young sailor was caught up in the spirit of the age, the competition for trade and colonies. He set his sights on a leadership role in the contest for empire. His apprenticeship on the ocean highways prepared him well. When he returned to England in 1746, he was offered command of a ship about to sail in a search for a northwest passage to the Orient.[34] That fact tells us much about Ellis at the age of twenty-five. He had met all the physical tests expected of a sailor. He could run up the rigging and slide down the ropes, walk along a swaying yard, reef a sail in a storm, and pull on a hawser with the best of them. He had learned how to read the stars, how to feel the wind on his cheek, how to calculate drift and tide. His intelligence and ability marked him for advancement. He was ready to become an empire booster.

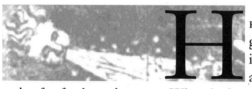

HENRY ELLIS returned to England from a voyage to Italy in May 1746 bursting with ambition, patriotism, and ardor for further adventure. When he learned that an expedition was about to sail in search of a northwest passage through North America, he immediately made up his mind to get aboard. Remarkably, eighteen hours later, he was on one of the two ships, and, even more astonishing, he had been offered command of the vessel.[1] Obviously, he could not have succeeded so well without the help of influential friends. It is quite likely that Arthur Dobbs was Ellis's patron.

Dobbs, the future governor of North Carolina, was an Anglo-Irishman from County Antrim. As a member of the Irish House of Commons, he had acquired a reputation for encouraging trade and colonization. He was largely responsible for the revival of interest in the search for a northwest passage. In 1731 he compiled and published abstracts of all previous attempts to find the water route west. Dobbs had friends in high places, including Robert Walpole, and their collective influence caused the Hudson's Bay Company to make a halfhearted search along the western coast of Hudson Bay. Dobbs was convinced that the company was not interested in finding a new route. Through another of his friends, Sir Charles Wager, first lord of the Admiralty, Dobbs obtained two ships. To command the expedition he selected Captain Christopher Middleton, who had sailed the northern waters for the Hudson's Bay Company. A second ship was engaged as an escort under Middleton's former first mate, William Moore. Dobbs's great expectations were dashed when Middleton returned in 1742 with the report that Hudson Bay was landlocked.[2] After reading Middleton's journal and talking to Captain Moore, Dobbs came to the conclusion that Wager Bay was really an outlet to the west. Dobbs persuaded himself that Middleton was involved in a conspiracy with the Hudson's Bay Company to conceal the passage. Dobbs's accusations led to a pamphlet duel between Middleton and him and an investigation of the captain by the lords of the Admiralty. The lords decided that Middleton was an honorable man, and his vindication was complete when the Royal Society gave him a medal. Dobbs was also a winner. A committee of Parliament was sufficiently impressed by his earnestness to propose a reward of £20,000 for the discoverer of a northwest passage. Parliament approved the idea, but Dobbs had to pay for the voyage. He did so by enlisting subscribers, each of whom invested £100. Prominent among the backers were Lord Chesterfield, Lord Southwell, and George Berkeley, the philosopher bishop of Cloyne.[3] Among the seventy-two subscribers was Henry Ellis. It is doubtful that the twenty-five-year-old Ellis would have managed to save a hundred pounds on his sailor's pay. He must have effected a reconciliation with his father by this time. Dobbs canvassed Ireland for subscribers, and Francis Ellis certainly knew of the project and probably put up the money. If Henry Ellis was offered command of one of the two vessels, and there is no reason to doubt his assertion that he was, Dobbs must have made the offer out of deference to Francis Ellis rather than on the basis of Henry's limited experience.

William Moore was engaged by Dobbs to return to Hudson Bay as master of the *Dobbs Galley*, a vessel of 180 tons. Francis Smith commanded the smaller *California*. Ellis would act unofficially as Dobbs's agent; officially he was the scientific observer with the impressive title of hydrographer. His duties included charting the soundings, rocks, and shoals of the western coast of Hudson Bay, mapping the area explored, and collecting metals and minerals that might be important trade items. Finally, he was instructed to do what he most preferred to do, take notice of "all kinds of natural curiosities." It was an ideal assignment, tailored to an intelligent, inquisitive, ambitious young man like Ellis. Such a role had made William Baffin famous and would do so again for Joseph Banks and, still later, Charles Darwin. As Dobbs's special agent, Ellis sat on the council, which included the captains, mates, and surgeons of the two ships. Because Captains Moore and Smith often disagreed, Ellis's vote was decisive. Moore's spirit of adventure matched Ellis's, and the two usually made the key decisions on this expedition.[4]

In spite of the hurried preparations for departure, Ellis was able to collect information on earlier voyages. Dobbs would have provided most of this material. In addition, Ellis had access to the 1740 reprint of a 1633 account entitled *The Dangerous Voyage of Capt. Thomas James in His Intended Discovery of a North-West Passage.* The pamphlet controversy between Dobbs and Middleton about the meaning of tidal flow in the western region of Hudson Bay would have been essential reading.[5]

Ellis reviewed the history of exploration in his own journal. The first man to explore the northern waters was Martin Frobisher, the Elizabethan "sea dog" who investigated the coast of Greenland, crossed the Labrador Sea, and entered the bay that bears his name. Frobisher thought he had found the passage but was distracted by a futile search for gold. The quest for the passage was taken up by John Davis. With a charter from Queen Elizabeth granted in 1585, Davis coasted up Greenland's western edge farther than Frobisher had gone, crossed the strait that was named for him, and entered another dead end, subsequently called Cumberland Sound. Curiously, both Frobisher and Davis sailed past Hudson Strait without recognizing its importance, although Davis reported an unusual flow of water between 62° and 63° latitude. Both captains lost men to hostile natives; both were in constant danger from ice, fog, and storms. Disease crippled many members of the crews. The enterprising Davis attempted a voyage up the west coast of North America in hopes of finding a western outlet to the passage. After a hazardous run through the Straits of Magellan, he made his way up the coast of South America but exhausted his provisions. Luck and skillful seamanship brought him back to England, where he wrote two tracts in 1594 and 1595 arguing for the existence of a northwest passage. His confidence caused a group of merchant adventurers to investigate the reported disturbance between 62° and 63°. They employed Henry Hudson, already famous for his voyages to America for the Dutch East India Company.[6]

In the fifty-five-ton *Discovery* Hudson located the strait that was named in his honor. The rising tide creates a surge that propels small vessels into the passage. The *Discovery* was thus carried deeply into the ice-strewn strait. The frightened crew nearly mutinied, but Hudson persuaded them to go on. It took thirty-seven days to navigate the narrows. Hudson's satisfaction in reaching what he thought was the western sea soon turned to disappointment as the land fell away to the south. The *Discovery* was frozen in by early winter ice, and the men barely survived. When the ice broke, the ill-disciplined crew put Hudson and a few others adrift in a shallop. Nothing was ever heard of them. The rebellious crewmen would have faced hanging in England, but the ringleaders were killed by natives before they reached the open sea. In all these early voyages, as Henry Ellis must have noticed, the natives were invariably hostile.[7]

Robert Bylot, a survivor of the Hudson expedition whose seamanship in bringing the *Discovery* home won him a reprieve from punishment, was sent out again in the same ship under command of Thomas Button in 1612. They navigated the strait without incident; however, when a party went ashore on Digges Island, the natives killed five men. The expedition continued due west across the bay but ran into the land mass instead of open water. Button was convinced that there was no western outlet; Bylot was not. The same sponsors sent Bylot out again in the *Discovery*, this time with William Baffin as scientific observer. They reported a northern exit out of Hudson Bay, but it led to the ice-choked bay later called Foxe Basin. They detected no surge of a tide from the west. Baffin concluded that the best prospect for an opening was farther to the north through Davis Strait. Out again went Bylot and Baffin in the small but sturdy *Discovery*. They sailed through Davis Strait into a new body of water to which Baffin gave his own name. Again, ice stopped them. Turning, they found an opening between Devon Island on the north and Bylot Island and Baffin Island, both to the south. They discovered the true passage, Lancaster Sound, but Baffin thought it was merely another inlet and reported it as such. The members of the expedition, terribly wracked by scurvy, returned to report its courageous failure. One more unsuccessful effort was made to explore Hudson Bay in 1631 by Captains Luke Foxe and Thomas James. James's account of the voyage was reputedly the inspiration for Samuel Coleridge's "Rhyme of the Ancient Mariner."[8]

The quest for a northwest passage slowed after the establishment of the Hudson's Bay Company in 1670. Henry Ellis noted the coincidence that the first Duke of Montague was ambassador to the court of King Louis XIV, who sponsored Pierre Radisson and his brother-in-law Médard Chouart, Sieur des Grossiliers in the formation of the Hudson's Bay Company, and the second duke was a sponsor of Ellis's expedition. Ellis agreed with Dobbs that the Hudson's Bay Company was more interested in establishing a lucrative fur trade than in sub-sidizing unprofitable voyages. In 1719 the company made a gesture at exploration and sent two ships out, not so much to find a northwest passage as to track down rumors of gold in the west. The wrecks of two ships were later found; it was assumed that natives had killed those who might have survived the wreck. The unhappy incident confirmed the company's determination to confine its operations to the land-based fur trade. The end of the company's interest in a passage marked the beginning of Arthur Dobbs's involvement in the search.[9]

Henry Ellis studied the successes and failures of his predecessors as he chronicled them in his journal. The proven dangers of fog, storm, shoals, ice, and disease seemed not to concern him. He was excited by the adventure and the fame that the voyage would bring.

The orders under which the 1746 expedition sailed were a mix-ture of the practical and the quixotic. The two ships would rendezvous in the Orkneys, then at Resolution Island at the entrance to Hudson Strait, and finally at Digges Island at the exit. They were to watch for whales going west, follow the whales as they wound their way across the continent, and emerge on the west coast of North America. The instructions reflected the confidence, however unwarranted, that everyone seemed to feel.[10]

The two ships left Gravesend on May 20, 1746. One of the mates went ashore at Scarborough and was left there when the warships con-voying the explorers sailed suddenly. The convoy, commanded by the same Christopher Middleton who had disappointed Arthur Dobbs, escorted the *Dobbs Galley* and *California* around to Kirkwall in the Orkneys and sixty leagues beyond until, presumably, they were out of danger of French men-of-war.

The passengers on the *Dobbs Galley* were ready for ice and cold, but they were nearly destroyed by fire. A neglected candle ignited a fire in a cabin directly under the helmsman and over the powder room. Even if the flames did not burn through, it was likely that the heat would touch off an explosion that would destroy the vessel and all in it. "It is impossible to express the confusion and consternation this accident occasioned," Ellis wrote. Prayers mingled with curses. Some struggled to lower the boats while others tried to hoist the sails and close up to the *California*. The captain nearly lost control of the situa-tion. The helmsman, feeling the heat of the fire, abandoned the wheel, and the ship turned into the wind, the sails flapping loudly. Ellis was coolheaded enough to organize a bucket brigade that contained and finally quenched the fire. He modestly played down his role, but the incident required courage and presence of mind. He earned the respect of his fellow adventurers.[11]

The two ships ran into ice on June 27, 1746, near Greenland. On July 5, Ellis recorded that the ice floes were of "prodigious size," six hundred or more yards thick. The ships were tiny and fragile by comparison. Resolution Island was the first rendezvous point and the site of another near disaster. Fog made the island invisible, and the *Dobbs Galley* was upon the rockbound coast before the lookouts saw it. The ship's boats were quickly lowered, and by frantic rowing, the vessel was towed away from danger. Ellis's account of the incident was almost casual.[12]

The most striking quality of Ellis's report, for anyone familiar with other accounts of conditions in the Far North, is the matter-of-fact tone, as though this voyage were a slightly less than comfortable pleasure cruise. The simple process of entering Hudson Strait was fraught with danger. A veteran sailor named William Coats, employed by the Hudson's Bay Company from 1727 to 1751, wrote interesting instructions to his sons as a kind of manual of navigation in northern waters. He warned against trying to enter Hudson Strait before July 6. To make his point, he described how, on July 3, 1736, his ship was caught by ice from both directions and crushed to pieces. In 1739 he tried six times to enter between July 1 and July 12 and was thwarted by the ice each time. Once inside the strait, the tide swells thirty feet and disturbs the ice in unpredictable ways. "Everywhere the ice is rude and troublesome and very dangerous," he warned.[13]

After mentioning his first astonishment at the size of the floating ice, Ellis felt it unnecessary to dwell on the continued danger of ice, even though that danger was very real. The ships sailed through the straits close to the desolate northern shore, where there was open water. On July 17 their way was blocked by solid ice. Captain Moore anchored to the ice, and the inquisitive Ellis walked about on the huge floe. He found that the melting pools of water in the crevices were potable, and the ship's casks were replenished while they waited. On the nineteenth the wind and tide broke the ice and the adventurers sailed through.[14]

An exciting incident for Ellis was their first encounter with the Eskimos, the Inuit people who had been hostile to strangers on past

1. Henry Ellis's map of Hudson's Bay demonstrates his skill as a cartographer and was the most accurate survey of the western coast of the bay at the time. (Hargrett Rare Book and Manuscript Library, University of Georgia)

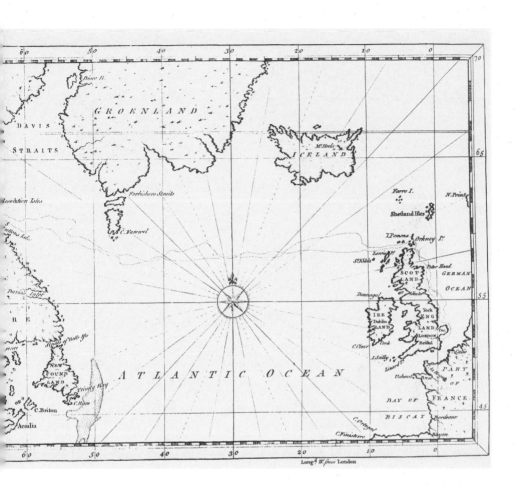

occasions. A flotilla of three large and twenty-six smaller canoes approached the wary English. Fortunately, they were intent on trade, not war. They exchanged whalebones and sealskins for hatchets, saws, and knives, even divesting themselves of clothing for pieces of iron. Ellis liked them. He thought they were cheerful and "sprightly," even if they were inclined to pilfer. A good observer, he described their kayaks, harpoons, and curious "snow-eyes." These were round pieces of wood or ivory with slits in them which fit over the eyes and eliminated the blinding ice glare. The Eskimos used them like telescopes to focus on distant objects.[15]

The passage through the treacherous Hudson Strait was completed in two weeks, a good showing. On August 2, the ships anchored at Digges Island. Hunters went ashore and shot wildfowl for provisions. From this point on the east side of Hudson Bay, the explorers sailed due west to the western shore and the hoped-for outlet. They passed between Southhampton Island to the north and Mansel Island to the south. On his chart Ellis depicted Southhampton Island as a long peninsula jutting out of the north shore of Hudson Bay instead of the true island it is. On August 11, apparently without incident along the way, they sighted the icebound western coast. A furious storm delayed close inspection for over a week. Finally, on August 19, Ellis and an eight-man crew, armed with ice-poles to fend off floes as well as rocks, went out in a longboat to investigate the narrows between Marble Island and Rankin Inlet in the 63° latitude.

Rankin Inlet, so named by Middleton in honor of one of his officers, was one of the most promising possibilities for a westward opening. Ellis discovered, however, that there was no surge of tide from the west; instead, the tide came from the north down the strangely named Roe's Welcome Sound. There was no time to search the most likely inlets, Chesterfield, Wager, and Repulse bays. The season of ice was at hand. The previous expedition, under prudent Christopher Middleton, was at 61° latitude on July 31, 1741, when the decision was made to go into winter quarters at the south end of Hudson Bay.[16] Ellis and his companions were farther north, and it was late August when the council met to decide whether to continue the search or go into winter quarters. These councils were held alternately on board the *Dobbs* and the *California*. Captain Smith of the latter vessel employed a clerk, Charles Swaine, who published an account of the voyage after Ellis's appeared.[17] Swaine was not aware that Ellis was an agent of the sponsors, and he was clearly annoyed by Ellis's assertions of leadership. Swaine seldom referred to Ellis by name; he called him "the draughtsman" and gave it a pejorative connotation.

Ellis argued for continuing the search for at least forty-eight hours. Captain Smith opposed the idea because of the danger involved. Swaine quoted the captain as describing the coast as one "where there was a number of Shoals and Rocks and all unknown when the Nights were dark and it was a season for thick weather and gales of wind." Nevertheless, the council approved Ellis's motion to search for two more days. The weather was so bad the next day that the decision was made to go south immediately. Ellis suggested that the notes of the previous council be discarded because they had not yet been signed. Smith insisted that the records remain intact. The two captains argued about where to put in for the winter, and Moore prevailed. They would anchor near the Hudson's Bay Company's fort at the bottom of Hudson Bay between the Nelson and Hayes rivers. The ships headed south through increasingly nasty weather, snow, sleet, and fog. The Hudson's Bay agent at the York Factory kept a beacon at the point of land as a warning to incoming ships to be aware of the shoals. As a stunning retaliation against Dobbs, who had criticized the company and sponsored this new expedition, the agent extinguished the beacon and the *Dobbs Galley* ran aground. By sheer luck no damage was suffered and the tide floated the ship again.[18]

Unwilling to believe that this incredible evidence of hostility was deliberate, Ellis and one of the mates were deputed to call on the agent and show him their credentials. They were received, Ellis reported, "in a very haughty and disrespectful manner."[19] The Inuit had been more gracious. The factor's attitude was unrelenting; far from assisting his countrymen during the ensuing months, he forbade Indians to trade with the visitors. Both Ellis and Swaine testify to the hostile attitude of the agent at York Factory. The publication of their criticisms, however, brought forth a published response by the factor, one James Isham. He explained that he cut down the beacon because he thought that the two ships were Frenchmen flying false colors. Even if Moore and Smith were aboard, he argued, they might have been prisoners of a hidden enemy. In his opinion, he had treated the visitors as respectfully as they deserved. He showed them where to store their beer and supplied them with bricks and lime to build a store. What more, he implied, could they reasonably expect?[20]

On September 12, 1746, the site of the winter camp was chosen, a cove near the mouth of the Hayes River. Tentlike log structures were built for the men with moss and clay as added insulation. A fire was kept burning inside, and a small hole was left in the roof for smoke to escape. Ellis was particularly proud of the "mansion" that was constructed for him and the officers and their servants because he had drawn the plans for the two-story house. The stove made with Isham's bricks was on the second floor, where the officers bunked. The building was ready for occupancy by November 1. By then, it was too cold to stay aboard ship. The river froze hard. All the bottled beer was solid even though it was stored near a fire. The ink Ellis used for his journal was black ice.[21]

Instead of huddling around a fire, Ellis adapted to the winter climate by imitating the Eskimos. He carefully dressed in several layers of clothing with a sealskin coat on the outside. He made snowshoes five feet long and eighteen inches wide and learned to walk on the snow with the ungainly footgear. He was thus able to venture out in search for small game. Rabbits were plentiful and could be caught easily in traps; wildfowl was also abundant. Ellis noted that a good hunter could shoot sixty to eighty partridges a day. He marveled at the way the Indians trained dogs to draw sledges, but the English were not yet accustomed to use that form of locomotion, nor were the dogs used to Englishmen.[22]

Venturing out of doors was risky. Snowstorms were so severe that at times the house was invisible from only a few feet away. Several men had faces, ears, and toes frozen, but fortunately, no one wandered far enough to get lost. Ellis and his fellow members of the council decided to make the best use of the time they had to fashion a new longboat, sturdier than any of those of the *Dobbs Galley*, for searching the labyrinthine coastline.

Although James Isham, the factor, disliked his unwelcome guests, he did not refuse their money. Two casks of brandy from the post were consumed as a Christmas celebration. It was the last joyful event. The dreaded scurvy made its appearance with the new year. The cause, according to Ellis, was "the constant attendant on the use of spirituous liquors." The progress of the disease was marked by livid spots, swollen legs, soft gums, and loose teeth. No cure had yet been found for the disease; ointments provided no relief. The only medicine that did any good was "tarwater," which was derived from urine. Ellis's journal assumed a somber tone as he chronicled the deaths, three in January, two in February, another in March, two more in April. Scurvy was the cause in all cases.[23]

Swaine's report reveals that the prolonged winter aggravated the strained relations between the two captains. The impatient Moore exhausted his men by trying to cut out of the ice in late February. Smith waited a month until the thaw began to cut the *California* loose. Smith blamed Moore for blocking his way. The deeper-drafted *Dobbs* could not get out of the harbor until June 2, and the mouth of the river was too narrow to permit the *California* to get around the *Dobbs*.[24]

It was only then that the captain and crew of the *California* learned of Moore's intention. In Swaine's version it seemed that a sinister conspiracy had been hatched. Moore "had formed a design with the persuasion of the Draughtsman, Ellis, of declining from his instructions and to execute this scheme (with the persuasion of the Draughtsman) he had raised and lengthened his boat in the winter." Their plan was to explore the coast from the winter camp to Marble Island, where they would meet the two ships. Smith was furious when he was told about the plan. He argued that the search would consume valuable time, that it would be dangerous, that the instructions were to search Rankin Inlet and Wager Bay, and that Moore stood to lose his £500 bond for not following instructions. Moore was sorry at Smith's displeasure, but he was determined to go with Ellis in the longboat. Evidently, Moore was confident that the sponsors trusted Ellis's judgment. And so it was that on June 30, 1747, the crews of the *Dobbs* and the *California* watched the longboat, now christened the *Resolution*, as it drew away, with Moore, the "Draughtsman," and eight men aboard. "We were now left to ourselves," noted the ill-humored clerk of the *California*.[25]

The *Dobbs* and *California* proceeded to Marble Island. There the morale of the *California*'s officers was lowered another notch when they learned from the first mate of the *Dobbs* that they were to wait until July 20 and if the longboat had not arrived by then to go searching for the passage during August and return to Marble Island by September 1, 1747. If Moore was not there then, the two ships should return to England without him. The message was a brave one, given by men who expected that they might not survive a dangerous mission. But it was not interpreted so by the suspicious men of the *California*. They thought that Moore and Ellis intended to "gain the whole Honour and Profit" for themselves by discovering the passage and sailing through it and back to England in their longboat.[26]

Ellis's journal reveals nothing of these dissensions and very little of the danger. The *Resolution* followed the coast, investigating every inlet. The floating ice and strong winds made navigation difficult. At Nevill's Bay (later named Dawson Inlet) the longboat ran aground, nearly wrecking the vessel. Suddenly a band of Eskimos appeared. As they approached on their snowshoes, the ten Englishmen must have recalled that other marooned sailors had been killed by natives like these. Ellis noted with relief and satisfaction that these people came to help. He paid tribute to their generous spirit, their industry, and their ingenuity. With their assistance, the *Resolution* was floated and resumed its mission.[27] Without further incident the longboat and its crew made the rendezvous at Marble Island on July 12, 1747. On the following day, Moore and Ellis came aboard the *California* to make their report and mend wounded feelings.[28] They had completed a search of a previously unexplored stretch of coast. Their next objective was Wager Bay.

Captain Christopher Middleton had chosen the name to honor Sir Charles Wager, first lord of the Admiralty. Middleton dared extremely hazardous conditions in his exploration of the inlet. His crew was incapacitated by scurvy and a worthless lot, even when healthy. Middleton's longboat was caught in the ice, and it was a "small miracle," in Middleton's words, that he survived Wager Bay.[29] His report of strong tides in the bay convinced Arthur Dobbs that there was a connection with the western sea.

As the *Dobbs* and *California* entered Welcome Sound and approached Wager Bay, the sense of anticipation increased. Henry Ellis went out in the longboat several times to chart the coast. He named one of the capes at the entrance of Wager in honor of Lord Montague; Middleton had already called its opposite Cape Dobbs. Wager was as dangerous as Middleton had said it was. Ellis, always understating the danger, noted that the water "raged, foamed, boiled and whirled." The turbulence was caused by the tide rushing through the narrow neck of Wager Bay and also by the summer thaws that caused great sheets of ice to break away from the cliffs on each side. The *Dobbs Galley* sailed farther into the bay than Middleton had and proved that it was a dead end, as Middleton had suspected. It must have been a disappointment to the members of the expedition to disprove the theory of their chief sponsor. Captain Moore bestowed the name Douglas Bay on a cove near the mouth of the Wager River, in honor of one of the sponsors of the expedition.[30]

The two captains were discouraged after Wager Bay. Many of the crew still suffered the effects of scurvy. Ellis and the surgeon of the *Dobbs* argued for a continuation of the search along the coast north of Wager. The captains reluctantly agreed. After several days of probing made increasingly difficult by fog and ice, a council was called. It was late in the season, already August 13, and they were farther north than Middleton had gone. The ice would imprison them if they delayed much longer. There was a note of exasperation in Swaine's comment that it was again proposed by the "Draughtsman" to go farther north. The mate of the *California* asked Ellis why he would suggest something that could not be done. Ellis replied calmly that it was not up to him to decide whether it could be done or not; that was the responsibility of the council. It is evidence of Ellis's standing in their regard that the council voted to continue the search a few days longer on the eastern coast of Welcome Sound.[31]

On August 25 another council was called. This time the mate of the *Dobbs*, who had never objected to anything before, declared that he would not go out in the longboat again unless the captain forced him to. Even Henry Ellis acknowledged that it was time to turn back.[32] Unaware that they might have taken a direct route north of Southampton Island, the two ships retraced their route down Roe's Welcome and around the south end of the island and back up to Hudson Strait. Though they might have not been particularly jubilant as they departed Hudson Bay, the explorers had every reason to give thanks. They had suffered casualties, but they fared far better than most Arctic expeditions, including Middleton's recent one.

Ninety years later, Captain William Back, an experienced sailor in northern waters, entered the same area visited by Ellis. Just to the north of Southampton Island he was caught by the September ice. The ship was twice the tonnage of the *Dobbs Galley* and specially constructed to withstand enormous pressure. Even so, she could not endure the crushing force of the ice pack. Her bow split and her keel cracked. For a month or so the ship remained stationary, then the whole pack of ice began drifting past Southampton Island, the imprisoned ship with it. The vessel was lifted out of the water by the force of ice below so that the carpenter was able to make the most essential repairs. It was not until the following July that the ice broke sufficiently so that the ship could be sawed loose from the floe to which she had been attached since the previous September. In August the badly battered ship reached the open Atlantic; she barely made the Irish coast.[33]

The most famous Arctic disaster happened a hundred years after Ellis's expedition and about 250 miles west of Repulse Bay. Sir John Franklin and his hundred-some men were caught in the ice and all of them perished. Franklin's disappearance touched off a massive international search in the course of which two different passages were discovered. Robert McClure went around Alaska across Beaufort Sea and fought his way along the very edge of the permanent ice around Banks Island and into McClure Strait. Halfway along Banks Island he took refuge in a cove. For a few hours open water separated him from Melville Island, which had been reached by Sir Edward Parry in 1820. The ice floes continually breaking away from the permanent ice cap on Beaufort Sea closed the opening. McClure made the crossing on foot. His triumph was diluted by the fact that his ship was hopelessly frozen in. He was trapped in his ship for three winters; the average loss of weight among his men was thirty-five pounds. He escaped Franklin's fate only because a rescue party approached from the south end of the island, and miraculously he was found. Even though McClure Strait was a river of ice, McClure received Parliament's long-standing award for finding a northwest passage. Henry Ellis would have been pleased at McClure's achievement and its recognition. McClure, knighted and feted upon his return, was from County Monaghan.[34]

McClure did not accomplish his primary goal, which was to solve the mystery of Franklin's disappearance. The man who succeeded magnificently in that was Francis Leopold McClintock. On his first attempt to follow Franklin's route, McClintock's ship was caught in the ice and for eight months drifted helplessly backward for thirteen hundred miles to Davis Strait. Finally freed from the ice, he tried again and this time succeeded. Not only did he find a note telling of Franklin's death, which occurred on June 11, 1847, but he found a comparatively ice-free way across the continent. The secret was in hugging the coast of Somerset Island and Boothia Peninsula and using Prince of Wales Island and King William Island as shields against the ice pack in McClure Strait. To the south of King William Island was an open channel between Victoria and Banks islands on the north and the mainland on the south. McClintock generously credited the dead Franklin with the discovery and lived long enough to learn that Roald Amundsen followed this route to the Pacific even though he was forced to spend the two winters of 1903 and 1904 on King William Island. Henry Ellis would have also felt a bond with Sir Francis McClintock, who was a native son of Dundalk, the nearest seaport to Monaghan County.[35]

Thus Henry Ellis played a part in the long drama that began with Frobisher and ended with Amundsen. He and his companions effectively put an end to attempts to find outlets from Hudson Bay. Subsequent searches concentrated on routes to the north. But because they did not make new discoveries and because they suffered no particular tragedies, they did not achieve the fame of some of the other explorers. Ellis was not knighted, but he was a celebrity.

After the *Dobbs Galley* docked at Yarmouth on October 14, 1747, Ellis was conducted to His Highness, Frederick, Prince of Wales, who seemed genuinely interested in Ellis's account of his adventures and asked a number of questions. The heir to the throne caught some of the infectious enthusiasm of the young explorer and expressed his interest in promoting future searches.[36] Ellis made important acquaintances at Leicester House, especially George Montagu Dunk, Lord Halifax, and William Wildman, Lord Barrington, an Anglo-Irishman from County Down. At the time, Barrington was one of the lords of Admiralty, and Halifax was about to begin his long tenure as president of the Board of Trade. Both men were ardent champions of trade and colonization and liked Ellis's talk about patriotism, glory, and especially profit to be derived from new commercial routes.

One who was less enchanted by Ellis's report was the prime mover, Arthur Dobbs, who hurried back to London from Ireland to interview Ellis and the two captains. He and they concluded that although there was no outlet in the region already explored, they ought to go on searching elsewhere. The energetic Dobbs began to lobby his high-placed friends to give a charter to the subscribers of the recent expedition under the title North West Company and to cancel the Hudson's Bay Company's monopoly. A select committee of Parliament seriously considered the matter and was subjected to an onslaught of petitions from merchants who were envious of the great company's profits. The committee members were sympathetic to Dobbs's petition but not convinced that they should tamper with a successful operation. Dobbs had to be satisfied with the committee's commendation for his public spirit. He gradually lost interest in finding a northwest passage and vented his considerable energy in settling his extensive landholdings in North Carolina. In 1749 he accused Governor Gabriel Johnston of maladministration. After looking into the matter, Lord Halifax and the Board of Trade agreed. Their solution was to name Arthur Dobbs governor of North Carolina on January 25, 1753.[37] It took him almost two years to assume the governor's chair; in another two years Henry Ellis would follow him to the southern frontier.

Meanwhile, Ellis improved the prospects for his own advancement by rushing into print with a book about his recent adventures, *A Voyage to Hudson's Bay by the Dobbs Galley and California in the Years 1746 and 1747 for Discovering a North West Passage with an Accurate Survey of the Coast and a Short Natural History of the Country*. A subtitle conveyed the message that the book included "a fair view of the facts and arguments from which the future finding of such a passage is rendered probable." The author signed himself "Henry Ellis, Gent." The voyage was a rite of passage; Ellis had gone as a sailor and returned as a gentleman. If the book lacked the dramatic impact associated with new discovery, it compensated by its attention to natural science. The book was translated into three other languages, and its author was inducted into the Royal Society. The recognition of his scholarly achievement must have been a source of great satisfaction to Ellis. A more tangible reward was his first government appointment; he was named deputy commissary of His Majesty's stores at Cheapside.[38]

Charles Swaine's account of the expedition, which was published a year after Ellis's, attracted the interest of certain enterprising Americans. Swaine was a resident of Maryland in 1750 when he obtained a permit from Governor Samuel Ogle to undertake another exploration of northern waters. Among Swaine's backers was the insatiably curious Benjamin Franklin, whose career touched Henry Ellis's at several points. Swaine's ship, the *Argo*, sailed on March 4, 1753, with instructions to explore the Labrador coast, to open trade and promote fisheries, and to cultivate the friendship of the natives. The *Argo* had none of the good fortune that the *Dobbs Galley* and the *California* had enjoyed. Ice blocked Hudson Strait, and Swaine's only achievement was a partial exploration of the coast of Labrador. He set out again in 1754 but had worse luck. Eskimos killed some of his men, and the rest of the crew forced him to return to Philadelphia.[39]

These were exciting times for men of imagination. In 1748 the war with France and Spain was concluded, but the competition for commercial supremacy continued. As the result of Vitus Bering's ill-fated voyage (he died of scurvy on an island near Kamchatka in 1741), the Russians established seal fisheries along the Alaskan coast. The Spanish government strengthened its claim to the west coast of North America by sending expeditions to map the terrain. The activities of Russia and Spain on the west coast were a challenge to England to continue its voyages of exploration.

On the eastern coast, the English strengthened their position by the establishment of Halifax in Nova Scotia in 1749. The project was the first scheme sponsored by Lord Halifax as head of the Board of Trade. Edmund Burke would later complain that the transformation of French Acadia into British Nova Scotia cost an exorbitant £700,000, but the Halifax colony was a popular venture in 1749. The first settlers, many of them discharged soldiers, did not adapt well to their new environment. They were described as "the King's bad bargains."[40] During the ten years that followed, Nova Scotia experienced revolutionary changes as the Acadians were removed, and, under Governor Charles Lawrence, a colonial government was established. Henry Ellis would have been astonished, if he had known in 1750, that in ten years' time he himself would be Lawrence's successor as governor of Nova Scotia.

In 1750, Ellis could not predict the future, but he could try to influence the shape of things to come. He wrote his second publication, *Considerations on the Great Advantages Which Would Arise from the Discovery of the North West Passage and a Clear Account of the Most Practicable Method for Attempting That Discovery.* His argument was that there was "a kind of moral certainty" that there was an undiscovered continent in the Pacific and a number of unknown islands westward of America. Increased competition with trade rivals in all the old routes to Africa and the Orient lessened the profitability of those channels of trade. The search for a northwest passage should be pressed. Its discovery would stimulate trade, increase shipping, reduce the national debt, promote manufactures, and provide for employment. Previous searches had been frustrated by ice and the opposition of the Hudson's Bay Company. Future searches should be from the west.

Ellis proposed a route that combined trade with discovery. He suggested taking a cargo by way of the Cape of Good Hope to the East Indies and Canton, China. From there the search for new islands in the Pacific would be made incidental to a crossing to the west coast of America. He cited Bering's explorations as proving that Asia and

America were separate continents. He knew also that the west coast was comparatively ice-free. California was inhabited; the natives were friendly. Even if the passage did not exist, the narrowest neck of land separating eastern from western waters should be located as a site for a trading center.

Ellis cited parliamentary precedents for encouraging such ventures, including premiums for promoting Greenland trade, bounties for exports, and, most important, the recent subsidization of the Halifax colony. Compared to the potential benefits, the cost of an expedition such as he described would be trifling.

In a bold challenge to the Newcastle administration, Ellis stated that where science, public virtue, and liberty prevailed, ministers would rise up and dare to "risk something in Favour of those who are willing to hazard themselves for the Good of their Country." [41] The historian Vincent T. Harlow wrote that this "was the age of theoretical speculation, of interest in the noble savage and in the distant parts of the earth as possible fields of commercial investment." [42] William Pitt was perhaps the most outstanding personification of the spirit and proponent of the policy of which Ellis was an eloquent spokesman. Harlow makes the point that the foundations of the "second" British Empire, that of the nineteenth century, an empire of trade rather than colonization, were laid in the mid-eighteenth century. The trading interests of England later welcomed the disposal of expensive colonies in the American Revolution. Whether Ellis's pamphlet caused it or was simply one of many factors, Parliament renewed its offer of £20,000 to the first ship to discover and sail through a passage between Hudson Bay and the South Sea in either direction. The measure was enacted in 1754 with the support of Lord Halifax and the Board of Trade. The Great War for the Empire delayed a search, but in 1764 Captain John Byron was instructed to explore the Falkland Islands on his way to America's western coast. He was to discover new lands in the Pacific and then locate a sea passage from the western side of North America. He was to return by way of China and the Cape of Good Hope, reversing Ellis's recommended route. The instructions reveal that the lords of the Admiralty shared Henry Ellis's imagination as well as his optimism. Byron was more realistic. He mapped the Falkland Islands and then exhausted himself working through the Straits of Magellan. Ignoring his instructions to proceed up the American coastline, he sailed home across the Pacific and around the Cape of Good Hope. He managed to avoid any discoveries.[43]

Byron had given England a claim to the Falkland Islands and sailed around the world, but he had failed to find a passage. Captain Samuel Wallis and Captain Philip Carteret were sent out on the same mission, but both followed Byron's example and sailed across the Pacific without attempting to explore the northern waters.[44] It was left to the incomparable James Cook to do the job properly. He was given the same instructions issued to Byron in 1764, that is, to look for a land mass in the Pacific and then proceed to investigate a western outlet for a northwest passage. On August 26, 1768, Cook sailed into history. With him was Joseph Banks in Ellis's role as scientific observer and, like Ellis, a member of the Royal Society. Admittedly, Cook did not do it all on the first try. On this voyage he merely mapped New Zealand, discovered Australia, proved that New Guinea and Australia were separate land masses, and returned by way of Africa in 1771. Nor did he look for the passage on his second journey, from 1772 to 1775. This time, however, he took the route suggested by Ellis and sailed around Africa and took an easterly course. He very nearly discovered Antarctica in the process; he reached 71° 10′ south latitude, farther than anyone had gone before, until he was stopped by polar ice. He proved that there was no continent between Australia and the southern ice cap and then sailed for home.

Finally, in 1776, Cook was sent out to complete his mission by coasting along California and to the northward in search of a western outlet for a passage. Again Cook's course was around the Cape of Good Hope and eastward across the Pacific; his ships were the *Resolution* and the *Discovery*. In a voyage free from the usual hazards associated with northern exploration, Cook methodically probed the western coast. He discovered Nootka Sound, made his way through the Aleutians, and probed around the shoulder of the continent, naming capes, rivers, and bays along the way.

Anyone familiar with the ice-choked eastern waters must be surprised when reading Cook's journal. By August 1 he had reached 60° 58′ north latitude and encountered no ice. On August 5, he anchored at Point Rodney at 64° 30′. He continued northward, still finding no ice, just mist and rain. By mid-August Cook reached 70° 44′ north, nearly matching his most southerly latitude on the previous voyage. There he ran into the permanent ice, which stretched as far as the lookouts could see. He could go no farther. He named the point of land that jutted out from under the ice Icy Cape and turned southward.[45] In the following year he was killed by natives on a beach in Hawaii. It has been said that the death of Cook marked the end of the second golden age of maritime exploration. The Elizabethans exploited the Atlantic and opened America for commercial ventures. The eighteenth-century explorers opened the Pacific for British entrepreneurs. Henry Ellis, explorer and promoter, played a not insignificant part in laying the foundation for the second British Empire.

Ellis, as a fellow of the Royal Society with a special interest in the exploration of northern waters, followed Cook's discoveries closely. Though his colleagues were convinced that Cook had demonstrated that there was no passage from the west, Ellis continued to hold to his opinion that there must be an opening. Cook had not followed the shoulder of the continent far enough to the east.[46] Ellis was right, as his countrymen McClure and McClintock would prove. It may have been that those hardy Irishmen were encouraged to continue the search even after Cook because they agreed with Henry Ellis's argument in his book on the northwest passage that "the most practical method for attempting that discovery" was from the west.

CHAPTER THREE *Captain Henry Ellis, F.R.S., and the African Trade*

ENRY ELLIS made a bold political statement when he dedicated the journal of his voyage to Frederick, Prince of Wales. The aging George II had no use for his son or for all those who gathered around the prince at Leicester House and Carleton Gardens. Frederick and his courtiers amused themselves with the fascinating pastime of composing and revising future ministries. If Henry Ellis hoped to be included in these ephemeral governments, his prospects were dimmed by the untimely death of Frederick in 1751. Frederick's friends had to make their peace with the Pelham-Newcastle ministry or bide their time until young George became the third king of that name.

The most important member of the entourage of the future king was James Stuart, Earl of Bute. Bute had been an intimate of the royal family ever since a chance meeting at a racetrack in 1747. A fourth at cards was needed, and Bute was introduced to the royal couple, Frederick and Augusta. W. S. Gilbert might have composed a ditty about how he played at cards so diligently that he became head of the ministry. There were those who said the reason Bute had caught the eye of Augusta was that he exhibited a well-turned calf. In addition, she might have liked his cultivated mind, his knowledge of the classics, and his keen interest in natural sciences. His wife could more than hold her own in polite conversation; she was Mary, daughter of the talented and often caustic woman of letters Mary Wortley Montagu.[1]

Robert Nugent, a wealthy Irish gentleman who became Viscount Clare in 1767, was a personal friend of the Prince of Wales. Frederick, reduced to a condition of chronic financial embarrassment by his unforgiving parent, borrowed money from his friends. He died in debt to Nugent. According to Nathaniel Wraxhall, a keen observer of the contemporary social scene, Nugent "was more than once destined to have filled an office in some of those imaginary administrations which were perpetually fabricated at Leicester House."[2] Nugent was a jovial Irishman who profited from successive marriages to wealthy widows. He was a boon companion, a quick wit, and a good debater in Parliament. His letters to his friend the Earl of Chesterfield are cleverly written.[3] Nugent's daughter married George Grenville, a rising star in the Leicester House firmament. Henry Ellis liked Nugent and dined with him at Bath, the favorite spa of the gentry.[4] A mutual interest was the West Indian trade. Nugent sat in Parliament as member from Bristol from 1754 to 1774 and represented the merchants of that busy port city of seventy-five thousand people. Henry Ellis sailed out of Bristol and contributed directly to the promotion of the trade.

The most politically important of Ellis's new friends was George Montagu Dunk, second Earl of Halifax. He acquired his name and fortune at the same time by marrying Anne, heiress to the estate of Sir Thomas Dunk. Because there was a stipulation that the inheritance must go to a man engaged in commerce, Halifax joined a London trading company. His conversion to the cause of trade was as sincere as his devotion to his wife. He was devastated when she died in 1753 at the age of twenty-eight.[5]

Halifax was a loyal frequenter of Leicester House and in 1742 was rewarded by a sinecure, the positions of lord of bedchamber in the prince's household and of royal forester at Hampton Court's Bushy Park. After his reconciliation with the ruling Pelham administration, a reconciliation made easier because he was a cousin of Henry Pelham and the Duke of Newcastle, he was elevated to the head of the Board of Trade and seized the opportunity to build up commerce with the American colonies. His most conspicuous achievement was the colonization of Nova Scotia and the establishment of the town in that province named after him. The policy of salutary neglect, deliberately followed by Walpole and inadvertently by Newcastle, came to an end with the appointment of Halifax in 1748 rather than with the Grenville administration in 1763.

Halifax was not so much Ellis's friend as his patron. In the sensitive sphere of high politics, the relationship between the conferrer of office and the conferee was like a publicly proclaimed attachment that was more important than friendship. Any success the protégé enjoyed reflected honor upon the patron. Because Henry Ellis invariably did well, offices and other benefactions were forthcoming. The first favor bestowed upon Ellis for his service in Hudson Bay was the post of deputy commissary general of His Majesty's stores. His duties took him to Southampton, where he helped outfit a regiment of Hessian soldiers. While there, he made the acquaintance of a major on the Duke of Cumberland's staff by the name of Jeffrey Amherst. Ellis would remind Amherst of their meeting later when one was governor of Georgia and the other was commander of the British forces in North America. Ellis realized that he owed his appointment to the Earl of Halifax. When he was given command of a ship by a group of Bristol merchants, he named the vessel the *Earl of Halifax*.[6]

Another important personage in Henry Ellis's circle of friends and associates was Irish-born William Wildman, Lord Barrington. Barrington served on the Admiralty Board in 1749, and after Henry Pelham's death in 1754, he joined the Newcastle cabinet as secretary of war. Barrington was a close friend of Halifax. As was the custom, he used his position to help his friends. He informed Francis Bernard, "I found Lord Halifax in the best disposition to shew his regard for you."[7] Bernard was named governor of Massachusetts.

Other acquaintances of Henry Ellis's included William Talbot, the lord steward, and Talbot's son-in-law, George Rice, who sat on the Board of Trade. Talbot was known for his skill in boxing and fencing rather than his intellectual prowess. He became the butt of London jokes as the result of an incident during the inauguration dinner for George III. Talbot, as lord steward, was in charge of the event. He had trained his horse to ride into the hall, pause while Talbot bowed to the royal table, and then back gracefully out of the hall. The horse became confused and backed into the hall, spoiling the effect.[8]

A listing of Ellis's friends should include Philip Carteret Webb, who in 1854 won the parliamentary seat from Haslemere, Surrey, a seat previously held by James Edward Oglethorpe, investigator of prisons and founder of Georgia. Webb gained unwelcomed notoriety by assisting his own cause through the creation of eight voting freeholds out of one alehouse called the Cow. A wag wrote a mock-heroic poem, which included the lines:

The Cow of fame
Then surely came
From Phil's prolifick Brain [9]

Webb was loyal to the Leicester House faction and was rewarded by Bute by appointment to the office of solicitor to the treasury. Like so many of his contemporaries, Webb was interested in science and botany. He maintained a conservatory for rare plants at Burbridge, his Surrey estate near Godalming. Because of his interest in plants, Webb was inducted into the Royal Society in 1749, the year Ellis was proposed for election to the distinguished company. A mutual friend of Webb and Henry Ellis was John Ellis, who helped Webb establish his conservatory.[10] The two Ellises, unrelated to each other, became close friends.

The president of the Royal Society, Martin Folkes, and a member of the council, Charles Stanhope, joined with two others to endorse Ellis for election to the society on November 9, 1749. Their resolution referred to Ellis as commander of a ship in the African trade and read in part, "We recommend him as a Gentleman of merit of great curiosity and an uncommon zeal for the making of discoveries and promoting Natural History, Geography and navigation and who will therefore we doubt not be a useful and valuable member of the Society." [11] It must have been a proud moment for Henry Ellis when, on February 8, 1750, he was welcomed into the fellowship of the society. He would never be a peer of the kingdom, but his status as a member was equal to that of other members, William Pitt, George Lyttelton, and Lord Egremont and the French members, Voltaire and Montesquieu. Ellis later paid visits to Voltaire on his trips to France, and the caustic Frenchman praised one of Ellis's suggestions about the management of police.[12]

A recent inductee at the time Ellis joined the Royal Society was Major General James Edward Oglethorpe.[13] Oglethorpe was a celebrity, his name forever linked to the most publicized philanthropy of the Walpole administration, the establishment of Georgia as a haven, not for debtors but for the moral, hardworking poor of England and for an assortment of foreign Protestants. Oglethorpe's reputation was blemished by a chorus of criticisms emanating from Georgia by the very folk who were supposed to be the grateful beneficiaries of Parliament's virtuous impulse. Oglethorpe had already given up Georgia as a failed experiment, and his fellow Trustees were in the process of handing the colony over to the king and, more specifically, to Lord Halifax and the Board of Trade. If Henry Ellis had known that Halifax would call upon him to rescue the distressed province, he might have made better use of his chance encounters with Oglethorpe at the society's meeting place at Crane Court.

A new inductee with Ellis was Edward Wortley Montagu, brother-in-law to the Earl of Bute. Another new member in 1750 was Charles Walmesley. Walmesley was admitted because he was one of the world's best mathematicians and also a Jesuit priest. If Ellis's invitation to membership indicated the society's interest in the curiosities of the New World, the admission of Walmesley was the result of the connection between the society and the Royal Observatory at Greenwich. As early as 1710 Queen Anne appointed the president and fellows of the Royal Society Visitors of the Royal Observatory. In 1748 the astronomer royal, Sir James Bradley, was awarded the society's Copley medal for his discoveries.[14] His close friend from college days, George Parke, Earl of Macclesfield, maintained an observatory at his country seat, Shirburn Castle in Oxfordshire, and spearheaded the successful campaign to bring the British calendar in line with the Gregorian calendar in use in the rest of the Christian world.

Walmesley, the Jesuit, was a prominent consultant in the preparation of a bill to reform the calendar. As a result, the new year was changed from March 25 to January 1, and the year 1752 began on the new date. Eleven days were simply erased from that year; September 2, 1752, was followed by September 14. The entire arrangement confused and worried the uninformed. Believing that their lives had been shortened by an edict of Parliament, a mob threatened Macclesfield shouting, "Give us back our eleven days!" Macclesfield and the other sponsors of the calendar change prudently concealed Walmesley's role in the affair. The bill was unpopular enough as it was. If the public knew that a Jesuit was involved, there might be a violent reaction. The admission of Walmesley to the fellowship of the society was all the recognition he would get and, perhaps, all he wanted. Macclesfield himself was rewarded by being elevated to the presidency of the society.[15]

Another issue of interest to the society when Henry Ellis joined its company was the cause and cure of a contagion known as "jail fever." In the year 1750 the lord mayor of London, two judges, and an alderman contacted the fever from inmates of Newgate who were brought into the Old Bailey for trial. Death was no stranger to Newgate, but when fatality spread to the judges' bench, the magistrates were roused to action. At least, they were roused to the point of asking the Royal Society to solve the problem. Dr. Stephen Hales, a companion of Oglethorpe's on the board of the Georgia Trust, headed the committee charged with looking into the matter. As the result, Hales invented a "ventilator" that worked like a modern exhaust fan but was manually propelled.

The erection of the machine at Newgate was a dangerous operation; of the eleven men employed on the job, seven contracted a fever and one died. The results were a triumph for Dr. Hales and the Royal Society. When fresh air replaced fetid, deaths at Newgate dropped from seven or eight a week to two a month.[16] It occurred to Hales and his friends, one of whom was Henry Ellis, that the ventilator might work as well aboard ship. Shipowners and masters were notoriously conservative and uninclined to experiment with newfangled devices of any kind, including ventilators. Henry Ellis promised Dr. Hales to take a ventilator along on his next voyage and give it a proper test.

Membership in the Royal Society was an opportunity for a liberal education. Regular meetings of the society were held in the rather confined headquarters at Crane Court, which served as a repository for the increasing collection of artifacts until the British Museum was opened in 1753. The meetings were attended by about seventy members; seating was at random, except for the president and secretary, who sat at a table at one end of the room. One of the members, William Stulkeley, the antiquarian, wrote of the "splendid company" at the gatherings: "Here we meet either personally or in their works, all the geniuses of England, or rather of the whole world, whatever the globe produces that is curious, or whatever the heavens present." [17] Henry Ellis would have been impressed by Stulkeley, the authority on England's ancient civilizations, whose books he had read in school. Stulkeley's fossils made up much of the society's collection, and there were those who murmured that Stulkeley was a better collector than he was a scientist.

Ironically, Stulkeley risked his reputation, not on fossils but on corals. He insisted that corallines were vegetables. "Whoever has eyes must see that they are vegetables," he proclaimed.[18] The man who challenged Stulkeley was the modest and comparatively unknown horticulturist John Ellis. The fellows of the society listened to Ellis's paper in 1753 in which he contended that corallines were animals and were so impressed that they invited him to become a member in 1754.[19] The prestigious Copley Medal for 1753 was conferred on Benjamin Franklin for his experiments on the electrical nature of lightning. Franklin was admitted to the society in 1756 and remained a member in good standing throughout the American Revolution.[20]

However congenial were his friends and fellow members of the Royal Society, Henry Ellis was by profession a sailor, and the sea called him away from the intellectual activities of London. Ellis combined his interest in the sea, science, and politics in his first voyage as a member of the Royal Society. It was politically important because Lord Halifax had approved the idea of experimenting with Hales's ventilator, and it was politically useful to cooperate with Lord Halifax. As captain of the *Earl of Halifax*, Ellis sailed from Bristol near the end of the year 1750 and wrote his first report to Dr. Hales from Cape Mount, Africa, on January 7, 1751, expressing his satisfaction at having the opportunity to work with a man whose greatest happiness lay in promoting the welfare of mankind. Ellis's detailed description of his experiments reveals more about his bent of mind than it does about ventilators. For example, he molded candles and measured them to an exact thickness and length. He burned a candle in the hold of the ship, which had not been ventilated in twenty-four hours, and found that it was diminished by sixty-seven grains in a half hour. After six hours of ventilation it burned ninety-four and a half grains in the same time.[21]

He conducted a complicated experiment involving reflected light to determine how much brighter it shone in a ventilated compartment. Finally, he found that a bell vibrated longer and slower in a ventilated compartment. Most important, as he emphasized, was that of the 130 people aboard, not a man was sick. The hold, which was usually moist, was dry as the result of using the Hales ventilators. The cargo, a shipment of arms, "came out as bright as from a recent polish."[22] Thus ventilation saved cargoes as well as lives.

Hales asked Ellis to do another experiment to determine the effect of depth on the temperature of water. Hales had invented a special bucket which he called a sea-gauge. It was equipped with valves that opened as the bucket descended and closed when the downward motion ceased in order to trap the water at the desired depth. Cords kept the bucket upright. The diligent Ellis tried various depths from 360 feet to a surprising 5,346 feet. He found that the cold increased in proportion to the depth until it reached 3,900 feet. At that level and deeper, the thermometer remained at fifty-three degrees Fahrenheit. The surface temperature of the water was eighty-four degrees. He discovered that the deeper water was heavier and saltier than water at the surface. Hales had not intended the experiments to have any practical application, but Ellis was an inventive person and put the deep-sea bucket to good use. It supplied cold baths, especially welcome in the tropics, and it chilled wines and drinking water.[23]

He had plants on board and carefully watched the effects of the change of climate on them. His report betrayed excitement when he described "a phenomenon which I saw last night and never before."[24] The unusual event was that the irises remained in bloom in the moonlight, rather than closing their petals as usual. There must not have been many aboard with whom Ellis could share this excitement for night-blooming irises. He had to be satisfied with giving his friend John Ellis a full report. At Ellis's request, Hales submitted the letter on ventilators to the committee on publications. It was approved and published in the 1752 *Philosophical Transactions*. The postscript was not published. In it Ellis asked Hales to convey his personal regards to Lord and Lady Halifax, Lord Barrington, Lord Dupplin (one of the members of the Board of Trade), and the bishop of Worcester.[25] A further indication of his close relationship with Halifax is that he collected a box of tropical plants for his patron during this voyage.[26]

On the passage to the West Indies Ellis intended to drop his sea-gauge to a depth of two miles, but he was unable to carry out another idea he and Hales had discussed because he did not have the necessary equipment to probe the ocean bottom.[27] Before he could undertake the crossing, he had other stops to make along the African Gold Coast. The polished guns he carried were to be bartered for a cargo of slaves. The *Earl of Halifax* was a slave ship, and Captain Henry Ellis, F.R.S., was a slaver.

The eighteenth-century slave trade was profitable to sellers, transporters, and buyers. Sugar plantations in the West Indies were labor-intensive. The native Americans were decimated by disease, and Europeans who migrated to America perished in large numbers. Africans were the most desirable workers because of their relative immunity to tropical diseases such as yellow fever and falciparum malaria.[28]

During the eighteenth century, when plantation laborers were most in demand, conditions in Africa made them available. For example, between 1746 and 1754, including the period when Ellis was involved in the trade, Senegal experienced a series of poor harvests. Senegalese refugees sold themselves into slavery in order to survive. Others put themselves at the mercy of neighboring tribes and were subject to being sold at the whim of their hosts. Intertribal warfare also helped make slaves available. During the eighteenth century the Asante had established themselves as the most powerful tribe on the Gold Coast. They carried on a series of wars to subjugate neighboring states and later put down rebellions among those subject peoples. Each war and each punitive action produced slaves for sale. Selling conquered enemies to distant places made good political as well as economic sense.[29]

Henry Ellis defended the slave trade three decades later when it came under attack from reformers. In his experience, the interior tribes were continually engaged in warfare for the purpose of taking slaves. These captives were at the mercy of their captors, whom Ellis described as "barbrous tyrants." Warfare was not the only avenue to enslavement. In Guinea a man might borrow money against the price he thought he might bring from a factor. If he could not repay the loan, he became the property of the chief or, more likely, the factor from whom he had borrowed. "I have often seen these wretches at the feet of the Captains of ships beseeching in the most pathetick manner to buy them," Ellis said.[30] Some whose defects prevented their sale were knocked in the head by their owners and thrown into the sea. Ellis's point was that those who were sold into slavery had already surrendered their freedom by crime, debt, or war.

Very few Englishmen ventured into Africa. Ellis did on several occasions, probably escorted by a trader who was well-known to the native chiefs. The comparatively few children he saw caused Ellis to believe that blacks were less prolific than whites. In one village he witnessed the ceremonial execution of a captive taken in war. At the climax of the ritual, the war captain cut out the heart of the victim and ate it to reinforce his own courage. Ellis saw heads of prisoners fixed on poles around the village. Life in Africa, as Ellis described it, was less than idyllic; it was fearfully cheap.[31]

It would do no good for England to refrain from trading in slaves, Ellis argued; the Dutch, French, or Portuguese would quickly take over the trade. Ellis saw the trade as a positive advantage to the British commercial interests which he represented. It stimulated British exports, which in turn created jobs in manufacturing. It was, like the fishing industry, a boon to the shipping interests and a nursery of seamen.[32] Ships and sailors were vital to England's control of the sea lanes, an objective promoted by William Pitt and the Earl of Halifax as well as by Henry Ellis and his fellow captains.

It would not have occurred to Henry Ellis to attempt to justify his involvement in the slave trade in his three voyages on the triangular routes from England to Africa to Jamaica and back to England. His arguments came later, when William Wilberforce influenced the younger William Pitt to raise questions about the propriety of the trade in humans. The prevalent opinion in 1750 was expressed in an anonymous pamphlet published in 1744. The writer explained the dire consequences that would arise from the collapse of the Royal African Company. The company maintained thirteen forts along the west coast of Africa in varying states of decline and decrepitude. The French, aided by government subsidies, were strengthening their posts and claimed a monopoly along four hundred miles of the Guinea Coast. The British company, burdened in debt, could no longer maintain the posts properly. France would be able to control the slave trade and might even deny slaves entirely "in order to distress and impoverish our British plantations."[33] French shipping and manufacturing would then increase at the expense of the British. Employment would be adversely affected. The writer's conclusion was calculated to strike fear in the soul of every British subject. If the national revenue were to be reduced by the diminution of the profitable triangular trade with Africa, then taxes on British subjects must increase.

A phobia about taxes was characteristic of Englishmen everywhere. Moral issues paled into insignificance when taxes were involved. Every man in the kingdom, in the opinion of the writer, had a stake in the preservation of the Royal African Company's posts.[34] The result of this and other lobbying was an act of Parliament of January 28, 1752, which compensated the old company £112,142 and abolished it. A new company was created under the title the Company of Merchants Trading to Africa. The governing body would consist of three London merchants, three from Bristol, and three from Liverpool. The company as such could not engage in trade; its purpose was to operate and maintain the African forts and factories.[35]

Public opinion as reflected by Parliament's activity was solidly behind the African trade, the most important part of which was traffic in slaves. Henry Ellis and his fellow captains were regarded by their countrymen as defenders of the British economy. Untroubled by the several hundred human beings crowded in the hold, Ellis could congratulate himself on providing proper ventilation for them and on maintaining England's commercial supremacy.

A few small voices wondered about the legality of slavery in a kingdom whose law did not know slavery. It had been questioned whether a slave who breathed the free air of England was thereby free. Philip Yorke, acting as attorney general, ruled not so in 1729. In 1749 that decision was reaffirmed, not surprisingly, by the same Philip Yorke, now Lord Hardwicke, acting in the capacity of lord chancellor.[36] The question of the legality of slavery in the colonies had not yet been raised.

As the *Earl of Halifax* probed along Guinea, Sierra Leone, and the Gold Coast, Ellis met a variety of dealers in slaves. In some places local kings did the trading; however, their supply of slaves was generally limited to criminals and debtors, and whether or not they traded, these potentates required a "custom," a bribe, before any negotiation could begin. Occasionally Ellis met a more powerful king from the interior, bringing slaves taken in raids against less powerful neighbors. The Mandingos, for example, were a Moslem tribe from the upper Niger River, whose religion encouraged the subjugation of the heathen. A Mandingo king's procession to the coast was a formidable sight, with the long line of slaves linked to each other in coffles and the guards, bearers, and personal household of the king extending the line. The bargaining, or "palavers," with such a dignitary followed an accepted ritual, marked by gift-giving, pipe-smoking, eating, and drinking. The experience Ellis gained in these African transactions prepared him for dealing with American Indians. The ritual was similar on both continents. Some of the slave traders Ellis met with were African, European, and men of mixed blood who had acquired wealth and a degree of independence from local kings. Their trading posts were forts, and their servants constituted a small army.[37]

The business of picking up slaves along the coast was not without risks. A journal by a contemporary of Ellis's provides a rare insight into the European attitude toward Africa. Nicholas Owen was an Irishman whose father had wasted a fortune and whose wealthy relatives turned their backs on the youth. Renouncing his native land, he took to the sea. His ship, which set out from Liverpool in December 1750, arrived at Cape Mount, Africa, while Ellis was there and picked up eighty slaves and a cargo of ivory. Then it encountered a French ship manned by slaves who had killed the whites and commandeered the vessel. The British attempted to overawe the slaves and claim them, but, in Owen's words "the slaves behaved so as to make us give over the attempt with loss on our side." Mutiny by slaves was not the only risk a European slave trader ran. Owen and several of his mates were seized by natives and enslaved in retaliation for the capture of several free blacks by a Dutch vessel.[38]

Owen settled on the African coast and became a minor slave trader, sending his servants into the country to purchase three or four slaves at a time for sale to passing ships. He lived in a crude hut with his woman and a few domestics, hoping someday to return to Ireland or England. Meanwhile, he consoled himself by writing in his journal, recording the customs of the people, and sketching scenes of life around him. As it happened, the Seven Years' War between England and France prevented Owen's return to his native land, and he died in Africa in 1758.

Ellis managed to avoid the hazards involved in trafficking along the African coast. The *Halifax* was a large ship, manned by a crew of thirty-four, and too well armed to fall prey to pirates and other enemies. The loading of slaves was a carefully organized operation. Ellis and his mates carefully examined the slaves before sealing the transaction with the trader. Each person was shaved and stripped. The trader's brand blistered each one's skin. Ellis looked for telltale signs of drugs given to simulate health, such as profuse sweating or unusual glossiness of skin. The slaves selected were brought to the ship in canoes; men and women were separated on deck and led to different compartments in the hold. In none of the British ships was there room to stand below deck, and slaves moved to their places in a squatting walk. Everyone faced the same direction, crowded closely together. There was a nightly struggle for an extra modicum of space. When Ellis had 340 souls aboard the *Halifax*, he hoisted sail for the dreaded "middle passage" across the Atlantic.[39]

The voyage quickly assumed a routine. During good weather, the slaves were brought on deck and the area below decks was washed. Every morning each person was given a dram of vinegar to prevent scurvy. Pipes of tobacco were circulated among the men. A half-pint of water per meal was allotted, about the same as in the Royal Navy.

While the slaves were on deck, singing was encouraged and exercising was required.[40]

In the evening the second mate and boatswain, each with whip in hand, stowed the human cargo below. In some ships, one slave in every ten was appointed constable and charged with maintaining order during the night. Meanwhile, the upper decks were swabbed down. It was the captain's responsibility to investigate every part of the ship every day. One slave trader believed that "no vessel, except a man-of-war, can compare with a slaver in systematic order, purity and neatness."[41] A clean ship lessened the chance of disease, which might strike white crew as well as black cargo. It made good business sense to take all reasonable precautions to maintain healthy conditions. A humane captain would have additional reasons. Ellis was both practical and humane. He informed Dr. Hales that the slaves recognized the advantage of ventilation and clamored for it when the fans stopped. The manual operation of the fans provided exercise for those slaves who were allowed to do that work.[42]

Ellis was puritanical in his condemnation of the use of alcohol on his ship. He had seen the debilitating effects of rum and brandy among the Indians of Hudson Bay. He blamed strong drink for the spread of scurvy among the crew of the *Dobbs Galley*. He was convinced that alcohol would do worse damage in the tropics and strictly limited its use. The crew respected his seamanship and accepted his strange experiments with sea buckets and ventilators although they regretted his attitude toward grog. Ellis attributed the health of his crew to the imposed sobriety.[43]

Kingstown, Jamaica, was the port of call for the *Halifax*. Slaves were brought on deck for the "scramble." Merchants came aboard to examine and purchase them for resale to planters.[44] The *Halifax* took on a cargo of sugar, molasses, rum, lumber, and a handsome profit in gold for its backers in Bristol. Upon his return, Ellis wrote Hales an enthusiastic report on the value of ventilators. He congratulated Hales for his efforts to find captains willing to try the device on their vessels and for the other worthy authorities who installed ventilators in hospitals and prisons. Ellis was pleased to be working with Hales "in promoting the public good."[45] He had lost only 6 out of 340 people, delivering 334 healthy bodies. To those who might observe that the people he transported faced a future of slavery, he would answer that they were slaves or criminals when he found them and that they would have fared worse in Africa. At least he had rendered their passage tolerable. He had promoted the public good.

Ellis took the *Halifax* out again in 1754 for a repetition of his former voyage. When he heard from Ellis after his return Dr. Hales was pleased to announce to the Royal Society that not one of the consignment of 312 slaves died en route. All thirty-six crewmen returned safely to Bristol in 1755.[46]

The greater glory of England by expansion of commerce was an objective Henry Ellis shared with his new acquaintances of high estate, Halifax and the Grenvilles. The West Indian merchants and their lobby applauded any policy aimed at this worthwhile goal. Such diverse interests as the country Whigs and the London crowds found common cause in the promotion of commerce. All the wars of the eighteenth century were related to competition for commercial advantage. The war that crowned the others, the Seven Years' War, was a global contest for trading advantages in America, Africa, and India. When the war began, Ellis was a captain of commerce. Before it ended, he was an adviser on imperial affairs. Ellis and the other English captains and merchants who brought Africans to America were engaged in another transformative process. The acculturation of Africans and Europeans produced a society that was distinctly American. In South America, the native inhabitants were included in the emerging social and cultural fabric. In North America, the fate of the native Americans hung in the balance. Their future relations with Europeans would be influenced by the decisions of men of Henry Ellis's generation. Ellis himself would have a significant role in determining British policy toward the natives.

When Ellis called on Lord Halifax after settling his accounts with the Bristol merchants, he learned that Governor John Reynolds was a disappointment in Georgia. Halifax wished Henry Ellis to take his place.

CHAPTER FOUR

The View from the Board of Trade

HEN HISTORIANS OF Georgia write about the Ellis administration, they assume a Georgia perspective. Henry Ellis suddenly appears on the stage, plays his part flawlessly, is applauded, and is gone. Ellis himself would have had a different point of view. For him, center stage, to continue the analogy, was in London. He knew the actors and the dialogue, and he knew how the plot should be played. The Georgia adventure, like his voyage to Hudson Bay, was a means of advancement, an opportunity to display ability, intelligence, leadership, and good sense. Ellis had those qualities, to which he added intellectual curiosity, charm, and wit, assets especially admired among the enlightened gentlemen of the eighteenth century.

Before his appointment to Georgia, Ellis had only a vague notion, gleaned from conversations with James Oglethorpe and Stephen Hales, of what the place was like. When he learned that he was going to Georgia, he made it his business to learn all he could about the colony and what was expected of him. The priorities of George Montagu Dunk, Lord Halifax, provided Ellis's agenda. In assessing his career there it is important to understand the colonial governor's relationship to the Board of Trade and the board's peculiar place in the British government.

The Board of Trade was established in 1696 as an experiment in mercantilism. Its purpose was to promote the trade of the kingdom and to inspect and improve plantations in America and elsewhere. The board was a royal creation, not Parliament's. Seven officers of the king's council were members along with eight other lords who did not hold office. The seven privy councillors were too busy with their own work or too grand to attend meetings so the eight other commissioners constituted the active membership. One of them was named first lord or president by the king's appointment. The board became the clearinghouse for information about the colonies, as the vast holdings of the Public Record Office collections under the title "Colonial Office" demonstrate. At first the board attracted the services of capable individuals who attempted to supervise the province, but after 1704 the secretary of state for the Southern Department assumed charge of the colonies and control of patronage. That worthy was usually too busy to bother much about colonial affairs. At times in the years that followed, the board was so out of touch that it was forced to ask the secretary the names of the colonial officers with whom it was supposed to correspond. When the Duke of Newcastle became secretary for the Southern Department in 1724, he diverted all colonial business to his office and the board became little more than a repository for colonial records. Lord Monson, president of the board from 1747 to 1748, acquiesced in the decline of its activity and importance.[1]

If the well-known phrase "era of salutary neglect" has any validity, it is with reference to those years when letters from colonial governors lay unopened for months. The Duke of Newcastle was busy with his principal preoccupation of playing politics, counting votes, managing elections, juggling jobs, placating office seekers, and ferreting out rumors. In fairness to the duke, American affairs were less important to him because the primary responsibility of the secretary of state for the Southern Department was southern Europe. The one consistent policy followed by Newcastle was a search for Continental allies to oppose France and Spain after those Bourbon powers entered into the Family Compact in 1733. The policy that came to be known as the "Old System" explains Newcastle's reluctance to abandon Prussia in 1762.[2] By then Henry Ellis had become an adviser on foreign policy and an advocate of an American system.

In 1748 a shuffling of the ministry occurred and Newcastle took Lord Chesterfield's place as northern secretary, the Duke of Bedford moved into the office of southern secretary, and his friend the Earl of Sandwich replaced Bedford as first lord of Admiralty. Bedford decided that greater attention should be paid to the management of the American colonies, then emerging from a war with their French and Spanish neighbors. He decided to reactivate the Board of Trade and nominated Halifax as one who would provide aggressive leadership and efficient management. Halifax took his seat as first lord of trade on November 11, 1748.[3] He proceeded to devote considerable energy, abetted by his powers of debate, to the administration of the colonies. He used his formidable personal influence to secure greater powers for the Board of Trade. When, at Halifax's initiative, the board assumed the unprecedented role of sponsor of the colonization of Nova Scotia, frustrating obstacles had to be overcome. Halifax could not ask Sandwich at the Admiralty to escort the transports; he had to go through Secretary of State Bedford. In 1751, when Halifax needed naval vessels to protect Nova Scotia, he forwarded his request through Bedford, who brought it before the cabinet council, which concurred. Sandwich balked, however, and Bedford had to choose between his old friend Sandwich and his recent colleague Halifax. Bedford chose Sandwich and denied the request.[4]

This, of course, was regarded as an affront not only to Halifax but to the Henry Pelham–Newcastle ministry, an affront the keener because Sandwich was a cousin of Halifax and the Pelhams. The result was that both Bedford and Sandwich were eased out of their offices. In the short run Halifax believed he was entitled to compensation, perhaps Bedford's vacated office, and he would hold a grudge against Bedford and Sandwich for as long as it was politically convenient. Henry Ellis needed to be aware of his patron's current friends and enemies. The Halifax-Bedford animosity would surface later during the negotiations for peace in 1763, when Ellis acted as adviser to the ministry, which included Halifax, and the Duke of Bedford represented the ministry in Paris.[5]

Newcastle was unable to persuade his brother Pelham to give cousin Halifax the secretary's position. Halifax then asked for the same right the secretaries enjoyed, that of direct access to the king on behalf of the Board of Trade. Newcastle relayed the request to the king, who refused his assent because he thought there were too many reporting to him already. Halifax then assumed the posture of an insulted noble lord and retired to his country estate, the Bushy Park ranger's residence at Hampton Court.

The king was informed that something would have to be done — the ministry dared not lose Halifax's influence in Parliament — and Barrington was sent to Bushy Park as a peace emissary. Halifax insisted as a condition of his return that the board be allowed to name all colonial officials and that the secretary of the Southern Department give up control of colonial affairs. Halifax also wanted to be present whenever the Privy Council discussed the colonies. By an order in council of March 11, 1752, Halifax got most of what he wanted. The board was given authority to name all colonial officials except those dealing with the Treasury or Admiralty. Further, all colonial correspondence would go through the board. This provision was more important than it might appear. The board became the most thoroughly informed agency regarding American affairs and began to take unprecedented steps in formulating colonial initiatives.[6]

In appointing governors, Halifax was no more free to name his own people than was the harassed Newcastle. Patronage was coin of the realm among the great lords by which they discharged debts and acquired credit for future use. Thus Halifax thanked Newcastle by appointing Arthur Dobbs to North Carolina. William Henry Lyttelton was given South Carolina as a favor to Sir George Lyttelton, chancellor of the exchequer. Francis Bernard went to Massachusetts because Barrington, secretary at war, asked Halifax to put him there, and Captain John Reynolds was sent to Georgia because he was the nominee of the respected Lord Chancellor Hardwicke.[7] Because Reynolds was not Halifax's man, however, he could be removed at the first complaints against him, a removal facilitated by Lord Hardwicke's retirement in 1756.

Despite the Duke of Newcastle's assertion in 1754 that he wished he knew the best men in England for colonial appointment "for we will have the best men we can find,"[8] it is impossible to detect any consistent pattern in Halifax's appointments, except that most were devotees of the new scientific philosophy. In the language of Newcastle, "best" meant most loyal to the Newcastle ministry, which was not necessarily the same as faithful to the instructions of the Board of Trade. Henry Ellis was unique in that he owed his appointment to no other patron than the noble lord to whom he reported. There was a personal tone to Ellis's letters to the Board of Trade. They were almost conversational.

One example of Newcastle's notion of fitness for colonial appointment was the case of William Grover. Henry Ellis, then in Georgia, desperately needed the help of a competent lawyer. Grover was recommended by Newcastle with the request that he be allowed to remain in England until after the local elections. However successful Grover was in turning out the votes, he was a disaster as chief justice in Georgia.[9] It was very likely his appointment that caused a critic of the administration to blast: "I can point you to a Chief Justice of a province appointed from hence for no other reason than publicly prostituting his honor and conscience at an election."[10]

Thus, because of the complex reasons for appointment, the colonial officials did not necessarily share Halifax's vision of welding a machinery of administration that would bridge the gap between Parliament and colonial governments. Even though Halifax did not gain the objective of a cabinet post, the board had become more than a clearinghouse. A careful student of the history of the Board of Trade concluded that it was at the height of its prestige under Halifax: "The power to nominate colonial officials, the power to monopolize colonial correspondence with them and the power to make representations and reports on the basis of such correspondence was, short of the establishment of an independent American department, the best arrangement that could have been made."[11]

Halifax continued to press Newcastle for the final necessary step, direct access to the king by admission to the Privy Council. Newcastle, who hated to say no more than any British minister before or since, assured him that it should be done as soon as an opportunity presented itself. The right moment came during another of those frequent rearrangements of ministers. William Pitt, in cooperation with the Duke of Devonshire, forced Newcastle out of government and assumed the office of secretary for the Southern Department in December 1756. The king heartily disliked Pitt, however, and the king's son the Duke of Cumberland refused to assume command of the British troops on the Continent with Pitt in power.

On April 6, 1757, the king ordered Pitt to return the seals of office. It was one thing to turn him out and another to find someone bold enough to set up a government which Pitt would certainly oppose. After three months of fruitless search, the king was forced to agree to a coalition between Pitt and Newcastle on June 29, 1757.[12] It was on this occasion that Newcastle told Halifax that he intended to give him a cabinet position equal to that of the two secretaries in rank. Halifax was delighted at the success of his long campaign and shared the good news with all his friends.

Then occurred an embarrassing scene described by George Bubb Dodington in his diary: Halifax went to court and met Pitt, the recently reappointed secretary of the Southern Department. Halifax talked confidently of the plans to remove America from under Pitt's jurisdiction. According to Dodington, "Pitt flared at him and told his Lordship very coolly and very truly that he never had heard one word of it." One can imagine the shock and surprise this caused Halifax. When he confronted Newcastle for an explanation, the poor duke could only say, "Pitt looked so out of humour, that he durst not." Halifax out of humor was only slightly less formidable than Pitt, and a bystander reported that he had never heard any man abuse another as Halifax did Newcastle.[13]

Halifax departed for Bushy Park to brood about the situation. Newcastle tried to get Lord Dupplin, a veteran member of the Board of Trade, to take the place of Halifax, but Dupplin had better sense than to be caught in a quarrel between Pitt and Halifax. Besides, Halifax was an old friend. Again Halifax was coaxed out of his retreat by Barrington and Chesterfield, and again he was rewarded for having been insulted. Pitt would not permit a partition of his office, but he agreed to give Halifax a place in the cabinet. So Halifax at last had direct access to the king, not as the first lord of trade, but as the Earl of Halifax. There lingered an unfortunate but understandable coolness between Pitt and Halifax. For Henry Ellis, who was so closely associated with Halifax, this turbulence on the highest levels was disturbing. He felt out of touch in Savannah and uneasy at hearing the rumors of Halifax's resignation. "I am concerned in his fate and consequently solicitous to know it," he told his friend Lyttelton, the governor of South Carolina.[14] During Halifax's protracted absence, Ellis's letters went unanswered. On all military matters Ellis had to report to Pitt. The lack of response from that office was singularly frustrating.

During the three months that Halifax was nursing his grievances in the country, there occurred one of those political incidents, trivial in itself, that highlighted a fatal flaw in colonial administration. It seems that William Henry Lyttelton was not happy in South Carolina. The Carolinians were far too independent and made his life miserable. William Henry asked his brothers Lord George Lyttelton and Sir Richard Lyttelton to take advantage of their close kinship with William Pitt to get Jamaica for him instead of Carolina. Richard wrote back that Pitt refused to fight for William Henry because, in general, Pitt abstained from the sordid business of jobsmanship. Newcastle, however, took advantage of the temporary absence of Halifax to persuade the board to name one of his creatures, a Colonel Haldane, to Jamaica. So it was, wrote Richard, that William was "freezing in Carolina with little more than your Public spirit and Virtue to warm you while Haldane . . . covered with fat, and bursting with debauchery and distemper must infest the air of Jamaica."[15] Haldane's only skill was in choosing the lucky minute when Halifax was away.

George and Richard Lyttelton continued to work on Halifax, and at last William Henry heard the good news that Jamaica was his and that Halifax wanted him to report to London for instructions. Evidently the noble lord had acquired a reputation as a ladies' man since the death of his wife in 1753. George made a tongue-in-cheek suggestion: "As Brigadier Townshend has brought over from Canada a young savage Boy for his friend Lord George Sackville, I think you should bring a young savage girl for your friend, My Lord Halifax. You will say we have wild girls enough in this country, but we have no copper-coloured ones, and men of pleasure you know are fond of variety."[16]

If anything, the incident reveals how shallow was Newcastle's boast that the best men would be chosen for the colonies and how the absorbing game of court politics took precedence over colonial considerations. William Henry Lyttelton was in the midst of a war with the Cherokees when he heard about his transfer; nevertheless, he packed his baggage for London. There is no evidence that he brought along an Indian maiden.

After he acquired cabinet status, Halifax had achieved nearly all his goals. From 1757 until his resignation in 1761, while the board was at the zenith of its power, Henry Ellis governed Georgia. Georgia, which began under a Board of Trustees, was transferred to a revitalized Board of Trade. Georgia and Nova Scotia were the special projects of the Halifax board. They would be examples of properly administered constitutional governments, to be held up as models before those colonies that ignored the prerogatives of the crown.

It was during the Halifax years that the board first formulated an Indian policy. The board's solicitation of information regarding colonial matters was an opportunity of which Edmond Atkin took full advantage. Atkin was a Charleston merchant who served as a member of Governor James Glen's council. He possessed encyclopedic knowledge of details about government, Indian trade, and the southern Indian nations. He had developed a violent antipathy for Governor James

Glen, whom he accused of conspiring with favored traders against the public welfare. Atkin wrote a long report and delivered it himself to Halifax on May 30, 1755. South Carolina's Indian commissioners were ineffective, he said; they never went out into the country. They got their information from traders, and Atkin distrusted all traders. No penalties for violation of trade regulations had ever been imposed, yet the traders cheated the Indians "most abominably."

Traders were supposed to live in the Indian towns to which they were licensed; instead, they lived in Augusta and sent their servants out. Some of the traders carried on a clandestine trade with the French at Fort Toulouse, the "Alabama Fort," even during the last war. After a litany of criticisms of the prevailing conduct of the Indian trade, Atkin concluded that there was no expectation that the colonies would ever unite to regulate trade, and the only solution was for the king to take over the supervision of Indian affairs through the agency of the Board of Trade.[17] Atkin's written arguments were compelling. In person, he exhibited the zeal and conviction of an evangelist, or, some might say, a fanatic.

Halifax considered Indian trade to be part of his responsibility, and he willingly enlarged the scope of the board's activities to include the complex and ultimately unsolvable problem of European and Indian relations. It is probably significant that the board's interest was in trade rather than settlement. The temptation is to read too much into the initial impulse that led the board into Indian affairs. Yet it can be demonstrated that Halifax and his friends, including the future American secretary Wills Hill, Earl of Hillsborough, followed a consistent policy of promoting trade over speculation and expansion. Henry Ellis was a good soldier in the implementation of the policy. It was ironic that Halifax was represented in America by two men who were interested in the Indian trade, Henry Ellis and Edmond Atkin, and the two were destined to become bitter rivals.

Their rivalry was complicated because Lord George Lyttelton was sufficiently impressed by Atkin's knowledge and zeal to urge that Halifax appoint him to the office of southern superintendent. In America, Governor William Henry Lyttelton would support Atkin's efforts, much to the annoyance of Henry Ellis, who considered the superintendent a busybody. Both Atkin and Ellis were appointed to their offices in 1756. On March 14, Atkin wrote to Lord Loudoun, the military commander in America to whom he was supposed to report, that the

Board of Trade had delivered his orders that morning.[18] He was still in London on May 20 when he informed Governor Lyttelton that his commission was in his pocket. Atkin was the sort to whom nothing came easily. He grumbled that Halifax would not give him any instructions and merely referred him to Loudoun. After a passage to New York marked by a running fight with a French privateer, he had to follow Loudoun to Albany and then to Philadelphia before Loudoun would authorize an expense account of £2,000.[19] Illness delayed his progress south, and he arrived in Charlestown over a year after Henry Ellis.

Ellis probably knew that Atkin was going to Georgia, but he was not aware of what Atkin was supposed to do. Indeed, Halifax himself knew too little about Indian affairs to give specific charges to the superintendents. During May and June the board considered complaints from Georgia directed at Governor John Reynolds. As the first royal governor, Reynolds was expected to mold Georgia into a model of a constitutional province, one in which the local assembly tended to local business and left other matters to the crown through the instrumentality of the Board of Trade or the secretary of state. It appeared from the letters and from the testimony of Alexander Kellet, a member of the Georgia Council who appeared in person before the board, that Georgia was off to a bad start.[20] The board, in a lengthy report to the king on July 29, 1756, concluded that government in Georgia was in disarray. Governor and council were at odds; records were not being kept; an Indian conference was bungled; a group of French Acadians, whose relocation was a matter of importance to Halifax, languished on the Georgia coast, their needs unattended. For these and other reasons, Reynolds was recalled to answer the charges against him. Because there was no person in Georgia who could act as governor, the board recommended Henry Ellis as "a person every way qualified for the station."[21] His confirmation as lieutenant governor was routine. Before the king's pleasure was known on August 4, 1756, Ellis's instructions had been copied out.[22] It was understood that after Reynolds had the courtesy of a hearing, Ellis would be named governor.

Henry Ellis went home to Monaghan that same August to tell his father the news of his promotion. Francis Ellis assured his son that he could count on his financial support to maintain himself as a royal governor should. It was agreed that John Ellis, the London naturalist, would act as agent for father and son.[23] While Henry Ellis was in Monaghan there would have been one or more of those social gatherings for which the Irish are famous. Almost certainly, Henry Ellis renewed the acquaintance of ambitious young William Knox, now twenty-four years old and ready to seek his fortune. Would he like to go to Georgia as Ellis's assistant? Indeed he would, but because he had no source of income or a wealthy father, Knox would require an office with a salary. Ellis thought that could be arranged. So it was worked out between Ellis and Halifax that Knox would be provost marshal in place of Alexander Kellet. When Knox arrived in London, Ellis conducted him to the office of the Board of Trade to meet his lordship. Halifax was gracious and told Ellis to be sure to bring his young friend to his house on Great George Street for a visit. Ellis took this to be one of those empty invitations common in polite society, but the sensitive and still insecure Knox brooded over Ellis's failure to accept Halifax's invitation.[24] For some time, Knox would complain to his journal that Ellis did not pay him enough attention.

Just as Ellis had taken the trouble to brief himself before his search for a northwest passage, he began to study up on Georgia as soon as he learned from Halifax that he was being considered for the appointment. He talked to Alexander Kellet and Patrick Graham, both members of the Georgia Council and both bitter critics of John Reynolds. He interviewed the aging and infirm Benjamin Martyn, the Georgia agent. He read the letters from Georgia at the Board of Trade office, including one of April 6, 1756, from Jonathan Bryan, describing how Reynolds had been received with "great satisfaction" when he first came to Georgia. People were then moving to Georgia in large numbers. Now that was changed; few came and some people of property were leaving. Trade had declined, "and I feer the colony will be reduced to as low an ebb as it was under the late unhappy Constitution under the Trustees," said Bryan.[25]

Ellis wrote a memorandum to the board on October 5, 1756, while still in London. He said he realized that the original purposes for founding Georgia were to produce commodities of value to Britain and to guard against the French, Spanish, and Indians. Now that a war was begun, Georgia's location made it of critical importance. Yet to his astonishment, the province was entirely defenseless. The only forts were in ruins, and even if they were not, there were no troops to man them. In all the province there was a single company stationed at Frederica, and it was under the command of the governor of South Carolina.

There was no artillery fit for service, no ships of war to protect the coasts, and the population was too scattered to constitute an effective militia. Ellis saw clearly that the only realistic defense lay in gaining and keeping the friendship of the surrounding natives. Presents were necessary to confirm an Indian alliance, and Georgia was too poor to supply presents. If it were only his own safety that was at risk by his undertaking this assignment, he would not bother the board with a request. But the safety of the colony and the interest of the country depended on him, and therefore it was his duty to ask for five hundred stand of arms, a ship of war to patrol the coast, and an appropriation for presents for the natives.[26]

The request demonstrates that Ellis had a quick grasp of the essentials and that he took his assignment seriously and responsibly. He did not concern himself with the criticisms leveled at Reynolds but looked beyond to the larger issues. The war for America had begun; if the busy French agents who were already among the Creeks and Cherokees were successful, Georgia would be at their mercy. John Reynolds had sent the same plaintive appeals for over a year without getting the attention and response given to Ellis's succinct statement. John Pownall, the board's secretary, quickly sent a request to the Treasury for funds for Indian presents.[27] James West, secretary to the lords of the Treasury, asked the board to be specific as to "the Nature and Quantum" of such presents. The board, with Ellis's concurrence, estimated that £1,500 would be about right. The lords of Treasury promptly agreed.[28] Meanwhile, the usually slow-paced agent Martyn was moved to ask the board for permission to place £500 in Ellis's hands for the encouragement of silk manufacture. He had had the money in his possession since April but had not sent it. Halifax approved the grant.[29]

Thus when Henry Ellis sailed aboard the *Andalusia* out of Portsmouth on December 8, 1756, his agenda was clear. The first priority was to conciliate the Indians of the interior; second, provide for the defense of the province; third, establish a constitutional government; and fourth, quiet the factionalism. There were other motives, slightly less important. Ellis would be impelled by his scientific curiosity as well as his awareness of the original reasons for establishing Georgia to experiment with the culture of silk and other exotic products. Patriotism played a part in his reasons for going to Georgia, as it did in his search for a northwest passage and in his experiments with ventilators;

he would do what he could to enhance British commercial supremacy at the expense of his country's rivals. Finally, down the list of motives was the knowledge that his future career depended on his performance in Georgia. Lord Halifax and the Lords of Trade would watch him closely.

CHAPTER FIVE   *The Transformation of Georgia*

HE HISTORIAN LAWRENCE
Henry Gipson noted that
the Halifax Board of Trade
attempted to impose uni-
formity upon the colonial administrations. He described a transforming process at work as provinces lost their original characteristics and
were molded into a uniform pattern of royal governments.[1] A set of
lengthy instructions to royal governors was an effective device used
by the board to bring about the desired result, a "constitutional government." Such a government was one in which provincial assemblies
were limited to a restricted range of local concerns while deferring to
the king in council on intercolonial and all external matters.

Thus the New England provinces were guided away from their
seventeenth-century attempts to legislate according to the prescrip-
tions of the Old Testament; Pennsylvania lost the traces of the gospel
according to William Penn; New York imposed an English system upon
Dutch foundations; Nova Scotia forcibly eliminated its French inhabitants as a reflection of the board's desire to erect a proper English
form of government. South Carolina had acquired a habit of independence under her careless proprietors. No one seemed to notice what
was going on in North Carolina until Arthur Dobbs arrived and asserted the royal prerogative. In retrospect it could be argued that the
American colonies had to go through an educational process in the
mid-eighteenth century to learn what the rights of Englishmen were.
Proof that they learned their lesson well was their rebellion against the
mother country in the name of those same rights.

Of all the colonies, Georgia was most in need of transformation.

Originally, Georgia was a much publicized experiment in humanitarianism with a strong underlying current of mercantilism. Unique among the American provinces, it had no government except for a Board of Trustees in London. Landholding was severely restricted, rum was forbidden, and slavery was banned. Inhabitants were expected to be satisfied with the cultivation of wine, hemp, and silk while guarding the valuable rice- and indigo-producing province of South Carolina.[2]

James Edward Oglethorpe, the only Trustee who visited Georgia, succeeded in winning the goodwill of the Indians and particularly of the powerful Creek Nation. In his diplomacy, he was abetted by the woman who called herself niece of Chigilly, brother of the great leader Brims, whom the English referred to as Emperor.[3] Her name was Coosaponakeesa and she was known to the English by the name Mary, to which was attached the names of her successive husbands, Musgrove, Matthews, and Bosomworth.

Oglethorpe antagonized the Spanish authorities in Florida by extending the limits of the colony to the St. Johns River, pretending that the Altamaha, the actual southern boundary, was connected somehow to the St. Johns. During the War of Jenkins's Ear, Oglethorpe failed in two efforts to take St. Augustine but succeeded in beating off a Spanish attack on Frederica, St. Simons Island.[4] In the last analysis, the Trustees' plan was a failure. Most Georgians moved across the river to South Carolina, where they could buy land and slaves, quite literally on the installment plan. Beginning in 1742 the Trustees relaxed their restrictions, allowing rum, then slavery, and finally, larger landholdings. In 1752 they gave Georgia over to the king, or rather, Georgia was handed by the Board of Trustees to the Board of Trade, from one set of parliamentary gentlemen to another. The same persons who held office under the Trustees were instructed to continue in office until the Board of Trade prepared a plan of government for the colony. In 1753 the board drafted a model plan which provided for a strong governor who represented the king in convoking an assembly, passing on legislation, erecting courts, granting lands, and otherwise administering the province. Other officers included an attorney general, a provost marshal, a clerk of the council, a receiver of quitrents, a surveyor, and various customs officials.[5]

The legislature would consist of an assembly composed of two representatives from each county. The counties were to be created as soon as possible. In addition, there would be a council which acted as an upper house as well as a court of appeals. Its members were nominated by the Board of Trade and approved by the king in council. The council, supposedly composed of the ablest men in the province, was an advisory body to the governor.

Captain John Reynolds was commissioned governor of Georgia on August 6, 1754, while Henry Ellis was at sea. Halifax was so impatient to get on with the Georgia experiment that he gave Reynolds ten days to get on board a ship for Georgia. Reynolds had no time to order the furniture and silver service to which every colonial governor was entitled. He reached Savannah on October 29, 1754, and was greeted with apparent enthusiasm.[6] It was not entirely his fault that the first euphoria was short-lived. His councillors were the same men who had held office under the Trustees and during the interim between 1752 and 1754. They were from Savannah and its environs and were interested in planting and commerce. Their primary objective was to secure their fair share of trade from Charlestown. Francis Harris and James Habersham, partners in one of Savannah's first mercantile houses, were members of the Georgia Council. The Georgia backcountry was so different as to constitute a separate province in all but name. Because Oglethorpe's treaty of 1739 with the Creek Nation permitted settlement only as far as the tidewater, the area above the tidal flow and west of the Savannah River was Indian country. With the consent of the Creeks, Oglethorpe had founded Augusta at the head of navigation on the Savannah River in 1736 as a traders' rendezvous with a fort as much to impress the Indians as to protect the traders.[7] Most of the traders were former Carolinians, and out of habit as well as convenience, they sent their deerskins to Charlestown for export. Backcountry people had never paid much attention to the Trustees' restrictions on rum, slavery, and landholding. They had become accustomed to managing their own affairs. Like classic capitalists, individual traders merged into one dominant company and brought an unusual degree of organization into the Indian trading business. Savannah merchants were annoyed at the fact that Georgia deerskins were sent to Charlestown and envious that Augusta merchants were part of the trade monopoly.[8] Savannah was not equipped to compete with Charlestown until Harris and Habersham constructed adequate docking facilities in 1751. Thereafter, the number of ships putting in to Savannah gradually increased.

By the time John Reynolds arrived in Georgia, two distinct groups of immigrants had added new dimensions to the polarity between Savannah and the backcountry. A community of Congregationals from New England by way of Dorcester, South Carolina, settled south of Savannah in a place called Midway and began to plan their own harbor on the coast at Sunbury.[9] Scattered on small rice plantations below Midway were the remnants of the Scots settlement at Darien. The town itself never prospered and was deserted by 1755. The second group of newcomers were from North Carolina; their spokesman was Edmund Gray, a charismatic individual who affected the plain manners and austere life-style of the Quakers. He may have been one of that gentle persuasion, but his enemies called him a "pretended Quaker." He and his followers carved farms out of the wilderness west of Augusta.[10]

Gray and his friends soon decided that the gentlemen who composed the interim council were too narrow and "aristocratical" in their interests. In dispensing land grants they were generous to themselves and their relatives but ignored the requests of outlying settlers. Furthermore, the members of the council were incompetent in their dealings with the Indians. Lulled into a complacent security by Oglethorpe's success in Indian diplomacy, they exhibited an arrogance toward their Creek neighbors which was entirely unwarranted by the reality of their exposed and helpless condition. They had forgotten that one of the reasons for Oglethorpe's success was his friendship with Mary, who claimed kinship with the acknowledged principal chief of all the Creek towns, Malatchi. In their treaty with Oglethorpe in 1739, the Creeks reserved the area near Pipemakers Creek, where Mary lived, and also the islands of St. Catherines, Ossaba, and Sapelo. On several occasions, most notably at a conference in 1753 with South Carolina governor James Glen, Malatchi stated that the islands belonged to the Creeks and the Creek Nation wanted Mary to have them.[11]

The Savannah council disregarded the Bosomworth claim and treated Malatchi rudely when he visited Savannah in 1754. Malatchi reacted by inviting a French delegation from Fort Toulouse of the Alabamas to visit him at Coweta. Mary and Thomas Bosomworth, more than ever determined to have their rights recognized, went to London to argue before the Board of Trade. By then, Reynolds was appointed and the board directed the Bosomworths to bring their case to him.[12] Opposition to the Savannah party was the bond that united Edmund Gray's followers, the Bosomworths, and many of the settlers in lower

Georgia. The realization that the goodwill of the Creeks depended on how the Bosomworths were treated was another link between the backcountry and low country, both of which were more exposed than Savannah. Later Henry Ellis would describe how the inhabitants of Savannah "awoke as from a dream" when the Indians took to the warpath and they realized how defenseless they were. During the Reynolds administration their dream remained undisturbed.

Even before Reynolds convened the first meeting of the Georgia Assembly in January 1755, Edmund Gray had formed Georgia's first political faction and put forward candidates opposed to the Savannah oligarchy. The Gray party seated six of its candidates and claimed that two others were defeated by fraudulent vote counting. They hoped to force new elections by boycotting the assembly and putting out flyers that called on the people to support their cause in the name of liberty. Instead, they were branded as outlaws by the rump assembly, and Governor Reynolds put out his own proclamations forbidding any demonstrations in the name of liberty or anything else. Protesting that they did not mean to be insubordinate to the governor, Gray and as many as three hundred others went below the Altamaha boundary and settled on the Satilla in the debatable land between Georgia and Florida.[13]

For the moment, Reynolds was a hero to his council. He soon alienated its members by giving his former naval surgeon, William Little, seven different appointive positions instead of distributing the sinecures among the councillors. The gentlemen of the council complained that Little neglected his many duties, and Little retaliated by taking Gray's place at the head of the anti-Savannah faction. Little was elected to the 1756 assembly, in which he controlled enough votes to gain the Speaker's chair. Reynolds was extraordinarily cooperative with the requests of the lower house while ignoring the increasingly hostile council. Reynolds planned to remove the seat of government from Savannah to a new town on the Ogeechee, which he named Hardwicke in honor of his sponsor. The governor sought the advice of Lachlan McGillivray, the most respected of the Augusta-based traders, and infuriated the Savannah faction by acknowledging the validity of the Bosomworth claims.[14]

Thus it was factionalism that brought John Reynolds down rather than any malfeasance of office. If he was guilty of anything, it was a lack of judgment in loading William Little with offices and other favors.

In his own defense, Reynolds complained that those who should have assisted him failed to do so because "they were unwilling to part with that power they had so long arbitrarily exercised." The members of the council were "the authors and promoters of every disorder." [15]

Two members of the council were in London to make certain that Henry Ellis heard their side of the story. Alexander Kellet remained in England and Patrick Graham returned to Georgia, coaching Ellis during the voyage. Ellis was impatient to be in Georgia and chartered a ship, the *Andalusia*, at his own expense. His party consisted of William Knox, his young Irish friend, who was Georgia's new provost marshal, and Ellis's personal secretary, Adam Wood. South Carolinians, as well as Georgians, had news of Ellis's coming, but they expected him on a vessel of the Royal Navy and were surprised when he disembarked from the *Andalusia* on January 26. The *South Carolina Gazette* expressed regret that "we had not an opportunity to receive him in a manner suitable to his rank." [16] Governor William Henry Lyttelton made up for any neglect, however, by lavish attention to his Georgia counterpart. Lieutenant Governor William Bull took his turn entertaining Ellis's party. For two weeks, Ellis was wined and dined in the manner for which Charlestown was renowned. Ellis met the naturalist Alexander Garden and the wealthy merchant Benjamin Smith and considered them friends ever after. Jonathan Bryan, a Carolinian who moved to Georgia to seek his fortune, was on hand to escort Ellis to Savannah. [17] William Knox complained in his journal that Ellis was ignoring him and that Adam Wood was jealous of him. He and Wood got into an open argument at William Bull's reception. Knox commented that nobody liked Wood and therefore everyone sided with Knox. [18] He guessed wrong. Within a few months, Governor Lyttelton advised the Board of Trade to appoint Adam Wood deputy provost marshal and it was done. It is doubtful that Ellis, who was conscientiously correct in all social affairs, either ignored Knox or tried to pit Knox against Wood as Knox suspected. On the occasion of Wood's appointment, Ellis wrote to Lyttelton, "I shall never oppose such people's inclinations, lest they should conceive I spoil'd their Fortune." [19]

Ellis returned a thousand thanks to Lyttelton when he reached Savannah. "To say in the cold language of the world that I am grateful will convey but an imperfect idea of the impressions you have made and the sentiments you inspire," he wrote. He reported that he was welcomed in Savannah with "tumultuous demonstrations of joy." By contrast, Reynolds was insulted and neglected. Ellis wondered if the same fate awaited him.[20]

Among the friends Ellis made in Charlestown was Peter Timothy, whose *South Carolina Gazette* continued to sing his praises. The journal described how nine-tenths of the people of Savannah were on hand to greet Ellis when the Carolina scout boat reached the bluff at Savannah. They welcomed him with loud huzzas. The new governor declined to acknowledge the cheers until he paid his respects to Governor Reynolds. In truth, Ellis was a bit embarrassed by the adulation. The celebration continued into the night. The few pieces of artillery in town were fired, and they were answered by the guns of all the vessels anchored in the river. A huge bonfire was kindled, and an effigy of William Little was tossed into the blaze.[21] Some unknown bard was moved to write an ode, which included the lines:

> How has this infant Province shook,
> Under a lawless Tyrants Sway;
> But lo: the iron Rod is broke,
> Ellis is come to cheer our Day.[22]

Charlestown shared the viewpoint of the gentlemen of Savannah, namely that Ellis, himself a gentleman of rare intelligence, was of their opinion regarding the wickedness of Reynolds and his henchman Little. The *Gazette* implied as much in stating that "it is so far believed that Governor Ellis perfectly understands and will readily pursue it [the colony's] true and real interests."[23]

William Knox, at least, had been convinced by all that he had heard, both on the voyage and in Charlestown, that Little was a consummate villain and that the assembly was filled with his creatures, and he urged Ellis to dissolve Little's assembly without giving that body the opportunity to embarrass him. Almost everyone who spoke to Ellis during the first hours and days in Savannah assumed that he would take sides against the Reynolds faction. William Knox, walking a tight line between a too obvious self-aggrandizement and too much modesty, suggested that some of the Savannah speeches of welcome include the request that the assembly be dissolved. Knox believed that this idea of his "proved of infinite convenience" because if he dissolved the assembly, Ellis could say it was at the request of the people, and if he decided not to dissolve, he could lay claim to the goodwill of the assembly by stating that he had confidence in it. Knox was eager to stand for election to the assembly if there was a dissolution and believed that Ellis was against the idea only because the young man "might make myself of too much consequence in that House."[24]

Ellis refused to be unduly swayed by the clamors of the Savannah party. "The assembly is much complained of by all who approach me, perhaps justly, but I am awary of Party prejudice," he confided to his friend Lyttelton.[25] So he listened to the speeches of welcome and graciously replied to them, all the while realizing that vested interests were represented. The freeholders of Midway, anxious for a port at Sunbury, looked for his encouragement of commerce and planting. The freeholders of the Ogeechee district stated that his appointment had prevented the ruin of the colony and that Ellis would have ample scope for displaying his "invaluable talents." The Georgia Society, taking its cue from the Royal Society, hoped Ellis would reward those making useful discoveries and promote the cultivation of silk and indigo. The freeholders of Savannah hailed him as "Father of His Country."[26] It is interesting that there were no speeches of welcome from the distant districts, which were represented by adherents of the Reynolds faction.

The assembly had been sitting since January 10, 1757, and had devoted much of its attention to a continuing feud with the council. To the credit of its leaders, it showed more awareness of the French-inspired danger on the frontier than the Savannah-based council demonstrated. On January 28, the House urged Governor Reynolds to fill the company of rangers already called up and to raise two more companies of seventy men each. But a residual anger over the perceived persecution of Edmund Gray was a strong undercurrent during the session. On January 14, the House resolved that whoever advised the governor that Gray was a troublemaker did so "with a bad and sinister design." All Gray and his followers wanted was "to procure a fair Hearing in a disputed Election." The main business of the session was a report on the state of the province. James Deveaux reported for the committee on February 1, 1757. The statement was a bald attack on the conduct of the president and assistants who had governed Georgia before the arrival of Reynolds. Among the accusations directed at the interim council were that it had neglected the silk culture, had mismanaged Indian affairs, and had deterred settlement below the Ogeechee River. According to the report, the president and assistants had granted large tracts to infant members of their families and absent relatives while denying land to qualified applicants. Because Benjamin Martyn, the veteran Georgia agent in London, had concealed the misconduct of the council in his reports to the Board of Trade, he was put down as no friend of the assembly. It was interesting that the report on the state of the province was a description of conditions three years earlier rather than a report on the Reynolds years. William Little was so pleased with the report that he announced on February 2 that he intended to hand carry it to the Lords of Trade himself.[27] This was the state of affairs when Henry Ellis appeared on the Georgia stage.

Ellis was thoroughly briefed when he attended the House two days after his arrival. In his responses to the welcoming speeches, he had resorted to conventional platitudes, and indeed, comfortable platitudes are all that are expected on such occasions. Ellis's address was surprisingly well-informed and direct. He began by stressing his "disinterested views"; he would be governor of all Georgians, not of one faction or another. He was certain that his listeners were as dedicated to the public welfare as he was. He urged them not to spend their time "in pursuit of the trivial" and called on them to "lay aside jealousies of each other." A war was raging in Europe and America. "Your religion, your liberty, your all is at stake." He acknowledged that they were few in number and that there were limits on what they could do for their own defense, but even that "should be done with spirit and chearfulness becoming Englishmen." They could erect log forts as places of refuge and should do that work immediately. Help was on the way; a supply of arms and ammunition was being sent from England as well as a supply of presents for the Indians.[28] Ellis's presentation was so open and sincere that he was able to disarm much of the potential opposition. He had gambled on his ability to do just that. At the conclusion of his address, he adjourned the House until March 8, 1757. The adjournment ostensibly was an opportunity for a recess during a long session, but it also prevented William Little from making a reply to the address. For the moment, Little was outmaneuvered.

There must have been tension in the air when Little came to call on the governor after the adjournment. Little suspected that Ellis had already taken sides with the Savannah crowd, but he had to move cautiously. Would His Excellency do the gentlemen of the House the honor of dining with them? Ellis explained that nothing would give him greater pleasure, but he had refused a similar request from the council and he wanted to avoid the appearance of taking sides.[29] Little was again thwarted.

William Little was not the only member of Reynolds's faction to approach the new governor. Patrick Mackay, who had been appointed senior justice by Reynolds, was a frequent visitor and repeated his willingness to be of service. In the evenings, Mackay met with Little and his friends to plan their next move. Ellis knew about these meetings. Most of Little's followers were not evil, he concluded, but ignorant and easily swayed. Moreover, many of them had stood for election because of promises of reward. Ellis was now in a position to bestow rewards. He decided that it would not be difficult to detach these "placemen" from their allegiance to Little. He would not dissolve the assembly but merely prolong the adjournment until May. He explained his thinking to Lord Halifax on March 11, 1757, stating that his intention was to heal the wounds caused by factions. The suspension "will give time for men's passions to subside and for truth to appear through the cloud of party prejudice that at present obscures it."[30] He was already thinking beyond that session to a more satisfactory solution. Reynolds's original instructions were to divide the province into counties at the earliest opportunity. He had never been able to manage such a politically explosive measure. Ellis planned to propose a redistricting, and a dissolution of the assembly would follow naturally.

The suspense of not knowing Ellis's intentions was too much for William Little. Ellis was sitting at his desk, finishing his report of March 11, when Little burst into the room and angrily dared Ellis to dissolve the assembly. It would do the governor no good, said Little, because he had taken steps to ensure that the same men would be reelected.[31] Ellis retained his composure and announced his intention of adjourning the assembly until May. Little would not be able to wait that long in Georgia. Reynolds needed him to prepare a defense of his administration, and Little would have to go with him to London. After leaving Ellis, Little huddled with Patrick Mackay and adopted a plan. Mackay would stand election for Little's seat in the assembly. Their friends would elect Mackay Speaker and he could present the address Little had prepared. Mackay immediately began a campaign for election to the May session of the legislature by circulating a copy of Little's address.[32]

Ellis already had decided that Mackay was an incompetent chief justice. Word of the governor's intention to remove Mackay from the bench was noised about. Mackay misinterpreted Ellis's even-tempered manner and openly boasted that there was no danger; Ellis "had neither the power nor spirit to do it." [33] Hearing that challenge, Ellis suspended Mackay from the bench and published his opposition to his candidacy for the Little seat in the assembly. As a result, Mackay was overwhelmingly defeated and left Georgia for South Carolina. Ellis later remarked that Mackay's defeat together with Little's departure for England dissolved the opposition: "That hydra faction seems to be at present subdued." [34] The laudatory *South Carolina Gazette* announced on May 26 that "all party spirits seem to have left the province with its Au[tho]rs some days ago." [35]

William Little's address, prepared for the May session of the legislature, was not delivered. Yet it was a striking effort and widely read. Because it expressed the deeply felt convictions of the dominant voice in Georgia politics before Ellis's arrival, it deserves the notice of history. If Ellis had not entered upon the scene, Little's voice would have continued to speak for many Georgians. The Commons House of Assembly would have continued to gain strength at the expense of the governor and council.

Little's message began by reminding the members of the House that he represented their true interest and that he and his friends had the support of the people. They should not expect their enemies to change their principles; they were true only to their selfish interests. He warned that lucrative employments would be offered to them if they conformed, but those who were devoted to the public interest would resist. They must be aware that their enemies would hide under the cloak of patriotism; they would say that nothing was wanted than to reconcile interests that had long been incompatible. But when the representatives of the people were lulled asleep, they would be deprived of their rights. A private association, the Georgia Society, was given more weight in London than the provincial assembly. These gentlemen stirred up trouble and then alleged that discontent was a reason to remove the governor. If private societies could gain notice by causing discontent, then "it's highly probable the people will upon other occasions claim that priviledge." They must oppose all efforts to weaken the assembly lest it cease to be the "resort of liberty and the barrier against wanton power." He called up the memory of the decemvirs of Rome and modern Venice to make his point that "an aristocratical form of Government is perhaps of all others the least eligible." [36]

The written address is a remarkable document; one can only wonder what would have been the effect if Little had delivered it. He was a radical twenty years ahead of his time. In fact, royal Georgia never again produced such a hotspur. The people he might have roused in the name of liberty watched him sail away and then compliantly fell in line behind Henry Ellis.

Ellis did not call the assembly together until June 17. He was aware of some lingering disaffection among Little's friends; William Ewen was one whose decisions as assistant justice were questioned by Ellis. Ewen attempted to rekindle the old factionalism, much to Ellis's disgust. The latter wrote to his friend Lyttelton: "These folks would give up the greatest priviledge of Englishmen for the sake of opposition. Tis amazing what a length that spirit will carry men. However we have but few such here." [37] Those few made no trouble when the assembly convened. David Montaigut was chosen Speaker, and he showed no intention of opposing the governor. The long-delayed reply to the governor's address of February 17 was delivered by James Deveaux, formerly a follower of Little. It was resplendent with empty rhetoric. Ellis was amused; the address was "foolish and fulsome enough," he told Lyttelton.[38]

No Georgia assembly had ever received such a barrage of proposals as Ellis laid before that summer session. The assembly dutifully approved bills for building log forts, for discharging the public debt, for establishing lookouts along the coast, for banning liquor to Negroes and Indians in public houses, for organizing the militia, and for preventing the sale of cattle and provisions to St. Augustine to deny their resale to the French. There was no opposition.[39]

In the welter of other business he attended to during his first year Ellis never lost sight of his plan to divide the province. He prorogued the assembly on July 28, and that body met again on January 11, 1758, to receive his instructions. It is not clear how much he had to do with the preparation of the bill to establish parishes, but it is likely that he sketched out the broad outlines of the measure. On January 16, 1758, a committee was named to work out the details. Word spread rapidly that the legislature was considering a bill to impose the Anglican religion on all Georgians. Pastor John Martin Bolzius spoke eloquently for the German Lutherans at Ebenezer; he begged the gentlemen of the assembly to remember that the reason His Majesty founded Georgia was so that "all sorts of Protestants" could enjoy liberty of conscience there. He recited the lengthy history of his Salzburgers, who had been forced to leave Austria because of their religion and had settled in Georgia some thirty years before.[40]

The bill was read by the House for the third time on February 8 and sent to the governor and council. It divided Georgia into eight parishes. The area around Augusta was the Parish of St. Paul. The area between Augusta and Ebenezer was known as the district of Halifax, and it became St. George Parish. The Ebenezer district was named St. Matthew. Savannah was Christ Church Parish. The proposed future capital of Hardwicke on the Ogeechee was St. Philip. Next to the south along the coast was St. John, the Midway settlement. The Scots in the Darien district were honored by the bestowal of the name of their patron saint, Andrew, on their parish. St. Simons Island, with its crumbling ruins of a fort, still manned by a garrison of South Carolinians, became the Parish of St. James.[41]

In the eight parishes there were only two churches, both Anglican and both completed within a few months of each other in 1750. They were St. Paul's in Augusta and Christ Church in Savannah. The legislation wisely refrained from imposing the established church upon dissenters. The old English tradition was maintained in the election of vestrymen by all freeholders in each parish. The vestry was empowered to levy taxes for poor relief and church maintenance. The vestries were the only form of local government except for the justices of the peace, or magistrates.[42]

The legislation, grandly entitled "A bill for the establishment of religious worship in the province of Georgia and for dividing the said province into parishes," did not do much to promote the cause of religion in the colony, but it accomplished Ellis's main objective of reconstituting the legislature. It was a year in the making, but Ellis succeeded in getting what he wanted. The legislation was an important feature in the transformation of Georgia.

While fortune smiled on Henry Ellis, it frowned on John Reynolds. After he and Little had gathered affidavits and testimonials, they left for England aboard the *Charming Martha*. Reynolds was under unusual difficulty in preparing his case because the Lords of Trade had not seen fit to tell him the nature of the accusations against him or the names of his accusers in their letter of August 5, 1756, recalling him. The *Charming Martha* was captured by a French privateer and taken into the port of Bayonne. Reynolds was treated courteously, but his journal and all other papers were taken from him. He arrived in London on July 7, 1757, and went immediately to the office of the Board of Trade.

During these months Lord Halifax was in the country brooding about Pitt's rejection of his bid for a cabinet position. Reynolds was hostage to court politics until matters were properly settled and Halifax resumed his seat at the Board of Trade. Only on March 8, 1758, was Reynolds acquainted with the charges against him, to which he made a lengthy reply on April 17.[43] His presentation was reasonable, his responses to the charges plausible. It did him no good. Halifax had made up his mind a year earlier that Reynolds would be removed, and the delay in naming Ellis governor was merely to give Reynolds the courtesy of a hearing and, incidentally, to oblige Lord Hardwicke, Reynolds's patron. Reynolds's case was heard by the board on April 17. On April 21, Halifax asked the Privy Council to approve the nomination of Henry Ellis as governor of Georgia. On May 8, the commission was drawn, and on June 16, 1758, it received the king's signature.[44] Henry Ellis was officially the captain general and governor in chief of the Province of Georgia. The decision of the board was a poorly kept secret. On April 21, the day he sent the nomination to the Privy Council, Halifax wrote Ellis to tell him the good news.[45] By May 1 John Ellis informed Henry that "everybody says Reynolds will never be sent again"; he planned to confirm the rumor in an interview with Lord Halifax.[46]

Captain John Reynolds resumed his interrupted career in the Royal Navy, and his advancement was aided by longevity if not by talent. He was made a rear admiral in 1775, a vice-admiral in 1778, and in 1787, at the age of seventy-four and despite being incapacitated by a stroke, he was promoted to the rank of admiral.[47] He died a year later. We can imagine that Georgia was only a dim recollection in his advancing years, a rather unpleasant shore duty in an otherwise placid naval career. The records are silent regarding the fate of his friend, the premature rebel William Little.

CHAPTER SIX

Indian Affairs

A CHANGE OF governors was an important matter to the Muskogee people whom the English called Creeks. The word spread swiftly throughout the Creek Nation that Georgia had a new governor. The French garrison at Fort Toulouse picked up the information and turned it into propaganda. This new Englishman, they told the Indians, intended to take their land and make slaves of them; his hands were red with the blood of people he had already killed. The Creeks were accustomed to hearing such things from the French and were curious to see for themselves what the new chief of the Georgians was like.

The Muskogees were a polyglot of various tribes who had wandered into the great river valleys that ran from the mountains into the Gulf. The English referred to those along the Coosa and Tallapoosa rivers as the Upper Creeks, those along the Chattahoochee as the Lower Creeks. About two-thirds of the eighteen thousand people lived in the Upper Creek towns. A detached band, later called Seminoles, took up residence in northern Florida in the early eighteenth century.

The Creeks regarded the English as a different threat than they were accustomed to from their other neighbors, the Cherokees in the mountains to the east, the Choctaws to the west beyond the Tombigbee River, and above the Choctaws, the Chickasaws. Creek warriors traditionally had tested their skills in raids against other Indians. These "wars" were usually reprisals for previous raids. The Spanish were the first Europeans to encroach upon Creek lands. Spanish missions reached into the region of Apalache, where the Chattahoochee and Flint rivers flowed together to form the Apalachicola. Many of the Indians who lived near the missions accepted Christianity. The French were the next intruders, forming settlements at Biloxi and Mobile at the turn of the century and establishing New Orleans in 1718. The French were clever in their dealings with the Indians, mainly because so many of them lived among the Indians and adapted to their customs. They benefited also because of the venality of the first English intruders into the Creek country.

At first, the Lower Creeks welcomed the Carolina traders. Their red cloth, called strouds for the town in England where it was manufactured, was so superior to anything the French or Spanish could offer that the English gained an advantage in the last decade of the seventeenth century. The British also traded in firearms and rum, commodities that forever altered the life-style of the Creeks, and they took slaves and sold them to the West Indian plantations. The Creeks knew about slavery; they enslaved captives from other tribes, but they were stunned by the number of slaves taken from Apalache by the Carolinians in 1704. They heard that the English were planning an attack on Louisiana through their country, and they were told by the French that the English wanted to enslave them all as they did the Apalache. The Creeks had long memories, and opposition to any English fort was a firm policy of theirs throughout the eighteenth century.

The arrogance of the British traders as much as the fraud they practiced caused the Yamassees to rise up against the traders among them in 1715. The titular headman of the Creeks, Brims of Coweta, called Emperor by the British, declined the Yamassee request to come to their assistance, and the Yamassees were driven out of Carolina and into Florida, where they sought protection from the Spanish. The French took advantage of the war to build a fort in the heart of the Creek country, where the Coosa and Tallapoosa rivers joined to form the Alabama. The fort was called Toulouse of the Alabamas because the Creeks who lived below the forks were the Alabamas. The English usually called it the Alabama Fort. The Creeks, though adamantly opposed to an English fort, admitted the French partly as trading partners and partly to counter the English influence.

Developments during the 1720s profoundly influenced the various peoples of the southern frontier. One was that the newly humbled British traders took up residence in the Creek towns. As the French had demonstrated in Canada and Louisiana, there was no better way to gain the trust of the Indians than to live among them, to cohabit with their women, and to father children who became living amalgams of the two cultures. A young agent of James Oglethorpe's was astonished at the number of children of mixed blood he counted in the Creek towns in 1736.[1] The Creek Nation was genetically altered by the British traders even as its economy was changed. Partly because they had learned a lesson in the consequences of bad behavior, and partly because of the competition of the French, the second quarter of the eighteenth century was the golden age of the British Indian trade on the southern frontier.

The South Carolina legislature through its Indian commissioners gave the traders a great deal of latitude. South Carolina's governor James Glen once tried to explain to a delegation of Creeks why he could not interfere in the deerskin business: "Trade is a Plant of a very tender and delicate Nature," he said. "It delights in Freedom and will not be forced."[2] Following a basic tenet of capitalism, the traders regulated themselves by forming partnerships and mergers until a few large companies dominated the trade. The largest was Archibald McGillivray and Company.[3] Its employees lived in the towns to which they were licensed, avoided trading in the woods, and if they were not entirely honest in their dealings, the Indians understood that it was part of the process. The Indians retaliated by trying to peddle off "green" skins and hides with hooves still attached to add weight. A certain amount of reciprocal dishonesty was expected.

James Oglethorpe appeared on the scene in 1733 as a champion of fair trade. He was persuaded by Tomochichi that the Carolinians used too much rum and had become too casual in their measurements. He believed that there was a real danger that the Creeks would turn to the French for their wares. Therefore, Oglethorpe and his fellow members of the Georgia Trust pushed an Indian Act through Parliament and followed it with a Rum Act. All trade west of the Savannah was to be controlled by Georgia; Carolina traders were required to obtain a Georgia license and post bonds as a pledge of good behavior, and the use of rum was forbidden. The authorities in Charlestown reacted angrily, but the pragmatic men of the trade solved the problem by moving across the Savannah River to the new village of Augusta in 1736. There Oglethorpe built a fort and put in a garrison to regulate the conduct of the traders as well as to impress the Indians.[4]

The Creek chiefs decided that they liked "Squire" Oglethorpe, especially when he did them the very rare honor of visiting them at Coweta town in 1739. None of the governors of Carolina had ever followed the great white road to the Creek Nation. They expected the Indians to do all the traveling. In token of their friendship with Oglethorpe, they made a treaty permitting white people to settle between the Savannah and Altamaha rivers, boundaries established by the king's charter, and from the coast upriver as far as the tide moved the waters. Reserved were the islands of St. Catherines, Ossabaw, and Sapelo and Mary Musgrove's trading post at Pipemaker Creek, west of the village of Savannah. Augusta was in the Indian country much the same as was its French counterpost at the forks of the Alabama, for purposes of trading convenience. Archibald McGillivray transferred his license to Lachlan McGillivray, who was a partner in the firm of Brown, Rae and Company, which soon dominated the Georgia trade.[5]

Another development that grew out of the decade of the 1720s affected the western fringe of the southern frontier. A small Mississippi tribe called the Natchez attacked some French settlers and fled for protection to the Chickasaws. The Louisiana governors became obsessed with the determination to punish the Chickasaws. They enlisted the traditional enemies of the Chickasaws, their near neighbors the Choctaws, in their campaign. For a quarter of a century the French and Choctaws waged intermittent warfare in an effort to destroy the Chickasaws. Incredibly, the vastly outnumbered Chickasaws beat off the repeated invasions, thanks to guns and ammunition supplied by the Charlestown traders.[6] A small band of Chickasaws moved to the Carolina side of the Savannah River near Fort Moore and opposite the site of Augusta, but most of the tribe stayed where they were and defied the French and laughed at the Choctaws.

Some of the Choctaws became disenchanted with their unproductive alliance with Louisiana and rose up against the French under the leadership of Red Shoes in 1746. Governor James Glen tried to take credit for instigating the Choctaw civil war, but few believed him. Edmond Atkin first came to the attention of the Board of Trade by his account of the Choctaw War and his criticism of Glen's role.[7] The Choctaws soon stopped fighting each other and, under French prodding, reluctantly returned to the campaign against the Chickasaws, who stubbornly refused to be exterminated. The single-minded and futile war against the Chickasaws by a succession of governors,

Bienville, Vaudreuil, and Kerlérec, was a miscalculation of such large dimensions that the French never seemed to grasp it. The Carolinians were convinced that the French intended to conquer the Chickasaws, then follow the Tennessee River into the Cherokee country. Carolina traders told the Cherokees that such was the goal of the Louisiana governors. More plausible was the likelihood that Louisiana needed a safe connection with Quebec. At any rate, the preoccupation with the Chickasaws meant that the Creeks were pampered, coaxed, and cajoled but not threatened by the French. Intrigue was their weapon, and the Alabama Fort was its point of dissemination.

The stage for Henry Ellis was set in 1756. Economic and cultural undercurrents were transforming the frontier, but individuals influenced the timing and direction of the changes. Among the dramatis personae of the southern frontier, beginning on the wings of the stage, were the European governors. With the departure of James Oglethorpe in 1743, James Glen of South Carolina dominated British policy during his long tenure from 1743 to 1756. Glen was a hardworking, pragmatic Scot who was frequently at odds with a recalcitrant legislature. Glen overstated his accomplishments, and those that he boasted most about were criticized by his enemies as mistakes. For example, Glen never tired of pointing with pride to the peace he arranged in 1753 between the Cherokees and the Creeks. His purpose was understandable; he meant to form a united front against the French. Veteran traders thought this a terrible idea, and the Indians themselves had serious doubts about it. One old chief told Lachlan McGillivray that McGillivray had sweated much in "our smoky townhouses" but that "our young mad people" would give him "a far worse sweat than you have yet had." The chief called the peace with his traditional enemies a "mad scheme" of the great English chieftain in Charlestown. He meant that the young warriors would probably attack whites if they could not test their prowess against the Cherokees.[8]

Glen was determined to follow the peace by building forts in the Cherokee and Creek country to establish British hegemony. The English faction among the Cherokees, headed by Attakullakulla, the Little Carpenter, agreed to the plan. Therefore, Glen had Fort Prince George built at Keowee in the lower Cherokee country and in 1756 was busy with the construction of Fort Loudoun on the Little Tennessee River among the mountain Cherokees when he was relieved by William Henry Lyttelton, who completed the project.[9] Both Glen and

Lyttelton attempted to impress the Indians with their importance by demands that were poorly received by the Indian visitors and lectures that were equally unwelcome.

Governor John Reynolds of Georgia was ineffective. He missed his one opportunity to meet with the Indians at Augusta in December 1755 and did not know how to deal with those who visited him in Savannah.[10] He deferred to Glen in everything, even acquiescing in Glen's command of the Independent Companies stationed at Frederica and Augusta in Georgia. The Augusta-based traders, like the Indians, looked to South Carolina for leadership. Henry Ellis's challenge was to recover for Georgia some of the prestige of the Oglethorpe era.

To the south, Florida enjoyed a decade of comparative quiet after the failure of Oglethorpe's second invasion in 1743. Its governor, Fernandez de Heredia, won Henry Ellis's admiration for his intelligence and good sense. In fact, Ellis was pleased when Fernandez was replaced by a less competent administration in 1758, which meant less danger of Spain's winning over the Indians.[11] A source of friction between Georgia and Florida was a colony of backcountry people who followed Edmund Gray to the Satilla River in 1755 and called their settlement New Hanover. The land between the Altamaha and St. Johns was claimed by both the Spaniards and the English. The bold Oglethorpe had pretended that the St. Johns was really a branch of the Altamaha and had laid claim to the region by building Fort William on Cumberland Island. To complicate matters, South Carolina regarded the territory below the Altamaha as part of South Carolina. John Reynolds did not challenge Carolina's claim. Edmund Gray's colony would be one of Ellis's thorniest problems, especially since England was studiously trying to avoid a war with Spain while fighting France. But Spanish ships out of St. Augustine supplied the Louisiana French, and it was a matter of time before Spain was drawn into the global struggle.

The governor of Louisiana in 1756 was Louis Belouart de Kerlérec. He was even more haughty and arrogant than the Carolina governors. He despised his allies, the Choctaws, as beggars and rascals and considered the Creeks "deceitful, mendacious and very mercenary."[12] He was no more innovative than his predecessors in his attempts to destroy the Chickasaws and propagandize the Creeks. He was, however, more successful in alienating the Cherokees from the English. He outdid Glen in his boasts to his superiors about the effectiveness of his allies among the Creek chiefs. After 1756 he was handicapped by a shortage of provisions as the result of the British blockade, and therefore his influence diminished.

The great men among the Creeks were equally important actors in the drama being played out on the southern frontier. Malatchi, son of Brims of the Lower Creek town of Coweta, was the honorary head of the Creek Nation. He was respected by the other chiefs as the first among equals, but he had no real authority over them except what came from prestige. Malatchi, like Brims before him, was dedicated to a policy of neutrality, and he was successful in playing one governor against another. By going to both Charlestown and Mobile, Malatchi was able to convince Glen as well as Kerlérec that he was the ally of each. He was received like the king he was in both places. Only in Savannah was he not treated with deference. He had gone there to see Mary Bosomworth, his cousin, as he complained to Glen, and his party was received in a "rude and uncivil manner, more like enemies than friends."[13] The members of the Georgia interim council regarded Malatchi with suspicion because they believed he meant to force them to recognize Mary's claims to the sea islands. Malatchi died in early 1756 after a lingering illness, and his death left a void which no one among the Lower Creeks could fill. His son Togulki, whom the traders called young Malatchi, tried to take his father's place with the help of Malatchi's brother Stumpe, and Henry Ellis would have to deal with the inexperienced and insecure Togulki.

Malatchi had no rivals among the Lower Creeks, although the Georgia council had foolishly tried to persuade the Long Warrior of the Oconees to lay claim to Malatchi's leadership. Among the Upper Creeks, however, there were several outstanding men, each one with a different personality and style. The best known was the man the French knew as the Wolf of Okchoys and the English as the Mortar. Both the French and the English had the impression that the Mortar was under French influence. He was certainly the instrument the French used in their intrigues with the Cherokees. More likely, the Mortar was, as one historian of the Creeks described him, a great nativist.[14] He strenuously opposed the building of English forts, and the construction of Fort Prince George and Fort Loudoun convinced him that the British threat was greater than the French. His partiality to the French put him in opposition to the headman of his own village, Enochtonachee, known by the British as the Gun Merchant. The Gun was frequently vexed at the conduct of the Carolina governor and the British traders, especially at their refusal to supply him with a set of stilyards or scales so he could verify weights of bundles of skins, and more so at their discrimination in prices in favor of Cherokee skins.

The Gun was a loyal friend of Lachlan McGillivray, the prominent Augusta trader, and used his considerable influence on behalf of the British. At a conference in Charlestown in January 1756, the Gun reluctantly yielded to Glen's urgent request that South Carolina be allowed to build a fort among the Upper Creeks. When the Gun returned to his country, the other headmen made it clear that he did not speak for them in this matter.[15] The issue still rankled in the minds of the Creeks when Henry Ellis landed in Savannah.

Another chief was the Wolf of Muccolossus, a small village on the Tallapoosa River, only a few miles from the Alabama Fort. He was an inveterate visitor to Savannah and Charlestown and enjoyed his rum as much as the next man. No one was a more steadfast friend of the English than he, and none was braver. He was the only chief who offered his own village as a site for the English fort. Once when a group of irate young warriors were chasing after the trader John Spencer with deadly intent, the Wolf shielded Spencer and shamed his attackers. His independent spirit was revealed when, during a solemn conference with Governor Glen, Malatchi asked for a reduction in the price of bullets. Glen made the usual excuses, whereupon the Wolf broke in to say that it was no wonder that traders could not afford to sell their goods cheaply when they gave away so much to the wives and women they kept. The blunt statement brought an apology from Malatchi and a reprimand from Glen that the dignity of the government suffered from such remarks.[16]

Henry Ellis would have had a far easier time dealing with the nervous Creeks and the increasingly disaffected Cherokees if it were not for two others who were his competitors, one of whom was also his friend. William Henry Lyttelton made it clear very early in their acquaintance that South Carolina would set Indian policy. Ellis did not object: "I can assure you Dear Sir that I have no sort of ambition of being principal Negotiator with the Indians. I have neither the abilities, or the means to support that character effectually." [17] Nevertheless, Ellis chafed at Lyttelton's presumption in sending a Carolina agent, Captain Daniel Pepper, on a mission to the Creeks without consulting authorities in Georgia. Lyttelton also took a high-handed attitude toward the Cherokees, which Ellis thought too harsh, and finally, the

South Carolina governor insisted that he was in charge of the Independent Companies in Georgia. The seeds of dissension were sown.

The other claimant to preferment in Indian matters was Edmond Atkin, whose slow progress brought him to Georgia in 1758, two years after his appointment as superintendent of Indians of the Southern Department.[18] Ellis disliked the idea of an Indian superintendent, and he disliked Atkin when he finally met him. He had to be guarded in his comments about Atkin, who was sponsored by the Lytteltons.

Another vexing problem was how to pay for the support of Reynolds's rangers. In 1756 a group of forty or so families from North Carolina settled without warrant on the Ogeechee River on Indian land above the tidewater. Governor Reynolds, calling them "a lawless crew," lamented that he was helpless to remove them.[19] On September 3, the squatters attacked a party of Creeks and killed two of them. This was exactly the sort of incident that provoked reprisals, and the residents of Augusta braced for a Creek attack. The Savannah River Chickasaws volunteered to live and die with their friends at Augusta. Governors Reynolds and Lyttelton sent out talks disclaiming any connection with the Ogeechee troublemakers and promising that the guilty would be brought to justice. Reynolds requested the legislature to authorize three troops of rangers. The frightened legislators agreed. Unfortunately, they neglected to provide for the support of the rangers. When Ellis arrived, he noted that all the officers had been named by Reynolds and that the enlistments had not been completed.[20] With the Independent Companies at Augusta and Frederica under Carolina control, the rangers constituted Georgia's only military force. Ellis's decision to retain the rangers began months and years of frustration in his efforts to get adequate funding for them from the British commander in chief in America.

As it turned out, the Indians were not as bothered by the Ogeechee incident as they might have been. The Lower Creeks objected to the white settlement on the Ogeechee but made the point that the slain Indians were Upper Creeks, and it was an Upper Creek problem. The Gun Merchant therefore sent Handsome Fellow of the Okfuskees to Savannah to demand justice. The mission was a formality. The dead Indians were known to be troublemakers and, in the opinion of the headmen, they deserved to be shot. Nevertheless, Handsome Fellow called on Governor Reynolds and politely asked life for life. The nervous Reynolds falsely claimed that two whites had been killed in the encounter. Handsome Fellow decided to accept that answer, knowing it was not true. When Handsome Fellow returned to Okfuskee, the Carolina agent Daniel Pepper was there. The chief told Pepper that the matter was settled.[21]

Henry Ellis was a fast learner. He had been briefed in London about the Indian situation by Patrick Graham, the Georgia Indian commissioner under the interim council. After his arrival, Ellis learned a great deal from veteran traders such as Lachlan McGillivray and George Galphin. And he learned from the Indians themselves. About forty Lower Creek Indians were camped outside Savannah when Ellis arrived. Reynolds had ignored them.[22] The contrasting styles of Ellis and his predecessor were evident in the way Ellis dealt with the visitors. After consulting with his council, he arranged a conference with the Indians. He appeared to be, and perhaps was, genuinely glad to see them. He gave their leader, Acouthla, a captain's commission, a gun, a drum, a hatchet, and a flag of Great Britain to fly over his village. He explained that a war to the finish was going on between the good King George and the wicked king of France. He said the governor of Louisiana was spreading lies about the English and had offered to buy scalps of English traders. Ellis promised twenty shillings for every French scalp and forty shillings for every prisoner. Acouthla and his band went away as British auxiliaries and spread the word that the new white chief of Georgia was a good man to talk to.[23]

It was surprising that Ellis offered money for scalps. Granted that the French were doing it, but he acted without authorization from Pitt, the secretary of state, or Lord Loudoun, the commander in chief, or even Lyttelton, who claimed precedence in all Indian matters. Perhaps he knew that Lyttelton had authorized the commanding officer at Fort Loudoun to offer rewards for scalps. Halifax cautioned Ellis about stirring up a war when he received Ellis's report.[24]

Before he left England, Ellis had ordered a supply of presents for the Indians. Therefore, he had to invite the chiefs to Savannah to receive them. How could he do this without interfering in Lyttelton's Indian affairs? The matter was especially sensitive because Lyttelton's agent, Pepper, was already out in the Creek country, broadcasting Lyttelton's invitation to Charlestown. Ellis wrote to Lyttelton on May 24, 1757, only two months after his arrival, to say that the presents had arrived in the warship *Juno*. What message should he send to the

Creeks? Should he act independently or in concert with Lyttelton? Should the Indians be invited to Augusta? [25]

Lyttelton quickly responded that he wanted the Indians to go to Charlestown. Indian strategy was too important a matter to be handled by correspondence, and he and Ellis should confer. Would Ellis meet with him at Beaufort between Savannah and Charlestown? Colonel Henry Bouquet was expected to arrive in Charlestown with two hundred Virginia provincials and half a battalion of Royal Americans. Bouquet's reinforcement was a response, albeit delayed, to the Ogeechee incident of the previous September.

Ellis would be glad to go to Beaufort or Augusta or anywhere else to meet with Lyttelton and Bouquet. He voiced the hope to Lyttelton that some of Bouquet's troops would be sent to Georgia: "There is scarce propriety in crowding troops into you and leaving us totally destitute." [26] Not one to take chances, Ellis wrote Bouquet on June 24, welcoming him on his arrival. He painted a dismal, almost comical, picture of Georgia's defensive capabilities. There were no forts in the province, although there were four places called forts: Augusta, Frederica, St. Simons, and Fort William on Cumberland Island. Augusta's fort was in ruins, Frederica's ditch was filled up, St. Simons's little wooden fort was "utterly decayed," and the same was true of Fort William. Considering Georgia's strategic location as a barrier to the French, he said, "I am astonished that it is left so defenceless." [27]

The meeting of the governors with Bouquet was delayed until August, but Ellis's Indian business would not wait until then. Curious Indians continued to visit Savannah, and Ellis was not the man to put them off. On May 18, a chief named Elleck brought a party of twelve Lower Creeks to visit. They had heard a talk that the Cherokees were angry about the English fort in their country and were going to join the French. The Cherokees wanted the Creeks to go with the French too. Ellis was able to assure his visitors that the fort had been built at the request of the Cherokees to protect them from the French. He displayed a talent for speaking in the exaggerated and allegorical manner which the best linguists or interpreters used and the Indians appreciated. He dwelled on the barbarous and inhuman campaign of extermination waged by the French against the Chickasaws. When the Chickasaws were finished, the Creeks would be treated the same way. The French, he proclaimed, were "notorious Enemies to truth and the

Disturbers of the World." [28] Then he invited the chiefs to have dinner with him in his house. An invitation to share a meal was an act of courtesy any well-mannered Creek chief would extend to his visitors, but English governors usually were too grand for such intimacy.

On July 30, an important chief from the Upper Creek town of Okfuskee was conducted to the council meeting by Lachlan McGillivray. John Reynolds had relied on McGillivray's information and employed him on important missions, and undoubtedly McGillivray tutored Ellis in Indian affairs. In coming to see the governor, the chief, Mad Warrior, had acted against the advice of other Creek headmen. He had decided to go only to Augusta to visit his friend McGillivray and tell him some things, but McGillivray thought it best to talk to the governor. Perhaps the governor might not know about the trouble caused by Pepper, the Carolina agent. Pepper's claim to regulate the trade "had given Disgust to the Chiefs . . . and greatly disquieted the Traders." [29]

Ellis told Mad Warrior that Pepper had exceeded his instructions, that trade with the Creeks was a Georgia matter. If regulations needed to be changed, a general congress of the chiefs would be held to do so. Ellis explained that he had spoken to the great Squire Oglethorpe before he left England and had been told that the Creeks were a wise and honest people. Ellis hoped that they would not let themselves be fooled by the French. Why was the French king keeping a fort among the Creeks? The small garrison there was too weak to protect the Indians and too poor to trade with them. No, the French meant to strengthen their claim to the land. The French had become so perfidious that even their usual allies, the Spanish, would not join them as they had in previous wars.

Mad Warrior agreed with everything he heard and said that upon his return he would relate it to the headmen of his nation. Ellis said that he was sending a messenger to invite the chiefs to Savannah, where he would have a strong talk with them and then divide the presents the king had sent them. When Mad Warrior asked if he might get his presents then rather than later, Ellis readily agreed. [30]

Joseph Wright, a reliable, self-effacing trader and an expert linguist, was selected to carry Ellis's invitation to the Creek chiefs. Wright was not to tell them what would be said in Savannah, merely that Ellis wanted to give a talk and that there were presents to be distributed. If the chiefs had already decided to go to Charlestown, they were requested to return by way of Savannah. Wright was cautioned to try to keep them all together and to avoid the settlements along the way. Wright's instructions were dated August 7, 1757.[31]

Thus Ellis had taken important initiatives before the Beaufort meeting in late August. At Beaufort the three dignitaries discussed the drift of politics at home and hoped for better things under the leadership of William Pitt. The course of the war in the North was going badly. The French general Montcalm had taken Fort Oswego the previous September and with an army of eight thousand French and Indians was advancing into New York by way of Lake Champlain. Lord Loudoun's poorly planned offensive against Louisbourg had been easily repulsed. Although the gentlemen at Beaufort were not aware of it, Fort William Henry on Lake George was surrendered to Montcalm on August 7, 1757. Loudoun would be recalled home and replaced by the equally ineffective James Abercromby.

The purpose of the Beaufort talk was to reach an agreement on Indian policy. Lyttelton and Bouquet agreed that firmness was the best approach to the Cherokee dissension. The Carolina legislature had already authorized the use of militia in case of war. The Creeks would be intimidated by the threat of force. Bouquet later achieved a certain notoriety by advocating the use of germ-laden blankets among the northern Indians.[32] He was insensitive, to say the least, about southern Indians and referred to Ellis's being "pester'd" with Indian visitors, saying that he himself was "heartily tired of America."[33] In the course of the meeting, Lyttelton made it clear that he should take the lead in all Indian negotiations. Ellis yielded the point but showed Lyttelton the instructions he gave Joseph Wright, observing that he had agreed that the Indians should go to Charlestown first.[34]

Most likely Ellis did not bring up one reason he had to confer with the Creeks because it was none of Carolina's business. One of the most delicate and potentially disruptive issues was that of the Bosomworth claims. Mary and her third husband contended that they owned three islands off the coast of Georgia because the Creek Nation had specifically reserved those islands when signing a treaty with Oglethorpe in 1739. Malatchi made it clear to Governor Glen in 1753 that the Creeks had given the islands to Mary. John Reynolds sided with the Bosomworths. The Georgians who had been rude to Malatchi were even ruder to the Bosomworths and refused to take their claim seriously. Several of these gentlemen sat on Henry Ellis's council. Ellis's problem was a legal one. In the opinion of the Board of Trade, only the king could grant land. The Indians could give the land to the king and then the king was free to dispose of it as he would, but private grants from Indians were illegal. Ellis realized that there was little likelihood that the Indians, who had the land before the king, would agree with this line of reasoning. Nevertheless, he had to do what he could to bring them around.

In the evening Lyttelton treated his guests to a dinner worthy of the son of Lord Cobham and the cousin of William Pitt. Henry Ellis was a connoisseur of fine foods but on the abstemious side. He broke his own rules at Beaufort. He later wrote to thank Lyttelton, remarking that he hoped his host was "now at liberty to indulge yourself in that temperance that both you and myself stood in great need of whilst at Beaufort. A little more of that good living, as it is called, would have soon made me incapable of living at all." [35]

Ellis reported to Lord Halifax on the meeting. He explained that Lyttelton was "solicitous" about having charge of Indian affairs. Ellis was not concerned about "preeminence," provided that their mutual goal of security was achieved. It was a neat trick for Ellis to walk the line between asking and complaining, but he did it with his usual adroitness. Ellis persuaded Bouquet to send a hundred Virginia provincials to Georgia. "The Affairs of that Province could not be in better hands," Bouquet advised Lord Loudoun. The Virginia Blues arrived in September, fortunately for Ellis and for Georgia, because a month later over a hundred Creeks came to Savannah.[36]

By good luck and timely planning Savannah's fortifications were ready to receive the Virginians. William De Brahm had come to Georgia in 1751 with a contingent of German Lutherans who settled in the German colony of Ebenezer, on the Savannah River, some forty-five miles above Savannah. De Brahm's expertise as a surveyor was recognized by his appointment as joint surveyor general of Georgia in 1754 with Henry Yonge. De Brahm prepared a scheme for the defenses of the province which Governor Reynolds transmitted to the Board of Trade in January 1756, but nothing came of it. De Brahm was then engaged by Glen of South Carolina to construct Fort Loudoun in the Cherokee mountains. His plans were criticized as being impractical, extravagant, and militarily indefensible, but like many other projects of the kind, it was built and soon proved to be a trap for its unfortunate garrison. When De Brahm's relationship with the commander of the

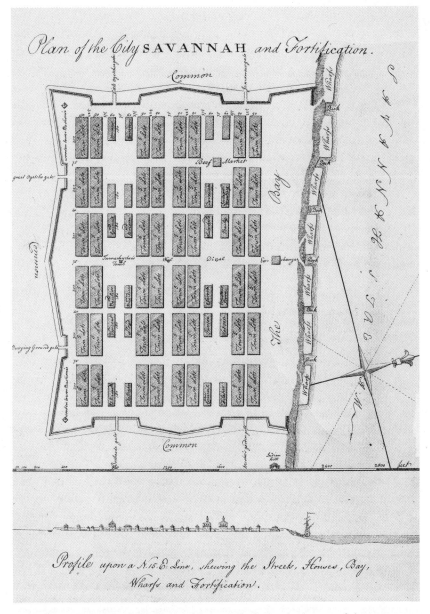

2. William G. De Brahm's map of Savannah shows the house of the governor near the Little Ogeechee Gate in the southwest corner of town. Ellis and De Brahm collaborated in planning the town's fortifications. (Kings 210, folio 54, British Library)

fort, Captain Raymond Demere, reached a breaking point, De Brahm prudently returned to Georgia.[37] Thus De Brahm was available when Henry Ellis wanted to discuss Savannah's defense works.

De Brahm, for all his contentiousness, was a man of many talents and interests, and he and Ellis had much in common. The German has been described as "a surveyor, engineer, botanist, astronomer, meteorologist, student of ocean currents, alchemist, sociologist, historian and mystical philosopher."[38] Ellis was most of these things, too, but he would have been uncomfortable if the conversation had turned to the occult.

It was decided to surround Savannah with an earthen wall, a relatively easy task because the town measured slightly over 500 yards south from the river and only 870 yards from west to east along the river. The town had not yet outgrown Oglethorpe's six squares. Ellis occupied a house in Heathcote Ward, in the southwest corner of town. The house followed the Charlestown style, two stories on a raised basement facing east to the square with a piazza or porch running along the north side.[39] Seven guns were mounted in the square to enhance the prestige of the otherwise modest structure. It was De Brahm's idea to fix sharpened pine logs on the exterior sloping walls of the earthworks. Ellis was responsible for the decision to erect wooden bastions at each corner of the works, each with its flag and battery.[40] Ellis had no trouble selecting the names of three of the towers, the King's, the Prince's, and Halifax's, but the fourth must have presented a problem. It should have been Pitt's, but he knew that there was no love lost between Halifax and Pitt, and so he chose the name of the commander in America, Lord Loudoun. It was ironic that two of the fortifications designed by William G. De Brahm honored the inept British general.

Ellis could not conceal his satisfaction when he announced to his council on October 25, 1757, that 150 Upper and Lower Creek Indians were at the forks of the Altamaha only two days from Savannah.[41] The Indians preferred Savannah to Charlestown, Georgia to Carolina, Ellis to Lyttelton. Ellis would now be the impresario of the grandest spectacle Georgians had ever attempted. Captain John Milledge was already on his way with a company of rangers to escort the Indians into town. The rangers and Indians would be met outside the town by the mounted militia commanded by Captain Jonathan Bryan. The line would enter the town through the little Ogeechee gate at the southwest side of town and proceed directly into St. James Square, past the governor's house, across the Perceval Ward with Tomochichi's tomb, along Bull Street, and then through Johnson Square and into Reynolds Square, where the council house and filiature building stood facing west.[42]

Everything worked as well as if everyone had practiced. Bryan's militia led the way with the Indians following in order of rank and the rangers bringing up the rear. When the procession came in sight of the town, the guns on each of the four bastions fired a salute. Colonel Noble Jones and the foot militia met the retinue at the Ogeechee gate and marched ahead into Heathcote Ward. The seven guns at the governor's house were fired, and at that signal, the ships in the harbor saluted with their cannon. It was a wonderful commotion, as impressive to the Georgians as to the visitors.[43]

At the council house on Reynolds Square, the Virginia Blues were drawn up in a line. They fired a welcoming volley and then executed a few professional maneuvers that capped the event. Some of Glen's receptions at Charlestown had been as splendid, but Georgians had never seen the like of the ceremony staged by Henry Ellis.

The governor's address was equal to the occasion. He bared his arms to show that they were white and not red as the French had said. If they could see his heart, they would know it was warm and true to those who were his friends. The French had said that whoever touched his hands would be struck dead. If they believed that foolish talk they should not touch him, but even if they did not, he was ready to embrace them. His visitors, of course, approached one by one to clasp his arms. It was a good beginning.

Then Ellis told them that he had built a large house for them to stay in while in Savannah and that he would not detain them because they must be weary after their long journey. He had given instructions to workmen to repair their guns and saddles if they desired it. In these arrangements Ellis followed the custom of the Indians, who provided for the comfort of visitors before doing business with them. In the absence of the Gun Merchant, the Wolf of Muccolossus spoke for the Upper Creeks. He said truly that he had made many visits to the English governors but was never received so well. Malatchi's son Togulki spoke for the Lower Creeks and said that he had been well treated in Charlestown but now met with even stronger tokens of friendship. Ellis invited the principal chiefs to dine with them at his house.[44]

It was not until November 3, 1757, that serious discussions began. Ellis asked if the representatives of the twenty-one towns were authorized to speak for the Creek Nation. He was assured that they were. Ellis then read a talk, purportedly sent by King George, with such dramatic effect that the Indians exclaimed aloud as each paragraph was interpreted. Ellis told them that the king had sent him to care for them. He said that they were better off since the English came: "We share what we have with you. We take nothing from you that you can enjoy. We leave you the Woods and all the wild Fowls and Beasts for your Subsistence. We draw our food from the Earth, we teach you to do the same, which increases your Plenty."[45]

Stumpe, guardian of Togulki, was appointed to respond. He proceeded immediately to the issue Ellis had not mentioned. The essence of his message was that his people had made a treaty with the great squire, reserving three islands, which were left in the hands of an old woman to keep for them, and now she pretended that they belonged to her. The assembled chiefs said that they had not sold them to her and they wanted Ellis to take them under his care to put an end to all disputes. Still speaking to the issues, Stumpe indicated that they were opposed to alterations in trading regulations advocated by the agent Pepper. Stumpe would not object to people settling on land above the tides; they might stay where they were because there were not many of them. Finally, his people would like a gunsmith to be sent to their country so that they would no longer have to go to the Alabama Fort to have their guns repaired.[46]

Ellis must have been greatly relieved to hear that the Bosomworths were not supported by the Creek Nation. There is little doubt that the traders had convinced the Indians that they should concede this point to Ellis. Regarding the regulation of trade, Ellis explained that he had agreed to abide by whatever was worked out with the governor of Carolina. Without mentioning Atkin by name, he told them that the king was sending a man to take care of their affairs and that he would tell him about their need for a gunsmith. A treaty was then translated, and each chief signed it with his own mark. The Wolf rose to say that it had been known in the past that some of his people agreed to a treaty and then when they reached home they denied it. If anyone present did such a thing, "I am the man that will call him a Lyar."[47]

The first three paragraphs of the treaty were platitudes reaffirming the treaty made with Oglethorpe and renewing pledges of friendship.

The fourth paragraph was the significant one. In it the Creek signers denied Mary Bosomworth's right to the sea islands and delivered the same islands "in trust" to his honor the governor of Georgia. The treaty, dated November 3, 1756, would last as long as the sun shone and the rivers ran to the sea.[48] It is of passing interest that the Georgians were so intent on securing the three sea islands that apparently it never occurred to them to ask for land above the tidewater for settlement.

On the same day the treaty was signed, Ellis found time to write to Governor Lyttelton and thank him for a large turtle that he had contributed for the delectation of the guests. Ellis wrote again a few days later saying that the Indians left very satisfied. The alliance with the Creeks needed careful nurturing, he warned, because the French and lately the Cherokees were constantly at work among them.[49]

The Indian conference of November 1757 did more than any other single event to raise Ellis's stature in London. He sent a transcript of the conference to his friend and agent John Ellis, who circulated it with unbounded enthusiasm. He told Henry that he "was in love" with the story. Philip C. Webb said that he should show it to as many people as possible because "wherever it is seen it will redound to your honour." Webb showed it to Lord Hardwicke, which was a bit bold because Reynolds was still technically the governor and Hardwicke was his patron. It was being said "in company" that Henry Ellis had all the "enterprising resolution" of Oglethorpe but that he was a much better manager both of civil government and of his temper. It was also said that no man was better suited than Ellis to be a proper governor for a "half-formed" province like Georgia.[50]

John Ellis was glad to report that he sent the account to Francis Ellis, Henry's father, in Monaghan, who derived great pleasure from it. Francis Ellis agreed with John Ellis that Henry should have all the money he needed for his essential expenses. They cautioned Henry against "getting the character of being too near which must greatly hurt every governor." No one liked a stingy governor. John expressed concern at the ministry's lack of support for Georgia. If Georgia's importance was really understood in high places, perhaps "our Darling Pitt" would do more to help.[51]

Ellis also earned the goodwill of the veteran Indian traders. He wisely solicited their help in persuading the Indians to come to Savannah, and he gave them credit for the Creeks' choosing Savannah over Charlestown. The Georgia traders did not care much for Daniel Pepper's interference in their affairs. They promoted a quiet revolution in Indian relations, a transfer of Creek allegiance from South Carolina to Georgia. That was the significance of the Savannah conference. James Adair recognized the part played by Lachlan McGillivray and George Galphin in arranging and conducting the conference. Ellis was held up by Adair as the model of what a governor should be. "When the governor saw that he could not shake hands with the Indians empty-handed, he cheerfully supplied their discontented head-men with his own effects and even his domestic utensils. They set a high value on each gift, chiefly for the sake of the giver, whom they adopted as brother, friend, father." [52] Adair did not hand out praise lightly; he had none for Glen or Lyttelton and only scorn for Edmond Atkin, when that worthy made his appearance on the southern frontier.

The euphoria that followed the conference did not last long. The uncommunicative Lord Loudoun was as silent on the matter of paying for the Virginia Blues as he was about paying for the rangers. In a moment of exasperation Ellis wrote to Loudoun, "It were greatly to be wished that you had more ample powers in what respects the defense of the southern provinces . . . especially as we are forbid to undertake anything of an expensive or military nature without the concurrence of your lordship." [53] Bouquet recalled the Virginians and declined to replace them on the excuse that Loudoun had not authorized that expense. Finally, before he gave over command to General Abercromby, Loudoun allowed Georgia enough money for Ellis to maintain the single troop of forty rangers and four officers. Those few were given the nearly impossible task of guarding Georgia's exposed settlements. [54]

The success of the conference brought a steady stream of other Indians, attracted by accounts of Ellis's extraordinary hospitality. By February 1758 1,287 by Ellis's exact count had been entertained. Ellis was £1,200 out of his own pocket and, as he confided to Lyttelton, "I am exceedingly wearied with such a succession of them." [55] At Ellis's request, the Georgia Assembly enacted a bill that imposed a £100 fine on any person who attempted to purchase land directly from Indians. A second act set a fine of £100 for anyone trading without a license and required the posting of a £2,000 bond for a license. On February 4, 1758, Ellis issued a proclamation calling attention to the new penalties. [56]

Ellis's initiatives in Indian affairs put a serious strain on his friendship with Lyttelton. Reports soon reached Ellis that the people in

South Carolina took offense at Ellis's proclamation. Lyttelton wrote to caution Ellis against restraining any licensed Carolina trader. It was not the licensed traders that he was worried about, replied Ellis. There was an unauthorized trading post at Pallachucolas, on the Carolina side of the Savannah River across from Ebenezer. Ellis did not doubt that Lyttelton would want to put a stop to that illicit business.[57]

Even while he was working on a compromise solution to the thorny issue of the Bosomworth claims, the settlement threatened to come undone. Togulki and Stumpe decided to pay Mary Bosomworth a friendly visit after the conference in Savannah. Mary was as fierce as a woman scorned. Young Togulki was no match for one who had scolded a council of chiefs and defied a council of Georgians. He left St. Catherines with the conviction that he had betrayed both Mary and the memory of his father. Therefore, he tried a time-tested method of securing a better bargain from the English by going to the Alabama Fort and saying that he would like to call on Governor Kerlérec. Kerlérec willingly hosted a conference at Mobile for Togulki and his Lower Creek entourage. A Spanish ship had recently furnished him with badly needed supplies, and he was in a position to rival Henry Ellis in generosity, if not in personality. In fact, Kerlérec disliked these meetings intensely: "It is work that is as difficult as it is unpleasant and disagreeable."[58] He usually insulated himself from direct contact with Indians. As a result, his reports to his superiors were optimistic guesses. He was convinced that Togulki was firmly on his side. Actually, Togulki, like Malatchi and his predecessors, Chigilly and Brims, were Creeks first and foremost and used the Europeans to their advantage.

Henry Ellis was as annoyed at Togulki's behavior as Kerlérec was pleased. "These savages are all mercenary," he complained to Halifax.[59] He felt that it was prudent to verify the Savannah treaty by making yet another one. He again enlisted the cooperation of the traders, and a conference was held at the Wolf's town of Muccolossus. The selection of the town was an honor to the chief, who had promised to stand up for the treaty in his own country. Again the chiefs assembled and approved the cession of the sea islands to the king. The new treaty was signed on April 22, 1758.[60]

On June 28, Ellis sent his plan to Halifax, who carried it to the Privy Council with his endorsement. On January 11, 1759, an Order in Council approved the plan. Finally, on July 26, 1759, Mary and Thomas Bosomworth sat down with Ellis and his council and agreed to his terms: they would receive a royal grant to the island of St. Catherines and a cash settlement of £2,000. The money for the settlement would be raised from the sale of Sapelo and Ossabaw islands as well as the tract along Pipemakers Creek.[61] The compromise was a triumph for Ellis. The Bosomworths were satisfied, probably for the first time since Oglethorpe's departure in 1743. Ellis was relieved. "No other event has happened here of late that has given such general satisfaction," he reported to Halifax.[62] He unburdened himself to Lyttelton: "I have at length finally accommodated the old and embarrassing dispute with the Bosomworths to their entire satisfaction, the accomplishment of which I had greatly at heart as it was an affair big with mischief and now as it is done we may expect some very beneficial effects from it."[63]

In addition to opening Ossabaw and Sapelo for settlement, he expected Creek relations to improve. He had to remain in Savannah during the summer of 1759 instead of leaving for the North as he had planned.[64] The settlement with the Bosomworths transcended narrow provincial issues. When the Cherokee War flared, the influence of Mary Bosomworth in preserving the neutrality of the Creeks was crucial.

For Henry Ellis the two years of constant personal involvement with Indian affairs was an education in imperial policy. He had so often repeated the message that the great king did not covet their land and that the French were liars for saying so that he convinced himself as well as his listeners. He had worked out an ideal theoretical relationship between the whites and the Indians, with each living in a separate zone guaranteed by treaty. There would be no private sales to confuse the clear line separating the two peoples. He would soon be in a position to translate his ideas into imperial policy.

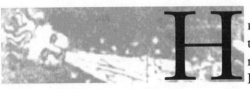

ENRY ELLIS'S four-year
tour of duty in Georgia
made him an expert on
Indian policy. He also re-
ceived an education in dealing with other extraprovincial issues, including those related to Spanish Florida, French Louisiana, and even
distant Canada. Anything that affected one part of North America set
up repercussions throughout the continent.

The transformation of Nova Scotia was a case in point. The first
experiment in colonization by the Halifax Board of Trade eventually
affected all of the American colonies, including Georgia. There were
already about 15,000 French Acadians in Nova Scotia when Governor
Edward Cornwallis arrived in June 1749 with a convoy of fourteen
ships bearing 2,576 colonists and established Halifax as the new provincial capital. Cornwallis issued a proclamation promising protection
of their land and religion if the Acadians took the oath of allegiance
to King George. The Acadians, a good, sturdy, honest people, with
unplumbed depths of stamina and stubbornness, replied that they had
already taken an oath not to bear arms and that was the only oath they
would take.[1]

During the following year there were repeated skirmishes between
the British army and the Micmac Indians, who supported the French.
Lord Halifax did not want a full-scale war, and he appointed a conciliatory governor, Thomas Peregrine Hopson, and cautioned against
enforcing the oath. Unfortunately for the cause of conciliation, Hopson had to return to England in 1753 because of poor health.[2] In his
absence the province was administered by the soldier who had been

fighting the Micmacs, Colonel Charles Lawrence. Despite instructions from Halifax not to alarm the Acadians or drive them out of the province, Lawrence proceeded to do just that. With the approval of the ineffective secretary of state, Thomas Robinson, Lawrence launched an attack on the French Fort Beausejour in June 1755. After the surrender of that and another smaller fort, the Acadians were without French protection. Lawrence presented them with an ultimatum to take the oath or be deported. With the concurrence of his provincial council and without reference to the Board of Trade or the secretary of state, Lawrence began the process of deportation. He notified the colonial governors that they would receive consignments of exiles who would make good indentured servants.

The army conducted the expulsion with a shocking disregard for the rights of the people. Nearly seven thousand people were forced from their homes and put on board ships. Some two thousand managed to elude the soldiers and escape to Quebec. As many as two thousand others hid in the forests and waited for a chance to return to their homes. Lawrence caught some of these refugees and deported four hundred in 1756. When General Jeffrey Amherst reduced the citadel of Louisbourg on St. John's Island, or Cape Breton, in 1758, he sent thirty-five hundred Acadians living on the island to France.[3] Connecticut and Maryland treated the exiles decently. Virginia and South Carolina deflected them to England, where they struggled to survive in enclaves in Liverpool and other port cities. After the war these people were allowed to join the Acadians who had been sent to France. From there many refugees were transported from France to Louisiana after the American Revolution to join some of their people already there.[4]

The arrival of four hundred Acadians in Georgia caused a mild sensation. Governor John Reynolds was about to leave Savannah and go to Augusta for a meeting with Creek Indians in December 1755 when he heard that a ship with 120 French women and children had anchored off Tybee Island at the mouth of the Savannah River. Reynolds, who was criticized for almost everything he did, was faulted for going off to Augusta when he should have dealt with the Acadians. He gave orders to permit the ship to land its passengers at Savannah and left instructions with Noble Jones, colonel of the militia and senior justice, to warn the pilot that no other transports were to put in at Savannah. He then proceeded to Augusta and fretted for ten days waiting for the Indians, who failed to appear. The Acadians required attention, and

Reynolds returned to Savannah. The same critics who said he should not have gone to Augusta blamed him for leaving.[5]

Reynolds was dismayed to discover that a second Acadian transport was at the Savannah landing, contrary to his instructions. He accused Noble Jones of deliberately embarrassing him by failing to deliver his message. In addition to the 120 women and children, there were now 280 men. The letter of Lieutenant Governor Charles Lawrence was delivered by Captain William Trattles, master of the *Prince Frederick*, which had transported the men. Lawrence explained that he had sent these French "neutrals" away for the greater security of his province.[6] John Reynolds was not clever enough to frame a proper reply pointing to the irony of bringing fiercely loyal French colonists to a desperately weak frontier province whose greatest enemy was the French in Louisiana.

Reynolds consulted with his council and decided to make the best of the unwelcome intrusion. Provisions were sent aboard to relieve at least the worst hunger pangs. The passengers were allowed to disembark and were allotted a pound of rice per person per day for ten days.[7] The Acadians must have wondered at the strange vegetation, the tall pines and giant water oaks, and the flat, sandy soil of the coastal plain. The one fortunate circumstance among a myriad of miseries was that January in Georgia was much like September in Nova Scotia. If the exiles had arrived in July, very few would have been able to make the adjustment to the climate. Henry Ellis never did.

Reynolds, as busy as he ever would be, ordered boats for the newcomers to disperse them around the outlying settlements, some down the intercoastal waterway and up the Ogeechee, some down the coast to Midway, and some to the ruined town of Frederica. The Acadians had a better idea. Once they had regained their strength, they suggested to Reynolds that they be allowed to build their own boats and set out for their homeland. They would not escape to join the French in Louisiana but would retrace their route along the Atlantic coast back to Nova Scotia. Reynolds liked the idea because, as he explained to the Lords of Trade, "they were all Papists and consequently enemies to our Religion and Government."[8] Three-fourths of the French people were gone before Henry Ellis arrived a year later.

The displaced Acadians left Georgia in April 1756 and stopped on Sullivan's Island near Charlestown to obtain passports from Governor Glen. When William Henry Lyttelton arrived on June 1, 1756, the

Georgia group had already gone; 273 others had been shipped off to London, over 100 had died, and he had to contend with the 645 who were left.⁹ The Georgia contingent reached New York in August. That province had recently enacted legislation that empowered justices of the various counties to place French refugees under the age of twenty-one with "Reputable Families." Under the terms of this act, 110 of those arriving from Georgia became indentured servants. Many served out their time and later returned to Canada. Some tried to escape and were put in jail. The Acadians from Georgia who were not stopped in New York continued their desperate journey northward. Their enemy, Lawrence of Nova Scotia, warned the Massachusetts authorities to be on the watch for them. The remainder of the Georgia group were arrested in Massachusetts and imprisoned; their boats were impounded. A few eventually reached Canada.¹⁰

More than a hundred exiled Acadians remained in Georgia when Ellis took charge of the province in February 1757. Ellis, who was different from Reynolds in so many ways, differed in his attitude toward these long-suffering people. He was surprised that Reynolds had let so many leave Georgia when the province needed settlers so badly. He found that a group of Acadians who lived near Savannah in huts they had constructed were "very useful" in making naval supplies such as oars, paddles, and hand spikes. These hand-crafted implements found a ready market in Savannah.¹¹ A month later, Ellis visited them for a second time and discovered that the high cost of food was a problem for the French people. He asked the Georgia legislature to grant them a tract of land for a garden, and he himself would provide them with "all manner of garden seeds." ¹² Ellis corresponded regularly with John Ellis about what would grow in Georgia and what would not. The French garden would give him an opportunity to do some experimentation in agriculture. The northerners found the summer heat enervating; in September Ellis was forced to ask the legislature for five barrels of rice to fend off starvation. Most of the Acadians were so sick they could not work. They were of sturdy stock, however, and it would take more than a Georgia fever to kill them. The exiles survived that summer and the next three. In April 1761 the legislature confirmed the Acadians' right to the land west of town and near the bluff.¹³ At last the long war, of which they were the first casualties, was over. By then the Acadians had been in Georgia for eight years. The French settlement resembled that of the Salzburgers at Ebenezer in that they formed a cohesive community, speaking a different language and worshiping in a differ-ent religion than most Georgians. There were thirty-seven families numbering 187 persons living on the commons west of the Savannah in 1763. The one great obstacle to their remaining in Georgia was that they had no priest to serve them; in a colony where Catholics were banned by charter, they were not likely ever to have the comfort of their rituals. When the French government offered to resettle them in French Sainte Domingue and to supply them with plantation tools and provisions for two years, they gladly accepted the offer. On January 12, 1764, the last of the Acadians left Georgia bound for Cape François. Perhaps some of them were among the refugees who came to Georgia when the blacks of the western part of the island rose in rebellion in 1793.[14] The French from Nova Scotia may have played no part in the formation of Georgia, but meeting them and learning from them was an important part of Henry Ellis's formation as an administrator in Georgia and later as governor of Nova Scotia after he left Georgia.

Another community of exiles, that of New Hanover on the Satilla River in the contested area between Georgia and Florida, also pro-vided Ellis with an opportunity for international diplomacy. Spain had indicated a willingness to recognize the Altamaha River as the bound-ary between Georgia and Florida, and the Altamaha was the boundary set by the original Georgia charter in 1732. The issue was confused by Oglethorpe's encroachments along the coast in an effort to enlarge Georgia's claims.[15] Oglethorpe's Fort William, in decrepit condition, still guarded Cumberland Island as a monument to his aspirations. Another cause of confusion was that Carolina's original charter was granted by a king whose generosity was not tempered by knowledge of the actual situation. The Carolina grant extended from the Atlantic to the Pacific and from Virginia to today's Daytona Beach, Florida. That the grant included St. Augustine and a chain of missions was of little importance to the English. The colony of Georgia, as Carolinians saw it, was within the boundaries of Carolina and should have reverted to Carolina at the termination of Trustee control in 1752. The Halifax board and the Newcastle ministry had judged otherwise, and Georgia became a royal colony instead. South Carolina accepted that decision but did not relinquish claim to an indeterminate area outside Georgia below the Altamaha River.

The apple of discord was the New Hanover colony. Edmund Gray, the charismatic individual who had frightened Governor Reynolds by protesting the results of the first Georgia legislative election in 1754 and had been declared a rebel, was the leader of the group, most of them debtors from North Carolina. When the French war began officially in 1756, the Gray colony gained importance. If Gray's people decided to accept the protection of the king of Spain and if Spain entered the war as an ally of France, as was expected, they would pose an immediate threat to Georgia's southern frontier, guarded only by the garrisons at Cumberland and St. Simons islands, garrisons that were, in Henry Ellis's words, "marks of our right rather than of our strength." [16] But if Spain believed that the New Hanover people were supported by the British government, Spain would be prodded into the war before England was ready. William Pitt, who had the ability to see the continent as an integrated whole, was the first minister to become alarmed at the dangerous possibilities posed by Edmund Gray. Henry Ellis would have to deal with Gray.

Ellis's counterpart in St. Augustine was Don Fernandez de Heredia, a professional soldier who had seen service in Central America and Jamaica before assuming the Florida post in 1755. Honest, bold, and imaginative, he was a worthy counterpart to Henry Ellis. Fernandez made enemies among his own people by enforcing laws long neglected. For example, Cuban vessels licensed to fish off Nova Scotia had learned that extra money could be made by stopping at Charlestown or Savannah and exchanging Cuban tobacco and sugar for English cloth or hardware and selling the cargo at St. Augustine. Although admirable as an example of free enterprise, the practice was contrary to Spanish regulations, and Fernandez put a stop to it. [17]

He startled Spanish officials by producing something of value for export for the first time in the history of the province. Under his encouragement, some Floridians began to manufacture pitch and tar. When a shipload of Florida pitch reached Vera Cruz, the customs officers were perplexed. The Floridians claimed an exemption from the usual port fees, but the novelty of a Florida ship with something to sell posed too large a problem for the locals to solve. The question of whether or not to tax was referred to the viceroy and then to King Charles III while the ship sat at Vera Cruz. Two years later, the answer came back that Florida products were exempt from port dues for ten years. [18] If nothing else, the incident reveals the inefficiency of the Spanish colonial system. An argument could be made that the British won North America because their system at the time was the least inefficient.

Governor Fernandez was in a stronger military position than his predecessors. The New Law of 1753 specified that the four hundred soldiers stationed in Florida were to be able-bodied and every year two hundred of them would be exchanged with the garrison of Santiago de Cuba. This regulation and the newly issued red and blue uniforms improved morale among the troops, for whom Florida was one of the least desirable assignments.[19]

Although Spain did not enter the war until 1762, there was covert cooperation between Fernandez of Florida and Kerlérec of Louisiana. Kerlérec had more difficulties to endure than either Fernandez or Ellis. His influence with the Indians was in direct proportion to the supplies he received. Because he never knew when the next shipment would run the English blockade, his mood ranged from extravagant expectations to grim despair. When well provisioned, he dared hope that he could organize all of the Indians of the Southeast as his predecessor in Louisiana, the Marquis de Vaudreuil, had done in Canada, where he now governed. Kerlérec's complaints about being neglected were more poignant than Ellis's. In October 1757 he counted fifteen dispatches he had written without receiving an answer to any. English privateers infested the Gulf and pounced on his ships at the mouth of the Mississippi. When a new commissary arrived with supplies in August 1758, Kerlérec's mood changed and he made plans to lead an invasion of Georgia and Carolina. Internal dissension was a characteristic of Louisiana politics, and Kerlérec and the commissary, Gaspard de Rochemore, were soon locked in a bitter dispute. Both men were guilty of questionable if not corrupt methods of making money, and both were called to Paris to answer charges.[20] The English colonies were fortunate in comparison to the French. There was no independent commissary in the English colonies, and there was far less opportunity for corruption.

In April Henry Ellis, on a tour of his province, chanced to meet "that odd character Gray" near Midway.[21] With Gray was a veteran trader, Ephraim Alexander, who had been forced to leave his post in Apalache by troops under orders from Governor Fernandez. Spain claimed Apalache and wanted no interference from English traders there. Alexander persuaded the Lower Creeks to threaten the Spanish with war if he was not allowed to return.

Instead of responding belligerently, Fernandez invited Alexander and Gray to open a trading post on the St. Johns, well within the jurisdiction of Florida. Gray and Alexander, however, preferred a license from Ellis. Ellis recognized a clever ploy when he saw one and in letters to Lyttelton and Halifax expressed praise for Fernandez's strategy. Bringing Gray's settlement to the St. Johns would give Florida a buffer against Georgia and opening trade would gain the cooperation of the Lower Creeks. Ellis was impressed with Gray; he characterized him as a "shrewd and sensible fellow" who affected an austerity of living that appealed to whites and Indians alike.[22] Perhaps Ellis should have waited for permission from London to act, as the Spanish and French governors were expected to do from their governments, but he decided to give Gray and Alexander a license if they would move to the St. Marys River across from Fort William on Cumberland Island.

Lyttelton was politely annoyed at Ellis's initiative because in his opinion the area in question was part of Carolina. Ellis begged Lyttelton's pardon and blamed "the natural impetuosity" of his temperament, if not "inadvertency or ignorance." But he felt constrained to observe that Gray held a grudge against the government of Carolina and refused to solicit a license there.[23]

Ellis furnished the ministry with useful intelligence regarding Florida. For example, he revealed that the British ships, which had the right by treaty to trade in the Bay of Honduras, stopped at Savannah as an alternative to Charlestown as they followed the Gulf Stream up the coast to catch the prevailing westerlies at Cape Hatteras. He supplied the Board of Trade with information about the number and nature of French ships bound for Louisiana.[24] He kept lookouts posted on the sea islands to watch for enemy vessels.

Ellis's new friends Gray and Alexander supplied him with news of Spanish activity. In July, it was said that preparations were being made to settle four hundred people from Cuba at Apalache in west Florida. Alexander inquired whether he should cause the Indians to attack the Spaniards and spoil their plans. Ellis relayed the report to the Board of Trade, explaining that he had told Alexander not to worry about the Spanish plans for Apalache. The barrenness of the land there and the hostility of the Lower Creeks to any incursions were obstacles enough; besides, the "natural indolence" of the Spanish would probably defeat the project.[25]

Ellis suggested a bold scheme to the board. The Spanish Guarda Costa had put a stop to the illegal traffic between Savannah and St. Augustine, but it occurred to Ellis that a flourishing trade with the Spanish might be conducted through New Hanover. Ellis admitted that his suggestion "did not square with the letter of the Navigation Act," but it was in accord with its spirit, which was to increase British commerce.[26]

A potential crisis arose in September 1757 when seventy Lower Creeks attacked outlying Florida plantations and killed four persons. Governor Fernandez was outraged and accused Gray and Alexander of instigating the attack and Ellis of knowing about it. Ellis might have assumed a haughty attitude common in such correspondence, but he advised Fernandez that, although he had nothing to do with the recent trouble, he would try to prevent a recurrence. Alexander at New Hanover was the most likely culprit, but he insisted that the Indians conducted the raid themselves to show their opposition to the proposed Spanish settlement in Apalache.[27] Ellis reported to the board that he had persuaded the Indians to release some Spanish prisoners but that now Fernandez was asserting Spain's claim to the St. Marys and wanted Gray's people to withdraw to the Altamaha. If Ellis agreed, he would seem to acquiesce in the Spanish claim. This was, he told Halifax, "ticklish business."[28] He explained to Halifax that it was not a good idea to urge the Indians to attack the Spaniards because the French would retaliate by instigating the Choctaws, Alabamas, or Shawnees, all under their influence, to attack the Lower Creeks, and the war would escalate, ruining the Georgia Indian trade. Ellis was under the impression that Kerlérec did not want to launch such a war. Actually, Kerlérec shared an ambition with his counterpart in South Carolina; each aspired to become a military hero, leading armies of Indians into the other's territory. Kerlérec was prevented only by lack of support from France.

Ellis received a letter from John McGillivray, a cousin of Lachlan's from the Upper Creek country, indicating that the Choctaws were growing impatient with the inability of the French to supply them with trade goods and wanted the English to open trade with them.[29] Just such a request to Lachlan McGillivray in 1746 had led to the Choctaw Revolt. Ellis might have taken the initiative, but Edmond Atkin was expected to arrive in Charlestown any day, and Ellis forwarded the message to Governor Lyttelton. The one achievement of Atkin's mission to the Indian country in 1759 was his treaty with the Choctaws, for which he claimed the entire credit but which could more easily have been arranged by Ellis with the willing cooperation of the Georgia traders.

William Pitt's leadership began to produce results in 1758 with Jeffrey Amherst's conquest of Louisbourg and John Forbes's occupation of the abandoned site of Fort Duquesne at the forks of the Ohio. Ellis learned from Lachlan McGillivray at Augusta that a party of Cherokees that had gone north to join Forbes's expedition clashed with whites in Virginia on their return. The Cherokees would be increasingly hostile during the coming year. Pitt's influence was felt in Georgia in an embargo on trade with France, imposed by his instructions. In May 1758, Ellis enforced the embargo by seizing a French ship flying a Dutch flag which had docked at Savannah.[30]

More significant was Pitt's concern about the Gray colony. It was ironic that Pitt, who later advocated a war with Spain, was so anxious to avoid friction in 1758. As soon as Pitt heard from Halifax about the protests of Governor Fernandez, he directed the board to make recommendations on the best way to avoid "bad consequences."[31] Halifax was embarrassed that his protégé was a source of concern to Pitt. In the same letter that informed Ellis of his appointment as governor, Halifax lectured his friend about the serious import of the Gray settlement, which the ministry saw as "a matter of a very extraordinary nature and of a very dangerous tendency." For one thing, it was subversive of government for English subjects to live outside the jurisdiction of the law, and, more important, it could easily lead to a dispute with Spain. Ellis should not have given Gray a license. That act negated all the other prudent steps Ellis had taken to conciliate the Spanish government. The matter was serious enough to be placed on the agenda of the Privy Council in April 1758.[32]

Meanwhile, unaware of the consternation in high places, Ellis took a second tour of the southern coastal region. At his initiative the church at Midway was enclosed with palisades, and a battery was mounted on an earthen fort at Sunbury, the port for the Midway district. A recent fire had destroyed most of the houses in Frederica, but the barracks were habitable for the thirty men stationed there under veteran Captain Raymond Demere. A detachment of South Carolina's Independent Company was stationed at Fort William on Cumberland.

While at Cumberland, Ellis had his second interview with Edmund Gray, who, as before, intrigued him. Gray was "shrewd, sagacious and capable."[33] Gray's judgment about others was sound, but he was "ridiculously absurd in every part of his own conduct." From Gray, Ellis learned that Florida had a new governor, Lucas Fernando de Palacio y Valenzuela. Palacio proved highly unpopular with his own people as well as with the Indians. In the opinion of one historian of Florida, "Palacio lacked judgment and tact and pursued a policy of tyranny." [34] Gray's people were alarmed at the reports that the new governor was building forts on the St. Johns River.

The immediate result of the change of government at St. Augustine was a worsening of relations between Georgia and Florida. French privateers began to make St. Augustine their base. On May 20 Ellis reported to the Board of Trade that three French privateers were cruising off the coast of Georgia. By July, they had captured five British vessels and outfitted one as a fourth privateer. The prizes were anchored at St. Augustine. Ellis warned Lyttelton that St. Augustine was becoming as troublesome as it was during Oglethorpe's war. Since his arrival in Georgia, Ellis had repeatedly asked for warships to be sent to Georgia. The board forwarded his requests to the Admiralty, but the Lords of the Admiralty were too preoccupied with the Louisbourg expedition to worry about Georgia. It was especially galling to Ellis that during the two months while the French ships cruised off Georgia's sea islands, there were three ships of the Royal Navy at anchor in Charlestown. He believed that the French supply line to Louisiana now followed the Florida coast into the Gulf and avoided the British ships in the West Indies.[35] Besides these causes of concern and frustration, he had not heard from the board in over a year (he had not yet received its reprimand for his handling of the Gray affair), and the heat of that July soared to 105°. While sensible folk sought the shade, Ellis went about with an umbrella and a thermometer, recording the temperature. He wrote an article about it which was printed in the *London Magazine* and inserted in the *Philosophical Transactions* of the Royal Society.[36] Unfortunately, his health broke under the stress of the Bosomworth negotiations, the constant stream of Indian visitors, the management of government, and finally, the immediate problem of a blockade by enemy ships.

In spite of the heat and his health and perhaps because of his frustration, he decided on the boldest action of his administration. Since the previous May, an impounded French ship had laid idle at a Savannah wharf. Ellis had her outfitted with fourteen swivel guns. He gave command to a Captain Robinson, and second in command was a Captain Demetre. He let it be known that he needed a crew willing to sail into the St. Augustine sanctuary to flush out the French and rescue the British ships held there. It was a desperately foolhardy venture, yet ninety "spirited young fellows" immediately signed on, among them two of Ellis's personal servants. The turnout was a tribute to his leadership. The ship, the *Tryall*, set sail during the last week of that torrid July. Ellis saw her leave with high hopes; the "officers are brave and the vessel sailed fast," he wrote Lyttelton.[37]

The *Tryall* was bold enough. Captain Robinson headed straight for St. Augustine and nearly made it without encountering an enemy vessel. At the entrance to the St. Augustine harbor, one of the French privateers issued a challenge. The two vessels exchanged broadsides and then locked together, the Frenchman's bow to the stern of the *Tryall*. Captain Robinson did not dare order his inexperienced crew of volunteers to board the other vessel, and they waited to be boarded while the French hurled grenades, flash bombs, "stinkpots," and other implements which, as Ellis put it, "mankind have been so ingenious to invent for the destruction of their species."[38] All the while, the bow guns of the French vessel fired into the English ship while the *Tryall*, with no stern guns, was unable to answer except with musket fire.

At last the Frenchmen clambered aboard the *Tryall*, swords and cutlasses in hand. In the first encounter Robinson was killed and Demetre fatally wounded. Even after he received his death stroke, Robinson killed two of the boarders. In a savage hand-to-hand melee, the Frenchmen were driven back to their ship. Darkness was falling and a fresh wind broke the ships apart. Bodies of men caught between the two vessels fell into the water. The cries of the wounded were a terrible sound. The *Tryall*'s crew, though badly mauled, fired a broadside into the Frenchman as the ships disengaged. Only three men of the Georgia vessel were killed in the engagement, but twenty-five were wounded and some did not recover. The *Tryall* limped back to Savannah with its sad story. Ellis sat with the dying Demetre and accompanied the body to the grave.[39]

The failure of his expedition and his worsening health made Ellis uncharacteristically irritable. He realized he was being importunate, he wrote to the board, but "I cannot avoid being so whilst my remonstrances to other branches of ministry seem to be disregarded. I have repeatedly urged these matters in the strongest terms to the Right Honorable the Secretary of State and to the Commanders in Chief of the King's forces in these parts, but hitherto with less effect than

I could wish."[40] No troops, no ships of war, no money for rangers, nothing was forthcoming from the ministry.

His complaints caused consternation among his friends. John Ellis warned Henry Ellis that Sedgwick, one of Pitt's secretaries, came to tell him that he could hardly find an inoffensive line to extract from a recent communication to Pitt. John Ellis cautioned Henry not to be "too open in writing severely on your being neglected by the ministry."[41]

Lord Barrington sent word to Henry Ellis that no requisition of his would be protested as long as he was secretary at war. John Ellis said that Barrington was "most zealously diligent in your interest; and that Lord Halifax was equally zealous and the two often conferred together." John Ellis shrewdly noted that "my frequent visits are necessary to put great people in mind," and he would continue to remind them of the governor's needs.[42]

Ellis heard from William Henry Lyttelton that William Pitt ordered a census of Gray's followers, whom he wanted removed to Georgia or South Carolina. Ellis concealed any displeasure he might have felt at receiving orders secondhand and tried to maintain the initiative by offering to send a messenger to talk to Gray. At the same time, he expressed doubts about the wisdom of removing Gray. To do so might give Spain the impression that England was abandoning the region to Spain.[43]

Lyttelton was more concerned that Georgia might claim the region than he was about Spain's pretensions. He informed Ellis that each province should name a commissioner, and the two would act jointly in dealing with New Hanover. If Ellis had aggrandizement in mind, and he probably did, he carefully concealed it from his friend and rival. He agreed that Lyttelton's method of dealing with Gray had "more dignity and propriety in it" than his own plan.[44]

On January 28, 1759, Ellis wrote to Halifax the news that the two commissioners were on their way to New Hanover. He did not agree with their mission, however, and suggested to Halifax the wisdom of extending Georgia's boundaries to the St. Johns, using Oglethorpe's claims as precedence. Why not simply remove Gray to Cumberland Island, where Georgia maintained Fort William?[45] The delay in communication with England and Lyttelton's determination to be rid of the Gray irritant ended Ellis's expansionist intentions for the moment. When the time came in 1763 to decide the boundary of Georgia, however, Henry Ellis would be the principal adviser to the secretary of state charged with making that decision. Meanwhile, Ellis took the precaution of sending a spy to map out the defenses of St. Augustine, just in case it might be needed. As it turned out, it was. As an additional concession to Lyttelton, Ellis introduced an act to prevent horses, cattle, and provisions from being conveyed overland to Florida.[46] The two southernmost provinces, one British, the other Spanish, were closer than ever to an open war.

James Edward Powell, Georgia's commissioner, reported that Gray and his people were very cooperative. The commissioner was kindly received at New Hanover, where he published the proclamation. Everyone seemed to expect the notice, and no objection was voiced. Powell then went to Cumberland Island to tell the settlers there that they must leave. Again there was no opposition. Ellis reported these results in a brief letter to Pitt without comment.[47] He was more open with Halifax, repeating that he would have preferred to leave the settlers on Cumberland Island. He thought that the apparent willingness of those people to abandon their settlement was a ruse intended to placate the authorities and that they would soon "steal back to their habitations."[48]

The war in the North had taken a turn for the better, and there was good news from the West Indies. On May 19, 1759, Ellis was able to inform Lyttelton that a British vessel ten days out of St. Kitts had docked at Savannah with the report that the British had taken the island of Guadeloupe from the French and that Martinique was on the verge of surrendering.[49] To many in England, including William Pitt, these two sugar islands were more important than Florida could ever be. Henry Ellis took the Georgia view that Florida in British hands was preferable. That argument would escalate in intensity before this war was over.

BY COINCIDENCE, colonial Georgia was the proving ground for two major initiatives of the Halifax Board of Trade: the effort to establish model provinces and the attempt to regulate the Indian trade. Henry Ellis represented one of these experiments, Edmond Atkin, the other. Before Halifax's term as president of the board ended in 1761, Ellis had successfully established a constitutional government in Georgia, and Edmond Atkin had failed as the first royal superintendent of Indian affairs of the Southern Department.

Nova Scotia was the other pet project of the Halifax board, and that province, too, was intended to be remodeled into an example of proper colonial behavior. The Acadians would have to be converted into English subjects or banished, and the latter alternative was quicker. Therefore, the board condoned the harsh policies of the military government, including the removal of the Acadians in 1756 and 1758. Because British subjects were needed to replace the French and compose a body politic, Governor Charles Lawrence, the most determined agent in the transformation of Nova Scotia, advertised in New England for settlers. His proclamation of October 12, 1758, announced the availability of two hundred thousand acres of free land. A second proclamation in 1759, the so-called Charter of Nova Scotia, exempted newcomers from quitrents for ten years and limited grants to one thousand acres per person. Dissenters were excused from the obligation to support the Church of England. The emigration from Massachusetts, Connecticut, and Rhode Island began in 1760. During the next three years, five thousand New Englanders became Nova Scotians.[1]

Contemporaries understood that a model province was being constructed in Nova Scotia. Benjamin Franklin warned in 1759 that the
province was intended to be a testing ground for policies the board
intended to impose on the other colonies. Indeed, the town of Halifax
was designated as the place of trial for violators of the Navigation Acts.[2]

No one, then or later, accused the board of having any such sinister design regarding Georgia. The best evidence that the Halifax board
meant to protect the rights of subjects rather than deprive them of
those rights is the board's approval of Ellis's administration. Halifax
tolerated a military regime in Nova Scotia during the removal of the
Acadians and the siege of Louisbourg; however, after 1758, the board
urged Lawrence to follow the example of Georgia and form a legislature.[3] Finally, convinced that a soldier was not the man to foster popular
government, Halifax appointed Henry Ellis to succeed Lawrence as
governor of Nova Scotia. The nomination was an acknowledgment of
a mission accomplished as well as a challenge to Ellis to bring Nova
Scotia into line. In England, where the game of empire was closely
watched, it was generally understood that Ellis had successfully carried
out Halifax's intentions in Georgia. John Ellis wrote to the Earl of
Hillsborough about one of his colonial appointments and expressed
the hope that the individual would be as "useful" to Hillsborough as
Ellis had been to Halifax in Georgia "and that he will meet your Lordship's favour as much as Govr. Ellis did Lord Halifax's."[4] It should be
possible, then, to learn what kind of model administration the Halifax
board approved by following the activities of Ellis as governor. From
this perspective, Ellis's years in Georgia take on a dimension and a
significance not generally understood.

Edmond Atkin, who represented the other major initiative of the
Halifax board, was able by his treatise of 1755 to persuade the board
to recommend a division of North America into two departments, the
northern and southern, and to name a superintendent of Indian affairs
in each department. Atkin drew upon his own experience as a Charlestown trader and merchant to make his case to the board. He argued
that the Carolina Indian commissioners were ineffective because they
never went out into the Indian country and had to take their information from the traders. He criticized the principal traders for forming
a company that dominated the trade, he accused them of manipulat-
ing the reports from the Indian country and of inventing crises, he
suspected some of trading with the French at Fort Toulouse, and he

believed that the traders opposed an attack on Fort Toulouse because it would disrupt their business. Because each governor granted licenses, it was unlikely that there would ever be a uniform policy of trade regulation. The only solution, as Atkin saw it, was to vest control in an agent who would report to the king through the board.[5]

Although Atkin dallied in Virginia for a time, his most important work occurred after his arrival in South Carolina in 1758. His visit to the Creek country in 1759 was his tour de force, his demonstration of the effectiveness of an independent Indian agent. The success of his mission depended on his ability to deal directly with the Indians, as he clearly understood. But he did not realize that success also depended on his having a cordial relationship with the governors and the veteran traders. The Lords of Trade watched Atkin's journey to the Creek Nation with interest. For that reason, Atkin's activities transcended the provincial in importance.

Henry Ellis had the advantage when he was named lieutenant governor of Georgia of knowing that he must avoid the mistakes John Reynolds had made. Reynolds was a decent, honest man, well suited for a career in the navy or any similar bureaucracy, but he was totally unsuited, as he demonstrated, for the role of colonial governor, model or otherwise. The lengthy instructions, which he diligently studied and to which he attempted to adhere, were not enough to ensure a successful administration. Reynolds showed incredibly poor judgment in dispensing patronage when he gave his former naval surgeon, William Little, seven of the positions at his disposal.[6] On the occasion of his first crisis, Reynolds panicked. When Edmund Gray and his friends announced their intention to march to Savannah and demonstrate against their political enemies, Reynolds decided that they must be dangerous incendiaries.[7] He was largely responsible for Gray's flight to the Florida borderlands.

Reynolds's worst failure was his inability to establish a harmonious working relationship among the three branches of government. During his second year, he quarreled continually with the council members, who were supposed to be his closest advisers and the chief supporters of his government. He encouraged factionalism, which adversely affected the morale of the people as well as the effectiveness of government. He yielded his prerogatives to William Little and the Commons House, especially in the initiation of legislation. He failed to show a grasp of finances, much less of a budget. Even though the province ran a large debt in 1756, he failed to propose new taxes in 1757.[8] Henry Ellis could compile an agenda for himself simply by avoiding Reynolds's catalog of mistakes.

From the outset, Ellis emphasized his interest in the welfare of Georgia and called upon the people to lay aside their jealousies of one another. He aroused them by asserting that their lives and liberties were at stake. He flattered them by assuming that their concern for the public welfare was as great as his. He reassured them that he understood their weakness in numbers and their collective poverty but insisted that "even if it is little that you can do it should be done with spirit and cheerfulness becoming Englishmen." He cautioned them against "the pursuit of the trivial."[9]

After raising the Georgians' horizons and exciting their patriotism, Ellis guided them in what needed to be done. At each session of the assembly, he described legislation and convinced the House of the importance of each measure. He told the delegates what the cost would be and left the painful business of raising money to them. On one occasion, after laying an estimate of expenses before the House, he said, "I desire nothing upon this occasion but what you yourselves shall think necessary to provide."[10] He observed, as though it was none of his business, that the previous year's revenue fell short. The assembled body expressed concern about the deficit and pledged to do better. A surprising and significant aspect of their attitude is the assumption of responsibility for self-taxation by these novices in government.

The precedent was set that the governor would propose legislation and recommend a budget and the legislature would work the program into law. That process was followed by subsequent Georgia governors and legislatures and is followed today. Those early Georgians would not have been surprised at the long-term implications of their work. They knew that they were building for the future, and they credited Ellis on behalf of posterity. "We will look upon any future good," they said, "as the happy consequence of the foundation you have laid for their welfare."[11]

Ellis set an example, for the first time in Georgia history, of an active constitutional chief executive. Among the litany of bills he proposed, the most important were those that established the public credit, reduced the disposition of public land to a manageable system, regulated Indian trade, and divided the province into parishes. In a display of evenhandedness that was difficult for future governors to equal, he succeeded in satisfying the various interests. The planters were grateful to him for clearing up the confusion in land titles. Ellis observed that one of Oglethorpe's "visionary ideas" was that "people might subsist and even become affluent upon such small parcels of land as the little farms in England" and he had "minced all the lands" into "Whimsical figures of five and forty-five acres."[12] As a result, Savannah was surrounded by a checkerboard of lots, many with no owners or absentee owners. Ellis was responsible for an act requiring that the land be developed within three years or be forfeited.

One of Ellis's infrequent quarrels with the board concerned the size of grants. The head of a family was entitled to five hundred acres plus fifty acres for each member of his family. Slaves were counted as family members. The number of slaves increased sharply during Ellis's administration, and he was concerned about too wide a dispersion of white planters. He attempted to reduce the amount of land awarded for each slave to ten acres, arguing that Georgia's immediate problem was security, but the board disagreed with him in favor of the larger grants. When he first came to Georgia, he estimated that there were not more than ten men who had £500 worth of property.[13] During his administration the number was radically increased because by 1760 most of the territory included in Oglethorpe's Treaty of 1739, that is, the tidewater region between the Altamaha and Savannah rivers, had been distributed.

The foundation for the plantation system that characterized Georgia for much of its history was laid during Ellis's tenure. The members of the council were among the leaders in the scramble for land grants. James Habersham, Patrick Houstoun, Noble Jones, Francis Harris, and James Edward Powell did well for themselves, and Jonathan Bryan led the way by acquiring an average of two thousand acres per year between 1755 and 1760.[14]

Ellis's personal friends among the rising gentry included Charles Pryce, whom he described as "a man of good disposition, independent fortune and bred to the law"; William Butler, "a considerable planter and universally esteemed"; Captain William Mackenzie, a recent arrival from North Carolina, who carried a recommendation from Ellis's old patron Governor Arthur Dobbs and who had a "sufficient fortune." William Clifton, the attorney general, knew something of the law, but Clifton's wife was a terrible termagant who was once jailed for disturbing the peace.[15] William Knox was among Ellis's closest acquaintances,

although Knox continued to nurse wounded feelings about being neglected by the governor. Ellis thought highly of the merits of Thomas
Burrington and made him clerk of the Commons House.[16]

The merchants, like the planters, approved of Ellis's administration. By accepting the paper money issued by the previous administration, Ellis raised the value of the currency. By establishing a budget, he
established the public credit of the province. Georgia's first and largest
mercantile house was that of James Habersham and Francis Harris,
both of whom were on the council. The partners built the first wharf
at Savannah in 1751, but neither the wharf nor anything else about the
town made a favorable impression on William G. De Brahm when he
disembarked in Savannah in that year. He found the town practically
deserted and so poor that he thought he could have bought up half the
property for £20 sterling. Three years later, in 1754, Governor John
Reynolds found a town of 150 houses, mostly small, wooden, and "very
old," although the oldest house was built by Oglethorpe twenty years
before. De Brahm took credit for the construction of a new wharf in
1759, which served as a model for others. A few years later the river-
side was lined with wharves from one end of town to the other.[17] The
South Carolina Gazette for June 30, 1759, noted that there were thirteen
vessels in Savannah harbor and commented that this was "proof that
the trade of that colony increases in proportion as it flourishes in other
respects."

The records of merchant Thomas Rasberry have been preserved
for the years 1758 to 1761. They reveal that rice was by far the principal export commodity but that deerskins were on the increase. Earlier,
Savannah merchants complained that the Augusta traders sent their
skins to Charlestown. By Ellis's time Savannah was beginning gradually to compete with Charlestown. When Rasberry injected into his
tedious listing of items that it was "A Matter of Joy" when Ellis's appointment as governor became known, he spoke for the merchants of
the colony. When Ellis left Georgia in 1760, the merchants tendered
an address of appreciation for his efforts on their behalf.[18] Savannah's
artisans joined the planters and merchants in singing Ellis's praises.
The Union Society, which was composed mostly of "mechanics," cited
the preservation of peace, the relief granted to debtors from provinces
other than South Carolina, and the legislation that barred slaves from
engaging in skilled crafts.[19]

A segment of the population that Ellis failed to help lacked a public voice and therefore registered no complaints. They were Georgia's blacks. A colony of free blacks lived below the bluff to the east of town. Some of them were riverboat men who paddled the dugout canoes called periaguas or poled the long, narrow barges upriver to Augusta and coasted down with the current. Others were manual laborers who helped build the new houses in town. But most were slaves, the number of whom increased dramatically from 1,066 in 1753, to 1,800 in 1757, 2,100 in 1758, and 3,578 in 1760. The increase occurred even though these were war years and importation was restricted.[20]

Ellis was concerned about the welfare of slaves, as he was about the Acadians living to the west of town. So was Joseph Ottolenghe, the supervisor of the silk filature, who conducted a school for them in Savannah. In the evenings, when the slaves had finished the day's chores, they gathered to learn how to read the Bible and to memorize the catechism. Ottolenghe wrote to a friend, "How often the present humane governor and I have commiserated their hard and forlorn fate." Ellis and Ottolenghe were unable to find a way to help the slaves without alienating the planters. As Ottolenghe phrased it, any measure for the relief of slaves would have as much chance of passage in a slave-owning legislature as a bill to curtail legal fees would have among a group of lawyers.[21]

Ellis himself provided a clue to one of the measures he favored. Many years later, during the debate in England over the slave trade, he recalled that he had recommended that mulattoes be freed to form a class in society between whites and blacks. Other slaves would be freed when they attained the age of thirty; "something of this sort I tried in Georgia," he said, "but could not accomplish."[22] The timing was wrong for any serious consideration of changing plantation slavery. When slavery was banned during the Trustee era, white Georgians became convinced that their lack of prosperity was directly attributable to the fact that slave labor was denied them. During the decade of the 1750s, they were determined to make up for lost time. South Carolina planters were their models, and the Georgia slave code, adopted in 1755, was based on Carolina's. In 1757 the assembly enacted legislation imposing a ten o'clock curfew on Savannah's slaves and free blacks. All white men between the ages of sixteen and sixty were to do patrol duty, and each night from five to ten men were to be designated as night watch. A second act extended the system to the countryside. Rural patrols were instructed to visit each plantation once a month and at discretion search the slave quarters for weapons. As historian Betty Wood observed, "All white males, including nonslaveholders, were being required to fulfill the additional function of safeguarding the property interests of the rapidly emerging planter elite."[23]

The Indian traders, headquartered in Augusta, joined the chorus of approval of the governor. From the start of his administration Ellis was careful to include the traders in his negotiations with the Indians. Aware that the traders were indispensable intermediaries between the two peoples, Henry Ellis took care not to interfere unduly in the trading business. He took the part of the traders when he objected to the missions of Daniel Pepper and Edmond Atkin. The established traders welcomed his efforts to eliminate clandestine trade, especially from isolated houses on the Carolina side of the river. They also supported Ellis's Indian Act, which required the posting of a £1,000 bond for a trading license, because it limited the number of traders. Most of all they admired Ellis's understanding of Indian culture and his manner of treating them with respect and consideration. When Ellis left Georgia in 1760, the inhabitants of Augusta, represented by Lachlan McGillivray, Edward Barnard, and John Graham, thanked him for his Indian diplomacy and for protecting the trade. Ellis replied that he had always felt that the people of Augusta were entitled to special attention because "they greatly contributed to the prosperity and security of this colony."[24]

There was another segment of society that was particularly indebted to Henry Ellis. It included planters and merchants, some traders, and possibly a few "mechanics." They were members of an organization modeled after the Royal Society in London, called the Georgia Society.[25] Their purpose was the promotion of trade and the advancement of knowledge, causes so dear to the enlightened gentlemen of mid-eighteenth-century Britain.

The naturalist John Ellis reflected the curiosity of England's scientists about the wonders of the New World. He asked Henry to tell him the names of all who would be interested in "our business," that is, natural science. Soon John Ellis's correspondents included William De Brahm, Henry Yonge, Pickering Robinson, Joseph Ottolenghe, William Clifton, and James Habersham, all of Savannah, and Dr. Alexander Garden of Charlestown. These men and a few others added an intellectual dimension to the emerging Georgia society. Libraries, as well as land, became essential property for gentlemen. Thomas

Burrington, clerk of assembly, had a private library of 425 volumes, including books in four languages. Most of them dealt with law, but also represented were works of Shakespeare, Milton, Pope, Smollett, and Swift.[26]

Henry Ellis communicated with the Royal Society through John Ellis. The account of the intolerable heat of the summer of 1758, which Henry sent to John, was reviewed by Dr. John Fothergill and read to the society. Like a good scientist, Henry Ellis went out in the noon-day heat, sheltered by the recent French invention the parasol, with his thermometer made by a member of the Royal Society, and recorded a temperature of 102°. Ellis told of the erratic changes in weather from day to day and the different degrees of heat in the various levels of his house. Georgia residents of today would not be surprised at a mere 102° in July, but Henry Ellis's London friends were appalled. John Ellis wrote that "the hot or rather hellish account you give me of the heat frightens me."[27] John changed his mind about going to Georgia and instead sent advice about plants he thought might grow in the Georgia climate. He categorized the plants under three headings: manufactures, drugs, and agriculture. Plants that could be used in manufacturing included madder, turkey galls, cork, safflower, yellow berries of avignon, turnsol, olives, rape, Turkish cotton, and kale. Items under plants for agriculture included lucerne, buckwheat, Indian millet, tea, capers, pomegranates, figs, almonds, grapes, plums, and pistachio nuts.[28]

Henry Ellis is credited with the introduction into Georgia of Bermuda grass, which under the name "wiregrass" spread rapidly over the coastal region.[29] Ellis urged certain gentlemen "of independent fortunes," who were friends of his, to try other plants. The best Savannah gardens belonged to James Habersham, Jonathan Bryan, Henry Yonge, and John Mullryne. Habersham was reluctant to be included in the circle of agricultural scientists. "My friend Governor Ellis mistakes in thinking I have any knowledge of or particular Passion for the cultivating of Plants," he wrote to John Ellis, adding, "I must own I revere and esteem Men who act out of the narrow sphere of self and communicate their knowledge for useful improvements for the Public good." Habersham employed an English gardener, who conversed with Ellis on the subject of exotic plants.[30]

Henry Ellis was able to report to John Ellis that figs did well in Georgia, olives not so well. Opium poppies grew to a large size and were a common feature of gardens. Gardeners were unsuccessful with almonds and dates. Sesamum grew everywhere, but no one would attempt safflower. In fact, the urge to grow the money crops of rice and indigo was so strong that few men could be persuaded to try anything else. "They are like the boy who resolved not to go into the water til he could swim," said Ellis. He continued to collect interesting specimens to send over to the Royal Society. He enlisted the traders to bring "all sorts of natural curiosities" to him from the Indian country. That he could ask this of these rough characters and that they would do it for him tells us a bit more about the relationship between the governor and the traders. Georgia was a frontier where even the traders were scientists.[31] Henry Ellis shipped acorns, cedar berries, seeds of the swamp cypress, palmetto seeds, and cones from tulip trees. John Ellis distributed them among Henry's high-placed friends, Halifax, Barrington, P. C. Webb, and James West, secretary to the Lords of Treasury.[32]

The shipping of seeds was not an easy task in the days before refrigeration. Many of Henry's specimens spoiled on the long voyage. How to send seeds became the subject of a lively dialogue involving the two Ellises, Alexander Garden, and even the great Dr. Carl Linnaeus. Linnaeus agreed with Henry Ellis that the great danger to seeds being spoiled was the heat of the deep holds of the ship. The consensus was that seeds should be coated with brewer's loam moistened with "gum arabick," encased in beeswax, and stored in casks carried on the decks of ships.[33] However appealing this procedure might have been to men of science, it was a bother to men of commerce.

This enthusiasm for plant experimentation by Henry Ellis and his friends revived one of the projects of the original Trustees, who had employed agents to collect tropical plants for cultivation in Georgia. The sloping hill to the east of town was laid out as the Trustees' Garden, and an "inspector of public gardens" was appointed. Like most of the Trustees' undertakings, the garden was a disappointment. By 1741 only a few mulberry trees and a scattering of fruit trees remained, and in 1755 the site was sold to the unimaginative Governor Reynolds.[34] Henry Ellis was aware of the history of the Trustees' Garden because of his friendship with Dr. Stephen Hales and Lord Shaftesbury, both former Georgia Trustees. John Ellis shared Henry Ellis's reports from Georgia with both men.[35]

Henry Ellis resurrected another favorite scheme of the founders of Georgia, the cultivation of silk. The Trustees had entertained the most extravagant expectations of eventually having twenty thousand Georgians on their little farms engaged in the production of raw silk while twenty thousand people in England would be employed in its manufacture. The Trustees' agents distributed thousands of mulberry seedlings and eggs of silkworms to the first Georgia settlers. In other climates the mulberry trees produced tender leaves just when the worms were hatched. Not so in Georgia. If the mulberry seedlings survived, and most did not, Georgia's frequent February frosts nipped the early shoots and left nothing for the worms to feed on. In spite of the contrariness of nature, however, some cocoons were produced. The next part was the hardest, unwinding silk from the cocoons. This task was performed in a special building in Savannah called a filature. A second filature was built in Ebenezer in 1751. A succession of silk experts was employed by the Trustees, the most obnoxious of whom was Mary, the wife of Jacob Camuse, who refused to show anybody else how to wind silk. She was dismissed by the Trustees in 1748. The greatest amount of raw silk produced in a single year under the Trustees was 496 pounds — not enough to promote manufacturing but enough to tantalize the silk enthusiasts in London. The Trustees sent Pickering Robinson over in 1751 to supervise the production of silk, but he soon had to return to England for his health and did not return to Georgia until 1760. Meanwhile, the pious Joseph Ottolenghe was responsible for storing cocoons in the filature and instructing workers in the art of spinning thread. Unfortunately, Ottolenghe showed signs of the Camuse syndrome, a reluctance to share his knowledge with others.[36]

Henry Ellis was genuinely excited about the possibilities of silk cultivation. His friends in the Royal Society deemed silk manufacture a greater accomplishment than his Indian treaty. "I must tell you that the silk culture was always a great object with me," Henry confided to John Ellis. But, most of the locals had given up the prospect of ever producing more than a token amount. When the energetic Ellis charged that the supervisor, Ottolenghe, held the position as a "job," a sinecure, without any incentive to produce silk, Ottolenghe was prodded into unaccustomed activity. On May 10, 1758, there was more than a hint of excitement in Henry Ellis's report that there were six thousand pounds of cocoons in the filature, more than ever before; "raising silk was no longer despaired of," he said.[37]

A letter from Henry Ellis to Benjamin Martyn dated June 27, 1758, sounded the same note of triumph as he counted seven thousand pounds of cocoons. Ellis thanked Martyn for his good work in getting the Royal Society of Arts to grant premiums for the production of silk. Ellis reverted to another of the Trustees' projects by inquiring about hemp, which he thought might be raised if the society offered an incentive. He himself had grown almonds, and his figs were as fine as any in the world. The only problem Ellis mentioned was that Ottolenghe seemed unable or unwilling to train enough people to spin silk into thread at the filature.[38]

On July 4, 1758, disaster struck. According to the *South Carolina Gazette*, "A dreadful fire broke out in the public filature and raged with irresistible fury." The filature faced Reynolds Square in the northeast corner of town. Next to it was the council house, which contained the public records and also the arms and ammunition for the militia. The heat was so intense that the side of the council house nearest the filature was scorched black. Fortunately, there was no wind or the entire town with its two hundred wooden structures would have gone up in smoke. The fire was contained by the heroic efforts of some sailors who happened to be in town. They entered the council house with its store of gunpowder when none of the townspeople dared approach it and doused the walls with water. The accident was a terrible blow to Ellis; he told Halifax that he was "extremely mortified." Only 350 pounds of wound silk were saved. Half the cocoons in the filature were lost. There is no doubt that a record amount of silk would have been produced if there had been no fire.[39] Some of these brave sailors went off to St. Augustine on the privateer *Tryall* later in July and were killed in the engagement with the French ship.

The disappointment over the loss of silk and the defeat of the *Tryall* coupled with the intense heat of July damaged Ellis's health. To find relief, he took a house on the water at Thunderbolt below Savannah. His illness was serious enough that he feared for his life. He may have suffered from malaria, as did so many in the mosquito-ridden climate.[40]

Halifax, who was as interested in silk production as Ellis, instructed Ellis to require Ottolenghe to hire assistants. A year after the fire, Ellis was able to report progress. A new filature had been completed on the site of the old, and twelve thousand cocoons were stored in it. A rule of thumb was that fifteen cocoons translated into one pound of silk. Therefore, a harvest of 800 pounds of raw silk was the result of the year's work. The raw silk brought a bounty of three shillings, nine pence per pound. In Henry Ellis's last year in Georgia, 1760, the production was 1,205 pounds of raw silk. There was no dramatic increase after Ellis left the province, the output dipping below 1,000 in 1763 and 1764, although 1767 was another good year with 1,961 pounds produced for manufacture. The bounty was discontinued in 1768, but production continued to hover around the 1,000-pound mark until the revolutionary war put an end to its production.[41]

Ellis's accomplishment in silk cultivation was modest in comparison to the aspirations of the Trustees, but under his encouragement silk production more than doubled and then held steady. John Ellis informed him that Georgia's success caused Benjamin Franklin to request and receive the same bounties for Pennsylvania and Connecticut "so that America will be the silk country and your silk will be the best."[42] Franklin failed to consider the requirements of the mulberry tree when he proposed the production of silk north of the Mason-Dixon Line.

Henry Ellis's interest in the experimental philosophy of the day helped make him the model governor Halifax wanted. Halifax, an enlightened gentleman himself, named two other members of the Royal Society to colonial governorships: Robert Hunter Morris was governor of Pennsylvania from 1754 to 1756, and Francis Fauquier was named lieutenant governor of Virginia in 1758. Thomas Pownall, whose brother John served as secretary to the Lords of Trade, was a favorite appointee, serving as lieutenant governor of New Jersey from 1753 to 1757, governor of Massachusetts from 1757 to 1759, and governor of South Carolina from 1759 to 1760. Pownall, an acknowledged scholar, was inducted into the Royal Society in 1772.[43]

According to William Knox, "establishing a British constitution" was Ellis's first objective upon arrival in Georgia. The two major obstacles Ellis had to overcome in his tenure of office were the inexperience of the members of the Georgia legislature and the example of the South Carolina legislature. Early in his administration Ellis asked that a competent lawyer be sent over from England to be chief justice and to supervise the amateurs who acted as judges in Georgia. Unfortunately, the Duke of Newcastle took advantage of the opportunity to reward one of his political hacks, William Grover. Ellis was concerned about Grover's good sense from the moment he met him. "His sentiments and mine differ on many things," he told Lyttelton.[44] William Clifton, the attorney general, and his difficult spouse were Grover's fellow passengers on the ship that brought him to Georgia. Within a month the chief justice and Mrs. Clifton were the subject of gossip for their "indiscreet conduct." Ellis reprimanded Grover, who then went to Carolina to complain to Lyttelton about Ellis. He got no satisfaction there. Ellis thanked Lyttelton for giving Grover short shrift and remarked that his chief justice and attorney general were a hindrance rather than a help to him.[45]

A more serious obstacle to Ellis's efforts to school Georgians in correct constitutional government was the behavior of the South Carolina legislature. Governor Lyttelton and both houses of his assembly were frequently at odds over questions of prerogatives. William Wragg, the Carolina chief justice, was even more of a nuisance to Lyttelton than Grover was to Ellis. Lyttelton was less compromising than Ellis and dismissed Wragg from his council without deigning to give a reason. After the incident, which occurred in November 1756, Lyttelton found it almost impossible to get anyone to accept membership on his council. The lower house was frequently uncooperative and used its power to set taxes as a means of controlling the governor.[46]

Ellis realized that the increasing number of emigrants from South Carolina brought with them a tradition of independence which threatened his efforts to convince Georgians that their liberty lay in following the constitution as set forth in the instructions of the Board of Trade. He wondered if his influence could counteract that of Carolina. "It would be happy for us," he wrote to Halifax, "if South Carolina was at a greater distance as our people are incessantly urging and aiming at all the priviledges enjoyed there."[47] Ellis framed the issue precisely. He was the model governor Halifax wanted because he made constitutional government, and therefore loyalty to the crown, acceptable and even preferable to the incessant bickering that went on in the older colonies. The great question that would be resolved during the two decades after Ellis's departure from Georgia was whether Georgians would remain content with the kind of constitutional government he had taught them or whether they would be swayed by their Carolina neighbors to cast off that constitution in favor of a new one.

The second major initiative of the Halifax board was the implementation of Edmond Atkin's plan to organize Indian affairs under two superintendencies, northern and southern. Atkin's reasoning was persuasive. Traders could not be trusted to do the king's business, and too many governors were involved in granting licenses and enforcing regulations. The ministry should control Indian affairs directly through an agent. Because America was too large for one man to deal with, two should be appointed, one for the North and one for the South. The Lords Commissioners must have had doubts about Atkin's suitability to act as southern superintendent because they did not grant him power to license traders. There was no doubt about who would be superintendent in the Northern Department. William Johnson of Johnson Hall, longtime friend of the Mohawks, was the only person considered. Indeed, Atkin may well have proposed two agents instead of one because he knew that if there were one, it would be Johnson.

For the same reason that Johnson was the logical choice in the North, Lachlan McGillivray was the obvious one in the South. He had taken a wife in the prestigious Wind Clan and fathered children of mixed blood, including the future spokesman of the Creek Nation, Alexander McGillivray. McGillivray's friend and partner George Galphin had nearly equal claims to the appointment. His influence among the Lower Creeks was as great as that of McGillivray among the Upper Creeks. Galphin lacked McGillivray's education, and although he felt comfortable among Indians, he was ill at ease in polite society.

Atkin understood that McGillivray's credentials made him a formidable rival and made it a point to discredit him at every opportunity. He accused McGillivray of trading with the French at the Alabama Fort, of distorting the news he sent in from the Indian country, and of bringing his "favorite" Indians to Charlestown for conferences.[48] If Governor James Glen had been asked, he would have recommended McGillivray without hesitation, as he did to Lyttelton, his successor.[49] But Glen had no noble lord as a friend and sponsor, and Halifax had grown weary of Glen's self-promotion. Atkin cordially disliked Glen and disputed his claims for credit in inciting the Choctaw Revolt against the French. He linked McGillivray to Glen, suggesting that the trader manipulated the governor for selfish reasons. Atkin had two advantages over McGillivray: he was in London, and he had the backing of Sir George Lyttelton. Halifax named Atkin superintendent for the Southern Department and gave him responsibility for proving that an imperial agent was really needed.

Atkin's original objectives were vague partly because he was out of touch with events in America. He left South Carolina in 1750, in the aftermath of the Choctaw War. When he returned to America in 1756, he explained to Lord Loudoun that his purpose was "to retrieve our declining interest" among the Choctaws. For that reason, he intended to visit the Choctaw country, 780 miles from Charlestown, every year.

In addition, he planned to make yearly visits to the Upper and Lower Creeks "to watch every Motion and Event and to do the best in my power for the general service." [50] The professed intention of traveling every year to distant tribes was an indication of Atkin's imprecise grasp of the possible.

The general terms in which he couched his objectives made it easier to achieve them. He did travel to the Creek country, where he met some Choctaws with whom he signed a treaty establishing trade relations. If one were to read Atkin's reports and nothing else, the agent's work would appear to be an unqualified success, even though it took him two years to complete his trip to the Creeks and he never reached the Choctaw villages. Those more familiar with the actual situation in the Indian country, the traders and the Indians, in particular, watched Atkin more in indignation than admiration. Henry Ellis reflected the opinion of Atkin's critics when he observed that Atkin was like the philosopher who put truth into a well and boasted of having found it there. [51] The Creeks had never been so quiet and well-disposed as they were at the time of the agent's visit. He left things in a turmoil. The Choctaws who signed the treaty were on their way to Savannah to ask Ellis to send them traders when they were halted in the Creek country with orders from Atkin to wait for him there. They had to linger all winter, and most of them went home before Atkin arrived.

Edmond Atkin was his own worst enemy and the enemy of the system he proposed. He was correct in his belief that the licensing of traders should be under control of a central authority. Halifax was not willing to assign this power to the new superintendent and left the matter to the individual governors. None of the governors—Robert Dinwiddie of Virginia, Arthur Dobbs of North Carolina, Lyttelton, or Ellis—were willing to give up their own authority to Atkin. Atkin asked Ellis to allow him to revoke the licenses of certain Creek traders. Ellis deferred to Lyttelton and told him privately that he doubted whether Atkin would use the power to license judiciously. Ellis did not question the agent's "probity, ability and good intentions" but thought that Atkin was too impetuous to deal with the people he wanted to reform. "I confess Mr. Atkin's projects alarm me, not less for their object, than the manner in which he will attempt to carry them into execution," Ellis confided. [52]

Atkin's behavior stemmed from his exalted notion of the office he held. He was continually frustrated because few others shared his opinion of his own importance. He was angry at the South Carolina Assembly because that body refused to provide him with a proper escort; it would pay only for an interpreter and a secretary. Atkin had a staff made and attached his standard to it. He entered Savannah preceded by his secretary carrying the standard.[53]

Ellis honored Atkin with an escort of rangers to Fort Moore, where Lieutenant White Outerbridge fired a thirteen-gun salute. Then Outerbridge hurried across to Augusta to repeat the welcome with powder provided by Atkin because there was none at Fort Augusta. Atkin solemnly read his commission to the assembled militia and traders. In Ellis's words, "Mr. Atkin is arrived at Augusta where he made a very pompous entry."[54]

From Augusta, Atkin issued several portentous proclamations announcing his impending march into the Creek country. A typical message was prefixed by the elaborate title, "Edmond Atkin Esquire His Brittanick Majesty King George's Agent for and Superintendent of the Affairs of His Allies, the several Nations of Indians inhabiting the Frontiers of His Colonies of Virginia, North and South Carolina and Georgia and their Confederates." One of these weighty announcements was addressed to the traders in Augusta, forbidding them to carry any goods to the Indians before Atkin held a conference with the Creeks. Another proclamation forbade the Choctaws' coming into Savannah or Charlestown "seeing I am so close to hand."[55] Then Atkin delayed his expedition until he recruited his escort. "I shall have such a troop as perhaps never was seen," he reported to Governor Lyttelton.[56] He delayed longer in an effort to incriminate Lachlan McGillivray for an illegal purchase of the Chickasaw lands across the river from Augusta. He was disappointed to find that the transaction was authorized by the Carolina lieutenant governor. He pretended to be shocked that the principal traders had not gone into their towns for years and that some had sold their licenses.

December 1758 came and went, followed by January, February, and March 1759, while Atkin made seemingly endless preparations for his journey. The Creeks complained at the delay in receiving their trade goods, most of the Choctaws tired of waiting, and the traders fretted loudly. James Adair accused Atkin of trifling away half a year "in raising a body of men with a proud uniform dress for the sake of parade."[57] At last, in April Atkin began his journey. Lachlan McGillivray reported from Augusta on April 25, 1759, that the agent was within forty miles of the site of his first rendezvous with the Lower Creeks, where he would "begin his procession." McGillivray added, "I think that gentleman is very lucky for he could not possibly meet with a more favourable opportunity to promote his Majesty's service than the present."[58] The *South Carolina Gazette* followed Atkin's progress. On July 21 the public learned from the *Gazette* that Atkin's entry into the Creek Nation was "very grand," but it was reported that he proceeded with such secrecy that no other news was available.

Ellis was already critical of Atkin's mission. He wrote to Halifax in July that Atkin's "dilatoriness" had several bad consequences. The French were forewarned, the Choctaws were disgusted with waiting so long, and the Creeks felt slighted. Ellis's comment to Lord Halifax, who was the final arbiter in deciding Atkin's fate, was devastating. He wished that "officers of the crown would be more attentive to the national service than the gratifying of pride, vanity or any other narrow ridiculous passion or humour."[59]

Henry Ellis had a firsthand report of Atkin's arrival in the Lower Creek town of Cusseta from Togulki, son of the great Malatchi and titular head of the Creek Nation. Mary Bosomworth accompanied the angry Togulki. His people waited for months for Atkin's arrival, said Togulki. They lost their winter hunts because they were uncertain when he would come. He had also stopped their annual shipment of goods. Atkin seemed not to care about the inconvenience he caused; he continued "to loiter in the Woods," Togulki thought deliberately. When he finally arrived at Cusseta, he called a general meeting of the chiefs. Togulki and his headmen paid a courtesy call on the distinguished visitor, as they would on any guest. Atkin told them to go about their business; he would send for them when he was ready. Togulki ignored the rebuff and entered Atkin's lodge, offering his hand in greeting. Atkin refused to take his hand. Togulki said that the governors of South Carolina and Georgia had taken his hand. Was Atkin greater than they? "Yes," was the reply, "I am the King's own mouth."[60]

This was Atkin's way of reprimanding Togulki for visiting Governor Kerlérec. All the same, it was an incredible display of arrogance and bad manners. Ellis, whose dealings with Indians were so different, could only sympathize with his visitors. He told them that Atkin was a stranger to their country and did not know how to act. The great king would call him to account. Atkin went further. Before going to the Upper Creek towns, he took the trade away from Okchoy, the Mortar's town. Escotchabie, the Young Lieutenant, reminded Atkin that white men did not like to hear bad things about their own great men and neither did he like to hear bad talk about the Mortar.[61]

At the Upper Creek town of Tuckabatchee, Atkin's manner nearly doomed him. Old Bracket, a friend of the English since the time of Togulki's grandfather, the emperor Brims, sent a talk to Ellis telling him what happened. He counted nearly forty talks Atkin gave in the Creek Nation, and they could make no sense of any of them, except that they contained much abuse. After the conference in Tuckabatchee began, Atkin again refused to shake hands with any of them and called them all Frenchmen. When he threatened to deprive the Cussetas of trade goods, a chief named Tobacco Eater decided he had heard enough; he attempted to club Atkin on the head. Atkin turned just in time, and the blow was deflected. John McGillivray, Lachlan's cousin, prevented the assailant from doing any further harm. The suddenly chastened Indians promised to do whatever Atkin wished.[62]

Togulki, the Mortar, and the Gun Merchant were with Ellis in Savannah when they heard about Tobacco Eater's assault on Atkin. Togulki was disturbed but understood how such a thing could happen. "I would have served him as much," he said. The Indians asked Ellis to restrain the whites from encroaching upon their hunting grounds west of Augusta. Ellis promised to issue a proclamation forbidding settlement on Indian land.[63] Three years later in London Ellis drafted such a proclamation, which bore the king's signature.

These events were important lessons in imperial policy for Henry Ellis. From Atkin's misadventures, he concluded that licensing power should remain in the hands of the governors. From the complaints of his Indian friends about white trespassers, he saw the need for an established Indian boundary. Ellis could no longer keep silent about Atkin in his correspondence with Lyttelton even though the Lytteltons supported Atkin. Ellis was annoyed that he was not told of the terms of Atkin's treaty with the Choctaws. "I should be glad to know about it," he advised Lyttelton. On October 11, 1759, Ellis wrote Lyttelton, "I heartily wish the agent would quit the nation for the Creeks that are with me complain bitterly of him."[64] On January 6, 1760, after Atkin had returned to report a successful mission, Ellis wrote a letter to the Board of Trade which must have influenced Halifax. Atkin prided himself on leaving conditions in the Creek country in a settled state when he actually "had greatly disturbed and embarrassed them." In Ellis's judgment, Atkin was "very ill calculated for the employment he is in." Ellis concluded that he was against the idea of managing Indians by "a general agent." [65] After Atkin's return, he continued to send messages to the Creeks, but Ellis thought the Indians disregarded them. "I question if they will signify a farthing," he said.[66]

Atkin lived in a world of his own. Just before his return from the Indian country, he drafted a long letter claiming complete success in spite of all the obstacles placed in his way. He asked for an interview with both governors in language that not even Halifax would have used. "Now is your time to serve me," he told them. He called upon the governors to restrain all traders until the following spring; he wanted to put a stop to the trade "to humble the Creeks." If the traders protested, too bad for them. It would serve them right for failing to cooperate with him.[67]

After his return, Atkin continued to portray his mission as a success. He took credit for ending the Choctaws' war with the Chickasaws and ending Glen's peace policy between the Creeks and Cherokees. All his reports contained complaints about a lack of respect due his office. He resigned from the South Carolina Council because he could not "suffer the mortification" of being the king's agent and outvoted by the majority. He accused the governors of trying to enhance their reputations by managing Indian affairs and observed that they ignored him and acted as they had before his arrival. He believed the Carolina Assembly was jealous of his authority. The traders were as bad as ever; "their lies are credited and propagated." Atkin was especially annoyed at Governor Ellis, whom he maintained never gave him any help. In fact, "the vilest trader who deserves severe punishment hath met with more countenance and credit." After making a final report to the Board of Trade, Atkin intended to resign. "I shall have no cause to desire to hold this invidious office any longer." [68]

But Atkin could not bring himself to resign. His death in May 1761 saved him from the embarrassment of being replaced. Among the applicants for his position was William Knox, the ambitious provost marshal. Ellis had offered other positions to Knox, who refused them on the grounds that he did not want to expose Ellis to charges of favoritism. As early as May 1760 Knox had heard from London that Atkin's job was in jeopardy. He wrote to his informant, probably Benjamin Martyn, the veteran agent for Georgia, that he hoped Halifax would award the superintendency to him because "I have served an apprenticeship under the second master in America." It was a nice compliment to Ellis. It may be assumed that Knox regarded Sir William Johnson of the Mohawks as first master. Knox would imitate the example of Ellis rather than Atkin: "I should rather seek the goodwill of the Indians by acts of kindness and hospitality than by an austere carriage aimed at exciting reverence." [69] Knox was unsuccessful in his application. Captain John Stuart, a hero of the Cherokee War and a friend of the new Carolina governor, Thomas Boone, was named as Atkin's successor. [70]

The short and troubled career of Edmond Atkin provided several lessons. An impressive title and pompous behavior did not ensure success. If a better diplomat had been appointed southern superintendent and taken the trouble to secure the cooperation of the governors and traders, the subsequent history of the Indian trade might have been different. For all his posturing, Atkin was right in his essential premises. He was right when he told Lyttelton, who was eager to launch an attack on the Alabama Fort, that the idea "about which the Charles Town politicians have for many years past almost run mad" was a great error. "Such an expedition would have cost the lives of all the King's subjects in this nation" because the Indians would unite to resist an invasion. [71] In the even more important matter of the regulation of trade, Atkin was right. The traders could not be depended on to do the king's business, especially after the removal of the French threat. The governors were too protective of their own prerogatives to agree on a consistent policy. An imperial agent with the power to grant and revoke licenses might have maintained order during the period after the French and Indian War, when the woods swarmed with unscrupulous traders. John Stuart had the temperament, if not the experience, to become an effective superintendent, but the governors were reluctant to give him the power he needed. Nor would the Board of Trade intervene to help Stuart, probably because the noble lords were soured by Atkin's experience.

Of the Halifax initiatives in colonial administration, the Ellis governorship was a success, the Atkin superintendency a failure. In both cases the results were lasting. Ellis's method of administration by leadership and suasion was continued by James Wright, and Georgia enjoyed a decade of prosperity. John Stuart followed Atkin's example of giving the Indians increasingly expensive presents as a means of controlling the tribes, with unfortunate effects on the ability of the tribes to remain independent. When the British lost the thirteen colonies, the United States government continued the position of Indian superintendent. Henry Ellis had a direct influence on the direction of Indian policy after he completed his term in Georgia. The lessons he learned while governor qualified him as an expert in American affairs when he returned to London.[72]

CHAPTER NINE *The Unfinished Campaigns*

I

T WAS THE unique fortune of Henry Ellis to experience the Great War for the Empire from both ends, from the frontiers on which the war was fought to the chambers in which it was concluded. His high-placed connections and the reputation he had made as governor assured him of a warm reception at Whitehall. Although Ellis was only on the fringes of Pitt's grand strategy for waging the war, he was the "oracle" on American affairs for Pitt's successor, Egremont. On the provincial level, several issues were raised by the war which Ellis could not resolve in Georgia. Among them were the location of Georgia's southern boundary, the question of military command in the province, and the problem of encroachment on Indian lands. Ellis had definite opinions on all these points when he left Georgia in November 1760.

William Pitt conceived the idea of an attack on Louisiana during his first year as war minister. The strategy was suggested by the excellent map made by Dr. John Mitchell in 1755, which clearly depicted Canada's dependence on the St. Lawrence and Louisiana's on the Mississippi.[1] If these great waterways were closed, the French would be trapped in the interior. Pitt would concentrate on the northern front first, then turn his attention to the South.

The southern strategy possibly originated in a chance comment by Governor James Glen of South Carolina to the Duke of Bedford in 1757. He mentioned that Captain John Colcock had sailed into Mobile Bay in 1736 and could serve as a pilot for an attacking fleet. He explained that the French forces were thinly spread, with garrisons at the Alabama Fort, on the Tombigbee River in Choctaw country, at Mobile, and guarding New Orleans.[2] Bedford must have relayed this information to Pitt. Pitt happened to be an in-law of William Henry Lyttelton—his brother married Lyttelton's sister—and Pitt trusted Lyttelton to advise him on the feasibility of a land and sea attack on Louisiana. Pitt's letter to Lyttelton, dated January 27, 1758, marked secret, stated that he had been informed that a Mr. Colcock knew the southern coast. He wanted Colcock to repair immediately to Halifax in Nova Scotia and report to Admiral Edward Boscawen. Pitt indicated that an attack on Louisiana might be made in the latter part of 1758.

By March 7 Pitt was more definite in his plans although still uncertain when they might be carried out. In addition to a naval assault on Mobile and New Orleans, he recommended to Lyttelton an expedition by land against the notorious Alabama Fort. The wording of the letter indicates Pitt's intense interest in the project. "Use your utmost endeavour to set on foot and encourage an expedition from your province against the Alabama Fort," Pitt urged, adding the cautionary phrase, "in case you judge it practicable."[3]

Such a summons from such a leader could not fail to galvanize even a lethargic officer of the crown. Lyttelton was anything but lethargic. Frustrated by the balking and bickering of the South Carolina Assembly, Lyttelton welcomed an undertaking that might unite his colony. As the son of one of the most respected of the old Whigs, Lord Cobham, he was eager to make a name for himself. But, he knew very little about the geography of the West and not nearly enough about the Indians who lived there. Therefore, he made an unannounced visit to Fort Moore in June 1758 to seek the advice of Lachlan McGillivray.

McGillivray was the authority on the Upper Creeks and the Alabama Fort; he had lived within a few miles of the French outpost. James Adair happened to be in Augusta at the time of the visit, and McGillivray suggested that he be consulted also. The result was a lengthy report by Adair written in his exuberant prose describing the hazards of a land war. At the appearance of an English army, all the Indians of the interior would join the French in opposing the invaders. An army of six thousand men, supported by hundreds of wagons carrying artillery and provisions, would be necessary. Rivers would probably be flooded, and pontoon bridges would be required. McGillivray and Adair did not predict that the expedition would be a disaster, but they raised so many questions that any but the most ardent militarist would have understood their meaning. To make their point, they reminded Lyttelton of what had happened to General Edward Braddock.[4] Lyttelton, however, had become an ardent militarist. He transmitted the advice of the traders to Pitt but disparaged their opinion on the grounds that as traders they were opposed to any interruption of the "tranquility with which they now carry on their trade."[5] Lyttelton outlined his own plan for a campaign by land, which was more ambitious than practical. Lyttelton would send ahead a proclamation explaining that his invading army was friendly; if the Indians opposed him, he would burn down their villages and put their women and children to the sword.

Despite Lyttelton's assurance that he had not disclosed the matter to "anybody whatsoever," rumors of an English invasion swept through the Indian country. Edmond Atkin, during his lengthy preparation in Augusta, dropped broad hints about an impending invasion. Governor Kerlérec of Louisiana informed his superiors in December 1758 that the English were planning a "surprise" attack on the Alabama Fort.[6] The French counterstrategy was to employ their allies among the Creeks to stir up trouble. Their argument to the Creeks was that the English intended to expel the French so that they might enslave the Indians. Kerlérec never had as much influence as he claimed. For example, Togulki, whom Kerlérec called "Emperor of the Kawitas" and considered a firm friend, merely flirted with the French during that year to gain better terms for Mary Bosomworth. The most reliable agent of the French was the Wolf of Okchoys, whom the English called the Mortar. For the Mortar it was not love of the French that drove him but fear of the English as the greater threat. He agreed to attempt to instigate the Cherokees to attack the English, using the building of Fort Loudoun in the heart of the Cherokee country as a pretext.

Henry Ellis kept Lyttelton's secret better than Atkin did. The importance of Pitt's message impelled Lyttelton to make his first and only visit to Georgia to tell Ellis the exciting news. Ellis thanked Lyttelton for the honor of his visit and hoped Lyttelton survived his journey through the "torrid zone." Privately, Ellis agreed with McGillivray that a land expedition would be a disaster. He was eloquent on the subject when he was asked for his opinion later in London. Henry Ellis laid his own plans in anticipation of a war with Spain. He pondered a way to attack St. Augustine and considered the advantages of annexing Florida.[7]

Meanwhile, Lyttelton's proposed southern campaign met with one delay after another. Lyttelton discovered that the navigator mentioned by Pitt, John Colcock, was dead. As the next best expedient he dispatched a brother, Captain Isaac Colcock, to Halifax. Admiral Boscawen thanked Lyttelton for sending Colcock and assured Lyttelton that he and General Amherst planned to turn their attention to Louisiana as soon as Louisbourg was taken. On July 29, the admiral reported that Louisbourg had capitulated but that Colcock had not yet arrived. On August 28 Boscawen wrote to say that Colcock had finally arrived but was not very knowledgeable about Mobile Bay or the Mississippi River. The problem was that despite his willingness to cooperate, Isaac Colcock was not an adequate substitute for his departed brother. He had never sailed into Mobile Bay. Boscawen said that the lack of sufficient information caused them "to lay aside any thoughts we might have had of an expedition to those parts" for the time being.[8]

Having missed the winter of 1758–59, the admiral and general looked forward to launching their campaign during the following winter season. Amherst shared Lyttelton's sanguine opinion that an attack on the Alabama Fort was feasible: "I make no doubt but it would have succeeded, for altho I am sensible it must have been attended with difficulties, yet I cannot forsee that they were insurmountable." Amherst informed Lyttelton on March 21, 1759, that he had been ordered to detach a portion of his troops under General James Wolfe to attack Quebec while he proceeded with the rest around about the Hudson River and Lake George through New York, the route Montcalm had made so difficult for the British army under Abercromby. Amherst held out to Lyttelton the possibility that the troops then involved in the attack on the French West Indian island of Guadeloupe might be employed in the campaign against Louisiana.[9]

Lyttelton must have been surprised to learn that Guadeloupe took precedence over Louisiana. One reason for Pitt's strategy was that Guadeloupe and its near neighbor to the south, Martinique, were bases for the French privateers that infested the Caribbean. It made military sense to clear the sea lanes before sending an armada to Louisiana. Pitt's other reason was that the London merchant William Beckford urged him to seize the French islands. Pitt liked to say that he was beholden to no one but the people. By "people" he meant the voters in the cities, especially London. Beckford was a longtime mayor of London whose trade in West Indian sugar was endangered by the French privateers. Insofar as he was guided by anyone, Pitt heeded Beckford and the London merchants.[10]

Ellis's friend Secretary at War Barrington opposed the expedition until Pitt selected John Barrington, the secretary's younger brother, to be second in command behind Major General Thomas Peregrine Hopson, former governor of Nova Scotia. The bombardment of Guadeloupe's capital, Basse Terre, on January 23, 1759, was followed by the landing of troops the next day. The French governor refused to surrender and withdrew to the interior. As the days turned to weeks, fever began to take its toll on the invaders. Hopson had to evacuate fifteen hundred sick men before the end of February; he himself became ill and died on February 27. General Barrington tightened the siege and offered generous surrender terms. Finally, on May 1, 1759, the French governor signed articles of capitulation. The inhabitants were permitted to keep their property, their laws, and the exercise of their religion. They were also given the commercial privileges enjoyed by people of the British islands. Guadeloupe was described by General Barrington as worth more for its sugar production than all the British Leeward Islands together. The British were as dazzled by sugar islands as the Spanish with gold, and Guadeloupe seemed a treasure. No one valued it more than William Pitt.[11]

The Louisiana operation was hostage to other of Pitt's priorities during the winter of 1758–59. The British navy forced the surrender of the French posts in Africa, including Senegal, Gambia, and the island of Goree. Next, there was the unfinished business of Martinique. Hopson did not attempt its capture as part of the Guadeloupe campaign. Pitt wished to have it and at the same time sent signals that an attack on Louisiana was pending. General Amherst had good cause to be confused when he received Pitt's message of December 27, 1760, stating that regular troops should be ready to go, "either against Mobile and Mississippi or Martinico, and the other French Islands in the West Indies."[12]

Meanwhile, the impatient Governor Lyttelton got his war, but not the one he expected. The powerful Cherokee Nation in the Appalachian highlands above South Carolina threatened open hostilities as the year 1759 lengthened into autumn. There had been a series of irritants, none of them sufficient to cause an outbreak, during the spring and summer. Several hundred Cherokee warriors had gone to Pennsylvania to join General John Forbes in his march against Fort Duquesne. Tiring of the inactivity, they returned to their country. When they passed through Virginia, they had clashed with the whites and several of their number were killed. The Cherokees retaliated against whites along the Yadkin River, killing seventeen. The French at the Alabama Fort tried to exploit the opportunity that this presented by sending the Mortar into the Cherokee country promising French help against the English. Encroachments by white settlers in the Long Canes region near the upper Savannah River were another irritant. On August 15, 1759, Governor Lyttelton sent seventy men to reinforce Fort Loudoun, raising the number of soldiers there to a formidable two hundred. Ninety others were stationed at Fort Prince George in the Carolina piedmont.[13]

In a dramatic testimony to their respect for Henry Ellis, the Cherokee chiefs sent him a talk, asking him to mediate their differences with the governor of Carolina. Ellis was thrust into an embarrassing position. He explained to Lord Halifax that Lyttelton would be "excessively jealous of our intermeddling." Ellis referred the Cherokee talk to Lyttelton and sent a message to the Cherokees urging them to cooperate with the Carolina governor.[14] Ellis tried to warn Lyttelton diplomatically not to be too arrogant or impetuous, urging his friend "not to think too contemptibly of these savages."[15] He hoped that Lyttelton would seize the opportunity to avert a war. He offered to serve as mediator; he was willing to meet with the Cherokees at Augusta or any other place if it would help.

Lyttelton was not inclined to be conciliatory, and his mood was not improved by the Cherokees' overture to the governor of Georgia. He issued a proclamation banning any trade with the Cherokees in arms and ammunition, and he had decided on a punitive expedition even before a Cherokee delegation arrived in Charlestown for a talk. The South Carolina governor delivered a stern lecture to the visiting Cherokee chiefs and dismissed them with the announcement that he would take a great many soldiers to their country and demand satisfaction for the whites killed by the Indians. Ellis was disappointed at the failure of his efforts to bring about a negotiated settlement.[16]

On October 27, 1759, Lyttelton left Charlestown as commander of a force of fifteen hundred men. He soon learned that the path to glory is filled with pitfalls. The march to Fort Prince George was tedious, the roads were terrible, and smallpox was rampant in the Catawba villages along the way. Lyttelton reached Fort Prince George near the Cherokee town of Keowee on December 9. He demanded that all Cherokees who were guilty of the murders of white settlers be given up or he would destroy their towns and take their women and children into captivity. This was precisely the ultimatum Lyttelton planned for the Creeks if they opposed his attack on the Alabama Fort. Unfortunately, Lyttelton's threat served to confirm what the French had been saying for years, that the English intended to enslave the Indians. Finally, on December 26, 1759, a treaty was signed by which the Cherokees promised to deliver up twenty-two guilty people. Lyttelton could not have waited much longer; smallpox had broken out in Keowee, and his militiamen were deserting in droves. The capitulation by the Cherokees enabled him to return to Charlestown with his dignity, if not his army, intact.[17]

Henry Ellis would have proceeded differently. He told Halifax that the treaty "was indeed a better one than I should have attempted" but was "too mortifying" to the proud Cherokees. General Amherst, however, thoroughly approved of Lyttelton's decisive action. He wrote to Henry Ellis that Lyttelton's expedition proved to the Indians "that His Majesty's Subjects are not afraid of them." He was against any show of leniency. Ellis tried to explain that the Indian situation on the southern frontier was unlike anything Amherst might be familiar with. The northern provinces were heavily populated, but the southernmost colonies were thinly settled and the Indians were numerous. "We are weak," Ellis said bluntly, "and they know it." [18]

As Ellis feared, the treaty did not last. Lyttelton had barely reached Charlestown when Cherokee warriors took up the hatchet in greater numbers than ever before. More than twenty traders were murdered. Forty settlers who were fleeing from their homes along Long Canes Creek were caught and killed. A thousand Cherokee warriors roamed the Carolina up-country. Terrified frontier people flocked to Fort Moore and Augusta for protection. Lyttelton sent frantic appeals to Amherst for help. The general responded by dispatching Colonel Archibald Montgomery's Highland Regiment, but this took time, and the regulars arrived two months after the height of the crisis.[19]

During those months, the exposed province of Georgia was in the greatest danger it had faced since the Spanish attack on Fort Frederica in 1742. Oglethorpe repelled that threat from the south; seventeen years later, Henry Ellis, more than any other single person, was responsible for saving his province from the wrath of the invaders from the mountains to the north. His campaign was a lesson in how to wage a defensive war without soldiers. It was complicated by a secondary theme, Ellis's effort to free Georgia from the military domination of Carolina.

Georgia in 1759, though still woefully weak, was better positioned by several of Ellis's initiatives for a defensive war than it ever had been. Ever since he had come to Georgia in 1757, Ellis had begged and pleaded for British support of two companies of rangers. He had importuned Loudoun, Abercromby, Pitt, and finally Amherst. On June 1, 1759, Amherst sent word that Ellis could maintain the number of rangers then on duty. Ellis replied that the present contingent of forty men and four officers was hardly sufficient. He needed two companies of seventy men each. By November, permission for the two companies had come, and Ellis quickly filled the ranks with recruits.[20]

For three years, Ellis had urged the magistrates at Augusta to rebuild their fort, which Reynolds had described as decrepit. By mid-October 1759 Lieutenant White Outerbridge, a veteran of Oglethorpe's regiment, reported that the construction work on the fort was nearly complete and the church would soon be enclosed by a stockade.[21] Thus there were places of refuge when they were needed in January. More important was Ellis's good relationship with the Augusta traders. He had involved them in his Indian diplomacy, taken their part against outsiders such as Pepper and Atkin, and generally followed their advice. Lachlan McGillivray and George Galphin would be enlisted to use their enormous influence to prevent the Creeks from joining the Cherokees. Finally, Ellis had satisfied the Bosomworths in time to use their good offices with Togulki and his people.

Ellis's differences with Lyttelton began when the Cherokees approached him instead of Lyttelton and grew when Lyttelton decided upon a harsh punitive policy. The first open argument stemmed from Lyttelton's peremptory summons to the Savannah River Chickasaws, all living on the Georgia side at New Savannah, to join his march to Fort Prince George. The Augusta magistrates threatened to imprison Lyttelton's agent, Captain Ulrich Tobler; Tobler complained to Lyttelton, who passed the complaint to Ellis. Ellis explained that the people at Augusta relied on the Chickasaws to guard against a Cherokee attack and that they objected to a Carolina militia officer recruiting in Georgia. Lyttelton could not have missed the defiant tone that underlay Ellis's polite language: "I must confess to you that it did seem a little surprising here that any person from your province should affect to exercise a peculiar jurisdiction over a people who had for some years past fixed themselves amongst us." [22] Ellis blamed the "officious-ness" of Tobler rather than Lyttelton, especially since Lyttelton had not mentioned the matter to Ellis. The point was made.

The tension between the governors increased during December when Lyttelton was at Fort Prince George. Ellis told Lyttelton he had heard that Lieutenant Outerbridge had been ordered to move his garrison from Fort Augusta to Fort Moore. Ellis had therefore sent orders to Lieutenant Colonel Edward Barnard of the Augusta militia to occupy Fort Augusta with twenty men. Outerbridge was surprised when he received Ellis's instructions to give up Fort Augusta to Barnard. Outerbridge told Barnard that he could march into Fort Augusta anytime he pleased, but that he (Outerbridge) would not give up command until he received orders from Governor Lyttelton.[23]

Ellis was astounded to learn that Outerbridge did not acknowledge Georgia's authority. He sent word to Outerbridge that he could remain at Augusta "since I find the officers of the Independent Companies stationed in this Province do not look upon themselves as subject to my authority." Nevertheless, the province of Georgia was in charge of posts, and he as governor had given command of Augusta to Barnard.[24]

Relations worsened when Ellis ordered Captain Thomas Goldsmith of the Independent Company at Frederica to send a sergeant and twelve men to Fort Barrington to permit the Georgia rangers there to go to Augusta. Goldsmith refused to obey on the grounds that he received his orders from Lyttelton. Ellis was clearly upset when he wrote Lyttelton on February 4 asking whether South Carolina claimed jurisdiction over Georgia. He hoped Lyttelton did not assume any authority over Georgia forts. Ellis's instructions were clear on the point that he was commander in chief in Georgia. Ellis conceded that after Oglethorpe left Georgia, the governors of Carolina exercised control of the regular troops in the province, but "whatever right the governors of South Carolina had to command the militia or regulars here during the Trustees' administration, they certainly have none at present," he declared. Ellis did not bother to conceal his irritation when he appealed to Amherst to settle the dispute: "Nothing can be more preposterous than the present situation of things." [25]

His correspondence with Lyttelton, which formerly had been characterized by friendly banter, assumed a frosty tone. When Lyttelton explained that he was merely exercising an authority his predecessor had enjoyed, Ellis replied that Glen's having done so did not make it right. "Your Excellency has certainly advanced all that can be alleged in defense of a claim which in my humble opinion is impossible to support with any degree of consistency or reason," he wrote, adding that he would rather command a cockboat than be viceroy of Mexico "under such degrading circumstances." Lyttelton had sent Lieutenant Lachlan Shaw with the commission of major to replace White Outerbridge at Augusta. Ellis replied that he was sending Captain John Milledge with his company of rangers to Augusta and declared, "If Lieutenant Shaw is by virtue of a major's commission to be superior of Capt. Milledge, I hope it will not be thought strange if I should make the latter a Lieutenant Colonel." He could not resist adding a postscript: "I hope Your Excellency will believe me incapable of applying to a Lieutenant of the Independents for leave to admit such Forces as I may think proper to order into a fort in my own Government." [26]

Meanwhile, the Cherokees were running amok on both sides of the Savannah. Edmond Atkin returned from his controversial mission to the Creeks to find Augusta beleaguered. "All things round here now wear a wretched aspect," he reported to Lyttelton. "The Cherokees have drove all before them downward to a few miles from Augusta . . . the fort, church, Mr. Macartan's and every other house of security crammed with people flying for shelter." [27] Lachlan McGillivray led fifty volunteers out to rescue the refugees. A band of Creeks, under the Young Lieutenant of Cusseta, volunteered to help McGillivray. They could not commit their nation to war, but they could protect their hunting ground against the Cherokees. The New Savannah Chickasaws swore that they would live and die with their friends in Augusta.[28]

Ellis's rangers reached Augusta at the height of the crisis, Captain Milledge's company on February 14 and Lieutenant Bailey's a few days later. The rangers brought Ellis's talk to the Creeks to Augusta, and McGillivray and Galphin dispatched it to the Upper and Lower Creeks. Wisely, Ellis did not urge the Creeks to go to war as Atkin had done. Instead, he asked the Creeks to keep the Cherokees on the other side of the river; the Cherokee dispute was with the people of Carolina. "I have had no quarrel with the red people," he said. "I never desire to have any." He knew that the French were urging the Creeks to join the Cherokees, but he hoped that they would not "turn fools and mad" and give up their trade and forsake their friends "for the sake of the Cherokees, your old enemies." [29] Ellis beat the French at their own game by employing the Mortar to tell the Cherokees to stop fighting. He presented the Mortar with a silver gorget and arm bracelet by way of a commission and did the same for the Wolf of Muccolossus, the Gun Merchant, Devall's Landlord, and the Young Lieutenant.[30]

Perhaps this successful employment of key Indian leaders caused Ellis to suggest a plan for organizing Indian affairs to William Pitt. In July 1760 Ellis proposed the commissioning of key men in each Indian village to be responsible for preserving the peace and protecting the trade. John Stuart later adopted a similar policy by awarding great medals to important chiefs and smaller medals to lesser chiefs.[31] Another suggestion Ellis made to Pitt was to get on with the plan to attack Mobile. If Mobile were taken, the Alabama Fort would be abandoned and the Cherokees would stop fighting. Two to three thousand troops and a half dozen barges carrying artillery should suffice to overwhelm the French defenders. Spain might object, but it should be done anyway. Ellis cautioned, "It must not be attempted otherwise than by water"; the Indians would oppose a land march. In giving this advice, Ellis agreed with McGillivray and Adair and differed from Lyttelton.[32]

The Cherokee War was still raging with Fort Loudoun under siege when William Henry Lyttelton was called away from Carolina to assume the post he preferred in Jamaica. Before Lyttelton's departure, Ellis made his peace with his rival, who was his friend in spite of it all. Ellis confided to Lyttelton that he had asked to be removed from his province because of his declining health.[33] In an earlier letter Ellis had said more on the subject: "I am pleased with my station and should highly enjoy it would I have my health, without which nothing is relishable. Philosophy does not require that we should hold any post longer than we can discharge the duties of it with credit to ourselves and advantage to our country." [34]

Lyttelton left Charlestown on April 5, and the popular Lieutenant Governor William Bull was left to settle the issue with the Cherokees. Bull was not pleased with the campaign of Colonel Archibald Montgomery, who destroyed some of the villages but failed to relieve the siege of Fort Loudoun. Montgomery was under Amherst's orders to return to the North as soon as possible so he and his regiment sailed away by mid-August. Bull complained to Lord Halifax that his situation was worse "than if they had never been sent in the first place." On August 18 Bull received the dreaded news that Fort Loudoun had capitulated and the garrison had been put to death. Only Lieutenant John Stuart among the officers had been spared, thanks to the intercession of Attakullakulla, the Little Carpenter.[35]

The Cherokee War was far from over when Henry Ellis left Georgia. The order in council authorizing Ellis's return was dated May 13, 1760, and on the same day James Wright, former South Carolina agent, was named lieutenant governor. Before he received the notice of the recall, Ellis penned a last appeal: "My health is in so poor a state as to render it impossible for me long to support myself under the accumulated load of business and fatigue."[36]

Ellis had one more trial to endure after some Okfuskee Indians, under French influence, suddenly murdered several traders. Ellis decided to treat the uprising as the work of a few and not the expression of the nation. He did not ban the trade, as Lyttelton had done in similar circumstances, but he accomplished the same thing by telling the Creeks that the traders would not take their goods into the nation when their lives were at risk. He held the chiefs responsible for the traders' security. There was not much else he could do except strengthen the bastions on Savannah's ramparts, at his own expense, and wait. His careful cultivation of the headmen paid off when the Creeks sent word that the mad deed was the work of a few and the guilty would be punished. The episode left Ellis discouraged as well as debilitated. He poured out his frustrations to Halifax: "It is inconceivable the pains I have taken these three years past to preserve the repose of these parts and keep the Creeks in good temper." During the same time, Carolina paid scant attention to the Creeks. Now "people start as from a dream," realizing that they are threatened by "such formidable Tribes of Merciless barbarians." People were leaving Georgia out of fear. He hoped that once the war in the North was settled "due attention will be shown to the defense of this important colony."[37]

Ellis clearly had made up his mind that he could do more for the southern frontier provinces in England than in Georgia. In his letter asking to be relieved, he suggested that he might be helpful to the Lords of Trade. He had "many things to lay before your lordships in reference to the Affairs of this Quarter highly deserving attention."[38] In its farewell address to Henry Ellis the Georgia upper house thanked him for his efforts to avoid war and asked him to inform the ministry of the dangers still facing the province. Ellis promised to do so.[39]

Ellis admitted to Lyttelton before the latter left Jamaica that "my judgment has been at variance with my ambition the greatest part of my life, but ill health, subsiding passions and a proper experience give me hope that the former will at last predominate."[40] Ellis's judgment gave way to his sense of duty when he decided not to go directly to England but to make a tedious detour to New York to describe to General Amherst the critical nature of the war in the South and to appeal for the help of the army. He later told William Pitt that "affairs of the Southern Provinces in general had taken so unfavourable a turn that their preservation seemed absolutely to depend on the assistance to be obtained from General Amherst which could only be expected from his being fully informed of their real circumstances." He therefore made the decision to go to New York even though the only vessel available was an unseaworthy shallop. Before he sailed from Charlestown, the *South Carolina Gazette* spread the good news that Ellis was going to get help from Amherst. He was saluted by the great guns of the Granville bastion as the small vessel *Bachelor* weighed anchor at Charlestown, and the salute was repeated by the cannon of Fort Johnson at the mouth of the harbor.[41] As Ellis watched the spire of St. Michael recede in the distance, he must have thought back to his arrival almost four years before. His perspective had been changed. He was not an American in the sense that he did not intend to make his permanent home in the colonies, but he had acquired an American point of view which his friends in Ireland and London did not have. He was identified with Georgia and for the rest of his life would be known by the title Governor Ellis. As time went on, he might have discarded the title and forgotten the province as Captain John Reynolds did, but he remembered Georgia and bore the title proudly as befitted one who had accomplished a worthwhile task. He had transformed a weak and ill-formed province into a proper, self-governing colony.

Ironically, another passenger aboard the sloop was Edmond Atkin, bitterly nursing his grievances and intent on reporting them to Amherst. He hoped his letter, written at sea, would reach Amherst in New York before Ellis arrived and had his interview. He expected nothing but "unfriendly offices" from Ellis; he had never received any assistance from him.[42] The Carolina Assembly was jealous of his powers, as he believed, and the policies of the governors of both South Carolina and Georgia were contrary to his. Atkin took credit for the neutrality of the Creeks and blamed others for the alienation of the Cherokees. The meetings of Ellis and Atkin at the captain's table must have been frosty. Atkin was neither willing nor able to disguise his feelings, but the urbane Ellis was a master of the art of dissembling. If they had compared ideas, they would have learned that they carried similar messages to Amherst. Both argued for an attack on the Cherokees from the north, and both recommended a naval rather than a land campaign against Louisiana. Ellis hoped that the Mohawks could be induced to enter the war against the Cherokees. If the French employed Senecas from New York in their campaign against the Chickasaws, as they did, why not bring Sir William Johnson's Mohawks down upon the Cherokees?[43]

Guy Johnson, Sir William's son, wrote from Trenton, New Jersey, to his father with the news that Ellis intended to ask Amherst for northern Indians. Moreover, he had heard that the general had orders from London to consult Ellis about all southern affairs, and Ellis was confident "of bringing him over to his opinion."[44] Amherst informed James Wright of Georgia that Ellis arrived in New York on December 26 and Amherst had informed him that troops under Lieutenant Colonel James Grant were under orders to sail from New York; moreover, a contingent of Mohawk Indians would go with them.[45]

Richard Shuckburgh, an agent of Sir William Johnson, and Lieutenant Hugh Wallace of the Fifty-fifth Regiment dined with Ellis in New York on December 27. Like most people who met him, Shuckburgh was impressed with Ellis's conversation. Ellis told him that he thought that those he had talked to had "too low an opinion of Indians." Shuckburgh later suggested that when Ellis gave his views to the ministry in London, they would "differ from some which may go from these parts." Other than their differences about Indian policy, Ellis thought the interview with Amherst went well. "The polite and confidential manner in which he treated me was sufficient to convince me my information was agreeable to him," Ellis informed Pitt.[46]

On January 1, 1761, Ellis wrote to James Wright from New York that Amherst had promised that the military under Grant would protect the exposed province of Georgia as well as Carolina.[47] Ellis pressured Amherst to get on with the Louisiana operation. At the same time, William Pitt at Whitehall sent instructions to Amherst to defer the Louisiana campaign until Martinique and the so-called Neutral Islands of St. Lucia, Dominica, Granada, and St. Vincent had been taken. The islands, Martinique in particular, were havens for French privateers. Pitt and his London constituency would not be content until the sea lanes in the Caribbean were cleared. The enormous investment in men and money in the campaign for the West Indies reflected their importance in Pitt's eyes and explains his preference for the sugar islands rather than Canada or Florida in the upcoming peace settlement. Martinique prevailed and a massive invasion force of fourteen thousand men was assembled for the island campaign.

On January 6 Grant arrived in Charlestown with twelve hundred men. An equal number of Carolina rangers and militia were recruited to accompany him. Some Catawbas and Chickasaws joined the Mohawks in scouting for the army. Although Grant penetrated into the Cherokee hills only as far as Montgomery had gone the previous year and, like Montgomery, failed to score a decisive victory, the Cherokees were growing weary of war. On December 17, 1761, a peace treaty was signed in Charlestown, and Grant was free to join the Martinique expedition. His Indians went with him.[48]

A stormy winter crossing brought Henry Ellis to a London titillated with gossip about the new king and Mr. Pitt. Lord Halifax may have welcomed his protégé with a reception at his handsome Georgian house on Great George Street. The Halifax connection would certainly have been on hand, including Barrington, the secretary at war, William G. Hamilton and George Rice from the Board of Trade, Charles Stanhope and P. C. Webb from the Royal Society, and John Ellis, the botanist. After questions about Ellis's poor health, the notorious Georgia weather, and the ever-fascinating subject of red Indians had been asked and answered, the conversation inevitably turned to politics, the favorite topic of the noble lords and their friends.

Ellis was told about the coolness between the young king and the great Mr. Pitt. It was said that the king, when he first assumed the throne, kept the minister waiting two hours. Then, on October 25, 1760, when the king addressed his council, he astonished everyone by inserting the phrase "bloody and expensive war" to describe the war on the Continent. The expression was regarded as a challenge to Pitt, who was deeply committed to the subsidization of Frederick the Great of Prussia. It was an open secret that George III wanted his former tutor, the Earl of Bute, in his council and William Pitt wanted to keep him out. The Duke of Newcastle, who still thought of himself as the "prime" minister, although few others did, tried to please everyone. The general election in March 1761 was the occasion for a reshuffling of offices, and Henry Ellis arrived just in time to be involved.

The most important change as far as the court was concerned was that the king got his wish and Bute joined the cabinet as secretary of state for the Northern Department, replacing the ineffective Earl of Holdernesse. The most important change as far as Henry Ellis was concerned was that his patron Halifax left the Board of Trade. The "Father of the Colonies" must have been disappointed that he could not carry out his plans to impose a constitutional conformity upon the American provinces. He had to be satisfied with limited success in Georgia and Nova Scotia. Actually, he had lost control of colonial affairs to Secretary of State Pitt as a consequence of the war. Pitt had always regretted the loss of colonial patronage by his office, and after the resignation of Halifax, the order in council of 1752 was repealed, leaving the board, as Horace Walpole put it, "reduced to its old insignificance," retaining only the correspondence of the colonial officials.[49] The board could henceforth recommend policy only if its opinion was asked. Halifax was willing to swap his board presidency for the position of lord lieutenant of Ireland, especially because it would displace his rival, the Duke of Bedford.

Before leaving office, and even before Ellis's arrival from New York, Halifax provided for Ellis's future by naming him governor of Nova Scotia. Halifax wished to reward Ellis, but he was also anxious for the success of Nova Scotia, his first colonial project. He knew that Ellis was an able administrator and was capable of completing the transformation of French Acadia to British Nova Scotia. As he had done when he received his appointment to Georgia, Henry Ellis made a thorough study of the state of the province of Nova Scotia that was to become his responsibility.[50]

Governor Charles Lawrence had been successful in banishing the Acadians but far less effective in establishing a constitutional government. Lord Halifax repeatedly urged him to hold elections for an assembly, even sending minutes of the Georgia Council to show how it should be done. Finally, on October 2, 1758, nineteen elected representatives met in Halifax to form the first House of Assembly. More British settlers were needed, and Governor Lawrence sent out an appeal for people from New England to colonize his province. A trickle of immigrants arrived in 1759 followed by a larger number in 1760. These newcomers occupied the fertile lands along the Minas Basin, where the French had constructed dikes to control the prodigious tides peculiar to the Bay of Fundy. Others settled to the west along the Annapolis

River. The influx of New Englanders was well under way when Governor Lawrence died on October 29, 1760, leaving the province in the hands of Jonathan Belcher, Jr., chief justice and president of the council. By 1761 there were about eight thousand people in the province, about one thousand of whom were Acadians who had taken the oath of allegiance and about two hundred who had not.[51]

Jonathan Belcher was not popular in Halifax, and after the appointment of Henry Ellis the people of the province eagerly looked forward to Ellis's arrival. A public reception was planned for July 1, 1761. On June 26, however, Ellis asked Pitt for a year's leave of absence. He had been in England only a month, his health was "far from being established," and he had matters to settle before he set out for Nova Scotia.[52]

Jonathan Belcher had some of Edmond Atkin's worst qualities. A historian of Nova Scotia stated that Belcher knew nothing of the art of managing men and that he was ignorant and careless in financial matters. He affected a pomposity of manner that alienated those who had to deal with him. Belcher certainly showed poor judgment in his frantic appeals for military assistance against the forty or so Acadian families who had not sworn allegiance to the crown. After sending petitions, the Nova Scotians dispatched an agent to complain of Belcher to the Board of Trade. They affirmed that Belcher was "so unskilled in the art of government and has behaved in such improper manner as to have occasioned a General Dislike to him." [53] The province was in distress because of Ellis's absence.

Perhaps it was fortunate for Ellis, if not for Nova Scotia, that he did not take up the reins of government in 1761. The historian John Bartlett Brebner doubted whether anyone could have satisfied both the Nova Scotians and the authorities in London. With the war coming to an end and Halifax out of office, parliamentary subsidies were sharply reduced. For years the people of Halifax had enjoyed exemption from prosecution for debt under an asylum act similar to one sponsored by Ellis in Georgia. Both acts were disallowed. One reason for Belcher's unpopularity was that he was instructed to repeal that legislation, which had the general support of most Nova Scotians.[54]

Ellis extended his leave of absence in 1762. By then his health had improved, but he had become an indispensable adviser to Pitt's successor. It soon became clear that someone other than Belcher was sorely needed in Halifax so Ellis resigned in favor of Montague Wilmot.[55] It is likely, in view of Ellis's role as adviser on American affairs, that he and Wilmot were on good terms. Politics being what it was, it is not at all surprising that Wilmot signed at least two grants of one thousand acres, one for Henry Ellis and another for Henry's nephew Francis. The grants were located in the fertile rolling hills on the eastern bank of the Shubenacadie River, where the rich red soil was evidence of a geological link to the red clay of Georgia at the other end of the Appalachian Highlands. A fort was established in that region and named Fort Ellis in honor of the absent governor. A history of the locality states that a family of Ellises later settled near Fort Ellis. Indeed, Henry Ellis left extensive holdings in Nova Scotia to his nephew Francis. The same local history remarks on the frequent appearance of the name Francis in generation after generation of the Shubenacadie Ellises.[56]

Ellis's main objective during most of the year after his return to England was the recovery of his health. There were several places in England where one could go to take the waters, but thanks to a dandy named Beau Nash, the favorite of the gentry was Bath. Philip Thicknesse, a sometimes caustic observer of the social scene and an acquaintance of Henry Ellis, described Bath as having recently experienced an increase in population. Men whose tastes inclined to reading found good libraries there; men who enjoyed good conversation found a variety of company there. For young ladies Bath was "the place where they have the best opportunity to improve and show their persons to advantage."[57] Nowhere, he suggests, were women permitted more liberty than at Bath.

Gout was the most respectable, if painful, of the usual indispositions of the privileged class. Pitt suffered from gout so badly that often he could scarcely hobble along on swollen legs. He was a frequent visitor to Bath in 1761. So were Bute, Halifax, Bedford, and many of the lesser nobility and hangers-on. Bath was a place where cleverness, wit, and charm were much admired, and one who could exhibit knowledge about the new scientific philosophy was entitled to a place of honor. Henry Ellis had all those attributes; at Bath he was in his milieu. If he took his own advice, however, he did more listening than talking at first. When William Knox came to England in 1762 as Georgia's agent, Henry Ellis gave him some fatherly counsel: "Success of most undertakings generally depends on setting out right." Knox should not do anything "of a public nature" until he had a chance to meet people and become known. "You must have time to look about you, to survey the ground you stand upon and to know the men you will have to do with and the way to avail yourself of them." Ellis himself followed that line of conduct successfully because by April 1762, a little more than a year after his arrival in England from America, he wrote to Knox from Bath that he was "now a veteran in soliciting and dancing attendance upon People in Office."[58]

At least one of Ellis's purposes in soliciting people in office was to recoup his wealth as well as his health. He wrote a letter to Benjamin Martyn, the Georgia agent, asking to be allowed to keep the surplus money from the sale of Bosomworth lands as compensation for his personal expenses in the public service. He described the Bosomworth litigation as a "vexatious business" that had been finally settled. He summarized the long delay in obtaining funds for the rangers and noted that he had to borrow money on his personal credit at interest to keep them in service. When the Cherokee War raged and the Creek killings occurred in May 1760, he again had used his own money to erect a bastion on the Savannah fortification and had not been reimbursed. He then had undertaken an expensive trip to New York to inform Amherst about the situation in the southern provinces. He estimated that his total expenses were greater than the £800 he had left from the Bosomworth sales but asked only to be allowed to keep that amount. Martyn sent Ellis's memorial to the Duke of Newcastle, president of the Lords of Treasury, who sought the advice of the Lords of Trade. This board judged that Ellis's statement was correct and that "his conduct in the administration of the government of Georgia has been such as entitled him to his Majesty's favour."[59] Ellis's request was granted. Other tokens of His Majesty's favor would soon follow.

When Henry Ellis wrote to William Pitt on June 26, 1761, asking for a leave of absence from Nova Scotia for reasons of health, the Great Commoner had more important matters on his mind. On that day he broke off peace negotiations with France and thereby caused a division within the cabinet council which rapidly deepened until he had to give up his office. Ellis could not have imagined that Pitt's resignation would result in his own elevation to the position of consultant to Pitt's successor.

URING THE same March 1761 when Halifax left the Board of Trade and Ellis was named to Nova Scotia, a letter from the French foreign minister, Etienne François de Choiseul, was delivered to William Pitt. The letter suggested that terms of peace between the two countries be discussed apart from the complications of the German war. As a starting point, France was willing to settle on the basis of *uti posseditis*. This would mean that England could retain Canada, Guadeloupe, and the African posts.

The proposal was greeted warmly by Bedford, cautiously by Bute, and suspiciously by Pitt. Pitt knew that the invasion of Martinique was under way. St. Lucia and the Neutral Islands were next, and then the twice postponed Louisiana campaign would be launched. More controversial was Pitt's plan, already being implemented, for the conquest of Belleisle, an island in the Bay of Biscay just off the French coast. The main unfinished business in Pitt's opinion was the closing of the Newfoundland coast to French fishing vessels. The French fishing fleet, Pitt argued, was the "nursery" of its navy. Deprived of its fisheries, France would be a "landlocked" nation. Most members of the cabinet disagreed, but only Bedford had the nerve to tell Pitt so. France had an extensive coastline, he observed caustically, and would have a navy even without fisheries. Regardless of logic, the city of London immediately accepted Pitt's position that the closing of the fisheries was a sine qua non for peace.[1]

Because the French announced that they were sending an emissary, Sieur de Bussy, England reciprocated despite Pitt's reluctance.

Hans Stanley was selected to go to Paris but was so restricted by his instructions that his mission had little chance of success. Stanley's first report revealed that Choiseul was willing to cede Canada, Cape Breton, and Prince Edward Island provided French fishing rights were retained. Bedford was strongly in favor of accepting the terms. Bute waffled, stating that Canada was "a barren country." [2] Pitt was adamant, and his reply on June 26, 1761, effectively broke off negotiations, much to the dismay of the king. Bute, following the king's lead, regretted the position Pitt was taking but was not willing to challenge him. Bedford, disgusted, stayed away from council meetings, and the respected Lord Hardwicke urged Pitt to be more flexible. Privately, Hardwicke wrote to Newcastle that Pitt's dispatch was in a "very haughty and dictatorial style, more strongly so than any which I remember to have seen of Louis the Fourteenth in the height of his glory and presumption." [3] Pitt's attitude toward his fellow ministers became increasingly distant.

France responded to Pitt's intransigence by forming a closer alignment with Spain, which in August resulted in renewal of the Family Compact by which each country pledged to defend the other against attack. Even before news of the alliance reached England, Pitt was determined to declare war on Spain. Ellis might have wondered why Pitt had been so nervous about Edmund Gray's colony offending Spanish sensibilities when now he called for a war that seemed unnecessary. The first sign of a break between Pitt and the others was a meeting at Newcastle's house to which Bedford was invited and Pitt was not. Pitt became more defiant than ever. He declared to the council that the moment for "humbling the House of Bourbon" was at hand. He was not accountable to the council; he had been called to the ministry by the voice of the people, and he held himself accountable to the people. If the council refused to support him he would resign; he would not remain in a situation that made him responsible for measures he was not able to direct. [4]

Lord Granville, the elderly president of the council, made an equally strong response. If Pitt ruled alone, "to what purpose are we called to this council?" he asked. Although Pitt was convinced of his infallibility, he said, he and the others would have to be convinced before they could yield to his opinion against their better judgment. In view of Granville's manly reply, it was unfair of Pitt to state publicly, as he did, that his demand for war was refused by "a trembling council." [5] The council sensibly hesitated to add a Spanish war to an already expensive German war. Only Richard Grenville, Earl Temple, brother of George Grenville and brother-in-law of Pitt, followed Pitt out of government. Pitt resigned on October 5, 1761, to the relief of the king and council. He was placated by a generous pension, and his wife was made a baroness. Bute offered Pitt's position to George Grenville, who declined but recommended one of his brothers-in-law, Charles Wyndham, Lord Egremont. On October 6, 1761, Bute offered Egremont the seals of office.[6]

Egremont's chief assets for his new position were that he was the son of Sir William Wyndham, the first Lord Egremont, chancellor of the exchequer under Queen Anne, that his sister Elizabeth was married to George Grenville, and that he was an honest, pleasant, polished, and likable man. Egremont's country house at Petworth, West Sussex, was one of the finest neoclassical mansions in England. In the eighteenth century architecture was meant to impress the viewer with the importance of the owners. Houses were memorials to the glories of Roman civilization, as interpreted by Andrea Palladio and translated in England by Inigo Jones, Christopher Wren, and Sir John Vanbrugh. Petworth was a slightly more restrained version of Castle Howard. Egremont filled its vast marble halls with ancient statuary from Greece and Italy, and it is one of only three such collections to survive intact. The master landscape architect of the age was Lancelot "Capability" Brown. Egremont employed Brown to transform Petworth's grounds into a bucolic park with serpentine lake, winding paths, and gothic follies. In 1757 Egremont engaged the architect Matthew Brettingham to design a second house for him in Picadilly. Brettingham, like his contemporary William Kent, avoided the exuberance of the baroque in favor of the severe classical design. The result was a dignified, unadorned, three-story building with a Palladian window above the modest front entrance. The interior was more daring; the central stairwell was lighted by a glass dome in the roof. Egremont House was ready for occupancy at about the time Ellis began his association with the Wyndham family.[7]

Egremont's wife was an Irish beauty named Alicia Carpenter. She bore him four sons and three daughters and presided elegantly over the frequent dinners which were among the most important preoccupations of the nobility. An indication of Egremont's importance in the social scale was that the sponsor at his firstborn son's baptism in 1752 was the king himself. The continuous entertaining took its toll. Egremont once remarked that he had "but three turtle dinners to come and if I survive them I shall be immortal."[8] His life was cut short by a heart attack at age fifty-three. The archives at Petworth House testify to his extensive correspondence, the bulk of it in connection with the conduct of the war and its settlement. Like most of the noble lords, Egremont was almost entirely ignorant about America.

When Egremont was introduced to Henry Ellis, probably by one of their mutual friends, Halifax or Barrington, he asked Ellis to advise him on American affairs. Ellis proved so useful that Egremont consulted him on a wide range of topics. Soon Ellis's name was bruited about as Egremont's "oracle."[9] The first indication of Ellis's involvement in the office of the secretary of state is a memorandum in Ellis's hand listing the royal officials in Nova Scotia and Georgia and dated November 1761.[10] Egremont now had the power of patronage, and Ellis would have some say in the assignment of offices. The first indication of Ellis's influence was a letter from Egremont on December 12, 1761, addressed to Amherst: "It is said that the Indians are often disgusted and their minds alienated from his Majesty's government by the shameful manner in which Business is transacted between them and our traders."[11] Undoubtedly, Henry Ellis was the source of Egremont's information; the letter reflects Ellis's sympathetic attitude toward Indians.

When Ellis did not know the boundaries of Canada, Egremont asked Amherst to find out "the extent and limits of Canada."[12] Amherst did not know either and inquired of his subordinate, General Thomas Gage, who gave this less than satisfactory answer: "I cannot discover that the limits betwixt Canada and Louisiana were distinctly described so as to be publickly known."[13] Here was another reason to conquer Louisiana rather than become embroiled in a dispute about boundaries between British Canada and French Louisiana. With Ellis at his shoulder, Egremont made up his mind to keep Canada, even though Bute considered it a "barren land" and a burden.

Egremont also reflected Ellis's conviction that a naval campaign against Louisiana was necessary. Egremont urged Amherst to get on with the expedition. Amherst replied that he had to wait for the conclusion of the Martinique operation because all available troops were occupied in that effort. Egremont was sorry to hear about the delay. "The King firmly relies on your exerting every possible effort for the success of that enterprise," he wrote.[14] Amherst suggested that an invasion of Louisiana from Canada might succeed if it were made in conjunction with a fleet at the mouth of the Mississippi. Before Amherst's letter was in Egremont's hands, Ellis's opinion was on record: "In regard to the project of attacking Louisiana from the north by descending the great rivers Ohio and Mississippi, the more I reflect upon it, the more I am astonished."[15] He cited the difficulties experienced by Forbes in his march to Fort Duquesne and insisted that the problems of an invasion of the Mississippi country would be incomparably greater. Ellis displayed a thorough knowledge of the geography of the interior, probably gleaned from John Mitchell's 1755 map. After reciting a litany of obstacles, he concluded, "I say, My Lord, whoever combines all these circumstances of danger and difficulty, must tremble for the consequences of so ticklish an enterprize."[16] By contrast, a naval campaign would face no such difficulties. Egremont decided upon a naval campaign that same March and so informed Amherst.[17]

Spanish relations fell within the purview of Egremont's office. It gradually became known that in a compact signed on August 15, 1761, Spain pledged to join France in her war against Britain by May 1762 unless peace had been restored by then. Grenville, Bute, and Egremont collaborated on a sharp note to the Spanish government demanding to know its intentions with regard to Great Britain. Spain considered the note an insult and refused to answer. Consequently, on January 4, 1762, Britain declared war on Spain, and on January 18, Spain reciprocated.[18]

Henry Ellis played an important part in his role as consultant concerning the strategy to follow upon the outbreak of war with Spain. Ellis urged Egremont to attack Havana, Cuba, and Egremont, knowing there would be opposition from the Europeanist Newcastle and possibly Bute, asked Ellis to put his thoughts on paper. On January 16, 1762, Ellis handed Egremont a remarkable eleven-page letter. England could not endure a protracted war with both Spain and France, he argued. Public credit was "at its utmost stretch." The longer we delay, Ellis said, the weaker we will become. It was better to go on the offensive than wait on the enemy. Spain was vulnerable in the straits of Florida, through which her commerce from South America passed. Havana (or "the Havannah" as it was called) controlled those straits.[19]

In Spanish hands, Havana posed a threat to Jamaica, the Bahama Islands, South Carolina, and Georgia. St. Augustine, the nest of privateers, was supported from Havana. The Florida forts at St. Augustine, St. Marks, and Pensacola must fall if Havana were taken. Ellis described

Georgia's vulnerability if Spain decided to launch an attack as it had in the last war. Havana must be taken before the Spaniards decided to invade Georgia, Ellis continued. Oglethorpe's failed sieges of St. Augustine proved how difficult it was to capture that fort when Havana was left free to reinforce it. Ellis was the first to suggest that Florida be annexed by Britain: "Should we have a desire to complete our American Empire by the addition of that Province, it may with the greatest ease and certainty be accomplished after reducing the Havana."[20]

Ellis then told Egremont how the task might be accomplished. After Fort Royal in Martinique was taken, advantageous terms should be offered to the inhabitants to induce them to end their resistance; he suggested that the blacks might be given land on one of the Neutral Islands. Then all the forces employed in the Martinique expedition should be sent against Havana, reinforced by troops from the northern colonies.

Ellis anticipated the arguments that could be raised against the expedition and answered them one by one. There was a landing place east of the harbor fifteen miles from town which could be safely used. The fort was not strong against a siege of heavy artillery; if closely invested by sea and land it would soon fall. The hurricane season began in July so the attack should be launched earlier. Ellis downplayed the danger to health, saying that the "air of an island is always purer" than that of a continent. Finally, the seizure of Havana would be the quickest way to gain peace. France was so worn out and exhausted that her only hope was with her Spanish ally; therefore, "tis in our power to disappoint and even to increase her present distress by distressing of Spain."[21]

In attempting to turn the Spanish war into an American one, Ellis and Egremont had to contend with those who, like Pitt, thought first of the European theater. Bute, Newcastle, and Grenville agreed that an army should be sent to Portugal to prevent Spain from seizing that impoverished country. Lord Loudoun, of dubious American fame, led six thousand troops from Belleisle to join the regulars already there. A desultory war with the Spanish followed. After much marching about and some sporadic fighting, the Spanish army left Portugal, and the king of Spain gave up his dream of ruling both countries.[22]

To Ellis's satisfaction, Egremont persuaded Bute and Grenville to approve the campaign against Havana. It is striking how closely Egremont's instructions to the general, Lord Albemarle, followed Ellis's memorandum and even more so that events fell out according to plan.

In a letter of January 6, 1762, Egremont alerted Albemarle to stand by for orders. Ellis's letter to Egremont was dated January 16, 1762. Egremont obtained the consent of the council and embodied Ellis's report in his instructions to Albemarle on February 15, 1762. The campaign went as Ellis had outlined. Albemarle landed at Martinique, where General Robert Monckton had won a timely victory, and was able to reinforce the invasion force. With twelve thousand men Albemarle reached Cuba on June 6, before the hurricane season. His army disembarked east of Havana as Ellis had suggested. The Spanish force of six thousand was quickly routed and Morro Castle was invested. There was little further progress until bombardment from British ships was added to that from the troops on land. Albemarle was reluctant to storm the fortress until Amherst's troops arrived in twenty-two transports from New York. The first of them landed on June 28. On June 30 the British troops stormed the citadel and won the "pearl of the Antilles." Terms of surrender were signed on August 13, 1762. The British were generous, as they were in all the West Indian conquests: the people could keep their property and continue to practice their religion.[23]

The American theater of operations was not the focus of attention for most members of the king's cabinet council during the first four months of 1762. On January 6, as Egremont and Ellis pondered an attack on Havana, Bute raised the question of whether to renew the annual subsidy to Prussia. If Newcastle stood for anything, it was to the Old System of employing European allies against France. Hardwicke convinced him that his honor was involved and that the commitment to Frederick the Great must be continued. The king, perhaps the staunchest opponent of further aid to Frederick, told Bute he would rather let Newcastle go than continue to send money to "that proud, over-bearing prince."[24]

On February 5, while Egremont composed his instructions to Lord Albemarle, the bold Bedford rose in the House of Lords to denounce the German war and to call for an end to British involvement. The Lords looked to Bute for the administration's position. Bute was not ready to break with Newcastle. He hedged, proposing that the war be brought "within a proper compass." Bedford lost the vote but won the point. At George Grenville's urging, a letter was sent to Frederick asking him to clarify his plans. That headstrong monarch returned an insulting answer as though his war was none of Britain's business. The council decided to act accordingly. The meeting of the council on April 30, 1762, was a major watershed, signaling a withdrawal from Continental concerns and permitting greater attention to American affairs. Only Newcastle, Hardwicke, and Devonshire voted in favor of continuing a subsidy to Prussia. In effect, the vote was a decision to support Egremont and the American war rather than Newcastle and the war in Europe.

Newcastle grumbled about the fanciful talk about Havana and St. Augustine and referred to Bute's "silly maritime war."[25] Painfully aware that he had lost the confidence of the king, Newcastle resigned as first lord of the Treasury on May 26, 1762, and Bute assumed the position. George Grenville took Bute's office as secretary of state for the Northern Department. Bute's conversion to American priorities was, like many of his positions, tentative. Bedford, the strong peace advocate, reflected Bute's views more accurately than anyone else. The fall of Havana in August actually embarrassed both Bute and Bedford because they saw it as delaying the peace process while more demands were put upon Spain. Shortly after easing Newcastle out of the council, Bute made an attempt to do the same to Egremont. Grenville scotched that plan in May. Nevertheless, Egremont's insistence on a hard line with Spain worried Bute so much that he actually approached Newcastle and Hardwicke about rejoining the government and, even more surprisingly, made overtures to Pitt.[26] Egremont and Grenville needed the support of a powerful political figure who would be sympathetic to their American policies. Fortunately, such a person was available in Ellis's patron Halifax, who accepted the position of first lord of the Admiralty at the end of May 1762.

Egremont was determined to secure either Puerto Rico or Florida as compensation for Havana. Henry Ellis pleaded the cause of Florida on March 3, 1762, in a letter written at Bath. He compiled a folder with all the documents he could gather relating to Florida, dating to James Moore's raids in 1702 and including accounts of Oglethorpe's invasions. He enclosed a map of the fortifications of St. Augustine to illustrate that taking it "would be a task of no great difficulty." He stressed the "incredible mischief" done to British commerce by the "swarms of privateers" sheltered at St. Augustine. Florida in British hands would give security to the southern provinces. It would also deprive runaway slaves of a sanctuary. He admitted that the harbor at St. Augustine was too shallow for large ships, but he thought that another suitable port might be found along Florida's unchartered coast which would be "as serviceable to our Fleets in distressing the Enemy as the Havana itself." [27]

Ellis concluded his recommendation by a comment which indicates that he felt comfortable enough in his relationship with Egremont to propose new initiatives. "I purpose writing to your Lordship soon upon other topics," he promised. One of these topics was far removed from Havana and Florida but reflected Ellis's continuing interest in the promotion of a commercial empire. The Canary Islands, Ellis argued, should be taken from Spain to secure the wine that otherwise cost specie and to deny Spain a rendezvous to replace Havana. British African and American commerce would be more secure if the Canaries were British. As he had done in mapping the Havana strategy, Ellis explained how the Canary Islands might be taken, enclosing a map of the town of St. Crux on the island of Tenerife.[28]

Bute, however, was intent upon narrowing the war rather than expanding it. Prodded by the king, he secured the agreement of the council to make a separate peace with France on roughly the same terms both countries had agreed to the previous year, that is, that Canada be retained and Guadeloupe returned to France, that there be a division of the Neutral Islands, and that France restore occupied territory on the Continent. The British ministers were willing to permit France to fish off Canadian shores by acknowledging French claims to the tiny islands of St. Pierre and Miquelon. The French minister Choiseul insisted on possession of St. Lucia in the West Indies. Bute persuaded Egremont to agree to make that concession, but Bute could not get Grenville and others to agree to negotiate separately with France. They insisted that if the French wanted peace they should bring Spain to the table.[29]

On July 28, 1762, the council reached a compromise; negotiations with France would start if France would give no further assistance to Spain. France sent a respected emissary in the Duc de Nivernais, and the king's choice to represent England was the most prominent advocate of peace, the Duke of Bedford, now the king's favorite minister next to Bute. Bedford sailed for France on September 6, 1762, with thirty retainers and twenty-three coaches. The grandeur was for effect. On September 29, Egremont received word that Havana was taken, and he and Grenville insisted that Spain would have to give up Florida if she wanted to keep Cuba. Bute, like Bedford, had been willing to settle for logging rights in Honduras. The king was upset with Egremont and Grenville for their strong stand and argued with Egremont about it. Richard Rigby wrote to Bedford describing the interview. The king said he did not want to bind Bedford by instructions, whereupon Egremont "flew into a passion" and insisted that Bedford be recalled if he did not seek compensation for Havana. Rigby, Bedford's friend and informant, wrote the duke that "not a single counsellor, not even Halifax will now consent to give up Havana without an equivalent, and Florida, his Lordship thinks will be the one proposed." [30]

Egremont did not trust Bedford to try for an equivalent and proposed that any terms agreed to at Paris would have to be voted on by Parliament. Robert Wood, Pitt's under secretary and now Egremont's, carried tales to Rigby about Egremont's dislike of Bedford, and the gossipy Rigby was delighted to relay them to Bedford. "I can assure you," Rigby wrote, "that his Lordship has a cordial hatred for you." [31] On October 29, 1762, Egremont wrote Bedford that "it is of indispensable necessity that a proper compensation should be obtained for the important restitution of the Havannah." [32] Egremont and Ellis had won the point.

Barrington, an old friend of Halifax's, with whom he "had lived from his earliest youth in the most entire and cordial friendship," as he said, and also a friend of Egremont's, was afraid that Egremont's position on Havana might cause negotiations to break off. He urged Bute "for God's sake to enlarge and strengthen" the administration. Bute asked Barrington to sound out Henry Fox, and Barrington did so. [33] As a result, Fox wrote to Bedford on October 13, "In short, I am this morning declared a cabinet counsellor and His Majesty's Minister in the House of Commons . . . I am a humble imitator of your Grace." [34] Halifax and Grenville exchanged positions, Halifax becoming the secretary of state for the Northern Department and Grenville first lord of Admiralty.

The French court helped the cause of peace by volunteering to compensate Spain for the loss of Florida by ceding to her New Orleans and Louisiana west of the Mississippi. That stumbling block removed, the terms of peace were quickly worked out, and on November 3, 1762, Bedford reported to Egremont that the preliminary treaty had been signed that morning. His only concession was to agree to demolish English forts in Honduras, but it was understood that logging by British subjects would continue. Bedford's tone was that of a man who knew he had done well and was proud of his achievement. Bute congratulated him on the "noblest and most essential service ever performed by a subject for his King and country. Our cabinet now appear almost as happy and satisfied as I am." [35]

With the crucial parliamentary debate on the treaty imminent, Egremont asked Henry Ellis to prepare a statement defending the treaty. The result was a document entitled "advantages which England gains by the present Treaty with France and Spain." Ellis cited the acquisition of Canada with its seventy thousand French inhabitants, which would be a valuable market for manufactures. With that vast country and its numerous Indian tribes came the fur trade. The acquisition of the Ohio and Mississippi rivers provided inland navigation for the older colonies, as well as greater security. With Isle Royal and St. Johns (Prince Edward Island and Cape Breton) came more extensive fishing coasts and a means of enlarging the British merchant fleet. The cession of Louisiana east of the Mississippi would put an end to French intrigue among the Indians. The navigation of the Mississippi and the acquisition of the port of Mobile were important for the commerce of the West. The addition of Florida "compleats our Empire in America." Pensacola "makes the parting with the Havana of much less consequence to us than it might otherwise have been." The possession of St. Augustine guaranteed the security of Georgia. The British claim to cut wood in Honduras was recognized as a right. Britain acquired St. Vincent and Dominica among the Neutral Islands and, instead of St. Lucia, the islands of Granada and the Grenadines, which were worth more. Tobago, situated near South America, had commodious harbors for commerce with that continent. Spanish commerce, both outward and homeward bound, would be subject to the control of strategically located British posts in the West Indies.

Britain obtained Senegal on the African coast and the exclusive right to the gum trade. France gave up any claim to erect fortifications in the Indian province of Bengal, and the British gained ascendancy in that province. Portugal was rescued from Spanish efforts to annex it. Britain gained Minorca and several other concessions. Ellis concluded by stating that the terms of the present treaty were superior to those on which Pitt had been willing to settle. [36] The report was descriptive rather than proscriptive, a convenient summary of essentials, equivalent to modern press releases and clearly intended to put the administration's position in the best light.

William Knox, Ellis's acquaintance from Monaghan and associate in Georgia, now Georgia's agent, became involved in politics at the time the preliminary treaty was presented to Parliament. William Petty, Lord Shelburne, a young friend of both Bute and Henry Fox, was selected to defend the treaty in the House of Lords. Fox, as administration spokesman in the House of Commons, realized that the opposition would criticize the acquisition of Louisiana and Florida as poor equivalents for Havana. Fox knew very little about those places and neither did Shelburne. Knox was introduced to Fox as one recently returned from America and was enlisted to draw up a statement Fox and Shelburne could use. Knox consulted Ellis in preparing his paper. Fox was so pleased with the result that he asked Knox to name the office he wanted in one of the new acquisitions; Fox expected "nobody to do anything for nothing." Knox's Presbyterian conscience would not permit him to be obligated "to a man with such a bad reputation."[37]

In fact, Fox did not have the authority to appoint to offices in the new acquisitions. Lord Egremont did, and the man who actually made a list of appointments was Henry Ellis. William Knox had no scruples about accepting a favor from Ellis. Among the Egremont Papers is an undated "list of new acquisitions and names of appointees" in Ellis's handwriting. Knox was named agent for Florida at a salary of £60 and retained his Georgia agency and office of provost marshal, raising his annual income to £540. There is little doubt that it was easier to turn down Fox's offer of assistance when one already had a guarantee of a sinecure. Knox felt comfortable enough with his financial situation to take a wife, Letitia Ford of Dublin, and to begin a family.[38]

Before Parliament met on November 25, 1762, rumors that the ministers had given away too much in the treaty began to circulate. Bute was blamed for the resignation of Pitt and now for a weak treaty. His coach was pelted with stones, its glass broken, and he was threatened with bodily injury. Even the king was insulted on his way to open Parliament. As the session began, Egremont spoke only to move the acceptance of the king's speech. The debate on the treaty began in earnest on November 29. The youthful Earl of Shelburne used some of the points made by Henry Ellis and Knox, emphasizing the gains made in America. "Having made very large demands in North America," he argued, "it was necessary to relax in other parts of the world." The debate made it clear that the administration turned its back on Europe by turning toward America. The point was stressed by Hardwicke in opposing the treaty: "By this desertion of the King of Prussia, we are left without any system or connection at all on the continent."[39]

William Pitt delivered a three-hour-and-twenty-minute speech as Richard Rigby timed it, claiming that his terms of the year before were far better than those of the treaty under consideration. The new treaty "obscured all the glories of the war, surrendered the dearest interest of the nation and sacrificed the public faith by an abandonment of our allies." Pitt left the hall as Fox rose to answer him. One of the assumptions that helped consolidate the emerging "Old Whig" faction of Pitt, Newcastle, Hardwicke, Temple, Devonshire, and their friends was that the peace was ignominious.

John Wilkes set a new standard for intemperate criticism by issuing a series of anti-Bute essays under title *North Briton* and particularly by asserting in the December 25, 1762, issue, "A wicked faction only would purchase an ignoble and inglorious peace by giving up to the perfidious French and to the feeble and insolent Spaniards our most valuable and important conquests." Wilkes's paper would not have deserved notice—it had only 120 subscribers—except that its financial backer was Richard Grenville, Earl Temple, Pitt's closest ally at the moment. Nathaniel Wraxall, a contemporary, echoed Wilkes's opinion in his memoirs: "All the achievements of that great Minister [Pitt] were sacrificed at the peace of Fontainbleau."[40] It became popular to complain that Florida and Louisiana were poor substitutes for Havana. Less was said about Canada for Guadeloupe because Pitt had been willing to make that swap.

The opposition had to explain why 319 members of the House supported the treaty and only 65 opposed it. They did so by exaggerating Henry Fox's powers of corruption. There is no doubt that Fox made liberal use of the ministry's secret fund, but the vote was too one-sided for bribes to have made a difference. The assessment of the careful historian Lawrence Henry Gipson is that the administration deserved praise for a notable achievement.[41] The peace was consistent with the British objectives at the outset: it provided for the security of the American colonies. Zenab Rashed, in an authoritative study of the Peace of Paris, acknowledged that English historians have generally echoed the opposition's opinion but concluded that the treaty was "extremely advantageous to England."[42]

Among the nineteenth-century Whig historians who were sweeping in their condemnation of Bute and his administration were W. E. Lecky, Thomas Erskine May, J. W. Fortescue, A. Ballatyne, George O.

Trevelyan, William Hunt, J. R. Green, and Goldwin Smith. Sir Lewis Namier dispelled the notion of Bute as the evil instrument of royal absolutism but bolstered the image of a man overwhelmed by petty intrigues. Recent scholars have rehabilitated Bute and in the process have agreed that the peace was an admirable one. As Karl Schweizer described it, "the Peace of Paris with France was in fact an honourable, advantageous settlement, rich compensation for Britain's global victories and eloquent testimony to Bute's concern for British imperial security."[43]

Largely overlooked by historians is the important role played by Egremont in formulating the peace terms. The mass of papers dealing with the treaty, including letters to Egremont from the king, Bute, Grenville, Fox, Hardwicke, and Mansfield, in the Egremont Papers testify to Egremont's essential involvement. Egremont continued to fret about Bedford while the final treaty was worked out in Paris. He made no attempt to disguise his concern that Bedford might try to weaken the treaty at the last minute.[44] He need not have worried. Bedford informed Egremont on February 10 that the final treaty had been negotiated according to instructions and that he had dispatched the document on that date. Bedford's messenger, Sir Richard Neville, arrived in London on February 15 and went immediately to Egremont House, Piccadilly, where he found Egremont and Grenville at supper. Egremont, in some excitement, insisted that they go see the king that evening. They were admitted at once and spent an hour and a half going over the treaty. "Why, my lord," exclaimed the king to Egremont, "this is greater than we could have hoped for. England never signed such a peace before, nor, I believe any other power in Europe; indeed, the Duke of Bedford has done greatly." Egremont knew the right words to say: "No prince had ever begun his reign by so glorious a war and so glorious a peace."[45]

Next morning Neville called on Bute at his house in Berkeley Square. Bute praised Bedford and expressed regret for the cabinet's lack of support for him. The reference was to Egremont. Neville told Bedford that Bute and Egremont had not spoken to each other for a fortnight because of their differing opinions regarding Bedford and the peace. Neville thought there would be little criticism of the treaty from Parliament. Even Wilkes had confided to him that "it was the damn'dest peace for the Opposition that was ever made."[46] Some nine

hundred merchants of London agreed that the peace had been concluded "on terms of real and solid advantage . . . marked with modera-
tion and equity" and said so in an address to the king.[47]

Without doubt, Egremont and his friends savored the moment.
Henry Ellis must have shared in the rejoicing at Egremont House.
The happy coterie did not know that even then Bute was plotting to
remove Egremont from his office. The revisionist historians are undoubtedly correct in reminding us that Bute had many good qualities
but one of his less admirable traits was his fickleness regarding his
closest colleagues, a trait he shared with his royal master.

The political by-products of the peace distracted the attention of
the king and his cabinet council from American affairs. The pragmatic
Henry Fox was given control of patronage, and he used it to dismiss all
those Newcastle appointees who sided with the opposition. Much was
made of the purge of the "Pelhamite Innocents," the commissioners
of treasury boards, customs officers, excise tax collectors, and other
minor officials who were appointed by Newcastle and refused to cooperate with the administration. They were comparatively few because
most of the civil servants had changed their allegiance from Newcastle
to Bute. The caustic Richard Rigby wrote to Bedford, "These turned-
out gentlemen are surprised that all the world are not as angry at their
removal as themselves, whereas, the truth is nobody cares a farthing
about them."[48]

The nucleus of a party began to gather around Newcastle, claiming the mantle of political virtue. Guests at a so-called coalition dinner
included Newcastle, Pitt, Temple, Grafton, Rockingham, Portland, and
Hardwicke.[49] They made much of the lack of morality of Henry Fox.
Even the king regarded Henry Fox as a bad man, and the administration
included the notorious Sir Francis Dashwood, who was incompetent
as well as corrupt, and Earl Sandwich, who was capable in public office
but profligate in private life.

With the final approval of the Peace of Paris by the council on
February 16, 1763, Bute decided that he had done his duty to his dear
friend, the king, and cast about for a successor who would do the king's
business. His first choice was Henry Fox. George III objected, saying
that he would rather have an honest man. Although Bute persuaded
the king to make the offer to Fox, Fox preferred to retire and enjoy the
rewards of his efforts. He was named Lord Holland and given a handsome pension. Next Bute offered the presidency of the council and

head of government to the hero of the recent negotiations, the Duke of Bedford. Bute explained to Bedford that the king was determined "never upon any account to suffer ministers of the late reign who have attempted to fetter and enslave him ever to come into his services."[50] He meant Pitt and Newcastle. Before the year was out, the king would approach both Pitt and Newcastle to reorganize his ministry. Bedford refused the honor because the ministry without Bute and Fox would be too weak. With Bute gone and "so many of those who wish me ill" still in government, he would be a madman to accept Bute's offer, he said. But he agreed that the ministry needed help: "For God's sake persuade his Majesty to widen the bottom of administration."[51]

Bute's rather curious choice to broaden the administration was the young Earl of Shelburne, who had earned marks by speaking for the treaty. Bute approached Grenville with the suggestion that Egremont be named lord lieutenant of Ireland and Shelburne be given the office of secretary of state for the Southern Department. If Bute had succeeded, Henry Ellis would not have played the part he did in American affairs. But Grenville was as staunch in his support of Egremont as he had ever been and was opposed to giving the inexperienced Shelburne such an important post.[52] The place to gain experience was the Board of Trade, and Bute's parting gift to his young friend Shelburne was the presidency of that body. If there had been bad blood between Egremont and Shelburne before, as William Knox asserted, relations were increasingly strained in 1763, when close cooperation between the secretary and the board was necessary in solving American problems.

Bute settled on Grenville to head the government as first lord of Treasury and chancellor of the exchequer, promising him the help of all "the king's friends," a phrase that became famous.[53] Grenville agreed to share patronage with the two secretaries, Halifax and Egremont. The administration came to be known as the "Triumvirate." The king regarded the three as equals and referred to them as the "Consilliabilum."[54] April 16, 1763, the date Grenville assumed his two important offices, marked the beginning of the ministry of the triumvirs and the apex of the career of Henry Ellis. For fourteen years at home and abroad he had been included in the circle of Halifax's friends, and for more than a year he had served Egremont well. Soon his friend William Knox began a long association with George Grenville. Therefore, the triumvirate had a Georgia connection with Ellis, the former governor, and Knox, still acting as both Georgia's provost marshal and agent. It is not surprising that some unfinished business regarding Georgia was attended to.

From the time he lost Bute until he acquired the services of Lord North ten years later, none of the king's ministers pleased him for long. The king believed that Egremont was offended when the king asked him to invite Hardwicke to take the presidency of the council, a position left vacant by the death of Lord Granville in January.[55] Hardwicke's account of his interviews with Egremont reveals the latter as cordial. On May 13, 1763, the first visit was described as marked by "respect and civility." Hardwicke was reluctant to join the ministry because he suspected that Bute was still guiding the king. Egremont assured him that there was no secret influence; he would resign if Bute interfered, and so would Halifax. Egremont spoke to Hardwicke again in August at the king's urging, but Hardwicke said he could not separate himself from his friends, Newcastle and the great Whig lords. Egremont expressed willingness to bring in Newcastle but asked Hardwicke not to say anything about it until he got back to him. Hardwicke commented that Egremont was "very jealous and uneasy with my Lord Shelburne" because he believed that Shelburne was scheming with Bute to undermine the administration.[56]

The young king was careful to show every sign of respect for his ministers because he knew that if he raised an eyebrow or kept one waiting for a few minutes, tongues would wag and anonymous broadsides would predict a change of government. The king seemed to be especially considerate of Egremont. When the youngest of Egremont's seven children was christened in May, the king and queen stood as godparents.[57]

At the moment of launching the new administration, there occurred a political tempest that distracted the attention of the ministers from more important business, including American affairs. The first official statement of the triumvirate was the king's speech delivered to Parliament on April 19, 1763. It dwelled on the benefits derived from the Definitive Treaty, mentioned that the king's good brother the king of Prussia had concluded a satisfactory treaty, and ended by stating that "the success which has attended my negotiation has necessarily, and immediately, diffused the blessings of peace through every part of Europe."[58]

Did Henry Ellis have a hand in the drafting of the address? If not, it is very likely that one of the subministers or ministerial advisers did. Bute's secretary, Charles Jenkinson, had gone to work for George Grenville, and he may have prepared the speech. At any rate, the simple statement of fact brought forth an unexpected reaction. On April 23, 1763, the *North Briton* Number 45 described the speech as "the most abandoned instance of ministerial effrontery ever attempted to be imposed on mankind." It went on to say that the magnanimous king of Prussia received no advantage from the treaty. "He was basely deserted by the Scottish prime-minister of England . . . and he was betrayed by us in the treaty of peace." [59]

The sober historian Gipson called the charges "irresponsible and uninformed outbursts of bravado." [60] The author, John Wilkes, was a thirty-eight-year-old member of Parliament from Aylesbury who was known for his reckless excesses even in this age of excess. In 1762 he was a member of the infamous Hell-fire Club with Dashwood, the chancellor of the exchequer, and Sandwich, among others. In that year he acquired a sponsor in the person of Lord Temple and began publishing the *North Briton* as a vehicle for attacking the Scottish prime minister. [61]

After securing the advice of the attorney general and solicitor general, the ministers decided to take a stand rather than risk accusations of cowardice or weakness. A general warrant was signed by the Earl of Halifax and placed in the hands of Robert Wood, Egremont's under secretary, and Philip C. Webb, Henry Ellis's friend and horticultural expert from Surrey and at the time Grenville's solicitor to the treasury. They searched Wilkes's home for evidence and carried off his papers. Wilkes himself was brought to Halifax's house on Great George Street for interrogation by Halifax and Egremont, then locked in the Tower of London. [62]

The opposition, with Earl Temple leading the way, seized the opportunity to attack the triumvirs. Wilkes was discharged on a writ of habeas corpus and brought to court. Chief Justice Sir Charles Pratt decided that there was precedence for Halifax's issuing a warrant but did not take up the constitutionality of general warrants. He ruled that libel was a matter to be decided by a jury. Finally, Pratt released Wilkes because he was entitled to immunity as a member of Parliament except in cases of treason, felony, and breach of peace. Wilkes was the hero of the moment and enjoyed himself immensely. Temple paid for issuing two thousand additional copies of *North Briton* Number 45. Wilkes sued Halifax, Egremont, Webb, and Wood for false arrest. Although very popular in the street, Wilkes was not supported in Parliament.

Grenville moved the resolution that declared Wilkes guilty of libel, and the House of Commons agreed 273 to 111. While the House prepared to consider the question of expulsion, Wilkes decided to retreat to Paris. Before he left, he fought a duel with a member of Parliament and was wounded. In Paris he assumed the pose of an invalid; it was widely suspected that any poor health he might have had was caused by riotous living. Wilkes was expelled from the House of Commons and chose to remain in exile for three years. Although the Wilkes case did not involve Henry Ellis directly, it disturbed his noble friends, Halifax and Egremont. Egremont challenged Wilkes to a duel, which prompted Wilkes's decision to prolong his sojourn in Paris. Wilkes wrote to Temple from Paris that Egremont's challenge "has dwelt on my mind ever since."[63]

As an additional distraction, the ministers were faced with the problem of reducing the war debt. Grenville, as first lord of the Treasury and chancellor of the exchequer, was principally responsible for economy in government. During 1763 Grenville succeeded in reducing the debt by £5 million to £13.6 million by maintaining wartime taxes on land, malt, and beer and by adding a new tax, four shillings a hogshead on cider and four shillings a bin on wines. Englishmen disliked taxes as much as Americans, particularly excise taxes, and the cider and wine taxes were excises. Excise inspectors were regarded as busybodies and nuisances, as the historian Steven Watson put it: "They pried into a man's business as no one else dared before the invention of an income-tax."[64] The new taxes contributed to the antigovernment feeling in London. It did Grenville no good to argue that they were necessary. If Grenville was stubborn or courageous enough to tax the people outside his window, it was only a matter of time before he taxed the British subjects across the sea.

The triumvirate faced unprecedented responsibilities in Europe, India, and Africa, as well as America, and at the same time had to deal with the cider tax protests, the Wilkes nuisance, and the vacillations of an insecure king. Some of the powerful who might have strengthened the administration, Hardwicke and Bedford, for example, believed that the government could not last. Others, including Newcastle and Pitt, waited to be invited back into power after the inevitable failure of the truimvirs. All the while, the king fretted, Bute plotted, and rumors multiplied.

Given the demands of his many social and political obligations, it is surprising that Egremont had time for America in the few months before his life was cut short by "apoplexy" on August 20, 1763. In fact, crucial decisions regarding the transformation of British North America were made before he died. Almost as though he anticipated his death, Egremont confided to Grenville on August 6 that he had gone to see the king and "availed myself to settle all my American affairs that I at all cared for." [65] The remark is significant. By August 1763, Egremont was satisfied with the way he had dealt with Canada, Louisiana east of the Mississippi, the Floridas, and the West Indies. Egremont's work was expedited by the man upon whom he relied regarding all colonial matters, Henry Ellis. Fortunately, Ellis's memorandums have been preserved among the Egremont papers so that Ellis's advice can be traced to its impact on policy. He had been influential in the decisions to attack Havana and acquire Florida. He had helped explain and defend the treaty of peace. Now he was called on to lay the foundation for the postwar American empire.

Henry Ellis was ready for the challenge that faced him. Everything he had done equipped him for the role of consultant on imperial policy. His explorations, his promotion of the search for new trade routes, his intimate knowledge of the American frontier, his familiarity with the geography of the West Indies, all stood him in good stead. To these advantages must be added those social graces essential to acceptance in the society in which Ellis moved. Ellis knew how to direct a great lord without giving offense and was shrewd enough to permit the noble lord to take credit for the policy.

CHAPTER ELEVEN *The Transformation of British North America*

EXTBOOKS GIVE William Pitt credit for winning the Seven Years' War and Bute for ending it and blame George Grenville for dealing with the postwar problems and thereby sowing the seeds of the American Revolution. During the crucial year 1763, however, as the postwar world began to take shape, none of the three ministers was specifically responsible for America. For the first eight months, Egremont was the American minister and for the last four it was Halifax. During the entire year the expert on American affairs upon whose advice the ministers relied was Governor Henry Ellis. He was involved in decisions that altered the course of American history: governments were established in Canada, the two Floridas, and the West Indies; Nova Scotia was enlarged by the addition of Cape Breton and Prince Edward Island; new boundaries were assigned to Georgia and the Floridas; an Indian reserve was established and a new trading policy was introduced; the course of westward migration was affected; the location of forts and the size of the military garrisons were determined; French New Orleans became Spanish; and the Mississippi and Iberville rivers traced the new western limits of British North America. Henry Ellis wrote memorandums that bore directly on all these decisions.

In December 1762, when Ellis was in London for the parliamentary debates on the preliminary treaty, he made a recommendation that anticipated the approval of the terms. The French would be banished from old Louisiana east of the Mississippi and Iberville rivers, and that huge expanse of Indian country would revert to British control. For years, ever since the brutal raids of James Moore early in the century and his capture and enslavement of Indians, the French had warned the Indians of the interior that the British wished to expel the French so that they might once again enslave the Indians. It was important, said Ellis, to seize the initiative by convoking a general congress of southern tribes and announcing the news of the British victory with the assurance that the British wanted only the peace and happiness of their red brothers. All this should be done "in the most prudent and delicate manner." Ellis meant that Atkin-like statements, those that were meant to awe and intimidate, should be avoided, and every means should be used "to quiet their apprehensions and gain their good opinion." The cruelties and treachery practiced in the past by the French should be stressed, and it should be emphasized that the Great Spirit was on the side of the British. Ellis had to explain to Egremont that the Indians' name for God was the Great Spirit. Ellis included in his letter not only the general ideas but the actual expressions that should be used in the official talk to the gathered tribes. Aware of the Indians' fondness for ceremony, Ellis suggested that all four southern governors should be on hand, each with his retinue of advisers. Nothing was to be demanded; on the contrary, all past offenses were to be forgiven and generous presents distributed. The congress should be held in a place where the Indians would be comfortable; Ellis suggested Augusta.[1]

The two French forts, Toulouse and Tombigbee, together with the ill-starred Fort Loudoun, should be demolished. In times of war, garrisons deep in the Indian country were hostages. As Ellis explained, "without the good will of the Savages such Forts are untenable and with it they are unnecessary."[2] This advice, if it had been followed in the newly occupied forts in the Northwest, St. Joseph, Miami, Owatonon, Mackinac, LaBay, Presquile, LeBeouf and Venango, would have spared British soldiers from Pontiac's warriors.

Egremont incorporated Ellis's recommendations in his instructions to Amherst and to the four southern governors, Francis Fauquier of Virginia, Arthur Dobbs of North Carolina, Thomas Boone of South Carolina, and James Wright of Georgia.[3] Edmond Atkin's death in 1761 saved him from the embarrassment of dismissal. John Stuart, a survivor of Fort Loudoun, was named his successor as a favor to Governor Boone, and the Augusta congress was Stuart's first important assignment.[4] Egremont heeded Ellis's advice to dispatch a shipload of presents to lure the Indians to Augusta and to send them away satisfied.

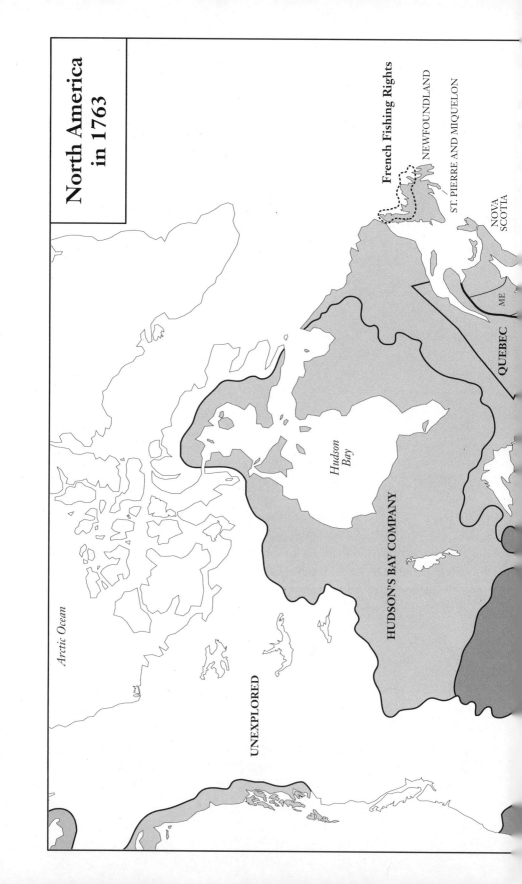

North America
in 1763

French Fishing Rights

NEWFOUNDLAND

ST. PIERRE AND MIQUELON

NOVA
SCOTIA

ME

QUEBEC

Hudson
Bay

HUDSON'S BAY COMPANY

Arctic Ocean

UNEXPLORED

3: The Proclamation of 1763 resulted in a transformation of British North America, including the ceded islands of the West Indies.

The governors were displeased about the selection of Augusta as a meeting place. They complained that the frontier town lacked the proper amenities and suggested that Charlestown would be more convenient. But the Indians preferred Augusta and sent a message that they would meet there or not at all. The governors went to Augusta in obedience to their orders from Egremont, wondering if the Creeks would actually show up.[5]

Ellis had insisted on haste because he knew that the French would upset the Indians with dire predictions about slavery and extinction. He was right. The French faction, led by the Mortar, tried to scuttle the conference by warning that the meeting was a ruse to extract more land from the Indians. On April 5, 1763, the Mortar sent Governor Wright a message that the Savannah River was the boundary set by the old emperor Brims. The white people were to drink on one side of the river and the red people on the other. This they still wished to be. Already the whites had driven away the buffalo, bear, and deer and had made the hunting poor.[6] The Gun Merchant sent a similar message in May. He had heard from the French that the English intended to take away their hunting grounds, and "it made their hearts cross to see their lands taken without their Liberty." The Gun Merchant said that he was tired of the English telling them to kill the French and the French saying that they should kill the English. He warned that those who told them to use sharp weapons might get cut themselves.[7] He was prophetic. Five British traders were murdered in the Upper Creek country between May and October. The Mortar was not responsible, nor were any of the principal chiefs, but they were certain they would be blamed. The Mortar reminded his fellow chiefs about the Cherokees who were taken hostage in Charlestown and then killed in cold blood.[8] The headmen of the Upper Creek towns decided not to go to Augusta, but a delegation of lesser chiefs and warriors did go to the congress, persuaded by the Augusta-based traders and drawn by the promise of gifts. Their leader was the then unknown Emistisiguo, who understood that he could not speak as "the mouth of the nation." He must refer any decision to the absent headmen.[9]

Some nine hundred Indians gathered in Augusta for the great congress. They were mostly Creeks from the upper and lower towns, a large representation of Cherokees, and smaller delegations of Chickasaws and Catawbas. A few Choctaws were brave enough to slip through the Creek country to Augusta.

The governors had good reason for grumbling about going to Augusta. The original purpose for holding the conference, to notify the Indians that the French were banished, had dissipated with the intervening months. The Indians were well aware that the war was over and that the French were leaving. The governors were supposed to tell their guests that past offenses were forgiven even though more recent offenses had occurred. The governors were to assure the Indians that they did not intend to ask for an inch of land. They were there, according to their instructions, to distribute presents, but John Stuart could do that; in fact, he did after the governors left Augusta. The only remaining reason for their going to Augusta was for the show. In an ironic turn of fate, Arthur Dobbs, who had dispatched Henry Ellis on a search for a northwest passage, was forced to journey to the frontier by the initiative of Henry Ellis.

The Indians were in Augusta well before the dignitaries reached the town on November 3, 1763. The arrival of the governors was announced by the firing of cannon and a parade of the Georgia rangers. With appropriate solemnity, Stuart announced to the assembled headmen that they were ready to begin. The officials were surprised to be told that the Indians were not quite ready; the Upper Creeks needed a day to confer with the Lower Creeks. The congress finally began on November 5 with a talk by John Stuart, touching on all the points in Egremont's instructions. Stuart and the governors must have been astounded when the Lower Creek chief Telletcher rose to speak and proceeded to offer the British a huge stretch of land between the Savannah and Ogeechee rivers. He described in detail where the boundary line should run; twice he was asked if he knew the lines, and twice he assured them he did.[10] Evidently, the agreement had been worked out between the Indians and the traders before the governors reached Augusta. The Georgia legislature later honored Lachlan McGillivray and George Galphin for their role in effecting the treaty. Significantly, both McGillivray and Galphin accompanied the surveyors who traced the line in 1768.[11] The governors were politicians enough to take some of the credit for the felicitous turn of events, but they made it clear to Egremont that the initiative for the cession came from the Indians. In a letter signed by all four governors, they explained that the Creeks were more tractable than they had expected and that the offer of land was voluntary.[12]

After the departure of the dignitaries, John Stuart distributed

Egremont's generous supply of presents. A listing provides a record of items which by 1763 had influenced the Indians' quality of life: the thick red cloth called strouds for the Cotswold town where it was manufactured, duffles, vermillion paint, shirts, guns, powder, balls, calico cloth, hoes, hatchets, brass pans, looking glasses, garters, trunks, gunlocks, saddles, bridles, stirrup leather, and cutlery. Stuart carefully listed each item and reported that his guests left Augusta "with all the marks of contentment and good humor."[13]

It remained for the absent Upper Creek headmen to ratify the Treaty of Augusta, and this they did on April 10, 1764, at Emistisiguo's town, Little Tallassee.[14] Why were the Indians willing to give up the Ogeechee strip when they had objected so strenuously to any encroachment? There is no clear answer; evidently, the traders convinced them that compensation had to be made for the recent killings. Besides, there were settlers at the Ogeechee already, and they could be restrained only by a line that would be like a wall, never to be passed. Emistisiguo remembered those words as spoken by Lachlan McGillivray.[15]

Henry Ellis set in motion a profound change in his former province by initiating the Augusta congress. The year 1763 was a watershed in Georgia history. Considerations of trade had dominated the backcountry since Georgia's founding, but the newcomers who poured into the Ogeechee strip had no intention of doing business with Indians. They soon clamored for more land. In a little more than a decade they would rebel against a government which they perceived as partial to the Indians and the Indian trade. The revolution in the backcountry was a war against the Indians, a war for land.

Ellis was able to assist his former province in several ways, many of them unnoticed by Georgians. At Egremont's request, the Admiralty belatedly dispatched a warship to guard the Georgia coast. Ellis's friend Charles Pryce replaced William Clifton as attorney general, and Clifton went to Pensacola as attorney general of the new province of West Florida, presumably taking his troublesome spouse with him. The obnoxious Grover, who stopped attending council meetings when Ellis left and was suspended from his office as chief justice by the long-suffering Governor Wright, was replaced by James Simpson. Ellis did a favor for his former province as well as for his Irish friend by securing for William Knox the Georgia agency.[16] One of Knox's first lobbying efforts on behalf of Georgia concerned the title to the debatable land between Florida and Georgia. Governor Wright protested that Governor Boone of South Carolina claimed that region for his province and had begun to distribute enormous grants to Carolinians. To add to the insult, when a Georgia resident requested a grant from Boone, he was denied. Wright was beside himself at the effrontery of the Carolinians.[17] Ellis was in a position to do something about the disposition of the land below the Altamaha, and he acted as Georgia's surrogate often without the knowledge of his friends in America.

Another troublesome issue that bothered Wright as much as it had Ellis was Carolina's claim to jurisdiction over the Independent Companies stationed in Georgia. Wright was unaware that Ellis was in Egremont's employ when he wrote a long complaint about the attitude of the governor of South Carolina. In the event of an Indian attack, Wright explained, Governor Boone expected Wright to notify him so that he could send orders to the Independents at Frederica. Boone threatened to arrest and court-martial any officer who took orders from Wright. Wright wrote Amherst about the patent absurdity of the situation. Amherst admitted that there was a problem but gave the same reply he had made to Ellis, namely, that the governor of South Carolina acted on instructions from the king and Amherst had no authority to interfere.[18] Actually, Amherst provided a solution to the problem of command before he turned over the responsibility to his successor, Thomas Gage, on November 17, 1763, by dispatching three companies of Royal Americans to South Carolina. The Royal Americans would replace the South Carolina Independent Companies in Georgia, and their officers were ordered to cooperate with Governor Wright.[19]

Although Georgia received Ellis's special attention during the last year of the war, it was in the context of continental concerns. Many of the king's ministers had ideas about one or another aspect of colonial policy, but few, if any, had as comprehensive a plan for the colonies as Henry Ellis proposed for the consideration of Lord Egremont in a series of papers written during the first weeks of 1763.

One memorandum bore the title "Hints relative to the settling of our newly acquired Territories in America."[20] It began with advice on the disposition of land in Canada. Canadians should have their holdings confirmed by the king so as to sever all connections with France. Ellis observed that such a system worked well in Georgia, where Trustee grants were registered and confirmed. This "judicious" Georgia policy should be followed in Florida and Louisiana, where the soil and climate were so like Georgia's.

Most of the paper was devoted to the West Indian acquisitions, which were prized because they "bid fairest to yield the most speedy and valuable returns to Great Britain," provided that they were managed properly. The French settlers on St. Vincent and Dominica should be allowed to continue in possession of their lands and should not be permitted to alienate their property for five years. Thus they would continue to produce sugar for the British trade.

An echo of Ellis's Georgia Asylum Act could be heard in his suggestion to offer protection to islanders who were debtors for a period of years together with a small grant of land on which they could support themselves. Ellis would limit grants to newcomers to five acres per person, black or white, in the settlers' families. Ellis had opposed overlarge grants in Georgia, and he insisted that no grant should exceed three hundred acres. That size was adequate for a sugar plantation in the Windward Islands. Of course, individuals could purchase land as they became more affluent. The poorer people on Barbados and the other islands should be granted small farms for raising indigo, cotton, coffee, cocoa, ginger, and such crops. Ellis's comments concerned the islands of St. Vincent and Dominica. The French planters on Grenada were protected by the terms of their capitulation in 1762 and by an article in the Treaty of Paris.[21]

The cabinet council adopted Ellis's suggested limit of three hundred acres in the case of Dominica but raised the maximum grant to five hundred acres in the larger island of St. Vincent. French inhabitants were permitted to lease land for twenty-five to forty years on the two islands. Ellis's main point, that it would be greatly to the advantage of Great Britain to encourage the French planters to remain on their plantations, was reflected by the Board of Trade in its report of November 3, 1763. A royal proclamation was issued in March of the following year, encouraging British colonization of St. Vincent, Dominica, and Granada.[22]

Another important paper Ellis wrote for Egremont was titled "Plan of Forts and Establishments proper to be made and kept up in North America for the Security of our Dominions and the Establishment of our Commerce with the Indians. The number of Regiments — their stations and in what manner the garrison's [sic] necessary in each Fort is to be kept up by Detachments from the said Regiments."[23] There follows a simple listing of regiments and the corresponding posts. The "grand stations" of the regiments were Quebec, Montreal,

Niagara, Detroit, South Carolina, Pensacola, and a new fort where the Iberville River joined the Mississippi. Two battalions of seven companies were listed for Nova Scotia. Evidently, Ellis took advantage of the opportunity to resolve the jurisdictional dispute between Georgia and South Carolina regarding command of the Independent Companies. He consigned the three Independent Companies and the two troops of Georgia rangers to St. Augustine. The suggestion was interesting but not very practical. The irascible Boone of South Carolina would not want to lose the services of the Independents, and the Georgia rangers would likely desert rather than serve in Florida. In any event, Amherst decided to disband the Independents.

Ellis's paper on the disposition of frontier defense was written sometime in December 1762 after the terms of the preliminary treaty were known but before news of the cession of Louisiana by France to Spain had reached England. One of his reasons for the western forts was to prevent "encroachments by the French." During that same month, Ellis's papers on the advantages of the treaty and the need to call a congress of Indians at Augusta were written.

Ellis's plan for the distribution of garrisons would decrease the number of western posts occupied since 1760. He did not recommend maintaining the French forts in western Pennsylvania, Presque Isle, LeBoeuf or Venango, Fort Vincennes on the Wabash, Fort Chartres on the Mississippi, Fort St. Joseph on Lake Michigan, Fort La Baye on Green Bay, and Fort St. Marie on the Straits of Michilimackinac.

According to Ellis's plan, the Montreal regiment would be responsible for Trois Rivières and Fort Frontenac on the St. Lawrence as well as Crown Point on Lake Champlain. The Niagara regiment would man Fort Duquesne (renamed Fort Pitt) and Oswego as well as Fort Niagara. The Detroit regiment would be responsible for Forts Michilimackinac and Miami and a fort to be constructed where the Illinois River joined the Mississippi.

A regiment would be assigned to a new fort at the junction of the Iberville and Mississippi rivers as well as a fort projected at the confluence of the Ohio and Mississippi rivers, at the Yazoo and Mississippi rivers, and at a point "where the Iberville joins the Sea." Ellis's plans for using the Iberville as an alternative to the Mississippi were based on a French map, copied in England and used by the Duke of Bedford in the peace negotiations.[24] The Iberville branched off from the Mississippi a hundred miles above New Orleans and was connected to

THE COURSE OF
MISSISSIPI RIVER
from Bayagoulas
to the Sea.

British Statute Miles

GULF   OF

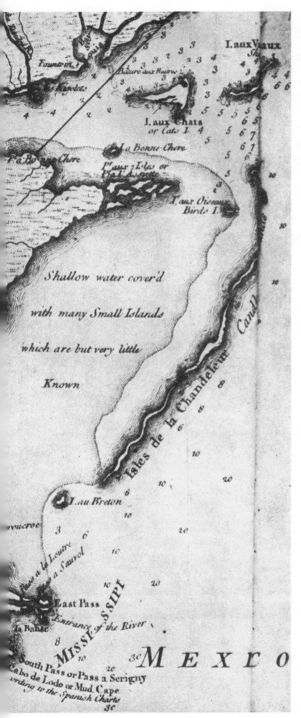

4. An English version of a French map prepared for the Duke of Bedford in his negotiations of 1762 shows the Iberville-Lake Maurepas-Lake Pontchartrain route as the shorter and apparently more practical link between the Mississippi River and the Gulf of Mexico. (From *Peace of Paris, 1763* by Zenab Rashad; courtesy University of Liverpool Press)

the Gulf by Lakes Maurepas and Pontchartrain. On paper the route seemed feasible, which explains why Bute and Bedford did not insist on possession of New Orleans in the treaty. Ellis, who gave cogent reasons for abandoning forts in the Cherokee and Creek country, recommended the new forts in Louisiana because he believed that the French would occupy New Orleans and western Louisiana. Ellis regarded the Yazoo fort as a protection for the brave Chickasaws: "They have a right to our protection, as being our ancient Allies, steady Friends and irreconcilable enemies to the French, who have long aimed at their extirpation."[25] In general, Ellis favored a policy of fortifying the borders of British territories instead of building forts in the interior. Settlement would be made safe by the screen of military posts on the perimeters.

Ellis outlined a rationale for his plan which became policy upon the council's acceptance of it. The system of posts would establish British authority in the new territories, Canada and Louisiana. The military establishment as a whole would facilitate the enforcement of British colonial policy; as Ellis put it, the posts would serve "to retain the Inhabitants of our ancient Provinces in a State of Constitutional dependence upon Great Britain."[26] Ellis, like Halifax, was hopeful that the older colonies would pay closer attention to the constitutionally correct provinces of Georgia and Nova Scotia. This reason for a military presence could and would be interpreted as a veiled threat to enforce conformity upon the American colonies.

The third reason for Ellis's proposal was to "create a proper respect for us amongst the Indians."[27] Except for Fort Duquesne in Pennsylvania and Crown Point in New York, all of Ellis's posts were located on the fringes of empire, the Great Lakes, the Mississippi, the Gulf. Therefore, he might argue that there was no contradiction between his memorandum on forts and the one of December in which he discouraged the idea of forts in the southern Indian country.

The fourth reason for his strategy was to prevent encroachments by the French. As Ellis was well aware, the French were dangerous neighbors. If he had known that Spain, rather than France, would occupy western Louisiana, he might have reduced the number of recommended forts. He had expressed the opinion earlier that Spain would be preferable to France on Britain's borders.[28]

The fifth reason given by Ellis was to be prepared for a future war, in which case the proposed posts would "protect our own and annoy the colonies and commerce of our Enemies."[29]

A nearly identical document has been attributed to General Amherst by Clarence W. Alvord and Clarence E. Carter. Most of the text is a verbatim copy of Ellis's plan. There is an insertion after the heading to the effect that the original was based on the supposition that regiments would be kept up to ten companies of seventy-five men each and on the assumption that South Carolina's Independent Companies would not be disbanded. In fact, they were, as part of Amherst's solution to the troublesome problem of jurisdiction over the Independents. Two paragraphs were added to the original; in one it was suggested that the vast interior be divided into northern and southern military districts, each under its own commander. In the other, it was noted that the plan was written when it was thought that France would control the west bank of the Mississippi. The additions were inserted after the exchange from France to Spain became known. The author saw no need to change the original suggestions; Spain might be "equally formidable in time of war." [30]

Alvord and Carter's identification of Amherst as the author of the memorandum on western forts influenced Robin Fabel, in a recent biography of West Florida governor George Johnstone, to ascribe to Amherst the idea of building a fort at the juncture of the Mississippi and Iberville rivers and clearing the Iberville channel for commerce. [31] Alvord and Carter attached a more sweeping interpretation to the document by noting that it "is one of the earliest statements by an official in favor of the rapid expansion of the settlements westward." [32] The two historians theorized that the radical expansionists wanted to encourage rapid western settlement for speculation or other reasons and the moderate expansionists favored a slower pace, which would allow tighter control of the frontier by eastern governments. One problem with their thesis is that the amended memorandum was almost certainly written by Henry Ellis and Ellis was not an expansionist. Another paper he wrote for Egremont was the genesis of the Proclamation of 1763, which prohibited settlement beyond the mountains. [33]

Ellis's suggestion about forts on the Iberville River led to an ambitious and expensive effort to open the route to commerce, which in the end proved impractical. Ellis, who had only maps to go by, was less at fault than those on the site who approved the plan. Captain James Campbell and Major Robert Farmar inspected the waterway and assured Governor Johnstone that an eight-foot channel could be opened in a month. Johnstone was convinced: "There is nothing on which

I would pawn my Reputation so soon," he wrote to John Pownall at the Board of Trade.[34] General Gage was similarly persuaded; he wrote Halifax on May 21, 1764: "It is judged that it may be cleared with much less Labour than was at first imagined."[35]

Among the Egremont Papers is an unsigned document entitled "Thoughts Concerning Florida." Robin Fabel referred to the report as "a detailed, informed, and optimistic memorandum." It was "unusually substantial" and, "despite a tendency to gloss over difficulties, impressive as positive analysis."[36] Fabel suggested that Governor George Johnstone either dictated it or had a hand in its composition. Donna T. McCaffrey found the same document among the Townshend Papers at the Clements Library in Ann Arbor, Michigan, and quoted extensively from it to illustrate Charles Townshend's plans for British East Florida. She concluded that the author of the document was on friendly terms with both Townshend and Johnstone.[37] Another candidate for authorship is Henry Ellis. It was written at a time when Florida was being disparaged by Townshend and others as a poor substitute for Havana or Puerto Rico, during December 1762 or the first part of 1763. It was a practical document on how to go about settling the Floridas, but it was also part of a promotion to justify the terms of the peace treaty.

Charles Townshend was president of the Board of Trade from March 1 to April 20, 1763. Egremont was in the habit of coaching the Board of Trade by sending advice to that body, and it is probable that the report reached Townshend by that routine process. Townshend was converted from a denigrator of Florida to a booster. He began to attend the monthly meetings of the East Florida Society of London. He became one of the most eager solicitors of grants, acquiring twenty thousand acres each for himself, his brother, and his stepson.[38] Townshend's plans for settling his property were ended by his death in 1767. The paper entitled "Thoughts Concerning Florida" might have been written by Ellis in anticipation of Lord Egremont's solicitation of advice from the Board of Trade dated May 5, 1763. When the board's authority to initiate policy was revoked in 1761, that body could offer advice only when asked. The procedure seems curious in retrospect. In effect, Egremont sent answers along with his questions and asked the board to pick one.

Egremont's questions were, What commercial advantages could be derived from the new acquisitions; how could these advantages be made permanent for "His Majesty's Trading Subjects"; what new governments should be established; what military establishment would be sufficient; what new forts should be erected and which demolished; how were the colonies to contribute to the cost of civil and military establishments; and how to retain or depart from past forms of government in Canada? Along with Ellis's papers, Egremont dispatched reports he had requested and received from Generals Amherst, James Murray, and Thomas Gage and Indian agent Sir William Johnson.[39]

Egremont's instructions to the board contained an interesting paragraph stressing the need to conciliate the Indians by mildness, by protecting their persons and property, and by "most cautiously guarding against any invasion or occupation of their hunting lands." Egremont sent instructions to the southern governors and Indian superintendent John Stuart forbidding private purchases of Indian land. The admonition to the governors and to the board was consistent with Henry Ellis's thinking and a caution against the advice in a paper attributed to Amherst that the British "should not consult the Indians pleasure."[40]

Egremont's instructions to the board continued with a request to consider the implications of the new arrangements regarding the fisheries and concluded by asking about the potential advantages of Florida. Egremont offered all the pertinent material in his office to the board. The extensive collection was saved by the meticulous Shelburne, who assumed the presidency of the board on April 20, 1763, replacing Charles Townshend.[41] Of all the papers delivered to the board, the one that commanded the attention of their lordships was one by Henry Ellis entitled "Hints Relative to the Division and Government of the Conquered and newly acquired countries in America." The importance of the document and Ellis's authorship were first recognized by Verner Crane and Clarence Alvord in 1922. R. A. Humphreys reaffirmed the attribution in his excellent article on the Proclamation of 1763 in the *English Historical Review* of April 1934. Lawrence Henry Gipson wrote that the "Hints" "was drawn up, it would appear, by Henry Ellis intimately associated with Egremont."[42]

The paper began by suggesting that Canada be divided into two provinces, Upper and Lower, with Quebec and Montreal as capitals. The civil government would consist of a governor and council at first; a general assembly would be formed later. Roman Catholics should be given the same conditions imposed in Ireland. They might retain their parish priests but would not be eligible for civil office.

The heart of Ellis's paper was the suggestion that a line be fixed upon for a western boundary for the existing provinces "beyond which our people should not at present be permitted to settle." Ellis hoped that the westward-moving settlers would be diverted to Nova Scotia in the North or Georgia and the Floridas in the South, "where they would be useful to their Mother Country instead of planting themselves in the heart of America, out of the reach of government." The military posts in the West would provide security in the Indian country, and the governors in the adjoining colonies would have jurisdiction in civil matters. Ellis's concern for Georgia and Nova Scotia is evident. The best mode of government for the new provinces, he said, was that of Georgia and Nova Scotia, "the latest formed and the freest from a Republican mixture and the most conformable to the British constitution." Georgia should be extended to the St. Marys and Florida divided into two provinces.[43]

Ellis went on to discuss the governments of the ceded islands. Granada and the Grenadines together with St. Vincent would be under the same government. Dominica and Tobago could have separate governments. The new fort in Senegal would be under the supervision of the Royal African Company, as the other African posts were.[44] R. A. Humphreys described Ellis's paper as "a remarkable document" which "enunciated important principles." He regarded as most important the two recommendations that the new governments be based on Georgia's and Nova Scotia's and that there should be a western boundary.[45]

Shelburne's personal secretary, Maurice Morgann, and the veteran secretary of the board, John Pownall, were involved in sifting through the documents submitted by Egremont and settling upon Ellis's "Hints." Pownall wrote the board's reply to Egremont dated June 8, 1763. A new element was introduced into the plan for an Indian reserve, namely, that the Indian country should be opened to free trade as opposed to the current practice of restrictive licensing. Ellis would not have made that recommendation. Pownall proposed one governor for Canada, assisted by a council, with lieutenant governors at Montreal and Trois Rivières. He agreed that Nova Scotia be enlarged by the addition of Prince Edward Island and Cape Breton and also agreed that Florida be divided into two provinces. The board would extend Georgia's boundary beyond the St. Marys to the St. Johns. Finally, all the new islands should be put under one government, with lieutenant governors for the individual islands.[46]

It was indicative of Egremont's relationship with and reliance on Henry Ellis that Egremont asked Ellis to inform him in what respects the board's reply differed from Ellis's original "Hints." Ellis quickly did so in a sharply focused memorandum. Canada would be one province instead of two. The West Indian islands would be under one government. Ellis thought that his proposals or the board's would be equally practical, and he advised following the board's suggestion. If it turned out that one government would not work well for Canada or the islands, they could be divided later.

Ellis acknowledged that the Chattahoochee would be a more proper boundary between East and West Florida than his proposal of the St. Marks River, but he strongly cautioned against giving the fertile land between the St. Marys and St. Johns to Georgia. Florida needed that region to attract settlers. In this paper, Ellis showed an objectivity free from pettiness. He did not cling to his own proposals, though he might have. In spite of his affection for Georgia, he would not extend that province farther than the St. Marys, a boundary he had fixed his mind upon long before in dealing with Edmund Gray.[47]

Ellis was quick to respond to Egremont, and as a result, Egremont was able to inform the board of his opinion only six days after the date of the board's letter to him. On July 14 he sent the message that the king agreed to the recommendation regarding Canada, the Floridas, Nova Scotia, Georgia, and the West Indian islands. He was ready with appointments: James Murray would be governor of Canada; James Grant, East Florida; George Johnstone, West Florida; and Robert Melville, the West Indian islands.[48] As was usual in such cases, the appointments represented political payoffs or favors to high-placed friends. Egremont agreed to the free trade provision in the region that was to be left unsettled. He pointed to the need for some form of government for the Indian country, however, and suggested that the governor of Canada be responsible for all the land not already included in the bounds of the old colonies. This recommendation foreshadowed the Quebec Act of 1774. It might have been a coincidence that Henry Ellis was the only royal official of Canada at the time Egremont made this suggestion. Ellis had himself named secretary of Canada as of April 30, 1763, even before Canada's form of government had been decided upon.[49]

By August 5, the board responded. It was not a good idea to give jurisdiction of the northern Indian country to Canada because it might seem an admission that French Canada extended that far. Besides, it would give one province too great an advantage over the trade of the Northwest. Instead, the military commander in chief should be given temporary jurisdiction over the Indian country. The board requested that a proclamation be issued to prevent any grant within a fixed line, leaving the West free for the Indians to hunt and "for the free trade of all your subjects." [50]

Egremont was pleased with the result of his negotiations with the board when he wrote to Grenville on August 6 that he had settled his American affairs with the king at St. James. The king was "placid and gracious." [51] In May, the king had copied the example of his predecessor by standing as sponsor to Egremont's youngest child. The christening was done in Lady Egremont's bedroom at Egremont House, Piccadilly, with the king and queen in attendance. In spite of that sign of favor, there were persistent rumors that the king was planning to replace the triumvirate. Egremont blamed Bute, "the fluctuating mind of the chief spring of all this confusion." [52]

Before August 20, the king called in Egremont and Halifax and told them he was pleased with the ministry and would not change it. The next day he told the same thing to Grenville; "he liked them all . . . he approved of their conduct," as Grenville quoted him in his diary. Grenville left the king just before noon and hurried to Egremont's house to tell him of the encouraging conversation. He met Egremont's doctor at the door and was told that Egremont had suffered a stroke of apoplexy and was beyond recovery. Grenville stayed with Egremont's family the rest of the day and sent messages to Halifax and the king. Halifax received the news at 4 P.M. and hurried to Egremont's house. Egremont died at 8 P.M. that night without regaining consciousness. Halifax and Grenville went together to St. James to tell the king. [53] The message Halifax wrote to his secretary would have been an appropriate epitaph on Egremont's tomb: "His Majesty has lost a faithful servant, I a dear and well beloved friend, and the world an honest and valuable man." [54]

Egremont's unexpected death put the American business on hold and threatened the collapse of the government. The insecure king, who had belatedly made up his mind to support his ministers, reverted to his chronic condition of uncertainty. Halifax bluntly explained the options available to him. The king could strengthen the present ministry, he could keep some of his ministers and bring in some of its critics, or he could turn the government over to Mr. Pitt. The king said he would never resort to the third option.[55]

The Duke of Bedford, who had resigned as lord privy seal earlier in the year, was invited to rejoin the government. He declined because he was not certain that Grenville and Halifax were strong enough to carry Parliament, even with his support. He urged the king to summon Pitt. The king again refused. Bute, however, persuaded the king to ask Pitt upon what terms he would join the government. This drama fascinated everyone connected with the court. Halifax noted that Pitt spent three hours with the king on August 27. He thought that was a sign that the king was not ready to capitulate to Pitt: "I should think that Carte Blanche might have been given in less than three minutes."[56]

Indeed, Pitt's terms were too high. Pitt would put Charles Townshend in Halifax's place, and he would assume his old post of secretary for the Southern Department. He would bring in Temple, Newcastle, and Hardwicke. He refused to serve with the treaty makers, Grenville and Bedford. The king asked if Pitt would abide by the terms of the treaty of peace. Pitt said he would "ameliorate" the treaty. The king was not sure what that meant. Bedford explained to a friend that he thought Pitt would disavow the peace and discard anyone who voted for it. Bedford understood that Pitt intended to prosecute him in criminal court for his prominent part in negotiating the treaty.[57] The irony was that Bedford had urged the king to approach Pitt.

To the king, Pitt merely hinted that he could not abandon his friends who had stood by him. The king asked how Pitt could expect him to abandon the ministers who served him faithfully. Pitt replied that the people would blame the ministers, not the king. The ministry, he said, was a "Tory Administration"; it was not founded on true principles of the revolution. In effect, Pitt told the king to reject his ministers because they were too much inclined to do the king's bidding. No wonder the king ended the interview by saying that Pitt's terms were too hard.[58]

Incredibly, Bute persuaded the king to have another talk with Pitt. He thought Pitt might form his own ministry if he would leave Temple out of it for a while; after six months or so, Temple might be brought in. If Bute actually made that suggestion, and Grenville believed that he did, it would have required the king to invite the sponsor of Wilkes to join his government. In any case, Pitt refused again to come in without

Temple, and the king had no choice but to put his reliance on Grenville. Although Grenville was later criticized for browbeating the king on the subject, one can understand why he insisted that the king have no further connection with Bute. He would ask Bedford and Bedford's ally Sandwich to join the government, but neither was his friend and they might be too strong for him. Grenville's only chance of success lay in the king's unwavering support, and the king was not capable of such steadfastness.

Grenville was surprised to learn from the king that Shelburne intended to resign from the presidency of the Board of Trade. The king explained that the business of the board was disagreeable to Shelburne because it was "attended with too many difficulties" and required "too close an attendance." [59] The business Shelburne found disagreeable certainly included the drafting of the proclamation concerning the American colonies. Perhaps he was overwhelmed by the mass of documents delivered by Egremont and he was not satisfied with the uncomplicated approach of focusing on Henry Ellis's "Hints" and disregarding other issues. William Knox came to know Shelburne well and said that he was difficult to please; he was "never satisfied with what anyone did, or even with what he did himself." [60]

On September 6, several days after learning about Shelburne's resignation, Grenville discovered that Bute had intrigued with Shelburne to topple the triumvirate. As early as August 8, about the time Egremont told the king that his American affairs were all but settled, Shelburne sent a message to Pitt that the ministry could not last.[61] According to Knox, Halifax and Egremont were aware of Shelburne's "intriguing and ambitious spirit." Pownall took Shelburne's side and "could not endure" Ellis's influence over Egremont.[62] Given the Byzantine politics of the time, it is surprising that any American policy was concluded. It would appear, however, that Grenville and Halifax were determined to follow through on Egremont's unfinished business. Halifax agreed to move from the Northern Department to become secretary of state for the Southern Department. The apparent reason was that he knew more about America than anyone else in government. It was agreed that Bedford would hold the honorific post of lord president of the council and Sandwich would move from the Admiralty to take the Northern Department. Sandwich assumed that he would replace Egremont in the triumvirate but soon learned otherwise. Grenville told him that "no man could stand to him in the degree of nearness and dearness of friendship that Lord Egremont had." [63] Bedford also wanted a share in the distribution of offices. Grenville secured Halifax's consent to keep control of patronage himself. Thereafter, Bedford and Sandwich were unhappy members of the ministry.

Halifax acted wisely in bringing in an ally to head the Board of Trade. He had worked with Wills Hill, Lord Hillsborough, in Ireland and liked and trusted him. Hillsborough kissed the king's hands on September 9, the same day Halifax and Sandwich assumed office. Halifax had a massive amount of work to catch up on, but as a member of the council and an intimate of both Egremont and Ellis, he was aware that an American policy was under consideration. Henry Ellis must have been of inestimable help to Hillsborough, who had not previously been involved. Ellis became and remained a warm friend of Hillsborough's. John Pownall had no choice but to become more cordial toward Ellis with the change in attitude of his superiors.

Halifax's papers are scattered, and Ellis's correspondence with his patron has not survived. It can be assumed, however, that Henry Ellis was at the height of his influence and his career in September 1763 when Halifax and Hillsborough took up their duties. Ellis had had a close relationship with Halifax since his return from Hudson Bay fifteen years before. Halifax had appointed Ellis to the governorships of the two provinces in America with which he was most concerned. Because of the absence of documentation, it is impossible to discover precisely what influence Ellis exerted, but that he did have influence is reflected in a comment about Ellis by a Pennsylvanian who was in London at the time: "Lord Halifax, who happens to be his godfather, it is said listens to him as though he was an Oracle of Truth. He has had no small share in the late events." [64] The godfather reference cannot be substantiated, but the general perception was that Halifax and Ellis were as close as godfather and godson.

With Ellis's help, Halifax prepared a report to the Hillsborough Board of Trade on September 19, 1763, which set in motion the last stages of the American proclamation. He agreed with the August 5 report of the board and its recommendation that Canada's jurisdiction be limited. He outlined the points to be covered by a royal proclamation: the prohibition "for the present" of any grant or settlement within an Indian boundary, the definition of the boundaries of the new colonies as well as Nova Scotia and Georgia, a description of their constitutions, a declaration permitting free trade among the Indian tribes, an order allowing the military to police the Indian country, and a policy on bounty grants in America to veterans residing in America.[65]

Did Ellis have a hand in the final drafting of the proclamation? There is a curious bit of internal evidence that he did. In the report of June 8 the board suggested the St. Johns River as the boundary of Georgia. Egremont clearly stated in his response of July 14 that he approved the bounds of Georgia "as suggested." Yet in the final draft of the proclamation, Ellis's boundary, the St. Marys, prevailed. There is also external evidence of Ellis's involvement. A contemporary of Ellis's, Francis Maseres, asserted that William Grant, who was then in London, saw the draft of the proclamation and it was in Ellis's handwriting. Maseres later referred to Ellis as the one "who drew that unfortunate proclamation."[66] As Halifax's resident authority on America and the initiator of the ideas in the proclamation, Ellis was a logical choice to finish the job. The draft was studied by the board on September 29 and 30. On October 1, 1763, Charles Yorke, the attorney general, gave the document his approval, with particular attention to the phrase that civil and criminal cases would be determined "as near as may be agreeable to the laws of England." The purpose of the provision was to encourage the migration of British subjects to Canada and elsewhere, but it created confusion among the French inhabitants, who were not accustomed to the laws of England.[67]

The finished product was approved by the cabinet council on October 5, and commissions were ordered for the governors, Murray, Grant, Johnstone, and Melville. On October 7 the proclamation received the royal assent. From first to last, no single individual played a more prominent role than Henry Ellis in initiating and enacting the proclamation. No other action of the British ministry except the treaty of peace had such an effect on the American colonies. British Canada was named Quebec and its boundaries were defined, two Floridas and the West Indian governments had their inception, Georgia's potential was enormously increased by the addition of the debatable land below the Altamaha and the addition of eastern Louisiana, and Nova Scotia was enlarged by Prince Edward Island and Cape Breton.

The Indian country was profoundly affected. Private purchases of Indian land were forbidden; if Indians disposed of land, it could be to the king alone. No grants were allowed beyond the heads of any rivers that fell into the Atlantic. Anyone settled beyond that line should "forthwith remove themselves." Trade was to be free and open to all persons who took out licenses and paid a security deposit. This meant that persons with licenses from Virginia, North Carolina, South Carolina, Georgia, or the Floridas could trade in the Creek country, which had previously been limited to a restricted number of Georgia and South Carolina traders. The proclamation thus inaugurated a decade-long policy of restricting westward migration in favor of exploitation of Indian trade. The policy was consistent with the overall promotion of trade and commerce, a cause to which Halifax and Ellis had long been devoted.

The restriction on westward movement was difficult to enforce, and the proclamation line was continually shifted by successive treaties arranged by the Indian superintendents. The opening of the Indian country to trade was an idea contributed not by Ellis but by Shelburne's board. The Indian country was quickly overrun by swarms of traders, many of them unlicensed, unscrupulous, and unaccountable. Governor Wright of Georgia was led to complain to the Earl of Shelburne that the new packhorsemen and servants of traders were "generally the very worst kind of people" and "the person who wrote that proclamation was unacquainted with Indian affairs." [68] The irony was that Wright did not know that Shelburne was probably responsible for inserting the open trade clause into the proclamation.

In an age when good deeds done for great men brought tangible rewards, it might be expected that Henry Ellis would be generously provided for, and, indeed, that was the case. A document in the Egremont Papers in Ellis's handwriting indicates that Ellis was able to take his choice of offices. He chose a combination of minor offices in Canada, secretary of the province, clerk of council, commissary, or steward general, and clerk of enrollments for registering of all deeds and conveyances. The offices returned him a total stipend of £1,012 annually, better than the governor's £1,000 salary, and were granted for life. Egremont secured the sinecures for him in April 1763.[69] In addition, Ellis was confirmed as provost marshal and marshal of the Admiralty for Granada, St. Vincent, Dominica, and Tobago, which brought in £1,650 annually. Under the circumstances, Ellis decided that he could afford to relinquish the governorship of Nova Scotia to Lieutenant Governor Montague Wilmot, and Wilmot was named governor on October 23, 1763.[70]

Joseph Read, an American student in London, reported that Ellis's patron, Lord Halifax, had procured sinecures for Ellis which "bring him near £800 per annum." Read would have been more impressed if he had known that Ellis received three times that amount. If Henry Ellis was aware of his own importance and began to comport himself accordingly, he had earned the right. Read noted that Ellis was "distinguished here for the romantic extravagant liberties he gives himself in conversation."[71] Read thought that there was little basis for Ellis's conversational extravagances, but Read did not know that Ellis had learned his lessons well as governor of Georgia, nor did Read realize that Ellis had played a key role in the transformation of British North America. Read did not explain the nature of the "romantic liberties" Ellis engaged in, except that they concerned America. The remark was the first critical comment about Ellis's deportment since Swaine, the clerk of the *California*, had objected to Ellis's airs. It was an indication that Ellis had taken on a role he would play with increasing skill, that of a man of many parts, a consummate conversationalist, a gentleman of the Enlightenment, a romantic who had risked his life in icy Arctic waters and had smoked the peace pipe with painted Indians.

CHAPTER TWELVE   *Echoes of the Proclamation*

HE PROCLAMATION of
1763 reverberated through-
out North America, setting
off repercussions that loos-
ened the fabric of the peace settlement. The prohibition on western
settlement beyond the mountains angered land-hungry frontier people
and profit-minded speculators alike and only delayed rather than prevented encroachment on Indian land. The Indian trade suffered as hundreds of unscrupulous characters invaded the Indian country south of
the Ohio River; in theory, they were answerable to one of the southern
governors but in practice responsible only to their employers, the merchant traders in Augusta, Mobile, or Pensacola. The promise of government by elected representatives caused unforeseen political turmoil
in Canada, the two Floridas, and Grenada. In the first three provinces
the governors quarreled with the chief justices, who insisted on convoking a general assembly as promised by the proclamation. A decade
of confusion was capped by a decision by Lord Chancellor Mansfield in
1774 that any and all ordinances, provincial or Privy Council, enacted
after 1763, were null because of the king's pledge in the proclamation
to grant representative government.[1]

   In the absence of a complete collection of Halifax papers, it is difficult to ascertain what part Henry Ellis played in the implementation
of the proclamation. Most likely he was consulted in the preparation
of the administration's plan for regulating the Indian trade proposed
in 1764. By it, trade was to be fixed north of the Ohio at the military posts, below the Ohio to designated towns in the Indian country.
The agent for the northern district would be allowed three deputies,

the southern, two. The southern agent would be permitted to assign a resident commissary in each Indian nation, as well as an interpreter and a blacksmith. A recommendation made by Ellis to William Pitt in 1759 was included in the plan. Superintendents in each district were advised to grant commissions to headmen in each village to make them responsible for the proper conduct of the trade on the part of the Indians.[2]

Although Ellis's connection with other aspects of the proclamation is not clear, his involvement in Canadian affairs is a matter of record. He was the first civil officer of Canada. His appointment to the multiple positions of secretary of province, clerk of council, commissary general, and clerk of enrollments dated from April 1763. In that year Canada was under military rule established by Amherst in 1760. General James Murray was military governor of Quebec, General Thomas Gage of Montreal, and Lieutenant Colonel Ralph Burton of the district of Trois Rivières. British merchants were invited to set up business in Canada, and Canadians were permitted wide latitude in maintaining their traditions and customs. Egremont complimented Amherst on December 12, 1761, on "the laudable gentleness and mildness with which you offer his [majesty's] royal protection to all." Egremont cautioned against alienating the French "habitants."[3]

Word that Egremont was preparing a proposal for a civil government for Canada reached Quebec by the summer of 1763. It became known that Henry Ellis had been appointed to his several sinecures and that he was acting as adviser to Egremont on American appointments. Any one of the recently arrived English merchants could have been the source of information. William Grant, who claimed to have seen a draft of the proclamation in Ellis's handwriting, might have been responsible for the rumor that Ellis was involved in establishing a government for Canada.[4]

As a result, Major Alexander Johnstone, Murray's nephew, wrote a letter to Egremont which provides unusual insight into Henry Ellis's reputation in the third year of the reign of George III. Johnstone had heard that the new governor of Canada would be Lieutenant Colonel Ralph Burton and not Murray. He argued that "naming an inferior who had acted under his command to supersede him" would disgrace Murray. He deserved better from Egremont. Johnstone then related what he had heard: "It is not it seems from your Lordship he is to receive this wound, but from a Gentleman (I mean Mr. Ellis) whose displeasure he has unhappily fallen under and who has for some time by past assumed a character without doors of acting as minister for North America." Murray did not know Ellis, and Ellis was ignorant of the general's merits: "One has been acting in the Field of North America while the other has been employed in private meditation for the good of the state nearer the Chambers of St. James where good men receive the reward of their Toils."[5] Johnstone had to contain his anger and not be too critical of Ellis for fear of offending Lord Egremont.

Ellis's objection to Murray, as Johnstone understood, was that three other Scots were being named governors of Florida and the ceded islands and therefore Canada should go to an Englishman such as Burton. "Mr. Ellis who uses this argument and who has not lately stirred out of London, has received offices worth all the four governments, and hardly any man knows where he was born," and therefore questions of birthplace should not be a consideration in appointments.[6]

Johnstone had also heard that Ellis was not pleased with Murray's temper and manners. "It cannot be expected he should possess all that politeness, condescension and affability for which this gentleman is so noted."[7] Evidently Ellis's reputation for urbane behavior was known by this time, even in Canada.

Johnstone concluded by assuring Egremont that "in contradiction to any evil impressions his enemy may endeavor to make," Murray would serve him faithfully and well as governor. The letter was dated July 13. Johnstone need not have worried. On July 14, 1763, Egremont sent to the Board of Trade the names of the new governors, including James Murray for Canada. Johnstone's letter is revealing in several instances. It indicates that Murray had already incurred the displeasure of the newly arrived English merchants, which would soon cause an open rupture. Murray had no love for Lieutenant Colonel Burton, and when Murray was named governor, he lost his military command to Burton, which caused him intense annoyance. Finally, Johnstone's letter demonstrates that Henry Ellis had become someone to reckon with in the chambers of St. James, an important personality in court circles.

Ellis and Murray were both caught up in the tangled web of Canadian politics. News of Murray's appointment as governor of the province of Quebec arrived in Canada on August 10, 1764, a date that marked the end of military and the beginning of civil government. Henry Ellis farmed out his offices to James Goldfrap as of July 20, 1764. Goldfrap also secured the post of deputy provost marshal from the patentee Nicholas Turner. As deputy provost marshal, Goldfrap had the important responsibility of summoning juries and executing court orders. Governor Murray complained that Goldfrap could neither read nor speak French.[8]

Whatever faults Murray imputed to Goldfrap, they were nothing in comparison to his successor. On January 15, 1766, Henry Ellis named George Allsopp deputy clerk of council and provincial secretary. Allsopp was one of the first English merchants to arrive in Quebec after the British victory on the Plains of Abraham. He first drew Murray's attention by protesting the "lantern order," which required civilians and private soldiers to carry lanterns after dark but exempted officers. Allsopp and his friends took exception to that and other examples of what they took to be military arrogance. They welcomed the proclamation and its guarantee of representative government. They objected when Murray allowed Canadians to practice law in the inferior courts and Catholics to serve on juries. They were angered by Murray's reliance on government by council and his reluctance to convoke an assembly. They took advantage of the grand jury session in the fall term of 1764 to outline their grievances. Among their recommendations was that all public accounts should be brought before the grand jury because it was the only representative body in the province.[9]

Murray was furious at Allsopp and the other British members of the jury and threatened prosecution. The merchants drew up a petition criticizing Murray and hired an agent to represent their cause in London. They complained that the Indian trade had not been opened as required by the proclamation. They said that Murray discounted the Protestant religion by not providing a place to worship; they listed "vexatious ordinances," "suppression of remonstrances," and a general "rudeness of language and demeanor" in the governor. They hoped for a governor "acquainted with other maxims of Government than Military only" and reminded the board that the proclamation promised a representative assembly composed of Protestants.[10] The petition was signed by a committee headed by George Allsopp. Murray denounced them all as "Licentious Fanaticks." By contrast, he considered the Canadian people the "bravest and best race upon the Globe." He defended his policy of admitting Canadians to juries and argued that they should have their own judges. The king's ministers agreed with Murray and by an ordinance of July 1, 1766, permitted Canadians to

sit as jurors in all civil and criminal cases and admitted them to practice law.[11]

Right or not, Murray became so embroiled in arguments with
his British subjects that he was recalled to answer the charges against
him. The final act that led to his recall was his refusal to recognize
Ellis's appointment of George Allsopp as deputy clerk of council and
secretary of the province. Even before Ellis actually entered into the
arrangement with Allsopp, Murray was prepared to contest Ellis's right
to assign deputies. The journal of the Board of Trade indicates that on
May 14, 1766, the board considered a letter Murray wrote on November 25, 1765, regarding a dispute he had with Ellis over the power
of appointment. Evidently, Ellis was not dissuaded from challenging
the governor because on January 15, 1766, Ellis named Allsopp as his
deputy. Allsopp paid Ellis £340 and agreed to annual payments of £300
per year. On April 11 Allsopp presented his credentials to Murray.[12] The
quick-tempered governor immediately suspended Allsopp and vented
his frustration in a letter to the Board of Trade on April 14, 1766. He
explained that Allsopp's behavior ever since the establishment of civil
government had been "most notorious." He blamed Allsopp for instigating the dissension between civilians and the military and for arranging the insulting grand jury presentment. Allsopp's chief occupation
in life, according to Murray, was troublemaking. The "meaness of his
character and the mediocrity of his parts" had rendered his efforts in-
effectual so far, but his elevation to a government post would provide
too wide a scope for mischief. Murray concluded with a defiant statement that nothing short of a direct order from the king himself would
prevail upon him to accept the unspeakable Allsopp. He dispatched a
copy of his letter to Henry Ellis.[13]

British merchants in Quebec did not share Murray's low opinion of Allsopp. Canadian historian Hilda Neatby characterized him as
"a man of ability and some education."[14] Indeed, Henry Ellis was too
conscious of his own reputation to appoint an unsavory character as
his deputy. On April 14, three days after his suspension by Murray,
Allsopp had already gathered signatures of thirty-seven English merchants stating that they had known the deputy designate for five years
and were ready to testify that he was an "upright trader and an honest
man." Two weeks later, the busy Allsopp had secured the signatures
of thirty-eight French Canadian merchants on his behalf. He then ob-

tained twenty-three signatures from Montreal merchants, ten from the English port city of Bristol, and four from London merchants, two of whom were members of Parliament. Henry Ellis gathered all these depositions and testimonials and presented them to the Board of Trade for its review. The board usually recalled governors from troubled provinces, ostensibly to give them a fair hearing but actually to remove them with minimal embarrassment. So it was in Murray's case. On April 1, 1766, Henry Conway, Halifax's successor as secretary of state for the Southern Department, instructed the governor to report to London forthwith.[15]

In preparation for the Murray hearing, Henry Ellis wrote a report summarizing Canadian affairs from the conquest in 1760 to May 1766. The history began with a reminder that Murray was instructed to institute a civil government and convoke a house of representatives as soon as the circumstances of the province would permit. In the meantime, the governor would issue ordinances with the consent of council; such ordinances were not to be repugnant to the laws of England. The levying of taxes was not permitted because that privilege required the consent of a representative assembly. With the advice of council, the governor was empowered to erect courts and appoint justices of the peace, using Nova Scotia as a model.[16]

The introduction of civil government, Ellis's report continued, "seems to have disgusted the military." Military officers who were appointed to civil posts alienated the British merchants. Ellis acknowledged that the governor must have found it difficult to please both military and the civilian officials; "by steering a middle course he seems to have disgusted both parties."[17]

Ellis noted that Murray continued the French practice of granting monopolies to trading and fishing merchants. He commented that it seemed to him "very extraordinary when a conquered country is wholly converted into an English province that it should retain any part of that servitude and vassalage which attended its conquest." The report then took up the religious question as one that had not been resolved. Ellis advised against extending the penal laws of Great Britain to any part of America. The only way to gain the loyalty of the Canadians was to treat them with the utmost leniency. Judges should be skilled in the French language. All official documents should be printed in French. Canadians should serve on juries. When an assembly was actually called, however, only the English language ought to be used. Ellis believed that such a requirement would prompt Canadians to learn English so they could be elected. He concluded with the hope that, "if the laws of Great Britain or an ill administration do not create a real Distinction in that Country between Roman Catholics and Protestants that all formal Distinctions will soon be forgotten, or at least be productive of no ill consequences." [18] Ellis's report was added to the accumulating Quebec file.

The lords commissioners listened as Murray answered the charges against him, and they agreed with him that the allegations were "groundless scandalous and derogatory," but they did not allow Murray to return to Canada. Instead, Lieutenant Governor Guy Carleton was confirmed as governor. [19] Francis Maseres, who went to Canada with Carleton in 1766 as a new attorney general, penned a harsh judgment of the previous administration. He accused Murray of following the policy of "divide and govern" by encouraging the "popish religion." "It will therefore be a dreadful Curse," said Maseres, "if ever he should come here again as Governor." [20] Murray, unlucky in a civilian role, had to be satisfied with a return to the military and promotion to the rank of lieutenant general.

George Allsopp and his fellow merchants rejoiced in Murray's departure and, indeed, were largely responsible for it. It could be argued that the authors of the proclamation, including Henry Ellis, were also responsible. Murray could not reconcile the promise of an English system of government in a province composed almost entirely of people who did not understand English law and who were barred from government by their religion. Murray might at least have ended the French practice of granting trading monopolies, as required by the proclamation, but he was reluctant to do even that. Therefore, Allsopp and his friends welcomed Guy Carleton in the fall of 1766 as the man who would enforce the Proclamation of 1763.

At first, the prospects were encouraging. Carleton reversed Murray's policy of granting monopolies. George Allsopp had set up a trading house on the upper St. Lawrence River in defiance of Murray's order. In Murray's absence, the council voted to tear the post down. Allsopp complained to Carleton, who hastily convoked a few members of the council and rescinded the order. The members of the council who had not been invited, mainly because they were friends of Murray, wrote a remonstrance. Carleton displayed some of Murray's impetuosity by dismissing the two principal remonstrators. Allsopp's victory was complete when his appointment was upheld by the Board of Trade, and he was installed as deputy clerk of council and secretary of the province.[21]

The constant human components in the transformation of French Canada into British Quebec were Allsopp and his fellow British merchants, the wealthy landowners called seigneurs whose favor both Murray and Carleton cultivated, the relatively few French merchants, the silent masses of French habitants, and, in London, Henry Ellis, his friend the Earl of Hillsborough, and the man Ellis heartily disliked, the Earl of Shelburne, whose interest in American affairs waxed when he was in office and waned when he was not.[22] Hillsborough succeeded Shelburne as president of the Board of Trade on September 9, 1763. He was replaced by the Earl of Dartmouth on July 20, 1765, but returned to his post on the board on August 16, 1766, in time to deal with Murray. Lord Clare, a mutual friend of both Hillsborough and Ellis, succeeded Hillsborough in December 1766. When the latter became secretary of state for the American colonies on January 20, 1768, he chose to preside over the Board of Trade. From August 2, 1766, until October 21, 1768, Shelburne was secretary of state for the Southern Department with responsibility for American affairs.

Shelburne and Hillsborough differed in temperament, politics, and policy. Hillsborough consistently followed the principles suggested by Ellis in his draft of the proclamation, particularly in the restriction on western settlement and in the regulation of Indian trade. Shelburne may have been responsible for the free trade clause in the proclamation, which was as impractical as it was ideal, and Shelburne was not averse to western land speculation and settlement. Neither man was quite sure what to do about Canada.

When he assumed office as secretary of state in 1766, the scrupulous Shelburne decided not to rely on the reports gathered by his predecessors. Instead, he sent his personal secretary, Maurice Morgann, to find out what reforms were needed in Canada. Francis Maseres, the attorney general, reflected the opinion of the provincial officials. He considered Morgann to be a busybody. "Mr. Morgann, the legislator, as we are to call him . . . is a well-bred agreeable man but not a lawyer, and he has a pompous way of talking that seems borrowed from the House of Commons."[23] Morgann later complained that his expense account was not adequate "to my situation in the ordinary character of a gentleman." He remained in Canada for a year, and by the time he returned, his patron was no longer in office. The unfortunate secretary did not receive the patronage or the honors he expected as a reward for his labors.[24]

Meanwhile, Carleton had become as thoroughly captivated by the Canadians as Murray was before him. On December 24, 1767, he wrote a strong note to Shelburne reminding the earl that Canadians were not "a migration of Britons." They had their own system of law and government, which had been suddenly overturned and strange new laws imposed. Carleton was moved to a flight of rhetoric; it was, he said, "a sort of severity, if I remember right, never before practiced by an Conqueror." The natural rights of men were violated in the case of the Canadians, even if they did not yet realize it. Judges sent over from England introduced "all the Chicanery of Westminster Hall into this impoverished Province." Carleton's solution was to repeal Murray's ordinance of 1764 and to restore Canadian laws, altered as needed.[25]

A month later, Carleton parted company with his new attorney general. Francis Maseres had "egged on" a tavern keeper named John McCord to get up a petition for an elected assembly. Carleton agreed with the "better sort" of Canadians who feared nothing more than popular assemblies, British or French. Carleton decided that the British model of colonial government was not suited to Canada.[26]

It fell to Hillsborough, who assumed the new post of American secretary on January 20, 1768, to reply to Carleton. He took exception to the accusation that the administration in 1763 had callously disregarded Canadian rights: "I certainly know what was the intention of those who drew the Proclamation, having myself been concerned therein." Hillsborough did not know Egremont well, but he was a close friend of Halifax, having worked with him in Ireland, and through Halifax he had met Henry Ellis. When he was brought into the ministry as president of the Board of Trade in September 1763, he was thoroughly briefed by Halifax and Ellis. "It never entered Our Idea to overturn the Laws and Customs of Canada with regard to Property," he said.[27]

Hillsborough invited Ellis to join the government when he became secretary of state for America. Ellis revealed the offer to his Irish friend William Knox on December 27, 1767, in a letter from Bath. Ellis told Hillsborough that he was grateful for the expression of confidence but that he had decided never again to take up public business. He did meet with Lord Clare, president of the Board of Trade, and together they agreed to nominate Knox and the veteran secretary of the board John Pownall to act as under secretaries to Hillsborough.[28]

When Knox was chosen by Hillsborough, Ellis sent his congratulations. Knox deserved the appointment, the public would benefit by his proven ability, and Hillsborough would be helped in the important work to be done in America. Ellis referred affectionately to Hillsborough as one "whose great kindness must ever interest me in his happiness." Ellis looked forward to a "confidential chit chat" with Knox. There were things he wanted to discuss which he preferred not to put on paper.[29] With Hillsborough and Knox managing American affairs, he expressed better hopes of resolving colonial problems than ever since they began.

Hillsborough's assumption of office coincided with Ellis's decision to resign his Canadian posts. The positions of provincial secretary, clerk of council, commissary general, and clerk of enrollments had been assigned to him for life in April 1763. If the offices were intended to be sinecures, they did not turn out to be. Ellis's deputies Goldfrap and Allsopp had involved him in their controversies. The Board of Trade called upon him from time to time for information and advice. By 1768, Ellis decided to relinquish the Canadian offices while continuing to hold the less demanding post of provost marshal of the ceded islands.[30] Even out of office, Ellis was identified with the administration. He wrote his friend John Ellis from the Belgian village of Spa, the new resort of the European gentry, to give the message to Hillsborough that "I have many a battle to fight for him here where we have an uncommon number of English." The Wilkes brand of factionalism was fashionable, and Ellis used his considerable talents as an authority and wit to contend against those he considered "extravagantly wrongheaded."[31] Ellis maintained his connections with America and particularly with Canada through William Knox.

Knox and John Pownall, Hillsborough's under secretaries, were inundated with advice about a Canadian policy. Maurice Morgann, Francis Maseres, and Governor Carleton submitted reports. Carleton disagreed with Maseres, whom he considered to be too anti-Catholic, and sent him home on a leave of absence. When the disgruntled British merchants named Maseres their agent, however, Carleton hurried to London to counteract Maseres's influence and lobby for a generous policy. Carleton had become the champion of the Canadians, just as Murray was before him. Not satisfied with the conflicting reports from

Canada, Hillsborough asked for opinions from the highest-ranking law officers, Attorney General Edward Thurlow, Solicitor General Alexander Wedderburn, and Advocate General James Marriott. Each composed lengthy reports which conflicted with the others. The multiplicity of reports delayed rather than expedited a resolution of the issue.

Meanwhile, Hillsborough was brought down by a different matter, which, like Canada, had its inception in the Proclamation of 1763. Henry Ellis had suggested in his original "Hints" that Canada be given jurisdiction over the old Northwest Territory. Pownall, in his response on behalf of Shelburne, objected on the grounds that the action would seem to validate the prewar French claims to the region. The result was that there was no civil government for the Northwest, yet there were French Canadians living there in Detroit, Kaskaskia, Cahokia, and Vincennes.

From this beginning, Shelburne was regarded as being well disposed toward Virginia's claim to the region and therefore to colonize the territory. Speculative companies were organized almost on an annual basis, among them the Ohio Company, the Susquehannah, the Loyal, the Mississippi, the Indiana, and, in 1769, the Grand Ohio. This last company included seventy-two shareholders, among whom were three members of Lord North's council, secretary for the Southern Department, Lord Rochford, whom William Knox described as "needy and dissolute"; the president of the council, Lord Gower; and the Lord Chamberlain Hertford. None were friends of Hillsborough, Halifax, or Grenville. Earl Temple was a shareholder, as were under secretaries Robert Wood, Richard Jackson, and Grey Cooper. Pennsylvanians Benjamin Franklin and Joseph Galloway were also members of the company. The company petitioned for a grant of 2.4 million acres in the Ohio country. The council referred the petitioners to the Board of Trade, which Hillsborough had presided over since taking office as secretary for America. A dramatic moment occurred when Franklin presented the company's request for the nearly two and a half million acres. Hillsborough's reply dripped with sarcasm. Why not ask for more, enough to make a province? Why not twenty million? In fact, he would present the request to the council himself, he said.[32]

Hillsborough's plan to defeat the company by making the request ridiculous boomeranged on him. Incredibly, the council approved the grant for twenty million acres for the same price the company had offered for 2.4 million acres. There was nothing for Hillsborough to do but to resign and fight the measure out of office. Henry Ellis applauded Hillsborough's decision as an honorable one. Benjamin Franklin was jubilant. "At length we have got rid of Lord Hillsborough," he wrote. Franklin wrote a savage attack on Hillsborough, which caused a sensation but probably hurt the cause of his company. By it, he drew upon himself the ire of Solicitor General Wedderburn, who found legal ways to thwart the Grand Ohio Company's oversized grant.[33]

So it was that the question of speculation in western lands became an issue at the same time the problem of civil government in Canada reached its resolution. The pious and amiable Lord Dartmouth, Hillsborough's successor as American secretary, inherited the responsibility of reaching a decision. No matter what was decided upon, there would be anger and disappointment from some quarter. The hundred thousand French Canadians would grow restless under English law or the few hundred British Canadians would protest the violation of their constitutional right to a representative government.

William Knox, who with John Pownall remained in office under Dartmouth, played a major role in formulating the final bill. John Pownall sounded a note of desperation in his message to Knox on December 3, 1773. Lord North wanted a summary of the various reports on Quebec immediately: "You know how little able I am to sit down to such a work and you know nobody but you or I can do it."[34] If Knox was annoyed, it was understandable. He complained that after all the trouble in compiling advice from the most informed and learned sources, in the end, Dartmouth was left to his own judgment. After all the years of dawdling, now everything had to be done in a hurry.[35]

By an interesting coincidence, Henry Ellis called on Knox during the same December when Knox most needed help in reaching a decision about Canada.[36] The "precis" requested by Dartmouth became the draft of the Quebec Act of 1774. It began with the proclamation that created Canada, West Florida, and Grenada and changed the dimensions of Georgia, Nova Scotia, and Newfoundland. It referred to the clause promising Canadians an assembly in due time and guaranteed the benefit of the laws of His Majesty's realm of England. By an ordinance of September 17, 1764, courts were established and commissions given. Since then, doubts had arisen as to whether the previous laws of Canada had been repealed and the new ordinances were valid. Therefore, the Proclamation of 1763 must be rescinded and the hundred thousand French Canadians be guaranteed freedom of religion and their traditional laws, customs, and usages concerning property and civil rights. Further, it was proposed to extend the boundaries of Quebec to include the French settlements in the Ohio country, which were without civil government.[37]

At Dartmouth's request, Knox sent the draft of the bill to Hillsborough. The reaction was prompt. "Every reason he had against the Ohio grant urges him with tenfold strength to oppose this proceeding," Knox reported. He had "insuperable objections" to extending the boundaries to the Ohio and Mississippi rivers with its assumption that it was right and proper to settle that region.[38] Carleton's reactions were generally positive, and Knox sent his comments along with Hillsborough's to Dartmouth on April 30, 1774. The next day, Dartmouth wrote a reply to Hillsborough explaining that the cabinet was unanimous in the opinion that there had to be a government for the French subjects in the Ohio country. It was not the intention of the bill to promote settlement, however. In fact, said Dartmouth, the application of French law in the region would discourage British subjects from entering the area. The assumption was that the Northwest could continue to be reserved for the Indian trade.[39]

Although the assignment of the Ohio region to Quebec would be greeted with outrage by the inhabitants of the older Atlantic provinces, there were historical and geographical reasons for the decision. The region was connected to Quebec by the water route of the Great Lakes and the St. Lawrence, by the fur trade, and by the language, religion, and culture of the inhabitants. The Quebec Act was not intended to be a retribution for the Boston tea affair. Nevertheless, the objections raised in the House of Commons by the opposition when Lord North presented the bill on May 18, 1774, were soon echoed in America. Isaac Barré, Thomas Townsend, and especially Edmund Burke argued that the bill violated the basic rights of Englishmen. The opposition demanded to see the reports on which the legislation was based. The ministry replied truthfully that the background material was too voluminous but might have added that it was also contradictory. The House went into committee on June 2 and questioned Carleton and Maseres. Next day they examined Quebec chief justice William Hey and the government's advocate general Marriott. By then the ministry decided that these hearings were simply delaying tactics, and a request to interview Murray was defeated ninety to thirty-six. It was obvious that the opposition lacked the votes to block the measure, and attendance dropped off. When the bill was presented for its final reading on June 13, it passed by a vote of fifty-six to twenty. In the Lords, William Pitt, now the Earl of Chatham, attacked the bill as a concession to popery and despotism, but he failed to prevent passage on the same day, June 16, 1774.[40]

In its final form the Quebec Act repealed the Proclamation of 1763 insofar as it applied to Canada. It granted legislative power except in taxation to a council which had no religious test for membership. Roman Catholics were entitled to the exercise of their religion and the clergy to their accustomed dues from their parishioners. Civil and property rights would be settled by the traditional laws, but English law would be followed in criminal cases except that there was no provision for habeas corpus. Quebec's boundary was extended through Lake Ontario and the Niagara River to Lake Erie, along the western edge of Pennsylvania to the Ohio River, and down the Ohio to the Mississippi.[41]

The losers in the decade-long struggle were the British merchants in Canada and the land speculators on both sides of the Atlantic. The winners were the hundred thousand French Canadians and, at least temporarily, the Indians of the Northwest and those who did business with them. Henry Ellis was pleased at the outcome. He wrote William Knox from Liége on July 15, 1774, to congratulate him. The act was, in his opinion, "a monument of British generosity and benevolence."[42]

Ellis was not as personally concerned with the other repercussions of the Proclamation of 1763. By 1774 the results were discernible. Nova Scotia and Florida were growing into proper British provinces as anticipated. Settlers poured into the Georgia backcountry, funneled by the proclamation line, much as had been hoped. The Indian boundary had been defined all along the western frontier by a succession of treaties with the Indians.

Other results were not expected. The anglicanization of Quebec had progressed much too slowly to permit the imposition of British government. The Indian trade had degenerated as the result of the removal of monopolies. The various ministers struggled to find a method of regulating the trade and finally agreed on one in 1774, much too late.[43] It proved impossible to prevent squatters from encroaching on Indian land. Finally, the Quebec Act, though the logical conclusion of ten years' experience, infuriated Americans. Thomas Jefferson expressed the general sentiment in the Declaration of Independence, when he blamed the king "for abolishing the free system of English laws in a neighboring province, establishing therein an arbitrary government, and enlarging its boundaries, so as to render it at once an example and fit instrument for introducing the same absolute rule into these colonies."

The negative effects of the proclamation, it could be argued, were partly responsible for the second transformation of North America, that which followed from the American Revolution.

CHAPTER THIRTEEN

The Inevitable Separation

I N JOHN SHY'S essay "The Spectrum of Imperial Possibilities," Henry Ellis is presented as the prototypical hard-liner in the decade before the American Revolution. "He was the most influential adviser to the Grenville ministry 1762–63," Shy wrote. "He was asked in vain by the notoriously 'firm' Earl of Hillsborough to serve as Undersecretary of State for the colonies in late 1767, and in 1774, on the eve of war, he urged the government to take coercive measures." In short, Ellis was the type of Tory against whom the Americans rebelled. Thomas Pownall, in contrast, represented those who took a conciliatory attitude toward America. After a careful examination of Pownall's position on the controversial issues of the day, however, Shy concluded that there was not much difference between the hard line and conciliation. He disagreed with the traditional opinion that wiser ministers might have saved America for Britain: "The impulse that swept the British Empire toward civil war was powerful, and did not admit of any real choice."[1]

If the separation was inevitable, there is little need to search for "what if" scenarios. Nevertheless, some explanatory generalizations have been offered for why things fell out as they did. Historians of the imperial school, like Lawrence Henry Gipson, tend to admire the work of the British ministers and fault the Americans for taking a parochial point of view. Sir Lewis Namier and those who follow him see the ministers as the petty ones, obsessed with gossip and court intrigue. America was lost while George III searched for ministers to his liking. Franklin Wickwire reconciled the apparent contradiction by emphasizing the importance of the role of subministers such as Charles Jenkinson, John Pownall, and William Knox in providing continuity and expertise during the changing and often distracted administrations.[2] The career of Henry Ellis bolsters Wickwire's contention. Jack Sosin observed that it was not fanciful theory spun out of Whitehall ruminations that framed Britain's policy toward America but the practical experience of royal officials in America.[3] Ellis bears out that point, also.

For Ellis there was a consistency, almost an inevitability, in the chain of events that led from the Great War for the Empire to the American Revolution. From the perspective of 1790, he reflected on the events of the three decades past in a letter to William Pitt the younger. "What did Britain gain by the most glorious and successful war on which she ever engaged?" he asked. Then he answered his own question: "A height of Glory which excited the Envy of the surrounding nations and united them in the late unnatural contest with our revolted colonies—an extent of empire we were equally unable to maintain, defend or govern—the final independence of those colonies which the dispossession of the French from Canada necessarily tended to promote and accelerate, and the enormous debt of two hundred and fifty millions."[4]

Ellis's interest in America was part of his early preoccupation with the promotion of British trade. In later life he referred to "that enthusiastic passion for national glory that used to inflame me."[5] He acquired an imperial view as a sailor. His voyage to Hudson Bay contributed to the continuing search for markets in the Pacific Ocean. His assignment in Georgia was to establish a colony that would be successfully integrated into the British trading empire. Ellis's policy papers were intended to promote similar colonial arrangements in the Floridas, Nova Scotia, Quebec, and the ceded islands.

The acquisition of Spanish and French territory presented new problems. Ellis demonstrated a comprehensive view in his advice on creating an Indian reserve, locating forts, and regulating Indian trade. The debt incurred by the war and by the garrisoning of American forts caused the ministry to search for ways to raise revenue, with each new effort bringing increased resistance by the colonists until the momentum for independence became irresistible.

If Ellis had wanted to console himself in his retrospection, he might have done so by observing that Canada, Nova Scotia, Grenada, and the islands remained loyal. So did the two Floridas, except that they were returned to Spain as part of the peace settlement of 1783. Ellis's Georgia was dragged into the Revolution by the example of Carolina, but much of Ellis's work endured in the new constitution of the state of Georgia and in a heightened sense of civic responsibility on the part of the people.

Ellis realized that the independent and growing United States was a rival and a threat to the commercial dominance of Britain. America offered inducements to English artisans and manufacturers to migrate and promised opportunity to the oppressed Irish.[6] He might have taken comfort in the thought that the voyages of exploration, in which he played a part, led to the colonization of Australia and British commercial supremacy in the Pacific and that even without the thirteen colonies, England entered the nineteenth century as the mistress of the seven seas. He helped establish the Second British Empire, as Vincent Harlow has called it.

The span from September 9, 1763, until July 12, 1765, while Halifax was secretary for the Southern Department and Ellis his American "oracle," was the climax of Ellis's political career. Since his return from Hudson Bay in 1747, Ellis had served Halifax in various ways. During most of those years, Halifax had striven for the authority over the colonies which he finally exercised as secretary. Though it suffered from the fits and starts of Halifax's career, his policy was fairly consistent. Since 1749 he had attempted to bring the colonies more closely under the supervision of the royal government. Unfortunately, Halifax's papers have been scattered or lost for this most important period of his life. A biographer of Halifax concluded that the records are silent for 1764.[7] Because there are no written memorandums from Ellis to Halifax, it is not possible to determine how Ellis would have administered postwar America, though Ellis must have been consulted in the preparation of the abortive plan of 1764 to regulate the Indian trade. The plan included a system of deputies, commissaries, and other officials who would live in the Indian country. The system was expensive and depended on the Stamp Act for financing. When the Stamp Act was repealed, the regulatory scheme was dismantled.[8]

General Thomas Gage reported that the plan to fix trade at northern forts "won't answer." He urged that the system of deputies and commissaries initiated by John Stuart be continued and that their authority to put a stop to fraudulent practices be strengthened.[9] The Grenville-Halifax ministry did not last long enough to enforce the plan of 1764. When Shelburne became secretary of the Southern Department, he preferred a policy of "leaving the Trade of each Province to the particular care of that Province."[10] The governors were uncooperative. When John Stuart attempted to regulate the practices of the Virginia traders, Governor Fauquier wrote to Stuart that he would not "Suffer the Traders to be Subjected to any regulation or restrictions whatsoever."[11] Stuart sent Fauquier a copy of the Proclamation of 1763 and observed that Virginia's rules did not govern the Indian country.

Ellis must have been consulted by Halifax regarding the causes of Pontiac's uprising in 1763. Halifax's letter to Gage of January 14, 1764, contained a confidential message: "I find many persons of consideration as well in America as here are of opinion that the Indians have of late years been too much neglected."[12] Ellis certainly thought so, and he was in a position to tell Halifax his opinion of Amherst's policy. Halifax hoped that the Proclamation of 1763 with its restriction on white encroachment would remove the principal cause of Indian discontent.

There is evidence that Ellis was consulted regarding Grenville's Currency Act. He and William Knox were invited to attend the meeting of the Board of Trade to give their opinion on the emission of paper bills of credit by colonial legislatures. Ellis had issued such bills in Georgia with positive results for the economy. It is likely that he would not have wanted to prohibit the practice. Nevertheless, the board had always frowned on paper currency and on February 9, 1764, condemned its use.[13] There is no indication in the records that Ellis had any direct influence on the Sugar or Stamp acts. Halifax dutifully informed the royal governors about the new measures, but it is not likely that either he or Henry Ellis had anything to do with formulating them.

Ellis's attitude toward the Stamp Act was probably like that of William Knox, who by 1765 had offered his services to George Grenville. Knox wrote a pamphlet justifying the imposition of the Stamp Act. Parliament had full and complete jurisdiction over the property and person of every inhabitant of a British colony, he argued. He rejected the distinction between internal and external taxes. It made no sense to him to admit Parliament's right to tax a commodity while it lay at the dock but not when it was rolled into a warehouse.[14] Knox's position on the Stamp Act cost him his Georgia agency. His friend James Habersham informed him that it had "given the greatest Umbrage" in Georgia.[15]

In a sense, the long, slow policy of bringing the colonies into the orbit of British government met its crucial test in the Stamp Act. The act could have been enforced in the new provinces, even in Georgia, where Wright was as popular as Ellis had been, but the old provinces of Virginia, Massachusetts, and South Carolina would not accept Parliament's right to tax them. Halifax's efforts to influence them by setting up model governments resulted in different definitions of a constitutional government. As James Habersham told William Knox, the idea that the colonists were virtually represented in Parliament was an insult.[16] Constitutional government was government by consent of elected representatives. Halifax interpreted the American attitude correctly when during the debate over the repeal of the Stamp Act he said, "It is not the Stamp Act that is opposed, but the authority of this legislature."[17]

Halifax's attention was distracted from American business by the same ongoing court intrigues that had occupied so much of Egremont's time. The Wilkes case dragged on as Halifax used various stratagems to avoid paying a fine for the arrest of Wilkes. Charles Townshend was amused at the idea of "the virtuous and popular Halifax, pursued through all his mazes of essoigns, privileges and fines, ordinary and extraordinary."[18]

A greater distraction for the ministry was the specter of Bute and the ever-recurring rumors that the king was about to call or was thinking about calling Mr. Pitt back into his service. Grenville had insisted as a condition of accepting the leadership of government that Bute leave London and not communicate with the king. In March 1764 Charles Jenkinson, Bute's former secretary, who now worked for Grenville, told Grenville "how mournful Bute was" at his country house at Luton and "how ill-used he felt."[19] Where Bute was and what he was doing was a constant preoccupation of the ministry for months. Finally, in May 1765, Bedford and Grenville went to see the king to complain that they had heard that Bute was negotiating with Pitt, Temple, and Newcastle through the king's uncle, Cumberland. They reminded the king of his pledge to back the present ministers.[20] Soon after that interview, the ministers heard that Bute was conniving to dump Bedford. Halifax then accosted Bute and to his face said that if there were any "evil counsellor" who would advise the king to show displeasure toward Bedford, "he would be the detestation of every honest man in the nation." [21]

Besides the nuisance of the Wilkes litigation and the incessant court intrigues, there were signs that Halifax had lost his earlier capacity for work and that his health had begun to deteriorate. He alternated between enthusiasm and lack of interest in the business of his office. Grenville noted in his diary that when he and Halifax were discussing how the salaries of American officials should be paid, Halifax became "extremely heated and eager." Later, the king told Grenville that he thought Halifax "too precipitate." A coolness developed between Grenville and Halifax during the summer of 1764. In September, the king complained of Halifax's inattentiveness and his "deadness" at council meetings.[22] When American affairs were on the agenda, the secretary of state was expected to open discussion by giving his opinion. Halifax no longer did that. His passivity after his overeagerness may have been a protest against Grenville, but more likely it was caused by a physical and mental decline which Halifax experienced during the last years of his life. Although he was only forty-nine years old in 1765, he had already begun to suffer terribly from gout and jaundice.

Added to physical problems were financial ones. After his wife died, Halifax took a mistress, a Drury Lane singer named Mary Anne Faulkner. He constructed a handsome house for her in the prevailing classical mode with baroque features. The house fronted on Hampton Green and backed on Bushy Park, on the other side of which was the ranger's lodge built for Halifax by King George II.[23] The expense of keeping up two houses at Hampton, in addition to his family estate at Horton and his three-story Georgian house in Great George Street, caused Halifax to remain in public service longer than he should have. His growing debility might not have been so apparent if he had remained out of public office after 1765, when the Rockingham administration replaced Grenville's. When his nephew Lord North became head of government in 1770, Halifax sought for and was given the post of secretary of state for the Northern Department. He died on June 8, 1771, five months after taking office, at the age of fifty-five.

Richard Cumberland, Halifax's scholarly secretary, who preferred poetry and playwriting to politics, displayed a keen insight in his memoirs. He had no use for John Pownall, who had an overblown notion of his own importance. Halifax also hurt Cumberland's sensitive soul on several occasions by his lofty manner, but Cumberland could overlook arrogance in great lords. Cumberland was genuinely saddened by Halifax's failure to live up to the promise of his early life. In a sentence remarkable for its length as well as for its perception, he wrote:

> I am persuaded he was formed to be a good man, he might also have been a great one: his mind was large, his spirit active, his ambition honorable: he had a carriage noble and imposing; his first approach attracted notice, his consequent address ensured respect: if his talents were not quite so solid as some, nor altogether so deep as others, yet they were brilliant, popular and made to glitter in the eyes of men: splendor was his passion; his good fortune threw opportunities in his way to have supported it; his ill fortune blasted all those energies, which should have been reserved for the crisis of his public fame; the first offices of the state; the highest honours which his sovereign could bestow were showered upon him, when the spring of his mind was broken, and his genius, like a vessel overloaded with treasure, but far gone in decay, was only precipitated to ruin by the very freight, that in its better days would have crowned it with prosperity and riches.[24]

It is ironic that when Halifax finally got what he wanted, the Southern Department, he did so little with it. The contemporary opinion is undoubtedly correct: his physical powers were exhausted, "the spring of his mind was broken." The Halifax who transformed the Board of Trade into a vital agency, who took bold colonial initiatives, and who corresponded with colonial governors in his own hand was not the same man who neglected giving his opinion on American affairs at council meetings. One is reminded of Pitt's strange malaise after the king called on him to form a government in 1766.

Ellis's career is a lesson in the operation of the two-tiered British political system. The top tier consisted of the great lords whose life centered around the court. The second tier was made up of the clerks who ran the offices of government and the advisers who supplied their patrons with information and ideas. The lords were expected to devote their talents and energies to court politics. To be successful, they had to keep up appearances by maintaining several residences, giving dinners, employing a retinue of servants, going about in coaches and riding chairs, and in other ways emphasizing their importance. Social stratification was a fact of life, and it was expected that those in the top stratum would dress the part. Lord Egremont was successful because he comported himself well, was complemented by a beautiful and capable spouse, indulged himself and his friends in fine food and drink, displayed temper on appropriate occasions, and cultivated the friendship of politically important men. The constant social activity left him little time or inclination to do research on current issues. Egremont needed someone like Henry Ellis to provide information and ideas. Henry Ellis in turn needed a great lord like Egremont to translate his ideas into policy. The result of their combined effort was an impressive series of accomplishments from the decision to attack Havana to the terms of the peace treaty of 1763, culminating in the Proclamation of 1763.

When Egremont died, a victim of patriotic overindulgence, Ellis was ready to serve Halifax as diligently as he had Egremont. The two men were at the apex of a partnership in public affairs which spanned fifteen years. The moment demanded the best efforts of the Father of the Colonies and the oracle on American affairs. Halifax failed, "a vessel overloaded with treasure, but far gone in decay," in the words of his secretary. His failure was his inability to maintain the extravagant life-style to which he was accustomed because of physical as well as financial ruin. He lacked the motivation and the energy to employ the talents of Henry Ellis. When his patron lost interest in policy, Ellis was unable to influence events. "I already begin to feel the insignificance of an idle man," Ellis confessed to Knox. He accepted his situation, but there was an understated poignancy in his remark to Knox: "You are sensible as well as I that our interest with the great ceases with our power of being of use to them. It is mortifying to our vanity to know this, but I have not concealed it from mine."[25] In 1769, Halifax thanked Ellis for sending boxes of plants to one of his daughters, but there is no evidence of the close relationship that had been compared to that of godfather and godson.[26]

Ellis refrained from taking an active part in the debates about America. He generally agreed with William Knox, who kept up a running defense of the Grenville policies even after Grenville left office. Knox, always serious and logical, scoffed at the idea that Parliament had a right to benefit the colonies but not to bind them, that it might give bounties but not impose burdens. The distinction between taxes for regulating trade and those for raising revenue was "of all absurdities the most ridiculous" because it asserted that Parliament had the right to impose a heavy tax (the Old Molasses Act) but not a small one (the tea tax). Nor did he agree with the notion that the laws of nature conferred special privileges on the inhabitants of Massachusetts. Whatever rights they enjoyed derived from their status as members of the British community or state. Otherwise, they could claim the rights and privileges of Dutchmen, Frenchmen, and Germans.[27]

In another publication Knox took issue with the argument that the Navigation Acts oppressed the colonists. On the contrary, he said, they guaranteed a market for colonial products. The acts bound the people of England to work for the good of the colonists. If the colonists were so oppressed, he asked, how did they become so wealthy?[28] Privately, Knox argued with Grenville to yield the point on taxing the colonies. He also recommended a relaxation of the Navigation Acts to give Americans access to foreign markets. Grenville thanked Knox for the advice but disagreed on both points. To give up taxation would be to give up sovereignty, and to abandon the Navigation Acts would play into the hands of Britain's commercial rivals. Knox suggested that provinces be permitted to tax themselves voluntarily. Grenville answered that they would never do it. Finally, Knox asked that the Americans be offered representation in Parliament. Grenville was amenable to that idea, but the plan lacked a sponsor, either in England or America.[29] All these efforts at compromise from Knox, who occupied an official position as under secretary to Hillsborough, Dartmouth, and Lord George Germain, indicate that he was less of a hard-liner in private than he was in his public expressions. So, very likely, was Henry Ellis, who assured Knox that his opinions "quadrated" with Knox's perfectly.[30]

By 1779 Knox seemed almost pro-American. The North administration had decided to send a peace commission to America offering generous concessions for reconciliation. Knox urged the ministry to "seize the present occasion to lay a new foundation . . . to erect a Constitution that by removing all Jealousy, and giving happiness to the Colonists, shall render it equally their Inclination and their interest to continue Members•of the British Empire." Knox severely criticized crown lawyers for not clarifying the constitutional rights of colonials. Colonial governors were never advised which past enactments applied to their particular province. He and Ellis had asked for clarification "upon this most essential business but no direction was ever given." Matters were made worse by "that treacherous act," the Declaratory

Act of 1766, which in effect informed the Americans that their rights were at the absolute disposition of Parliament.[31]

Ellis kept up a commentary on developments in America in his correspondence with Knox. In March 1774 he wrote from Marseilles that he was most anxious about the critical situation in Boston. He approved of the North ministry's coercive acts. By June he expressed the fear that these measures would have only a temporary effect: "The seeds of discontent will necessarily remain so long as the point in contest is left undecided."[32] That point was the constitutional relationship between colonies and Parliament.

Ellis spent the war years shuttling between Marseilles and Spa in Belgium. Knox kept Ellis informed of the progress of the war, and Ellis reported on France's efforts to assist the Americans. Ellis rejoiced at General John Burgoyne's progress and was puzzled at General Sir William Howe's decision to take Philadelphia instead of joining Burgoyne. He suffered with the surrender of Burgoyne and congratulated Knox upon the restoration of Georgia in 1779. Ellis appealed to Knox to use his influence to secure the exchange of certain French prisoners. The news of the defeat at Yorktown was followed by worse news as far as Ellis was concerned. Lord North's ministry was turned out and Lord Shelburne brought in to make the peace. Ellis was not one to hold a grudge, but he did not like Shelburne or his policies. He called Shelburne "that Factious Chief," holding him responsible for "those dangerous principles which threaten a general subversion of every system, religious or civil, hitherto respected by mankind." He wondered how the "Jesuit Earl" would treat the civil servants appointed by Lord North. His own offices in the West Indies were for life; he was not personally concerned because he was "above the reach of a minister." He thought Shelburne's peace treaty was "marked by ignorance and negligence."[33]

If Ellis was out of Shelburne's reach, William Knox was not. Knox was under secretary along with the veteran John Pownall when Shelburne took office in 1781. Knox noted in his memoirs that Shelburne was impossible to please; he knew nothing about the geography of America, and Knox had to point out places on a map and describe the terrain. Knox knew that his chances of retaining office were slim because of his connection with Grenville and North; however, he was not prepared for the manner of his dismissal. Shelburne first promised him that he would be continued in office, then told him that the under secretary's position was discontinued and that he was terribly sorry. Other subministers were given pensions; Knox got none.[34]

Henry Ellis's observations on the loss of the American colonies were expressed in a series of articles sent to a newspaper in 1790 when it seemed that England and Spain might engage in a war over Nootka Sound on the west coast. "Has not dear-bought experience taught Britain that her victories in America have produced her no better rewards than transient glory and durable distress?" He urged an alliance with Spain rather than hostilities; the rising power of the American states threatened the mines of Spain as well as the commerce of Britain. "It is not its existence," he said of the new nation, "but its exuberance which the British and Spanish nations have cause to dread."[35] For Ellis, who had followed the quest of commerce and empire all his adult life, it must have been frustrating to realize that programs he had helped shape created the seeds of discord and division of that empire. He had helped raise up an exuberant rival made in the image of Britain.

ELLIS's withdrawal from public service in 1768 when he
resigned his Canadian offices
was the beginning of a new
career, that of a gentleman of the world. The title "Governor" did for
his reputation what Benjamin Franklin's beaver skin hat did for his; it
advertised him as an expert on the New World and its people, places,
and things. His standing in the Royal Society gave him entrée into
scientific circles, and his wealth ensured him a place in polite society.

His impaired health was a reason for going to watering places
like Bath and Tunbridge Wells, and he continued to visit the resorts
because he liked the company there. He once wrote to Knox that because few of his friends were in London he intended to visit "Bristol,
Badminton, Beckett and Bath," where he knew he would meet many
old friends. Bristol was the port he shipped out of while captain of
the *Earl of Halifax* and the location of Lord Clare's residence; Badminton was Lord Beaufort's country house, which gave its name to
the game invented there; Beckett was Lord Barrington's estate; and
Bath was where Henry's brother Robert lived at Lansdowne Crescent
with Penelope, his wife, and their eight children, the oldest of whom
was Francis, born in 1772.[1] Henry took a special interest in his nephew
Francis; he referred to him in 1795 as "really a very deserving young
man of uncommon abilities and possessed of more scientific and other
knowledge than one could expect at his years."[2] Francis returned the
sentiment; he wrote to his uncle about his disappointment at not seeing
him "who unites my love, duty and gratitude."[3]

When Ellis developed what he called "rheumatic complaints" he spent less time in England and more in sunnier climates. Marseilles was his winter retreat during the 1780s, Pisa for most of the 1790s, and Naples after that.

Ellis had become a celebrity and an object of curiosity by 1786, when Joseph Cradock included him in his book about famous contemporaries. "Governor Ellis was a rich old bachelor, one of the greatest humourists I ever knew," he wrote. Ellis "regularly took his flight from North to South like certain birds." On his travels through France, Ellis visited Tissot and Voltaire and "was as free in all opinions" as the famous Frenchmen were. He published a tract on organizing the police that was admired by Count Vergennes, the foreign minister. Ironically, when Ellis returned to England to publish the pamphlet, he was robbed in Pall Mall.[4]

Cradock described how he went to buy groceries with Ellis in Marseilles in preparation for "one of those splendid dinners which he meant should be talked of by all the strangers then resident." Ellis "ransacked" all the vessels in the harbor for rarities, wild boar from Algiers, choice wines from Greece, and the richest liqueurs from Trieste and Venice. Ellis was especially particular about his tea, which he ordered exclusively from his friends the Twinings of London.[5]

Cradock described one dinner in Marseilles to which both Ellis and Thomas Pownall were invited. Cradock considered himself an authority on most subjects, but he dared not challenge the opinions of either Ellis or Pownall. Pownall was "splendid and magnificent in his dress," as Cradock saw him, whereas Ellis, always spare in physique, "was covered with a Scotch plaid cloak and the cut of his coat beneath had not been changed for the last thirty years." Apparently such social occasions were like the jousting matches of the knights of old. Various topics were advanced, and both men demonstrated their intellectual acumen; they "kept the uninitiated at an awful distance." The subject of antiquities in the south of France was one of Pownall's favorites, and he waxed eloquent on the nature of prehistoric remains until his "antagonist" turned all "his minute investigations into ridicule." Ellis apparently won that tournament. When not challenged by a rival, Ellis and Pownall were as polite as the next gentleman, or as Cradock put it, "our two great dictators, though totally unlike, were always attentive to their countrymen."[6]

Ellis explained to a friend how his hospitality to fellow Britishers sometimes got him in trouble. He had a carriage specially built for himself in Brussels and traveled in it from Brussels to Marseilles and to Pisa. He was generous in letting his friends use it. A lady named Mrs. Wall took advantage of his courtesy and used his horses, carriage, and driver frequently. Then Mrs. Wall's female relatives visited Ellis, and, as he said, "flattered me with particular attention," the object of which Ellis understood to be to gain equal access to his carriage. The problem was that the women had quarreled with Mrs. Wall, and there was no way Ellis, as a gentleman, could oblige them without seeming to take sides against Mrs. Wall. Therefore, he decided that neither Mrs. Wall nor her relatives could use his carriage in the future. The result was "great resentment and much backbiting" by all the women involved and a tongue-lashing of Ellis by Mr. Wall. Ellis took some comfort from the fact that those whom he referred to as "persons of distinction" sympathized with him, but he concluded, "It was unpleasant to one who through life has studied to avoid giving offence or having quarrels with anybody." [7]

The well-known, sometimes caustic, observer of the social scene Philip Thicknesse had words of praise for Ellis. "This Gentleman's success in life is a proof that merit does not always pass unrewarded," he wrote.[8] He had seen Ellis in the capacity of an ordinary sailor and followed his subsequent career with interest. Another popular author, Lord Gardenstone, wrote in some detail about Ellis in his *Travelling Anecdotes*. On November 7, 1786, he was introduced to Ellis at Marseilles and considered it "a singular favor" to meet one about whom he had heard so much. He was as impressed by Ellis's "uncommon talents" as by his "considerable fortune." The governor was "remarkably agreeable" in his conversation. No one entertained his guests with greater hospitality or set a finer table. Ellis himself was almost abstemious; he ate no meat and though his wine and cordials were the finest money could buy, he took only a little with a glass of pure water. Ellis's travel habits had settled into a routine, London or Bath in the summer, Marseilles or Pisa in the winter, and Spa in the spring. Ellis was well-known as a bird of passage in Brussels, Paris, and Lyons. Gardenstone recommended Ellis as one well able to "give prudent and proper lessons to genteel travelers." [9]

The impression Ellis made on his friends is evident in a letter he received from Marseilles: "Since your departure a fortnight ago, we have lived in the greatest loneliness. Comforts of every kind are gone with you. No cheerful morning teas, no friendly and pleasing dinners, no social evenings have taken place, much less enlightened, gay and sprightly conversation." [10]

On that occasion, Ellis was on his annual visit to the Belgian resort that gave its name to all later watering places, Spa. Thicknesse described Spa in 1776 as recently grown from a wretched village into a populous town, with excellent provisions and crowded with persons of high rank from all over Europe. The resort was in mountainous country on the banks of a stream, and everything necessary had to be carried from Liége, twenty miles away. Gambling was the favorite occupation, and fortunes were made and lost at the dice tables. An employee of one of the gambling clubs met newcomers as they arrived in town and offered to announce their presence to all the right people. Thicknesse warned that only the counterfeit nobility indulged in that antic. [11]

In 1777 Ellis wrote Knox that "you would think all Ireland had flown from their country to drink these waters," so many were at Spa. He was enjoying the company of "respectable and sensible people" such as Charles Jenkinson and George Rice; the latter was a former member of the Board of Trade and since 1770 treasurer of the king's chamber. Ellis was careful to tell Jenkinson any news Knox sent him, saying that Knox wanted him to be first to know. "I observed that this flattered him and was useful in supporting the idea he seemed to wish should be entertained of him." [12] After serving as secretary to Bute and Grenville, Jenkinson was given several offices by Lord North and was often consulted by the king. He was rewarded by being made Baron Hawkesbury in 1786 and the Earl of Liverpool in 1796.

In 1780 Ellis pretended to Knox that his status as a celebrity was becoming inconvenient. During the season at Spa, he had the tiresome honor, as he put it, of being much distinguished by the great of all countries. The king of Sweden had asked to be introduced to the famous Governor Ellis. They met in the large public hall and conducted their first conversation on a raised platform before an audience of 150 people. Ellis and the king enjoyed themselves so much that they met again several times privately. Ellis decided that His Majesty was "one of the most amiable and captivating persons I ever met with." In 1781, the prince and princess of Liechtenstein competed for Ellis's attention. He wrote Knox, "I have the honor to be the first favourite with them and in consequence receive constant and abundant food for my vanity." [13]

Ellis maintained a correspondence with his fellows of the Royal

Society and attended the society's dinners at the Crown and Anchor in the Strand when he was in London. His friendship with John Ellis and interest in botany brought him into contact with Dr. John Fothergill, sponsor of William Bartram's investigation into the flora and fauna of the southern frontier during the years 1773 to 1777.[14]

The discovery of the planet Uranus by Sir William Herschel in 1781 brought honor to the Royal Society and caused Henry Ellis to acquire a telescope and learn all he could about astronomy. The pious William Knox wrote to Herschel and asked where in the heavens "the seat of bliss" was located. Herschel replied politely that "an attempt to assign a space for the seat of bliss does not fall to the lot of astronomers, who keep always within the range of facts that may be ascertained."[15]

The decade of the 1780s was one of stormy debate in the society provoked by the arbitrary tactics of Sir Joseph Banks, the president. He took upon himself the right to veto candidates. If he did not like the applicant, he would not introduce him to the board of the society. The opposition to Banks reached its height when he rudely dismissed the society's secretary, Sir Charles Hutton, without a hearing. The leader of the movement to oust Banks was Francis Maseres, the former attorney general of Quebec who was admitted to the society in 1771 as a mathematician. Maseres called for a vote of confidence in the president. After a bitter debate before 170 members, Banks won by a vote of 119 to 42.[16]

Henry Ellis had his own dispute with Banks in 1789. He was excited about his new theory on the nature of hurricanes. He described when and how hurricanes appeared as he had observed them, then gave his opinion that the cause was the hot air rising from volcanoes which set the dense air rushing in to take the place of the lighter air. He noted that typhoons resemble hurricanes and they rise in the Sea of Japan, which abounds in volcanic islands. Ellis wrote the paper in Marseilles and delivered it himself to the Royal Society to Banks's attention with the note, "Governor Ellis presents his most respected compliments to Sir Joseph Banks."[17]

In return, Ellis received this rather ungracious reply: "Sir Joseph has read over with care the Governors conjectures on the causes of hurricanes but is not so fortunate as to be able to agree with them."[18] Ellis was a proud and sensitive man and felt constrained to present a defense. He explained that he had been urged to publish his theory by distinguished Frenchmen such as Abbé Mann and Abbé Raynal. Banks's arrogant answer was that he wanted to spare Ellis the embarrassment of reading his paper and then having it deemed unworthy of publication. After another exchange, Ellis gave up the effort. He believed that he could buttress his opinion if he worked at it, but his "indifference with regard to any little reputation which might be acquired thereby" caused him to refrain from doing so.[19] His polite capitulation concealed the sting to his vanity caused by the arbitrary Banks.

The Abbé Raynal was one of several French scholars whose friendship Ellis enjoyed. Ellis wrote Knox in 1781 that he had many interesting discussions with the abbé.[20] Guillaume Thomas François Raynal, eight years Ellis's senior, was ordained a Jesuit but later dismissed from that order because of conduct unbecoming a clergyman. Raynal joined Diderot and the philosophes in attacking the throne, the church, and the nobility and in exaggerating the benefits of American democracy. Ellis had a less favorable opinion of the American masses and attributed Raynal's views to Shelburne, with whom Raynal stayed in London.

Raynal's magnum opus was a ten-volume work entitled *A Philosophical and Political History of the Settlements and Trade of the Europeans in the East and West Indies.* A perusal of the massive history reveals topics on which he must have received help from Henry Ellis. For example, Raynal displayed a detailed knowledge of the history of the search for a northwest passage, as well as for the geographical conditions in Hudson Bay. Raynal discounted the value of the reports previous to Ellis's and referred to Ellis's voyage as "the famous expedition of 1746" and the first clearly to delineate the interior of the bay. Raynal reflected Ellis's opinion that there was a passage and called upon men of enterprise and spirit to go find it. Raynal's description of Eskimos was so like Ellis's that Ellis must have been at his ear or Ellis's book at his elbow. Raynal's description of postproclamation Canada displayed an inside view of the politics leading to the Quebec Act.[21]

In addition to his learned discussions with Raynal and others, Ellis turned to writing poetry and sent some samples off to a publisher. He sat for his portrait by the famous and expensive Sir Thomas Lawrence. His life settled into a pleasant pattern; as he described it in a letter to a friend from Pisa in 1796, "I enjoy a kind of still life here in a good climate and tolerable good society which at my years is all I ought in reason to expect." He was not a religious person, but he took consolation in the belief that "he who made the world governs it and consequently that things will finally terminate as they ought."[22]

Ellis could not have maintained himself in the style he did if it were not for the revenue from his Irish lands. He might have lived comfortably on his governor's pension and the emoluments from his West Indian offices, but his Irish holdings allowed him the extra amenities. Ellis's Irish affairs were in a tangle when his father died on June 15, 1773, leaving Henry all his assets and liabilities. Ellis made one of his infrequent visits to his hometown to sort out his affairs. He learned that his father, Francis Ellis, had grown very careless with his money in his old age and very generous. In 1768 he donated £4,000 to the town to build a hospital, and in his will he stipulated that £7,000 be invested and the interest used for the poor of the town. He had lent money to friends and promised loans to others, which Henry felt obliged to make good. After lending £600 and paying £3,000 in various legacies, Henry did not have the £7,000 for the poor fund. He never forgot that obligation, however, and provided for the payment in his own will. Henry was so short on cash that he was in the embarrassing position of borrowing money from his brothers James and Robert. James, a farmer in Kilkenny, he scarcely knew, but he was close to Robert and his wife, Penelope, who had taken up residence at Bath, in England.[23]

Ellis left Monaghan with mixed feelings. He almost wished he had been disinherited rather than be "made heir to such a load of vexation." Still, it was good to see old friends like the Thompsons and the Pringles. Ellis told William Knox, his fellow county man, that he had been well received in Monaghan; "to do my townsfolk justice, I experienced from them the utmost attention and civility."[24]

Examples of the nature of Henry Ellis's financial arrangements are preserved in the heavy leather-bound ledgers in the National Registry of Deeds in Dublin. Ellis's father had lent £1,000 to Francis Lucas of Castleshane at a moderate interest of 6 percent. The loan was for Francis Ellis's lifetime, and Lucas was not able to come up with the money when it was required. Therefore, he deeded over to Henry the manor town and lands of Castleshane.[25] Monaghan County was divided into five baronies, one of which was Monaghan. In turn, the barony was composed of twenty-one "ballebetaghs." A ballebetagh was defined as "a town able to maintain hospitality."[26] Thus Castleshane was a ballebetagh. Monaghan's ballebetagh contained sixteen taths (or tates) of sixty acres each, and each of the taths was distinguished by its own Gaelic name.

The deeds listed not only the towns or ballebetaghs but also the lands or taths. In November 1773 Alexander Montgomery of Ballyleek and his son John deeded over to Henry Ellis the town and lands of Lisillee and then listed names such as Ballyleek, Drumadeen, Tullymarny, Dronagelvin, and Killelune—musical, mysterious names evocative of the ancient Celtic cultures.[27]

Henry Ellis hired John Harrison of Monaghan as his agent and continued to acquire property. In 1778, Harrison purchased twelve taths in Ballyfreeman, fourteen taths in Loughevene, and the town and lands of Lisdrumtools and Drumhillagh. Alexander Montgomery, formerly of Ballyleek and in 1781 of Rosefield, sold Ellis the towns or ballebetaghs of Torregarve, Skenegive, Beldarrige, Mullaghbene, and Aughalogan. Two years later, Thomas Tarrison surrendered for debt the town of Lisnelong with its mill. Also in 1783 Ellis acquired lands in the barony of Cremorne from Cornet John Ker of the Eighth Regiment Dragoons. In 1792 Henry paid £6,000 to Lord Baron Andrew Thomas Blayney for extensive holdings in Castleblayney, including several islands on Lake Muckro, the greatest of the county's 184 lakes. By the end of the century, Henry Ellis was one of the largest landowners in the county.[28]

During the same period, there was a gradual improvement in the social and political condition of the people of Ireland. In 1773 Ellis wrote that "the poverty and distresses of the people surpass all description." He predicted that unless something were done for them by the government "it's hard to say what may be the consequences."[29] In 1771 the Irish Parliament passed the Bogland Act, which permitted Catholics to lease up to fifty acres of bog (considered worthless by landlords) for up to sixty years. That such a miserable concession could be seen as a measure of relief illustrates the profundity of the plight of the mass of Irish people. In 1778 Catholics were allowed to lease land for 999 years, and four years later the next logical step was taken to permit them the outright purchase of land. The ban against bishops was lifted, and Catholics were permitted to open their own schools. The emerging Catholic middle class learned that their best hope of advancement was through the British Parliament, rather than the conservative Irish Parliament. Under pressure from Whitehall, the Irish Parliament in 1793 extended the right to vote to Catholics. In addition, Catholics were permitted to join the army, enter the professions, and enroll in Trinity College.[30]

Unfortunately, concessions to Catholics alarmed the Irish Protestants, and in 1795 the Orange Society was organized; its members swore to support the king only as long as he safeguarded the Protestant ascendancy. Armed bands of Protestants roamed Ulster, including Monaghan, attacking Catholics. Wolfe Tone organized the United Irish movement and agitated for independence from England. The government considered the United Irishmen a threat and in 1798 called out the militia to break up the organization. An estimated thirty thousand people were killed. Ironically, most of the militiamen were Catholics and most of the United Irishmen were Protestants. Tone himself was arrested for treason in connection with the abortive French landing at Lough Swilly and was found dead in his jail cell.[31]

John Thompson wrote to tell Henry Ellis that Cornwallis, the lord lieutenant of Ireland, had suppressed the movement for independence. He thought that "Catholic emancipation," the opening of political office to Catholics, was a false issue. Most Catholics did not care about office but resented high rents and the enforced payment of tithes to support the Protestant church. Among the Protestants "Papistphobia" was stronger than ever, and he was afraid nothing constructive would be done.[32]

William Pitt's administration took advantage of the moment to bind Ireland more closely to England. A liberal use of bribes helped persuade the Irish Parliament to abolish itself, and on August 1, 1800, an Act of Union was passed at Westminster. Thereafter Ireland was represented by its delegates to the Parliament of the United Kingdom. In general, the absentee landlords, Henry Ellis among them, favored the Act of Union as the best means of economic and political advancement for the Irish people.

By 1800 Monaghan County was a much improved place to live than in the time of Henry Ellis's youth. A published survey of the county described the town of Monaghan as "remarkably neat, but is rather whimsically built"; the streets were narrow but kept very clean. The county infirmary, which Francis Ellis built, was cited as a dominant feature of the town. The landowning gentry were praised for providing excellent roads. The improved condition of the county and its people redounded to the financial advantage of Henry Ellis in faraway Italy.[33]

Anyone who has followed Ellis's career this far must have wondered whether there was a woman in his life. A girl in Monaghan claimed that Ellis was her father. Ellis denied that, blaming the mother for the allegation, and left the girl a small legacy in his will. Ellis was very popular with the ladies, as the many invitations and "thank you's" in his papers attest. A close friend for almost ten years was Lady Bolingbroke, whose husband left her with three children when he ran off with a German countess. In a letter dated Pisa, April 22, 1796, Ellis mentioned to a friend that Lady Bolingbroke and her companion were leaving and it was "a great loss to me."[34] Charlotte Collins, the companion, wrote Ellis on May 1, 1804, to tell him Lady Bolingbroke had died. She assumed that the wretched husband would have to marry the German woman, who by then had produced five children for Bolingbroke. Her brother, a hot-tempered baron, had sworn to kill Bolingbroke if he did not marry the countess.[35]

There is the possibility that the young man whom Henry Ellis adopted was his natural son. John Joyner took the name Ellis after his adoption. Ellis owned land in Kempsey, near Worcester. We would have to assume that he met the boy's mother there and had a child by her around 1750. It is possible that Ellis went off to sea before the boy was born. The woman married a man named Joyner, and the lad was reared as John Joyner. Young John's first known association with Ellis was a letter to his parents written from London on December 2, 1762, telling them about a trip he had taken through Holland, France, Germany, and Flanders in the company of Ellis and conveying to his parents the best regards of the governor.[36] Shortly after that the boy was adopted by Ellis and took his name. Henry Ellis secured an ensign's commission for John in the Royal Irish (the Eighteenth) Regiment. The Eighteenth was sent to garrison the forts in the American Northwest in 1767, and as of September 2, 1771, seven companies of the regiment were stationed at Fort Pitt. During that year Ensign John J. Ellis joined his regiment. Henry Ellis asked his friend Lord Barrington, the secretary at war, to recommend the young officer to General Thomas Gage, commander in chief in America. Barrington did so, and Gage replied cordially on May 6, 1771, "I shall omit no occasion to do Service to Mr. Ellis of the Royal Irish."[37]

Ensign Ellis was stationed at Fort Pitt until 1773, when the Eighteenth was removed to Philadelphia. In January of that year he was promoted to lieutenant and granted permission to return to England by General Frederick Haldimand, who replaced Gage as commander while Gage was on leave. Haldimand's kindness to young Ellis brought an effusive letter of thanks from Henry. "The repeated marks of civility and friendship with which you have condescended to distinguish my nearest relation, Lieut. John J. Ellis, demand my particular acknowledgements," the governor wrote. Lieutenant Ellis had "constantly" informed Henry of Haldimand's goodness to him. Henry referred to John as "one whose happiness I have very much at heart." [38]

The historian of the Royal Irish Regiment noted that it was stationed in Boston "when the unfortunate misunderstanding occurred between Great Britain and her North American colonies on the subject of taxation." [39] Three companies of the Eighteenth marched with John Pitcairn to Lexington and Concord and were almost annihilated by the Massachusetts Minutemen before they were rescued by Earl Percy and escorted back to Boston. The regiment was so decimated that its officers, including Ellis, were sent home to recruit in 1775. The regiment was stationed in various places in southern England from 1776 to 1779. On February 26, 1779, Ellis was promoted to captain lieutenant and in May of that year was transferred to the Eighty-ninth Regiment. [40]

Another example of Henry Ellis's watchful concern for his adopted son is his letter to Charles Jenkinson, then secretary at war, on January 14, 1780, asking if Captain Ellis could sell his commission in the Eighteenth. Jenkinson sent a courteous reply that the practice had been discontinued. [41]

Captain Ellis took advantage of the military inactivity to marry a Miss Walton from Worcestershire. When their first son was born in 1783 and named Henry for his grandfather and Walton for his mother's family, he was immediately enrolled in the Eighty-ninth as an ensign, entitled to draw half-pay. The Eighty-ninth was disbanded that same year. John was listed as a major in the "late 89th foot" from 1785 through 1787. [42]

Major Ellis was named to the reorganized Forty-first Foot and given responsibility for inspecting the men of the old Forty-first and selecting those he thought fit to enlist in the new regiment. A junior fellow officer who served with Ellis in the Forty-first was Lieutenant Arthur Wellesley, later Duke of Wellington. The regiment had trouble recruiting in Ireland, but Major Ellis found a number of new men in his native Worcestershire. On March 12, 1789, the regiment received its colors and was assigned to Cork in Ireland. Of its 262 privates, 205 had under one year's service. By 1791 the regiment had attained full strength with 333 private men, 13 drummers, 33 officers, 30 sergeants, and 29 corporals. In 1792, nine-year-old Henry Walton Ellis joined the regiment as a lieutenant on full pay.[43] The practice of allowing children to be officers in the royal army was almost as strange as permitting newborn infants to be listed as ensigns.

By 1793 England was again at war with France, and the Forty-first was sent to Barbados as part of the fifteen-thousand-man army under Lieutenant General Sir Charles Grey for the campaign against Guadeloupe, Martinique, and St. Lucia. John was transferred to the Twenty-third, the Royal Welch Fusiliers, as a lieutenant colonel. He commanded the regiment from December 6, 1793, until September 1, 1795. The regiment served with distinction in the conquest of Martinique and French Sainte Domingue. Fever was a worse enemy than the French, and by 1795 the Twenty-third Regiment numbered only thirty healthy men. It was ordered back to England in 1796. Henry Walton, the boy officer, survived the campaign, but the Forty-first was almost entirely wiped out by fever. On January 20, 1796, the fourteen-year-old Henry Walton joined his father's regiment at Worcester as a captain lieutenant.[44]

Henry Ellis's letter from Pisa on April 22, 1796, congratulated John on the recovery of his health and his promotion to full colonel. Henry expressed delight at some compliment paid to young Henry Walton by the Duke of York. He agreed with John that both father and son were extremely fortunate to have survived the twin dangers of war and disease. Henry predicted greater honors in store.[45] John was promoted to major general in 1798, and when he retired from the service, he represented Worcester in Parliament until his death in 1804. His son Henry Walton paid tribute to his father's memory in a ceremony in Worcester: "His talents and urbanity of manners endeared him to an amiable and intelligent society; with less ability but an equal warmth of heart, I hope, some future day, to solicit a transfer of those bonds of affection and to live into the same social habits which my father enjoyed in this city and neighborhood."[46] Gallant words from a gallant son.

As his grandfather watched proudly, Henry Walton Ellis outdid his father in gallantry and became a legend in the Royal Welch Fusiliers. At the age of eighteen, while serving in Egypt under Major General John Moore, Ellis led his company in taking an almost impregnable position with bayonets and was severely wounded. After receiving another wound in the siege of Copenhagen in 1807 he went to Nova Scotia as lieutenant colonel of the First Battalion. In 1809 his battalion was ordered to join the campaign against Martinique. General George

Beckwith rode up to Ellis's position to inquire whether his men could take the strong French positions on Mount Sourier. "Sir," replied Ellis, "I will take the flints out of their firelocks and they shall take them." True to his boast, he led the bayonet charge and took the hill without the support of artillery.[47]

Ellis and his battalion then returned to Halifax. Henry Walton's sojourn in Halifax prompted Henry Ellis to provide in his will that his "considerable tract" of land in Nova Scotia be divided between Henry Walton and nephew Francis.[48]

Duty called, and on November 10, 1810, the Fusiliers embarked for Portugal to serve under the Duke of Wellington. Ellis saw action immediately; he led his battalion in a bloody bayonet charge up a hill at Albuera and was wounded. He was wounded again at Badajoz but stayed with his battalion as Wellington advanced into Spain. He was wounded a third time at Salamanca.[49]

The French forces fighting for Joseph Bonaparte were forced out of Spain. When they tried to break through the Pyrenees, the British defense line stood firm. Henry Walton wrote to a friend that when the French attack began, he had 254 men. He lost 105 in fighting off the assault. A week later, when the pursuit of the French began, his regiment was reduced to 108. Wellington combined the decimated regiments into a brigade and gave Henry Walton overall command. Henry was wounded again in the successful attack on the French lines. The British went into winter quarters at Toulouse for badly needed recuperation. Henry Walton was promoted to colonel and recognized by the king with the rank of Knight Commander of Bath. He was henceforth Sir Henry Walton Ellis.[50]

On December 19, 1814, the city and county of Worcester honored Colonel Ellis at a public banquet. The Earl of Coventry said that he was "justly esteemed an ornament to his country." Henry Walton gave a graceful and modest reply filled with praise for his father and the hope that he might follow his example.[51]

After Napoleon's escape from Elba, the Royal Welch Regiment went with Wellington to Bruges, Ghent, and Waterloo. During the epic battle with Napoleon, Ellis's foot soldiers were attacked by enemy cavalry, and Ellis formed them into a square with him in the center astride a white horse. He was struck in the chest with a musket ball and calmly ordered an opening in the lines to permit him to ride to the rear.

The rest was tragic. He was thrown from his horse while trying to leap a ditch. His men found him "much exhausted" and brought him to a barn to rest. During the night the barn caught fire, and Ellis was badly burned before being rescued. An officer who was with him at the end testified that his last words were, "I am happy; I am content; I have done my duty." He was buried on the mound of the only windmill at Braine-L'Alleud. One of his men asked about him anxiously. He was told that the colonel was dead, but why did he care — had not Ellis caused the man to be flogged? The soldier answered, "Sir, I deserved the punishment, else, he would not have punished me," and burst into tears.[52]

A monument was erected to the memory of Colonel Sir Henry Walton Ellis in the great cathedral at Worcester. The sculpture, one of the most impressive among the many memorials in the ancient edifice, depicts the hero falling from his horse into the arms of an officer kneeling on the ground, while an angel hovering overhead holds a laurel wreath. The inscription claims Henry Walton as a native of Worcester, recites his exploits, and concludes that the monument was erected by the Royal Welch Fusiliers "as a tribute of their respect and affection to the memory of a leader not more distinguished for his valour and conduct in the field than beloved for every generous and social virtue." Colonel Sir Henry Walton Ellis was thirty-two years old when he died.[53]

His only son, Francis Joyner Ellis, followed a military career. He attained the rank of major in the Sixty-second Regiment when he died of a fever in Moulmien in the East Indies. William Joyner of Berkeley in Gloucestershire, the brother of John Joyner Ellis, then took the name of Ellis.[54] Whether or not John was the governor's natural son as well as adopted, Henry was a loving parent and mourned when John died in 1804. Henry was eighty-three in that year and an established member of the English colony at Naples.

There is an old expression, old even in Henry Ellis's time, "See Naples and Die." The saying loses something in translation from the Italian and sounds more like a curse than a commendation. The meaning, of course, is that Naples is so beautiful that only heaven can surpass it. No other earthly scene can match it. Henry Ellis probably did not intend to die when he went to Naples in 1798, but that is what happened.

The real world kept intruding into Ellis's idylls. The French Revolution in 1789 put an end to his coach trips between Spa and Marseilles. He sought the comparative safety of northern Italy until the army of the French Directorate invaded Tuscany. So Ellis went to Naples for safety rather than scenery. By doing so, he became a player in one of the most celebrated dramas in British history; the hero was the incomparable Lord Horatio Nelson, the heroine was the beautiful Emma, Lady Hamilton. A key actor was Sir William Hamilton, age sixty-eight, who doted on his thirty-three-year-old bride and whose admiration for Nelson was boundless. Sir William would have been considered old by almost everyone but Henry Ellis, who was seventy-seven in the year 1798.

Sir William Hamilton, the British minister to the Kingdom of the Two Sicilies, had been a boyhood companion of George III and had embarked on his diplomatic career in 1764 as one of Lord Halifax's appointees. His wife died in 1782, and in 1786 he agreed to do his nephew a favor by taking his mistress off his hands to allow the young man to enter respectable wedlock. She was a "cleaner, sweeter bedfellow," the nephew explained.[55] Thus Amy Lyon became Emma Hamilton. She was twenty-one when Sir William brought her to Naples in 1786, and three years later, when he was sixty, they were properly married.

Henry Ellis paid his respects to the minister upon his arrival and found out, if he did not know it already, that he and Sir William had much in common. In addition to being protégés of Lord Halifax, they were both members of the Royal Society, both were friends of Sir Joseph Banks (though Ellis was smarting from Banks's rejection of his paper on hurricanes), and both were insatiably curious about antiquities. Sir William was a collector, Henry Ellis a scholar. Sir William wrote a learned paper on volcanoes, a subject that interested Ellis. Living as they did in the shadow of Vesuvius, they could not help but pay close attention to the nature and workings of volcanoes.

The British colony at Naples clustered around the court of King Ferdinand and Queen Maria Carolina. Ferdinand was dull-witted and athletic. Fortunately, Sir William liked hunting and fishing as much as the king did, and the two were boon companions. The queen was of the Austrian imperial family, the sister of Marie Antoinette, and was more intelligent than her husband. Her favorite occupation was motherhood, and she kept at it, producing seventeen royal children in all. Emma became the queen's companion as Sir William was the king's.

The events of the French Revolution, particularly the beheading of Louis XVI and Marie Antoinette, made the king and queen of the Two Sicilies very nervous and caused them to look to Britain for protection and to become even better friends with the Hamiltons. The symbol of British power in the Mediterranean was the small man, already one-armed and one-eyed, named Horatio Nelson, and the greatest event of the year 1798 was his victory over the French fleet at the Nile on August 1. Nelson had visited the Hamiltons five years before and was smitten by Emma's charms almost immediately. He was pleased to accept the invitation of the Hamiltons to stay with them for rest and recuperation after the Battle of the Nile.

Nelson proceeded to fall hopelessly in love with Emma and she with him, and Sir William loved them both. We do not know what Henry Ellis thought about Emma. Most members of the English colony considered her vulgar. She had put on weight, and she spoke with a Liverpool accent. The same critics admitted that she was a talented actress. Lacking parts to play, she struck "attitudes," assuming poses from well-known paintings and sculptures. Once at dinner she struck an attitude rather suddenly, collapsing on the floor. A visitor, not knowing her habit of doing such things, splashed her with water. Sir William chided the stranger for spoiling one of Emma's best poses.[56]

Having Nelson as his guest caused King Ferdinand to decide to become a hero also. He led his undisciplined mob of an army against the French and caused them to withdraw temporarily from Rome. Unfortunately, the French counterattacked, and the Neapolitan army ran back to Naples, the king in disguise.

Nelson had to rescue the king and queen, the Hamiltons, Henry Ellis, and the other members of the English colony and deliver them to Sicily, the other part of Ferdinand's domain. A mob took over Naples and made high carnival until the French army entered the city on January 22, 1799.[57]

Ellis's tea merchant friends, the Twinings, wrote to tell him that they and his other friends in London (William Knox, certainly) were worried about his safety. They need not have. Ellis rented a house in Palermo and bought furniture to suit his taste. Palermo was a beautiful place. Many preferred it to Naples, but it was not a place Ellis would have chosen for the summer.[58]

The king and queen were especially solicitous to the Hamiltons because Lord Nelson was their only hope of returning to Naples, and Emma was their key to Nelson. Nelson was in no particular hurry to leave Palermo, and the winter lengthened into spring. Palermo was as near as Nelson would ever get to a honeymoon.

By June the situation had changed for the better, at least for Ferdinand and Maria Carolina. An Austro-Russian army invaded northern Italy, and most of the French troops withdrew from Naples rather than risk being cut off from France by land. With Nelson patrolling the Mediterranean, the French could not risk a naval operation. Ferdinand asked Nelson to take charge of the return of the royal family and court to Naples. He agreed to do it, and the Hamiltons would go with him.

On June 24 Nelson's eighteen warships entered the Bay of Naples for the purpose of restoring order to a mob-ridden town. Emma shared the poop deck with Nelson because the queen had appointed her a special agent and because Nelson wanted her there. She urged Nelson to treat Naples like an Irish town in rebellion. British marines went ashore and imposed martial law. Ferdinand was brought up from Palermo to join Nelson on his flagship. Emma entertained the king, Nelson, Sir William, and everyone within earshot by singing "Rule Britannia."[59]

Then the fleet went back to Palermo to fetch the queen and to celebrate the victory. The garden of the royal palace was the scene of the party honoring Nelson. All the English refugees were there; Henry Ellis would not have missed it. There was a fireworks display which was supposed to represent the Battle of the Nile and the blowing up of the French flagship. Pavilions were set up for the allies—Britain, Portugal, Russia, and Turkey. In the center was a temple, and at the top of the stairs were life-size wax figures of Nelson, Sir William, and Emma. In the center, mounted on a chariot, was the wax figure of King Ferdinand, more heroic in effigy than in life. The orchestra played "Rule Britannia" and everyone had a grand time. Henry Ellis must have wondered how it happened that he had sought serenity and found one of the least serene places in Europe.

Lord Keith, the commander of the British forces in the Mediterranean and therefore Nelson's superior, visited Palermo in February and said, "The whole was a scene of fulsome Vanity and absurdity all the long eight days I was at Palermo."[60] Keith sailed for Malta on February 12, 1800, and Nelson went with him.

By then Ellis was back in Naples, putting his residence in order. A friend, Abraham Gibbs, kept his house in Palermo for him on the chance that Ellis might have to return. The elderly Ellis had become fond of Gibbs's little daughter Mary and left her a keepsake. Gibbs relayed the thanks of "your little sweetheart." The queen had invited Mary to a dance, and the proud father said, "I can assure you your little favorite is taken great notice of which I think you will believe." Gibbs was also a good friend of Nelson and the Hamiltons and entrusted little Mary to Emma's care when the Hamiltons went to London in 1800. "Our worthy friends" (Gibbs meant Sir William and Emma in his letter to Ellis) "are well, but in low spirits at the departure of our two gallants, Lord and Admiral, for Malta." Gibbs informed Ellis that Lady Hamilton just learned that Emperor Paul of Russia had awarded her the Cross of Malta for her services as deputy of Queen Maria Carolina.[61]

The English colony at Naples began breaking up in 1800 because travel, though not safe, was at least possible. One of Ellis's friends, Emma Scott, wrote a farewell note to him: "Adieu My dear sir. Allow me to wish you much health and comfort and to thank you for the many pleasant hours we have passed in your society. I once thought of calling on you this morning but on consideration prefer this mode of taking leave. Be assured I shall always enquire after you with much interest and beg you to believe me tho but a new acquaintance."[62] She signed it "your sincere friend." From Naples to Palermo and back again, Emma Scott, Ellis, and their friends had participated in an unforgettable adventure which bound them more closely. Though Nelson was the focus of attention and his affair with Emma the topic of common gossip, Ellis was a conspicuous figure at court in Palermo and Naples. He wore his title "Governor" as proudly as Nelson wore his stars. Nelson had the Nile, Ellis had the northwest passage. He could talk about African princes and Indian chiefs that he had known. He could tell the inside story of the peace settlement of 1763 and his essential role in it. He had written books and was written about in books. He was clever and kind and now elderly enough to occupy that privileged position reserved for those who embody history.

Nelson and the Hamiltons traveled through Europe to London. British society, titillated by rumors from Naples about the hero and Lady Hamilton, decided Emma was no lady and sided with Nelson's jilted wife, Fanny. As dramatic as his personal life was, Nelson was involved in a grander role. For the fourth time in Henry Ellis's life England had to face a challenge from France to save its empire; a trading empire required control of the sea lanes. Henry Ellis was intensely interested in Nelson's campaign because he had devoted his life to promoting the commercial supremacy of Britain. He was personally involved because Major General John Joyner Ellis and Captain Henry Walton Ellis played distinguished roles in the unfolding drama. Young Captain Ellis followed Nelson to Egypt and nearly died there of a wound. Joyner Ellis died in 1804, before the last act. Henry Ellis lived long enough to hear the glorious news of Trafalgar, a victory that ensured Britain's maritime supremacy and effected the apotheosis of Horatio Nelson. Even then it was not finally settled until Waterloo, where Colonel Sir Henry Walton Ellis played his heroic part and ended it with almost the same final words spoken by Nelson, "I have done my duty." [63]

Henry Ellis's last close acquaintance was the new British minister to the court at Naples, Hugh Elliot, son of Ellis's old friend Sir Gilbert Elliot. When the new diplomat and his lady arrived in Naples in 1803, the eighty-two-year-old Ellis was dean of the British colony and a model of courtesy. Instead of waiting for overtures from the much younger man, he took the initiative and sent word that he would "have the honor and pleasure of waiting upon the Minister when he is settled and more at leisure." [64]

Now and again, Nelson put in at Naples as he searched for a decisive fight with the French fleet. The British colony was grateful for Nelson's "campaign of protection," as Elliot called it, but Nelson's welcome was not so warm as before at the court. The rise of Napoleon muted the strains of "Rule Britannia." Despite her seventeen children, Queen Maria Carolina had fallen in love with a French officer, and the king was occupied with his hunting and fishing. Elliot, a proper Englishman, was shocked at the low level of morality exhibited by the royal family. "I do not believe that there ever existed a more indolent, dissipated, frivolous or dissolute court," he said. [65]

Ellis was a welcome relief, and the two saw a great deal of each other. Ellis was as delighted at the birth of the Elliot's daughter as if the child were a member of his own family. "No one more sincerely wishes the happiness of yourself, your Lady and your amiable family, than him who has the honor to subscribe himself . . . Henry Ellis," he wrote to the proud parents. [66]

The year 1805 was marked by the Battle of Trafalgar. On July 26, there was a violent earthquake and Vesuvius began to spew lava, as if nature's drumroll were announcing a grand finale. Henry Ellis suffered a violent fall and a paralytic stroke that deprived him of the use of his voice for several weeks. His mind was as keen as ever. He declined an invitation to dine with the Elliots because "I am obliged to wear a Night Gown and to be carried up and down stairs and put in my carriage by two servants." He explained that Mrs. Elliot would not like the sight of him in a nightgown.[67]

By September, Ellis had almost completely recovered, as he informed his old companion William Knox. He regretted that Knox had never received the recognition and rewards his long public service merited. Knox needed money, and Ellis arranged a £5,000 loan from his £20,000 account in a London bank. Most of his fortune, Ellis explained, was tied up in Irish lands.[68]

History crowded in on Ellis's last few months of life. The weak Bourbon rulers of the Two Sicilies brought trouble on themselves by signing a treaty of neutrality with Napoleon and almost immediately inviting Tsar Alexander to send Russian troops to protect them from Napoleon. A momentous chain of events was thus unleashed. The British army stationed at Malta was ordered to cooperate with the movement of a Russian force from the Ionian islands to Naples.[69]

Napoleon learned of the joint operation and ordered his fleet out of Cadiz and into the Mediterranean to prevent the allied expedition from reaching Naples. The vigilant Nelson was waiting for just such an opportunity. He found time to write to Abraham Gibbs, Ellis's merchant friend at Naples, with the news that he had sighted the French fleet and was giving chase.[70]

On October 21, 1805, Nelson caught his prey near the shoals of Trafalgar on Spain's southern coast. Never mind that Villeneuve, the French admiral, outnumbered him thirty-three ships to twenty-seven, Nelson ran up the famous signal, "England expects every man to do his duty." He broke the French battle line in two places as he had planned and ensured the victory before a French sharpshooter took aim at his chest, conspicuous with his stars and medals, and fired the fatal shot.

All England mourned Nelson's death as they rejoiced in the unprecedented triumph—not a ship lost and mastery of the seas secured. At Naples, Henry Ellis must have felt a stirring of the ardor that had carried him into the icebound waters of Hudson Bay hoping, as he wrote then, "It will redound to the Glory of the British Nation."[71] Heroes were those who opened new avenues for commerce and those who protected them. Commerce and glory marched arm in arm.

A month after Trafalgar the ponderous Anglo-Russian expedition began disembarking at Naples. Eight thousand British troops and over eleven thousand Russians provided a welcome sense of security to the court of Naples and to the British colony. Unfortunately, the relief was of brief duration. The rout of the Austro-Russian army at Austerlitz on December 2, 1805, caused the tsar to recall his army from Italy. By the end of January 1806 the allied troops had abandoned Naples. The indolent king, his querulous queen, Hugh Elliot, and the British colony were forced once again to retire to Palermo. The curious military adventure would have been ridiculous except that, inadvertently, it brought on Trafalgar.

Death came peacefully to Henry Ellis on January 21, 1806, in the eighty-fifth year of his life and spared him the indignity of a second exile.[72]

Epilogue

HUGH ELLIOT witnessed Ellis's will, made out on March 30, 1805. Ellis was able to be generous, and he was. He gave his sister-in-law Penelope Ellis a lifetime annuity from the rents of some of his lands in Ireland. His nephew Francis, as principal heir, received £10,000 and the Irish estates. Francis's brother Henry received £2,000 and each unmarried niece £2,000. His "old and worthy friend" William Knox of Soho Square, London, was given one hundred guineas and William's son Henry a like amount. Samuel Marshall of Sergeants Bank, who handled Ellis's finances for over thirty years, was awarded one hundred guineas. One hundred each went to John Thompson and William Henry Pringle of Ireland. Henry carried out his father's last wish by leaving £3,000 to the Monaghan hospital and £3,000 to the poor fund of the county. Henry, the natural son of James Ellis of Kilkenny, received five hundred pounds, and one hundred each went to James's two daughters. Twenty pounds were awarded to the woman in Monaghan who claimed to be his daughter. Ellis's retainers, clerks, and servants were all remembered. His Nova Scotia lands were divided equally between Henry Walton Ellis and Francis.[1]

Francis Ellis of Lansdowne Crescent, Bath, was able to live comfortably on his inheritance. His son Robert Leslie became a fellow of Trinity College, Cambridge, and was recognized as a brilliant mathematician. His oldest daughter, Everina Francis, married Sir Gilbert Affleck. When he died, she married Reverend William Whewell, master of Trinity College, and joined her brother in Cambridge. Lady Affleck, as she continued to be called, acquired her father's papers, among which were many of Governor Ellis's letters from his later years.[2]

Because his papers are so scattered and incomplete, Ellis's role in British history has not been noticed. He is remembered as a successful governor of Georgia and nothing else. Yet, if the Georgia years are viewed in the context of his entire career, they can be seen as preparation for Ellis's role in the transformation of British North America.

Ellis was interesting because he was typical of the gentlemen of the British Enlightenment, an explorer, scientist, and man of letters. But he was important because of the contributions uniquely his. He rescued the struggling province of Georgia from a chaotic condition and turned it into a respectable province and thereby earned the title of Second Founder of Georgia. He established an alliance with the Creek Nation which ensured the security of Georgia during the Cherokee War. The knowledge of French and Spanish colonial activity, together with his familiarity with the Indian nations, equipped him to become an authority on American affairs. He was called the "oracle" for one minister and the godson of another. He influenced the course of the war and the terms of peace. He had a major part in the epochal Proclamation of 1763 and influenced the subsequent history of Quebec, Nova Scotia, the Floridas, and the British West Indies.

During Ellis's lifetime he was compared favorably with James Edward Oglethorpe. Oglethorpe was better known and more historically important because of his role in the establishment of Georgia. The Georgia over which Oglethorpe presided was a curiously improbable affair, an aberration among colonies, without a government and without the rights of Englishmen elsewhere. Ellis swiftly and efficiently taught Georgians to govern themselves properly, and they thanked him for it and have been doing so ever since.

No other governor of the American colonies exerted as much influence on British American policy as did Henry Ellis. No Georgia governors who followed were more highly acclaimed while in office, and only one was as involved in international affairs after leaving office.[3]

If Americans began to think of themselves as "a people" during the 1760s, as Jack Greene and others have argued, it may have been because British policy began to treat Americans as a whole.[4] Halifax tried to impose a uniform colonial administration, and Pitt's military strategy was continental in scope. The first comprehensive American plan, however, was contained in the Proclamation of 1763. Insofar as he was instrumental in the formulation of that plan and its policy, Henry Ellis contributed to the dawning awareness of Americans that they were one people.

Notes

ABBREVIATIONS

CO   Colonial Office, British Public Record Office
CRG   *Colonial Records of Georgia*
Ms. CRG   Manuscript Colonial Records of Georgia
GHQ   *Georgia Historical Quarterly*
HMC   Historical Manuscripts Commission
PRO   British Public Record Office
T   Treasury, British Public Record Office
WLCL   William L. Clements Library, University of Michigan, Ann Arbor
WO   War Office, British Public Record Office

CHAPTER ONE   *A Monaghan Lad*

1 Sir Bernard Burke, *A Genealogical and Heraldic History of the Landed Gentry of Ireland* (London: Harrison and Sons, 1912), 205.

2 Peadar Livingstone, *The Monaghan Story: A Documented History of the County Monaghan from the Earliest Times to 1976* (Enniskillen: Clogher Historical Society, 1980), 100–101, 476.

3 Ibid., 118; the remark was made by Canon Terrence Mattingly Golding, Scotshouse, County Monaghan, Ireland.

4 Conversation with Geraldine O'Grady of Glynch House, Newbliss, County Monaghan, Ireland, December 5, 1990; see also map of the County of Monaghan, made in the years 1790, 1791, 1792, and 1793 by William McCrea, National Library of Ireland, Dublin.

5 Denis Carolan Rushe, *History of Monaghan for Two Hundred Years, 1660–1860* (Dundalk: William Tempest, 1921), 339.

6 Livingstone, *Monaghan Story*, 143–48, 239–40.

7 Ibid., 141; Constantia Maxwell, *Country and Town in Ireland Under the Georges* (Dundalk: Dundalgan Press, 1949), 113–19.

8 Conversation with Canon Golding, Scotshouse, County Monaghan, December 6, 1990.

9 Thomas Ellis's will mentions his parks in the Corporation of Monaghan, Book 23,

p. 37, item 12495, National Registry of Deeds, Dublin; see map of Monaghan town in 1787 in Ulster Architectural Heritage Society and An Taisce, County Monaghan Branch, *List of Historic Buildings . . . in the Town of Monaghan* (1970), National Library of Ireland, Dublin; The Applotment Book for Monaghan Parish, 1826, p. 53, shows Ellis Field of seven acres.

10 Thomas Ellis's will, Book 23, p. 37, 12495, National Registry of Deeds, Dublin; Henry Ellis's will, March 1, 1805, PROB. II, 1450, Public Record Office, London. Ellis's will contained two codicils dated April 10, 1805, and May 5, 1804 (should be 1805).

11 William Smith Ellis, *Notices of the Ellises of England, Scotland and Ireland from the Conquest to the Present Time. . . .* (London: Privately printed, 1857–66), 138, 272; Henry Ellis's will, March 1, 1805.

12 Henry Ellis's will, March 1, 1805.

13 Livingstone, *Monaghan Story*, 273–74; for comment on Stulkeley see Basil Williams, *The Whig Supremacy, 1714–1760* (Oxford: Clarendon Press, 1962), 395.

14 Livingstone, *Monaghan Story*, 274.

15 Oration at Trinity College by Reverend Canon Hannay, *Irish Times*, June 9, 1914; Denis Carolan Rushe, *Monaghan in the Eighteenth Century* (Dublin: M. H. Gill and Son, 1916), 18–19.

16 Robert Lynam, ed., *The Complete Works of the Late Reverend Philip Skelton*, 6 vols. (London: Richard Baynes, 1824).

17 Ulster Architectural Society and An Taisce, County Monaghan Branch, *List of Historic Buildings*, 21, 26.

18 William Knox to Philip Skelton, October 5, 1780, in HMC, *Report on Manuscripts in Various Collections* (Dublin: John Falconer, 1909), 6:449.

19 Samuel Burdy, "The Life of the Reverend Philip Skelton," in Lynam, ed., *Complete Works*, 1:lviii–lix; Henry Ellis's will, March 1, 1805.

20 Codicil to Henry Ellis's will, May 5, 1804 (1805), PROB. II, 1450, Public Record Office, London.

21 Rushe, *Monaghan in the Eighteenth Century*, 85.

22 Livingstone, *Monaghan Story*, 151; Maxwell, *Country and Town in Ireland*, 31.

23 *Northern Standard*, September 29, 1963, cited in Livingstone, *Monaghan Story*, 478.

24 Maxwell, *Country and Town in Ireland*, 128.

25 Oration at Trinity College by Reverend Canon Hannay, *Irish Times*, June 9, 1914.

26 Francis Ellis, Henry's nephew and heir, was the source for the story that Henry ran away from his father's severity. See John Nichols, *Illustrations of the Literary History of the Eighteenth Century Consisting of Authentic Memoirs and Original Letters of Eminent Persons and Intended as a Sequel to The Literary Anecdotes* (London: Printed for the author, 1817), 477. Later, when Ellis was governor of Georgia, his father followed his career "with great pleasure" (John Ellis to Henry Ellis, May 1, 1758, John Ellis Papers, Linnean Society Library, Burlington House, London).

27 Details regarding life at sea are taken from John Kenlon, *Fourteen Years a Sailor* (New York: George H. Doran, 1923), 18–22. Kenlon was an Irish lad from County Louth, adjacent to Monaghan, who began his career in a ship out of Dundalk.

28 Ibid., 52–55.

29 Ibid., 30–35.

30 Ellis to Lord Hawkesbury, March 27, 1788, Liverpool Manuscripts, British Library.

31 Lawrence Henry Gipson, *The British Isles and the American Colonies: Great Britain and Ireland, 1748–1754* (New York: Knopf, 1958), 4–5.

32 Ibid.

33 There is a growing literature dealing with Oglethorpe and Georgia. For the military aspects, see Phinizy Spalding, *Oglethorpe in America* (Chicago: University of Chicago Press, 1977); and Larry E. Ivers, *Drums on the Southern Frontier: Military Colonization of Georgia, 1733–1749* (Chapel Hill: University of North Carolina Press, 1979).

34 Henry Ellis, *A Voyage to Hudson's Bay by the Dobbs Galley and California in the Years 1746 and 1747 for Discovering a North West Passage with an Accurate Survey of the Coast and a Short Natural History of the Country* (London: H. Whitridge, 1748), 104.

CHAPTER TWO *The Northwest Passage*

1 Ellis, *Voyage to Hudson's Bay*, 104.

2 Desmond Clarke, *Arthur Dobbs, Esquire, 1689–1765, Surveyor-General of Ireland, Prospector and Governor of North Carolina* (Chapel Hill, University of North Carolina Press, 1957), 48–53.

3 Ibid., 64–65; Ellis, *Voyage to Hudson's Bay*; a list of subscribers is given at the beginning of Ellis's book.

4 Clarke, *Arthur Dobbs*, 65–66. Clarke cites the journals of James Isham, the factor at York Fort, to make the point that the two captains, Moore and Smith, were continually at loggerheads (ibid., 70); Ellis, *Voyage to Hudson's Bay*, 101–2.

5 Christy Miller, *The Voyages of Captain Luke Foxe of Hull and Captain Thomas James of Bristol in Search of a North-West Passage in 1631–32* (New York: Burt, Franklin, 1893). "Captain Middleton's Voyage to Hudson's Bay for the Discovery of a North-West Passage 1741–42" is printed as an appendix to John Barrow, ed., *The Geography of Hudson's Bay: Being the Remarks of Captain W. Coats in Many Voyages to That Locality Between the Years 1727 and 1757* (London: Hakluyt Society, 1852).

6 Ellis, *Voyage to Hudson's Bay*, contains a review of previous explorations in the first hundred pages; for a recent summary, see Leslie H. Neatby, *In Quest of the North West Passage* (New York: Thomas Y. Crowell, 1958).

7 Neatby, *In Quest of the North West Passage*, 16–29.

8 *The Dangerous Voyage of Capt. Thomas James in His Intended Discovery of a Northwest Passage into the South Sea 1633*, reprinted in Miller, *Voyages of Foxe and James*; Neatby, *In Quest of the North West Passage*, 40.

9 Barrow, ed., *Geography of Hudson's Bay*, ii–vi; Ellis, *Voyage to Hudson's Bay*, 80–82, 99–100.

10 Ellis, *Voyage to Hudson's Bay*, 118.

11 Ibid., 122–23.

12 Ibid., 131.

13 Barrow, ed., *Geography of Hudson's Bay*, 19.

14 Ellis, *Voyage to Hudson's Bay*, 142–43.

15 Ibid., 131–32.

16 Ibid., 146–50; "Captain Middleton's Voyage to Hudson's Bay for the Discovery of a North-West Passage, 1741–1742," in Barrow, ed., *Geography of Hudson's Bay*, 109.

17 [Charles Swaine], *An Account of a Voyage for the Discovery of a North-West Passage by Hudson's Streights to the Western and Southern Ocean of America Performed in the Years 1746 and 1747 in the Ship California Francis Smith, Commander, by the Clerk of the California*, 2 vols. (London: Jolliffe, Corbett and Clarke, 1748).

18 Ibid., 1:102–3, 122–23; Ellis, *Voyage to Hudson's Bay*, 146–50.

19 Ellis, *Voyage to Hudson's Bay*, 151.

20 James Isham, "Notes and Observations on a Book Entitled A Voyage to Hudson's Bay . . . , " in E. E. Rich, ed., *James Isham's Observations on Hudson's Bay, 1743* (Toronto: Champlain Society, 1949), 204–5.

21 Ellis, *Voyage to Hudson's Bay*, 156.

22 Ibid., 160.

23 Ibid., 199–205, 213; see also James Isham, "A Journal of the Most Material Transactions and Copys of Letters Between Mr. James Isham and Council at York Fort and Captain William Moor, Captain Francis Smith and Their Council During Their Wintering in Hayes River Commencing 26 August 1746 Ending 24 June 1747," in Rich, ed., *James Isham's Observations*, 242–308. It is interesting that the request to store goods was signed by the two captains and Henry Ellis, another claim to preferment that must have annoyed Swaine.

24 [Swaine], *Account of a Voyage*, 2:33–34.

25 Ibid., 201, 204.

26 Ibid., 225.

27 Ellis, *Voyage to Hudson's Bay*, 230–31.

28 [Swaine], *Account of a Voyage*, 2:228.

29 "Captain Middleton's Voyage," in Barrow, ed., *Geography of Hudson's Bay*, 114–16.

30 Ellis, *Voyage to Hudson's Bay*, 257–58.

31 [Swaine], *Account of a Voyage*, 2:272–75.

32 Ibid., 318.

33 Neatby, *In Quest of the North West Passage*, 116–21.

34 Ibid., 147–60, 163. Theo MacMahon, historian of Monaghan County, identified McClure as a native son of Monaghan.

35 Neatby, *In Quest of the North West Passage*, 167–70.

36 Ellis, *Voyage to Hudson's Bay*, dedication.

37 Clarke, *Arthur Dobbs*, 78–81, 100.

38 Ellis's friendship with Lord Barrington and W. G. Hamilton and his appointment to the post of commissary general, Cheapside, is in Tom Waller, "Henry Ellis, Enlightenment Gentleman," *GHQ* 64 (Fall 1979): 364–76. No source is given. In a letter Ellis later wrote to Jeffrey Amherst, however, he mentioned his holding the position of deputy commissary of stores under a Mr. Hume (Ellis to Amherst, December 10, 1758, Amherst Papers, PRO, WO 34/34). Abraham Hume was commissary general in the year 1747 when Ellis returned from his voyage and again in 1756. It is possible that Ellis acted as deputy commissary in the latter year (Alan Valentine, *The British Establishment: An Eighteenth-Century Biographical Dictionary*,

1760–1784, 2 vols. [Norman: University of Oklahoma Press, 1970], 477). A document entitled "Commissary of the Provisions," dated June 26, 1685, gives detailed instructions as to the duties of a commissary general (PRO, WO 26/6).

39 Leonard Labaree, Whitfield J. Bell, Helen C. Boatfield, and Helene H. Fineman, eds., *The Papers of Benjamin Franklin*, Vol. 4 (New Haven: Yale University Press, 1961), 381–82.

40 W. S. MacNutt, *The Atlantic Provinces: The Emergence of Colonial Society, 1712–1856* (Toronto: McClelland and Stewart, 1968), 53.

41 Captain Henry Ellis, *Considerations on the Great Advantages Which Would Arise from the Discovery of the North West Passage and a Clear Account of the Most Practicable Method for Attempting That Discovery* (London, 1750).

42 Vincent T. Harlow, *The Founding of the Second British Empire, 1763–1793*, 2 vols. (New York: Longmans, Green, 1952), 1:33. A recent historian of British foreign policy supports Harlow's interpretation while describing it as "occasionally controversial and overdrawn" (H. M. Scott, *British Foreign Policy in the Age of the American Revolution* [Oxford: Clarendon Press, 1990], 103).

43 Harlow, *Founding of the Second British Empire*, 1:25–27.

44 Ibid., 38–40.

45 Captain James Cook and Captain James King, *A Voyage to the Pacific Ocean Undertaken by Command of His Majesty for Making Discoveries in the Northern Hemisphere*, 4 vols. (London: John Stockdale, 1784), 2:332–37, 3:19–40.

46 Bertrand to Ellis, August 6, 1789, Whewell Papers, Trinity College, Wren Library, Cambridge.

CHAPTER THREE *Captain Henry Ellis, F.R.S., and the African Trade*

1 Nathaniel William Wraxall, *Historical Memoirs of My Own Time* (1815; rpt. London: Kegan, Paul, Trench, Trubner, 1904), 259–60.

2 Ibid., 77.

3 Bonamy Dobree, ed., *The Letters of Philip Dormer Stanhope, Fourth Earl of Chesterfield*, 6 vols. (London: Eyre and Spottiswoode, 1932), 2:378–79, 6:2952; Ninetta S. Jucker, ed., *The Jenkinson Papers, 1760–1766* (London: Macmillan, 1949), 161.

4 Ellis to Knox, December 30, 1767, William Knox Papers, WLCL.

5 Alan Valentine, *The British Establishment: An Eighteenth Century Biographical Dictionary, 1760–1784*, 2 vols. (Norman: University of Oklahoma Press, 1970), 1:277–78.

6 Ellis to Amherst, December 10, 1758, Amherst Papers, PRO, WO 34/34.

7 Edward Channing and Archibald C. Coolidge, eds., *The Barrington-Bernard Correspondence and Illustrative Matter, 1760–1770* (Cambridge, Mass.: Harvard University Press, 1912), 7.

8 J. C. Long, *George III: The Story of a Complex Man* (Boston: Little, Brown, 1961), 83.

9 Rodney Baine, "James Oglethorpe and the Parliamentary Election of 1754," *GHQ* 71 (Fall 1987): 460.

10 Spencer Savage, ed., *Catalogue of the Manuscripts in the Library of the Linnean Society of London, Part IV, Calendar of the Ellis Manuscripts* (London: Taylor and Frances, 1948), 178.

11 Raymond Phineas Stearns, "Colonial Fellows of the Royal Society of London, 1661–1788," *William and Mary Quarterly* 3d ser., 3 (April 1946): 241–42; Sir Archibald Geikie, *The Record of the Royal Society of London* (London: Royal Society, 1912), 344.

12 Pitt, Lyttelton, Egremont, and Voltaire were inducted in 1743, Montesquieu in 1744 (Geikie, *Record of the Royal Society*, 341); for Ellis and Voltaire, see Joseph Cradock, *Literary and Miscellaneous Memoirs*, 4 vols. (London: J. B. Nichols, 1828), 1:253–54.

13 Oglethorpe was admitted to the society on November 9, 1749, four months before Ellis (Geikie, *Record of the Royal Society*, 344).

14 Charles Richard Weld, *A History of the Royal Society with Memoirs of the Presidents*, 2 vols. (London: John W. Parker, 1848), 1:504, 516; Geikie, *Record of the Royal Society*, 35.

15 Weld, *History of the Royal Society*, 1:517–18, 525.

16 Ibid., 508–9.

17 Ibid., 526; Geikie, *Record of the Royal Society*, 37.

18 Weld, *History of the Royal Society*, 1:527.

19 Geikie, *Record of the Royal Society*, 346. John Ellis was awarded the Copley Medal in 1767 (ibid., 210). For a discussion of Ellis's study of corallines, see Savage, ed., *Calendar of the Ellis Manuscripts*, iv–v.

20 Weld, *History of the Royal Society*, 2:8.

21 "A Letter to the Rev. Dr. Hales, F.R.S., from Captain Henry Ellis, F.R.S., dated January 7, 1750–51 at Cape Monte, Africa, Ship Earl of Halifax," in Royal Society, *Philosophical Transactions* 47 (London: Printed for the Society, 1751 and 1752), 211–14.

22 Ibid.

23 Ibid.

24 Ibid. It is possible that the plant was a night-blooming cereus.

25 Ellis to Stephen Hales, January 7, 1751, Royal Society Library, Carleton House Terrace, London.

26 Savage, ed., *Calendar of the Ellis Manuscripts*, 8.

27 "A Letter to the Rev. Dr. Hales," Royal Society, *Philosophical Transactions*, 211–14.

28 Philip D. Curtin, *The Tropical Atlantic in the Age of the Slave Trade* (Washington, D.C.: American Historical Association, 1991), 10–11.

29 Ibid., 11–16.

30 Ellis to Lord Hawkesbury, March 27, 1788, Liverpool Manuscripts, British Library.

31 Ellis to Lord Hawkesbury, March 31, August 25, 1788, ibid.

32 Ellis to Hawkesbury, March 27, 1788, ibid.

33 *The Importance of Effectually Supporting the Royal African Company of England* (London: M. Cooper, 1744), 3; the pamphlet is in the New-York Historical Society, New York City.

34 Ibid., 4.

35 "An Account of Our Trade to Africa," *London Chronicle*, April 16–19, 1757, newspaper collection, New-York Historical Society.

36 O. A. Sherrard, *Freedom from Fear* (New York: St. Martin's Press, 1959), 104–5. Ellis's friend William Knox was troubled by the morality of slavery and in 1768

wrote a pamphlet about it addressed to the Society for the Propagation of the Gospel in Foreign Parts. He denounced the "disgraceful neglect by every administration" of the question of the rights of slaves. See Knox, *Three Tracts Respecting the Conversion and Instruction of the Free Indians and Negroe Slaves in the Colonies . . .* (London: J. Debrett, 1768), 29.

37 Sherrard, *Freedom from Fear*, 61–62; Malcolm Cowley, ed., *Adventures of an African Slaver, Being a True Account of the Life of Captain Theodore Canot, Trader in Gold, Ivory and Slaves on the Coast of Guinea* (Garden City, N.Y.: Garden City Publishing Co., 1928), 96–107.

38 Eveline Martin, ed., *Nicholas Owen, Journal of a Slave-Dealer*, (New York: Houghton Mifflin, 1930), 24, 37.

39 Cowley, ed., *Adventures of an African Slaver*, 98–107.

40 Ibid.; Sherrard, *Freedom from Fear*, 64–65.

41 Cowley, ed., *Adventures of an African Slaver*, 110.

42 Ellis to Hales, December 26, 1753, Royal Society, *Philosophical Transactions at Large* 49, pt. 1 (London: Printed for the Society, 1755), 336–38.

43 Ibid.

44 Sherrard, *Freedom from Fear*, 67.

45 Ellis to Hales, December 26, 1753, Royal Society, *Philosophical Transactions* 49, pt. 1 (London: Printed for the Society, 1755), 336–38.

46 "An Account of the great Benefit of Ventilators in many Instances in preserving the health and Lives of People in Slave and other transport ships by Stephen Hales D.D., F.R.S., read December 18, 1755," Royal Society, *Philosophical Transactions* 49, pt. 1 (London: Printed for the Society, 1755), 338.

CHAPTER FOUR *The View from the Board of Trade*

1 For the history of the Board of Trade, see Arthur Herbert Basye, *The Lords Commissioners of Trade and Plantations Commonly Known as the Board of Trade, 1748–1782* (New Haven: Yale University Press, 1925); also Duncan McArthur, "The British Board of Trade and Canada, 1760–1774," *Annual Report* (Ottawa: Canadian Historical Association, 1932), 97–113.

2 Scott, *British Foreign Policy in the Age of the American Revolution*, 43–44.

3 Gipson, *The British Isles and the American Colonies: Great Britain and Ireland*, 16–18.

4 Basye, *Lords Commissioners*, 63–65.

5 For a detailed history of the Paris negotiations, see Zenab Esmat Rashed, *The Peace of Paris, 1763* (Liverpool: Liverpool University Press, 1951).

6 Basye, *Lords Commissioners*, 68–72.

7 George Lyttelton to William Henry Lyttelton, December 4, 1759, Lyttelton Papers, Hagley Hall, Stourbridge, England; Barrington to Bernard, November 14, 1759, in Channing and Coolidge, eds., *Barrington-Bernard Correspondence*, 7; John Ellis to Henry Ellis, May 1, 1758, John Ellis Papers, Linnean Society Library.

8 Gipson, *The British Isles and the American Colonies: Great Britain and Ireland*, 98–99.

9 Basye, *Lords Commissioners*, 81; Henry Ellis to William Henry Lyttelton, Lyttelton Papers, WLCL.

10 Basye, *Lords Commissioners*, 103.

11   Ibid.

12   Ibid., 93–94.

13   Henry Penruddocke Wyndham, ed., *The Diary of the Late George Bubb Dodington Baron of Melcombe Regis, from March 8, 1749 to February 6, 1761* (Salisbury: E. Easton, 1784), 396–97.

14   Basye, *Lords Commissioners*, 98. Dupplin was a friend of Henry Ellis; see Ellis to Stephen Hales, January 7, 1751, Royal Society Library, Carleton House Terrace, London. In a postscript, Ellis asks Hales to present his compliments to Lord Dupplin, among others (Ellis to William Henry Lyttelton, December 10, 1757, Lyttelton Papers, WLCL).

15   Richard Lyttelton to William Henry Lyttelton, December 21, 1757, Lyttelton Papers, Hagley Hall.

16   George Lyttelton to William Henry Lyttelton, December 4, 1759, ibid.

17   Edmond Atkin to the Right Honourable the Lords Commissioners for Trade and Plantations, May 30, 1755, (A Report on) the Regulation and Management of the Indian Trade and Commerce; An Account of the Situation; Characters and Dispositions of the Several Indian nations that have Intercourse or connection with South Carolina: A Plan of a general Direction and Management of Indian Affairs throughout North America, Earl of Loudoun Papers, Huntington Library, San Marino, California. See also Wilbur R. Jacobs, ed., *Indians of the Southern Colonial Frontier: The Edmond Atkin Report and Plan of 1755* (Columbia: University of South Carolina Press, 1954).

18   Atkin to Loudoun, March 14, 1756, Loudoun Papers, Huntington Library. Atkin was mistaken. His commission did not receive royal approval until May 14, 1756 (PRO, CO 324/38).

19   Atkin to William Henry Lyttelton, May 20, October 13, 1756, Lyttelton Papers, WLCL.

20   Memorial of Alexander Kellet to Board of Trade, July 7, 1756, *CRG* 27:117–20.

21   Halifax, James Oswald, Andrew Stone, and William G. Hamilton to Henry Fox, July 29, 1756, in Letterbook of Board of Trade, PRO, CO 5/672, 388–425.

22   Ellis's commission, dated August 4, 1756, is in Letterbook of Board of Trade, PRO, CO 5/672, 427–28, and also in CO 324/38. A copy is in the DeRenne Collection, Hargrett Collection, University of Georgia Libraries, Athens. His instructions are in CO 324/38.

23   John Ellis to Henry Ellis, May 1, 1758, John Ellis Papers, Linnean Society Library.

24   "Reminiscences, Georgia," William Knox Papers, WLCL. Knox's appointment to the office of provost marshal was extended to last his lifetime in 1775 (PRO, CO 324/43).

25   Jonathan Bryan to the Earl of Halifax, April 6, 1756, *CRG* 27:114–15.

26   Ellis to Board of Trade, October 5, 1756, *CRG* 27:121–22; the letter is in PRO T1/367.

27   Board of Trade to James West, Secretary to Lords of Treasury, October 9, 1756, Board of Trade Letterbook, PRO, CO 5/672, 433; also in PROT1/367. On the same day John Pownall, secretary of the Board of Trade, forwarded Ellis's request for a warship to the Lords of the Admiralty and Halifax, Stone, and Oswald en-

dorsed Ellis's application for five hundred stand of arms. That requisition would follow a complicated route through the secretary of state and the commander in chief in America (PRO, CO 5/672, 436–40).

28 John West to Board of Trade, October 15, 1756, *CRG* 27:124; N. Hardinge to John Pownall, November 5, 1756, ibid.

29 Halifax et al. to Martyn, November 16, 1756, Board of Trade Letterbook, PRO, CO 5/672, 446.

CHAPTER FIVE   *The Transformation of Georgia*

1 Lawrence Henry Gipson, *The British Isles and the American Colonies: The Northern Plantations* (New York: Knopf, 1960), 273–80.

2 Rodney M. Baine and Phinizy Spalding, eds., *Some Account of the Design of the Trustees for Establishing Colonys in America by James Edward Oglethorpe* (Athens: University of Georgia Press, 1990).

3 Rodney Baine argues that Mary's claim that she was Chigilly's niece was a falsehood. When Brims's son Malatchi called her sister and cousin, he used the terms loosely (Baine, "Myths of Mary Musgrove," *GHQ* 76 [Summer 1992]: 428–35).

4 Phinizy Spalding, *Oglethorpe in America* (1977; rpt. Athens: University of Georgia Press, 1984), 110–50.

5 For an excellent description of Georgia's new government, see Trevor Richard Reese, *Colonial Georgia: A Study in British Imperial Policy in the Eighteenth Century* (Athens: University of Georgia Press, 1963), 18–28.

6 Reynolds to Board of Trade, December 5, 1754, *CRG* 27:32–34; his complaint about leaving hastily is in a letter to Thomas Robinson, August 2, 1755, PRO, CO 5/16.

7 Heard Robertson and Thomas H. Robertson, "The Town and Fort of Augusta," in Edward J. Cashin, ed., *Colonial Augusta: "Key of the Indian Countrey"* (Macon: Mercer University Press, 1986), 59–74.

8 President and Assistants to Martyn, February 28, 1751, *CRG* 26:168–72. For the traders' opinion, see Brown, Rae, and Company to Trustees, February 31, 1751, ibid., 152–55.

9 Kenneth Coleman, *Colonial Georgia: A History* (New York: Charles Scribner's Sons, 1976), 224.

10 Joseph Ottolenghe to Martyn, November 25, 1754, giving an account of the defeat of Gray's plan to take over the Assembly, *CRG* 27:39–43; John Reynolds to Board of Trade, February 28, 1755, ibid., 56.

11 *South Carolina Gazette*, July 11, 1753; James Glen to Board of Trade, July 10, 1753, South Carolina Records in the British Public Record Office, microfilm Vol. 25; South Carolina Department of Archives and History, Columbia; "Abstract of the proceedings at Augusta, December 15 to 18, 1755, between William Little, acting for John Reynolds, Governor of Georgia, and the head men and deputies of the Upper Creek Nation of Indians," *CRG* 27:213–19.

12 *South Carolina Gazette*, November 7, 1754.

13 John Reynolds to Board of Trade, April 7, 1755, *CRG* 27:61–62.

14 John Reynolds to Board of Trade, December 5, 1754, *CRG* 27:32–34; *South Carolina Gazette*, October 31, November 7, 1754.

15 John Reynolds to Board of Trade, April 17, 1758, *CRG* 28:154.

16 *South Carolina Gazette*, January 27, 1757.

17 Ibid., February 17, 1757; William Knox, "Reminiscences . . . Georgia," William Knox Papers, WLCL, printed in HMC, *The Manuscripts of Captain Howard Vincente Knox*, from Vol. 6 of *Report on Manuscripts in Various Collections* (Boston: Gregg Press, 1972), 245–50.

18 Knox, "Reminiscences . . . Georgia," Knox Papers, WLCL.

19 Ellis to Lyttelton, February 18, 1757, Lyttelton Papers, WLCL.

20 Ibid.

21 *South Carolina Gazette*, April 28, 1757.

22 "On Governour Ellis's Arrival in Georgia," Henry Ellis Papers, Hargrett Collection, University of Georgia Libraries, Athens.

23 *South Carolina Gazette*, April 28, 1757.

24 Knox, "Reminiscences . . . Georgia," Knox Papers, WLCL; Ellis to Board of Trade, March 11, 1757, *CRG* 28:2–14.

25 Ellis to Lyttelton, February 18, 1757, Lyttelton Papers, WLCL.

26 *South Carolina Gazette*, April 28, May 12, 1757.

27 House Minutes, January 28, 1757, *CRG* 13:138–39; House Minutes, January 14, 1757, ibid., 111; House Minutes, February 1, 2, 1757, ibid., 147–48, 152.

28 House Minutes, February 17, 1757, ibid., 167–68.

29 Knox, "Reminiscences . . . Georgia," Knox Papers, WLCL.

30 Ellis to Board of Trade, March 11, 1757, *CRG* 28:2–14.

31 Ibid.

32 Ellis to Board of Trade, February 10, 1759, *CRG* 28:180–84; Knox, "Reminiscences . . . Georgia," Knox Papers, WLCL.

33 Ellis to Board of Trade, February 10, 1759, *CRG* 28:180–84.

34 Ellis to Lyttelton, July 8, 1757, Lyttelton Papers, WLCL.

35 *South Carolina Gazette*, May 26, 1757.

36 Little's Address, May 25, 1757, *CRG* 28:36.

37 Ellis to Lyttelton, June 6, 1757, Lyttelton Papers, WLCL.

38 House Minutes, June 20, 1757, *CRG* 13:174; Ellis to Lyttelton, June 23, 1757, Lyttelton Papers, WLCL.

39 Ellis to Lyttelton, July 8, 1757, Lyttelton Papers, WLCL.

40 House Minutes, January 16, 1758, *CRG* 13:248; House Minutes, January 26, 1758, ibid., 257–58.

41 House Minutes, February 1, 3, 6, 8, 1758, ibid., 265–66, 268–69, 271, 274; Coleman, *Colonial Georgia*, 231.

42 Coleman, *Colonial Georgia*, 231.

43 Reynolds testimony before Board of Trade, April 17, 1758, *CRG* 28:132–54.

44 Order in Council, May 8, 1758, ibid., 154.

45 Halifax et al. to Ellis, April 21, 1758, Board of Trade Letterbook, PRO CO 5/673, 2–37.

46 John Ellis to Henry Ellis, May 1, 1758, John Ellis Papers, Linnean Society Library.

47 Kenneth Coleman and Charles Stephen Gurr, eds., *Dictionary of Georgia Biography*, 2 vols. (Athens: University of Georgia Press, 1983), 2:835–36.

CHAPTER SIX   *Indian Affairs*

1 The agent, John Tanner, was a neighbor of Oglethorpe's from Surrey who had gone to Georgia "for his amusement." He counted about four hundred children of mixed blood (Robert G. McPherson, ed., *The Journal of the Earl of Egmont* [Athens: University of Georgia Press, 1962], 272–73). For a brief history of the Creek Nation see Louis A. De Vorsey, Jr., "The Colonial Georgia Backcountry," in Cashin, ed., *Colonial Augusta*, 3–26, and Charles M. Hudson, "The Genesis of Georgia's Indians," in Harvey H. Jackson and Phinizy Spalding, eds., *Forty Years of Diversity: Essays on Colonial Georgia* (Athens: University of Georgia Press, 1984), 25–45. For a more complete treatment though marred by minor mistakes, see David H. Corkran, *The Creek Frontier, 1540–1783* (Norman: University of Oklahoma Press, 1967).

2 Minutes of Conference with Creek Indians, June 2, 1753, in William L. McDowell, Jr., ed., *Colonial Records of South Carolina: Documents Relating to Indian Affairs, May 21, 1750–August 7, 1754* (Columbia: South Carolina Archives Department, 1958), 403.

3 Verner W. Crane, *The Southern Frontier* (1929; rpt. Ann Arbor: University of Michigan Press, 1959), 127; *South Carolina Gazette*, January 12, 1738, September 8, 1739.

4 For the founding of Augusta, see Heard Robertson and Thomas H. Robertson, "The Town and Fort of Augusta," in Cashin, ed., *Colonial Augusta*, 59–74.

5 Edward J. Cashin, "The Gentlemen of Augusta," ibid., 29–56.

6 Headmen and Warriours of the Chickasaw Nation to the King of Carolina and his Beloved Men, April 6, 1756, in McDowell, ed., *Colonial Records*, 109–10.

7 In spite of Glen's disclaimer that "an awkward modesty hindered me from claiming the merit that I knew was justly due to me," he claimed it anyway, saying that "it was entirely owing to me that any of the Choctaws ever declared War against the French" (Glen to Board of Trade, December 1751, South Carolina Records in the British Public Record Office, microfilm vol. 24, South Carolina Department of Archives and History, Columbia; Atkin's refutation of Glen's claim was printed in pamphlet form, *Historical Account of the Revolt of the Choctaw Indians in the Late War from the French to the British Alliance and of Their Return Since to That of the French* (London, 1753). A copy is in the British Library.

8 Samuel Cole Williams, ed., *Adair's History of the American Indian* (New York: Promontory Press, 1974), 299–300.

9 William R. McDowell, Jr., ed., *Documents Relating to Indian Affairs, 1754–1765: Colonial Records of South Carolina* (Columbia: University of South Carolina Press, 1970), xxiii–xxiv.

10 McGillivray blamed the Indians for not keeping their appointment with Reynolds (McGillivray to Glen [December 22, 1755], ibid., 89).

11 Ellis to Lyttelton, September 6, 1758, Lyttelton Papers, WLCL.

12 Kerlérec to Machault, December 18, 1754, in Dunbar Rowland, A. G. Sanders,

and Patricia Kay Galloway, eds., *Mississippi Provincial Archives: French Dominion, 1749–1763*, 5 vols. (Baton Rouge: Louisiana University Press, 1932–84), 5:154–59.

13 McDowell, ed., *Colonial Records*, 405.

14 David Corkran characterized the Mortar as a "nativist," *Creek Frontier*, 161.

15 James Germany to Messrs. Rae and Barksdale, June 10, 1756, in Outerbridge to Lyttelton, July 17, 1756, Lyttelton Papers, WLCL.

16 Minutes of Conference, May 31, June 2, 1753, in McDowell, ed., *Documents Relating to Indian Affairs*, 406–8.

17 Ellis to Lyttelton, August 25, 1757, Lyttelton Papers, WLCL.

18 Ellis to Board of Trade, May 5, 1757, *CRG* 28:16–28.

19 Reynolds to Lyttelton, September 8, 1756, Lyttelton Papers, WLCL.

20 Ellis to Board of Trade, March 11, 1757, *CRG* 28:7.

21 Ellis to Board of Trade, November 25, 1757, ibid., 85; Ellis to Lyttelton, October 31, 1757, Lyttelton Papers, WLCL.

22 Ellis to Lyttelton, February 18, 1757, Lyttelton Papers, WLCL.

23 Council Minutes, February 25, 1757, *CRG* 7:494.

24 Board of Trade to Ellis, November 24, 1758, PRO, CO 5/673.

25 Ellis to Lyttelton, May 24, 1757, Lyttelton Papers, WLCL.

26 Ellis to Lyttelton, June 23, 1757, ibid.

27 Ellis to Bouquet, June 24, 1757, Ellis Papers, Hargrett Collection, University of Georgia Libraries.

28 Council Minutes, April 4, 1757, *CRG* 7:506–7.

29 Council Minutes, July 30, 1757, ibid., 613–17; Ellis to Lyttelton, July 21, 1757, Lyttelton Papers, WLCL.

30 Council Minutes, July 30, 1757, *CRG* 7:613–17.

31 Governor Ellis's instructions to Joseph Wright, August 7, 1757, in John T. Juricek, *Georgia Treaties, 1733–1763* (Frederick, Md.: University Publications of America, 1989), 258.

32 Ray Allen Billington, *Westward Expansion: A History of the American Frontier* (New York: Collier-Macmillan, 1967), 138.

33 Bouquet to Ellis, December 10, 1757, Ellis Papers, Hargrett Collection, University of Georgia Libraries.

34 Ellis's instructions to Wright, August 7, 1757, enclosed in Ellis to Lyttelton, August 25, 1757, Lyttelton Papers, WLCL.

35 Ellis to Lyttelton, August 25, 1757, ibid.

36 Ellis to Board of Trade, September 20, 1757, *CRG* 28:68–70; Bouquet to Loudoun, August 25, 1757, in S. K. Stevens, Donald Kent, and Autumn L. Leonard, eds., *The Papers of Henry Bouquet*, 2 vols. (Harrisburg: Pennsylvania Historical and Museum Commission, 1972), 1:172–76.

37 John R. Alden, *John Stuart and the Southern Colonial Frontier: A Study of Indian Relations, War, Trade, and Land Problems in the Southern Wilderness, 1754–1775* (New York: Gordian Press, 1966), 59–60.

38 The historian Charles L. Mowat is quoted in Louis De Vorsey, Jr., ed., *De Brahm's Report of the General Survey in the Southern District of North America* (Columbia: University of South Carolina Press, 1971), 7.

39   In his letter to John Ellis of July 17, 1758, about the heat in Savannah, Ellis mentioned the piazza on the northern side of the house, a cellar, and two stories above it. John Ellis had the account printed in the *London Magazine or Gentleman's Monthly Intelligencer*, July 1759, pp. 371–72 and also in Royal Society, *Philosophical Transactions*, 50, pt. 1 (London: Printed for the Society, 1757), 754–56. William G. De Brahm's plat of Savannah's defenses shows a lot designated "governor" in Heathcote Ward (De Vorsey, ed., *De Brahm's Report*, facing 155). De Vorsey cautions that this drawing is not entirely consistent with Ellis's description of the defense works (ibid., 26).

40   De Brahm acknowledged that the bastions were Ellis's idea (De Vorsey, ed., *De Brahm's Report*, 154).

41   Council Minutes, October 25, 1757, *CRG* 7:643–44.

42   Council Minutes, October 29, 1757, ibid., 644–45.

43   Ibid., 645.

44   Ibid., 645–47.

45   Council Minutes, November 3, 1757, ibid., 658–61.

46   Ibid., 661–64.

47   Ibid., 664.

48   Ibid., 665–67; see also Juricek, *Georgia Treaties*, 270–71.

49   Ellis to Lyttelton, November 3, 11, 1757, Lyttelton Papers, WLCL.

50   John Ellis to Henry Ellis, March 10, 1759, John Ellis Papers, Linnean Society Library.

51   Ibid.

52   Williams, ed., *Adair's History*, 400–401.

53   Ellis to Loudoun, September 20, 1757, Loudoun Papers, Huntington Library; Ellis to Board of Trade, October 25, 1758, *CRG* 28:165–66.

54   Loudoun allowed Ellis credit of £850 on the account of the deputy paymaster at New York (Loudoun to Ellis, June 19, 1757, Loudoun Papers, Huntington Library). Two days before, Loudoun informed Pitt of his intended action and asked for instructions (Loudoun to Pitt, June 17, 1757, PRO T1/376).

55   Ellis to Lyttelton, February 20, 1758, Lyttelton Papers, WLCL.

56   Ellis to Board of Trade, February 18, 1758, *CRG* 28:123–24.

57   Ellis to Lyttelton, February 20, March 17, 1757, Lyttelton Papers, WLCL.

58   Kerlérec to Machault d'Arnouville, September 15, 1754, in Rowland, Sanders, and Galloway, eds.,*Mississippi Provincial Archives*, 151–52.

59   Ellis to Board of Trade, December 7, 1757, *CRG* 28:89–91.

60   Creek Declaration Ceding the Yamacraw Tract and the Islands of Ossabaw, St. Catherine, and Sapelo, April 22 and May 1, 1758, in Juricek, *Georgia Treaties*, 277–79.

61   Ellis to Board of Trade, June 28, 1758, *CRG* 28:158; Board of Trade to Ellis, November 24, 1758, PRO, CO 5/673/182; Order in Council, January 11, 1759, *CRG* 28:173.

62   Ellis to Board of Trade, July 26, 1759, *CRG* 28:210.

63   Ellis to Lyttelton, August 3, 1759, Lyttelton Papers, WLCL.

64   Ibid.

CHAPTER SEVEN   *International Affairs*

1   Gustave Lanctot, *A History of Canada: From the Treaty of Utrecht to the Treaty of Paris, 1713–1763* (Cambridge, Mass.: Harvard University Press, 1965), 92.
2   Ibid., 94.
3   Ibid., 99.
4   The travails of the Acadians sent to France are chronicled in Oscar William Winzerling, *Acadian Odyssey* (Baton Rouge: Louisiana State University Press, 1955).
5   Reynolds defended himself against these charges in his testimony to the Board of Trade, March 6, 1758, *CRG* 28:136–54.
6   E. Merton Coulter, "The Acadians in Georgia," *GHQ* 47 (March 1963): 69.
7   Council Minutes, December 14, 1755, *CRG* 7:301–2.
8   Ibid.; Reynolds's testimony to the Board of Trade, March 6, 1758, *CRG* 28, pt. 1:143.
9   Glen to Board of Trade, April 14, 1756, Lyttelton to Henry Fox, June 16, 1756, Lyttelton Papers, WLCL.
10 John Frederic Herbin, *The History of Grand-Pre* (St. John, New Brunswick: Barnes and Company, n.d.), 130–33.
11 Ellis to Board of Trade, March 11, 1757, *CRG* 28:7.
12 Council Minutes, April 4, 1757, *CRG* 7:506–7.
13 Council Minutes, September 6, 1757, ibid., 625; Journal of Commons House, April 1, 1761, *CRG* 13:491–93.
14 Coulter, "Acadians in Georgia," 73–74.
15 Louis De Vorsey, Jr., has demonstrated that Oglethorpe altered existing maps to show a nonexisting branch of the Altamaha flowing into the St. Johns in order to strengthen England's claims to that river ("Oglethorpe and the Earliest Maps of Georgia," in Phinizy Spalding and Harvey H. Jackson, eds., *Oglethorpe in Perspective: Georgia's Founder After Two Hundred Years* [Tuscaloosa: University of Alabama Press, 1989], 22–43).
16 Ellis to Bouquet, June 24, 1757, Ellis Papers, Hargrett Collection, University of Georgia Libraries.
17 John Jay TePaske, *The Governorship of Spanish Florida, 1700–1763* (Durham: Duke University Press, 1964), 17–18, 73–74.
18 Ibid., 106–7.
19 Ibid., 156–57.
20 Charles Gayarré, *History of Louisiana*, 2 vols. (New Orleans: James A. Gresham, 1879), 2:82–84, 90, 95.
21 Ellis to Lyttelton, May 1, 1757, Lyttelton Papers, WLCL.
22 Ellis to Board of Trade, May 5, 1757, *CRG* 28:19.
23 Ellis to Lyttelton, May 1757, Lyttelton Papers, WLCL.
24 Ellis to Board of Trade, May 25, 1757, *CRG* 28:28–29.
25 Ellis to Board of Trade, October 22, 1757, ibid., 71–72.
26 Ibid.
27 Ellis to Lyttelton, October 6, 1757, Lyttelton Papers, WLCL.
28 Ellis to Board of Trade, October 22, 1757, *CRG* 28:74.
29 John McGillivray to Ellis, December 2, 1757, enclosed in Ellis to Lyttelton, December 10, 1757, Lyttelton Papers, WLCL.

30 Extract of McGillivray to Ellis, October 24, 1758, in Ellis to Lyttelton, November 5, 1758; Ellis to Lyttelton, May 9, 29, June 5, 1758, ibid., Ellis to Pitt, February 8, 1758, *CRG* 28:128.

31 Pitt to Board of Trade, March 7, 1758, *CRG* 28:129.

32 Board of Trade to Ellis, November 24, 1758, PRO, CO 5/673.

33 Ellis to Board of Trade, May 20, 1758, *CRG* 28:155–57.

34 TePaske, *Governorship of Spanish Florida*, 38.

35 Ellis to Board of Trade, May 20, July 20, 1758, *CRG* 28:155–57, 161–64; Ellis to Lyttelton, June 5, 25, July 3, 1758, Lyttelton Papers, WLCL.

36 "An Account of the Heat in Georgia," *London Magazine or Gentleman's Monthly Intelligencer*, July 1759, pp. 371–72; also in Royal Society, *Philosophical Transactions* 50 pt. 1 (London: Printed for the Society, 1757): 754–56.

37 Ellis to Lyttelton, July 21, 29, 1758, Lyttelton Papers, WLCL; Ellis to Board of Trade, July 20, 1758, *CRG* 28:163.

38 Ellis to Lyttelton, July 29, 1758, Lyttelton Papers, WLCL.

39 Ibid.

40 Ellis to Board of Trade, October 25, 1758, *CRG* 28:165–66.

41 John Ellis to Henry Ellis, March 10, 1759, Linnean Society Library.

42 Ibid.

43 Ellis to Lyttelton, November 22, 1758, Lyttelton Papers, WLCL.

44 Ellis to Lyttelton, December 23, 1758, ibid.

45 Ellis to Board of Trade, January 28, 1759, *CRG* 28:174–77.

46 Ellis to Lyttelton, December 15, 1758, Lyttelton Papers, WLCL.

47 Ellis to Pitt, March 1, 1759, *CRG* 28:186.

48 Ellis to Board of Trade, March 1, 1759, ibid., 187.

49 Ellis to Lyttelton, May 19, 1759, Lyttelton Papers, WLCL.

CHAPTER EIGHT   *The Halifax Initiatives*

1 George A. Rawlyk, *Nova Scotia's Massachusetts: A Study of Massachusetts–Nova Scotia Relations, 1630 to 1784* (Montreal: McGill-Queen's University Press, 1973), 218–21. Another Halifax initiative, not treated here, was the convoking of the Albany Congress in 1754 to consider a plan of colonial defense.

2 Ibid., 228.

3 Lawrence Henry Gipson, *The Triumphant Empire: New Responsibilities Within the Enlarged Empire, 1763–1766* (New York: Knopf, 1956), 130–31.

4 John Ellis to Hillsborough, 1963?, John Ellis Papers, Linnean Society Library.

5 Edmond Atkin, "A Plan of a General Direction and Management of Indian Affairs Throughout North America," May 30, 1755, London Papers, Huntington Library, San Marino, California.

6 Reynolds to Board of Trade, April 17, 1758, *CRG* 28, pt. 1:149.

7 Coleman, *Colonial Georgia*, 181.

8 Ellis to Board of Trade, March 11, 1757, *CRG* 28, pt. 1:4.

9 Ellis's address of June 16, 1757, *South Carolina Gazette*, July 14, 1757.

10 Ellis's address of October 25, 1759, *South Carolina Gazette*, November 3–10, 1759.

11   Address of Commons House, October 13, 1760, *South Carolina Gazette*, October 25–November 1, 1760.

12   Ellis to Board of Trade, May 5, 1757, *CRG* 28, pt. 1:24.

13   Ellis to Board of Trade, April 24, 1759, ibid., 200–209; Ellis to Pitt, August 1, 1757, PRO, CO 5/18.

14   Alan Gallay, *The Formation of a Planter Elite: Jonathan Bryan and the Southern Colonial Frontier* (Athens: University of Georgia Press, 1989), 101. Gallay refers to the period 1755 to 1760 as "the most competitive" (ibid., 91).

15   Ellis to Board of Trade, February 10, 1759, *CRG* 28, pt. 1:180–84; Thomas Rasberry to Samuel Lloyd, May 7, 1759, "Letter Book of Thomas Rasberry, 1758–1761," *Georgia Historical Society Collections*, 8:55.

16   Ellis to Lyttelton, March 21, 1757, Lyttelton Papers, WLCL.

17   De Vorsey, ed., *De Brahm's Report*, 141, 158–59; Reynolds to Board of Trade, December 5, 1754, *CRG* 27:32–34.

18   Thomas Rasberry to Samuel Lloyd, November 1, 1758, *Georgia Historical Society Collections*, 8:17–18.

19   Address of Union Society, *South Carolina Gazette*, November 15–22, 1760.

20   Harold Davis, *Fledgling Province: Social and Cultural Life in Colonial Georgia, 1733–1776* (Chapel Hill: University of North Carolina Press, 1976), 32; Coleman, *Colonial Georgia*, 230; Ellis to Board of Trade, January 28, 1759, *CRG* 28, pt. 1:178.

21   Davis, *Fledgling Province*, 142, Ottolenghe to Rev. Mr. Waring, July 12, 1758, quoted ibid., 98.

22   Ellis to Hawkesbury, March 31, 1788, Liverpool Manuscripts, British Library.

23   Betty Wood, *Slavery in Colonial Georgia, 1730–1775* (Athens: University of Georgia Press, 1984), 124.

24   Address of inhabitants of Augusta and Ellis's reply, *South Carolina Gazette*, November 15–22, 1760.

25   Address by Georgia Society, *South Carolina Gazette*, October 25–November 1, 1760; Davis, *Fledgling Province*, 97.

26   Davis, *Fledgling Province*, 182.

27   John Ellis to Henry Ellis, November 20, 1758, John Ellis Papers, Linnean Society Library. Ellis's account of the heat was reviewed by Dr. John Fothergill and read to the Royal Society on November 16, 1758.

28   John Ellis, "A Catalogue of Plants . . . that would grow in the Climate of Georgia. . . . ," Guard Book 4, Royal Society of Arts, London.

29   Paul Tabor, "Bermuda Grass: A Georgia Name?" *GHQ* 52 (June 1968): 199–202.

30   James Habersham to John Ellis, October 18, 1770, in "The Letters of Hon. James Habersham, 1756–1775," *Georgia Historical Society Collections*, 6:91–93.

31   Henry Ellis to John Ellis, June 29, 1758, Guard Book 4, Royal Society of Arts.

32   John Ellis to Henry Ellis, September 12, 1758, John Ellis Papers, Linnean Society Library.

33   John Ellis's Notebook, November 17, 20, December 14, 1758, ibid.

34   Coleman, *Colonial Georgia*, 113.

35   John Ellis to Henry Ellis, May 1, 1758, John Ellis Papers, Linnean Society Library.

36   Coleman, *Colonial Georgia*, 113–16.

37   Henry Ellis to John Ellis, May 10, June 29, 1758, Guard Book 4, Royal Society of Arts; Henry Ellis to Board of Trade, May 20, 1758, *CRG* 28, pt. 1:157.

38   Ellis to Benjamin Martyn, June 27, 1758, Guard Book 4, Royal Society of Arts; Ellis to Board of Trade, May 25, 1757, *CRG* 28, pt. 1:29.

39   *South Carolina Gazette*, July 28, 1758; Ellis to Board of Trade, July 20, 1758, *CRG* 28, pt. 1:161–62; Ellis to Lyttelton, July 21, 1758, Lyttelton Papers, WLCL.

40   Ellis to Lyttelton, July 21, 1758, Lyttelton Papers, WLCL.

41   Ellis to Board of Trade, July 26, 1759, *CRG* 28, pt. 1:218; H. Kennan to Dartmouth, December 31, 1765, Dartmouth Papers, American Section, Vol. 2, p. 133, Staffordshire Record Office, Stafford, England; Coleman, *Colonial Georgia*, 209.

42   John Ellis to Henry Ellis, November 20, 1758, John Ellis Papers, Linnean Society Library.

43   Stearns, "Colonial Fellows of the Royal Society," 243–44, 255.

44   Ellis to Lyttelton, April 25, 1759, Lyttelton Papers, WLCL; Ellis to Board of Trade, May 5, 1757, *CRG* 28, pt. 1:21.

45   Ellis to Lyttelton, June 6, September 8, 1759, February 5, March 14, 1760, Lyttelton Papers, WLCL.

46   Kinloch Bull, Jr., *The Oligarchs in Colonial and Revolutionary Charleston: Lieutenant Governor William Bull II and His Family* (Columbia: University of South Carolina Press, 1991), 46.

47   Ellis to Board of Trade, March 15, 1759, *CRG* 28, pt. 1:192–93.

48   Atkin to Halifax, May 30, 1755, Loudoun Papers, Huntington Library; Atkin to Lyttelton, May 20, 1756, Lyttelton Papers, WLCL.

49   Glen to Lyttelton, January 23, 1756, Lyttelton Papers, WLCL.

50   Atkin to Loudoun, March 8, 1756, Loudoun Papers, Huntington Library; Atkin to Amherst, May 20, 1758, Amherst Papers, PRO, WO 34/47.

51   Ellis to Board of Trade, January 6, 1760, *CRG* 28, pt. 1:226.

52   Ellis to Lyttelton, February 24, 1759, Lyttelton Papers, WLCL; Council Minutes, March 8, 1759, *CRG* 8:5–8.

53   Atkin to Amherst, May 20, 1758, Amherst Papers, PRO, WO 34/47; charges of carrying on the Indian Service in the Southern District from October 6, 1756, to March 24, 1760, Amherst Papers, PRO, WO 34/47.

54   Ellis to Lyttelton, November 5, 1758, Lyttelton Papers, WLCL.

55   *South Carolina Gazette*, December 29–January 5, 1760; Proclamation given at Mucollossus, September 7, 1759, Amherst Papers, PRO, WO 34/47.

56   Atkin to Lyttelton, November 24, 1758, Lyttelton Papers, WLCL.

57   Williams, ed., *Adair's History*, 268.

58   McGillivray to Lyttelton, April 25, 1759, Lyttelton Papers, WLCL.

59   Ellis to Board of Trade, July 26, 1759, *CRG* 28, pt. 1:212.

60   Council Minutes, October 10, 1759, *CRG* 8:160–67.

61   Ibid.

62   Council Minutes, October 11, 1759, June 5, 1760, ibid., 168–70, 319–23; *South Carolina Gazette*, October 13, 1759.

63   Council Minutes, October 11, 1759, *CRG* 8:168–70.

64   Ellis to Lyttelton, August 27, October 11, 1759, Lyttelton Papers, WLCL.

65 Ellis to Board of Trade, January 6, 1760, *CRG* 28, pt. 1:226.
66 Ellis to Lyttelton, February 16, 1760, Lyttelton Papers, WLCL.
67 Atkin to Lyttelton, November 30, 1759, ibid.
68 Atkin to Amherst, November 20, 1760, Amherst Papers, PRO, WO 34/47.
69 Knox to Martyn(?), May 20, 1760, Knox Papers, WLCL; Historical Manuscripts Commission, *Report on Manuscripts in Various Collections*, 6:84–85.
70 Alden, *John Stuart*, 135–36.
71 Atkin to Lyttelton, November 30, 1760, Lyttelton Papers, WLCL.
72 If readers of the *South Carolina Gazette* followed the adventures of Edmond Atkin, they might have noticed an item in the July 7, 1759, issue. Field Marshal Keith, on the staff of Frederick the Great, was killed in the Battle of Hochkirchen. According to a report, Keith "received a shot in his breast and fell dead in the arms of Mr. Tibuy, a gallant English gentleman, who had made the campaign as a volunteer, and was himself shot through the shoulder." The readers could not have known that the gallant English gentleman was James Edward Oglethorpe, Georgia's founder. See Rodney M. Baine and Mary E. Williams, "James Oglethorpe in Europe: Recent Findings in His Military Life," in Spalding and Jackson, eds., *Oglethorpe in Perspective*, 112–21.

CHAPTER NINE *The Unfinished Campaigns*

1 The Mitchell map is in the Hargrett Collection, University of Georgia Libraries, Athens.
2 James Glen to John Forbes, June 8, 1758, in Henry Moore to Lyttelton, Lyttelton Papers, WLCL.
3 Pitt to Lyttelton, January 27, March 7, 1758, ibid.
4 The twelve-folio-page letter has several references to Adair's willingness to be of service. It is in Adair's style and the signature is misspelled "Lauglin McGilvery." The boisterous Adair was under a cloud in Charlestown and thought his advice would be better received if it came from the respected McGillivray. He need not have bothered with the deception. McGillivray sent a covering letter to Lyttelton, stating that he was enclosing Adair's opinion. The letter signed "Lauglin McGilvery" is dated July 14, 1758, McGillivray's covering letter is July 18, 1758; both are in Lyttelton Papers, WLCL.
5 Lyttelton to Pitt, November 4, 1758, PRO, CO 5/18.
6 Kerlérec to Berryer, December 1, 1758, in Rowland, Sanders, and Galloway, eds., *Mississippi Provincial Archives*, 5:199–202.
7 Ellis to Lyttelton, July 3, 1758, Lyttelton Papers, WLCL; Ellis to Egremont, n.d., PRO, 30/47/14/2.
8 Boscawen to Lyttelton, July 5, 29, August 28, 1758, Lyttelton Papers, WLCL.
9 Amherst to Lyttelton, March 21, 1759, ibid. Amherst referred to the contents of his letters of April 15 and 16, 1759, to Lyttelton.
10 Lawrence Henry Gipson, *The Great War for the Empire: The Culmination, 1760–1763* (New York: Knopf, 1953), 83.
11 Ibid., 105.

12 Ibid., 186.
13 Lyttelton to Board of Trade, September 1, 1759, PRO, SC, 28. Lyttelton kept the board informed of Cherokee activities in reports dated February 21, April 14, and May 8, 1759, PRO, SC, 28.
14 Ellis to Board of Trade, September 6, 1759, *CRG* 28, pt. 1:216–17.
15 Ellis to Lyttelton, August 27, 1759, Lyttelton Papers, WLCL.
16 Lyttelton to Board of Trade, October 16, 1759, PRO, SC, 28; Ellis to Lyttelton, October 30, 1759, Lyttelton Papers, WLCL.
17 Lyttelton to Board of Trade, October 23, November 24, December 10, 29, 1759, PRO, SC, 28.
18 Ellis to Board of Trade, February 15, 1760, *CRG* 28, pt. 1:227; Amherst to Ellis, December 21, 1759, PRO, CO, 5/57; Ellis to Amherst, April 14, 1760, Amherst Papers, PRO, WO 34/34.
19 Lyttelton to Board of Trade, February 22, 1760, PRO, SC, 28.
20 Amherst to Ellis, June 1, 1759, Ellis to Amherst, July 20, 1759, PRO, CO 5/55; Ellis to Lyttelton, November 25, 1759, Lyttelton Papers, WLCL.
21 Outerbridge to Lyttelton, October 14, 1759, Lyttelton Papers, WLCL.
22 Tobler to Lyttelton, November 7, 1759, Ellis to Lyttelton, November 25, 1759, ibid.
23 Ellis to Lyttelton, December 7, 1759, Ellis to Outerbridge, December 7, 1759, Outerbridge to Lyttelton, December 19, 1759, ibid.
24 Ellis to Outerbridge, January 4, 1760, ibid.
25 Ellis to Lyttelton, February 4, 1760, ibid.; Ellis to Amherst, January 12, 1760, Amherst Papers, PRO, WO 34/34.
26 Ellis to Lyttelton, February 16, 1760, Lyttelton Papers, WLCL.
27 Atkin to Lyttelton, January 9, 1760, ibid.
28 Outerbridge to Lyttelton, February 12, 1760, Ellis to Lyttelton, February 3, 1760, ibid.
29 *South Carolina Gazette*, February 23–March 1, 1760.
30 Ibid., July 19–26, 1760.
31 Ellis to Pitt, July 10, 1760, PRO, CO 5/19.
32 Ibid.
33 Ellis to Lyttelton, February 27, 1760, Lyttelton Papers, WLCL.
34 Ellis to Lyttelton, September 8, 1759, ibid.
35 Bull to Board of Trade, July 20, August 31, September 9, 1760, PRO, SC, 28.
36 Order in Council, May 13, 1760, PRO, CO 324/39; Ellis to Board of Trade, May 15, 1760, *CRG* 28, pt. 1:249.
37 Ellis to Board of Trade, June 7, 1760, *CRG* 28, pt. 1:252.
38 Ellis to Board of Trade, November 25, 1759, ibid., 218.
39 *South Carolina Gazette*, October 25–November 1, 1760.
40 Ellis to Lyttelton, August 3, 1759, Lyttelton Papers, WLCL.
41 Ellis to Pitt, June 26, 1761, Chatham Papers, MG 23, Vol. A2, 66–67, National Archives of Canada, Ottawa; *South Carolina Gazette*, November 1–8, November 22–29, 1760.
42 Atkin to Amherst, November 20, 1760, Amherst Papers, PRO, WO 34/47.
43 Guy Johnson to William Johnson, February 2, 1761, in Milton W. Hamilton and

Albert B. Corey, eds., *The Papers of Sir William Johnson* (Albany: University of the State of New York, 1951), 10:208–10.

44   Ibid.

45   Amherst to Wright, December 28, 1760, PRO, CO 5/60.

46   Richard Shuckburgh to Johnson, December 29, 1760, in James Sullivan, ed., *The Papers of Sir William Johnson*, vol. 3 (Albany: University of the State of New York, 1921), 293–95; Ellis to Pitt, June 26, 1761, Chatham Papers, National Archives of Canada.

47   Wright to Amherst, February 20, 1761, Amherst Papers, PRO, WO 34/34.

48   Bull to Board of Trade, December 17, 1760, PRO, SC, 28; Bull to Board of Trade, January 29, April 30, May 16, 28, June 19, July 17, September 23, 1761, PRO, SC, 29.

49   Basye, *Lords Commissioners of Trade*, 107. The sobriquet "Father of the Colonies" graces Halifax's monument in Westminister Abbey.

50   Ellis was named governor by the Halifax board on March 17, 1761 (*Journal of the Commissioners for Trade and Plantations* [London: His Majesty's Stationery Office, 1935], 11:180); the appointment was confirmed by Order in Council, April 14, 1761, PRO, CO, 324/40.

51   Gipson, *Triumphant Empire*, 132–33, 144.

52   Beamish Murdoch, *A History of Nova Scotia or Acadie*, 2 vols. (Halifax: James Barnes, 1866), 2:405; John Bartlett Brebner, *The Neutral Yankees of Nova Scotia: A Marginal Colony During the Revolutionary Years* (New York, Columbia University Press, 1937), 66; Ellis to Pitt, June 26, 1761, Chatham Papers, MG 23, Vol. A2, 66–67, National Archives of Canada.

53   Brebner, *Neutral Yankees*, 67, 85.

54   Ibid., 67; Gipson, *Triumphant Empire*, 151.

55   Ellis's second leave of absence from Nova Scotia was dated May 12, 1762, and signed by Egremont (PRO, CO 324/40); Francis J. Audet, "Governors, Lieutenant-governors and Administrators of Nova Scotia, 1604–1932," 137–38, typescript, Nova Scotia Public Archives, Halifax. On March 13, 1763, Wilmot was commissioned lieutenant governor and, on October 5, 1763, as governor.

56   Old Deed Book 5, Public Archives of Nova Scotia, 403–5; Centennial Project, *The Town of Stewiacke, Nova Scotia* (1967), 46–47, Stewiacke Public Library.

57   Philip Thicknesse, *The New Prose Bath Guide for the Year 1778* (London: Printed for the author, n.d.), vi–vii.

58   Ellis to Knox, April 20, 30, 1762, Knox Papers, WLCL; Ellis was at Bath but indicated on the latter date that he would meet Knox in London.

59   Memorial of the late Governor of Georgia, June 11, 1761, PRO, T1/409; *Journal of the Commissioners for Trade and Plantations*, 11:207.

CHAPTER TEN   *The Option for America*

1   Rashed, *Peace of Paris*, 70–75; Gipson, *Great War for the Empire*, 209–23.

2   Gipson, *Great War for the Empire*, 218.

3   Hardwicke to Newcastle, August 2, 1761, in Philip C. Yorke, ed., *The Life and Cor-*

respondence of Philip Yorke, Earl of Hardwicke, Lord High Chancellor of Great Britain, 3 vols. (1913; rpt. New York: Octagon Books, 1977), 3:318.

4   Newcastle to Bedford, October 2, 1761, in Lord John Russell, ed., *Correspondence of John, Fourth Duke of Bedford,* 3 vols. (London: Longman, Brown, Green and Longmans, 1846), 3:46–47.

5   Gipson, *Great War for the Empire,* 224–25.

6   Newcastle to Bedford, October 6, 1761, in Russell, ed., *Bedford Correspondence,* 3:48–49. Alan Valentine wrote: "Pitt's place as secretary of state was taken by Granville, while Halifax left the Board of Trade and Plantations to fill Bedford's place as lord lieutenant of Ireland." Egremont, of course, replaced Pitt, and Halifax left the board seven months before; the index mistakenly lists John Perceval, Lord Egmont, as Egremont (Valentine, *Lord North,* 2 vols. [Norman: University of Oklahoma Press, 1967], 99, 563).

7   Egremont House was later the residence of the Duke of Cambridge, sixth son of George III. In 1757 it was acquired by Lord Palmerston, prime minister and foreign secretary. There is a marker on the front wall identifying the house as the residence of Palmerston. After the prime minister's death, it became the Naval and Military Club. Bold "in" and "out" signs at each gate caused it to be known locally as the "in and out club." In 1878 a more imposing portico and decorative balcony were added to the plain front facade.

8   Robin Fedden, *Petworth* (London: Curwen Press, 1973), 6; Horace Walpole to George Montagu, January 9, 1752, in W. S. Lewis, ed., *A Selection of the Letters of Horace Walpole,* 2 vols. (New York: Harper and Brothers, 1926), 1:66–69. Petworth House and Park are under the protection of the National Trust; see Lydia Greeves and Michael Trinick, *The National Trust Guide* (New York: Weidenfeld and Nicolson, 1989), 246–48. Anyone wishing to use material from the Petworth House Archives must order it two weeks in advance. The documents are delivered to the West Sessex Public Record Office in Chichester for study. The arrangement discourages use of the Petworth holdings.

9   The expression was Francis Maseres's; William Knox said the same thing differently: Egremont was "guided in all colonial affairs by Governor Ellis," he wrote ("Anecdotes and Characteristics, Lord Lansdowne," July 6, 1785, Knox Papers 10/35, WLCL).

10   "A list of offices in America in the recommendation of the Secretary of State for the Southern Department made in November 1761," Egremont Papers, PRO 30/47/14/5.

11   Egremont to Amherst, December 12, 1761, Egremont Papers, Petworth House Archives, West Sussex, England.

12   Ibid.

13   Gage to Amherst, March 20, 1762, in Amherst to Egremont, May 12, 1762, Egremont Papers, Petworth House Archives.

14   Egremont to Amherst, July 10, 1762, ibid.

15   Amherst to Egremont, April 6, 1762, ibid.; Ellis to Egremont, March 3, 1762, Egremont Papers, PRO 30/47/14/6.

16   Ellis to Egremont, March 3, 1762, Egremont Papers, PRO 30/47/14/6.

17 Egremont to Amherst, February 13, 1762, Egremont Papers, Petworth House Archives; Gipson, *Great War for the Empire*, 274.

18 Ibid., 251–53.

19 Ellis to Egremont, January 16, 1762, Egremont Papers, PRO 30/47/14/6.

20 Ibid.

21 Ibid.

22 Gipson, *Great War for the Empire*, 257–60.

23 Ibid., 262–68.

24 Ibid., 292.

25 Bute to Bedford, January 3, May 1, 1762, in Russell, ed., *Bedford Correspondence*, 3:72, 75; Hardwicke to Newcastle, April 14, 1762, Newcastle to Joseph Yorke, May 14, 1762, in Yorke, ed., *Hardwicke Correspondence*, 3:348–49, 355–57.

26 Newcastle to Hardwicke, October 3, 1762, in Yorke, ed., *Hardwicke Correspondence*, 3:419; see also editorial comment, 368–69.

27 Ellis to Egremont, March 3, 1762, Egremont Papers, PRO 30/47/14/6.

28 "Reasons for Attempting the Conquest of the Canary Islands," undated, Egremont Papers, PRO 30/47/14. The document is in Henry Ellis's hand.

29 Gipson, *Great War for the Empire*, 302.

30 Rigby wrote two letters to Bedford on the same date, September 30, 1762, in Russell, ed., *Bedford Correspondence*, 3:130–33.

31 Rigby to Bedford, September 29, 1762, ibid., 128.

32 Egremont to Bedford, October 26, 1762, ibid., 139.

33 Shute Barrington, *The Political Life of William Wildman, Viscount Barrington, Compiled from Original Papers by His Brother Shute, Bishop of Durham* (London: W. Bulmer and Company, 1814), 78, 90.

34 Fox to Bedford, October 13, 1762, in Russell, ed., *Bedford Correspondence*, 3:133–35.

35 Bute to Bedford, November 10, 1762, ibid., 152; Rashed, *Peace of Paris*, 181.

36 "Advantages which England gains by the present Treaty with France and Spain," Egremont Papers, 30/47/14. The document is in Ellis's hand.

37 William Knox, "Anecdotes and Characteristics, Lord Lansdowne," July 6, 1785, Knox Papers, 10/35, WLCL.

38 Undated list of appointees in new acquisitions, Egremont Papers, PRO 30/47/14/6; Knox to Lyttelton, February 10, 1762, HMC, *Reports on Manuscripts in Various Collections*, 6:86.

39 Gipson, *Great War for the Empire*, 308. Some of Ellis's ideas were paralleled in Shelburne's speech. For example, "By the acquisition of Florida, Great Britain has obtained the cloathing and the command of several Indian Nations, who have long been the Terror of the Inhabitants of South Carolina and Georgia and a great hindrance to the settlement of the latter." Shelburne stressed the greatest security to the colonies and the advantages to trade as results of the treaty (Shelburne Papers, 165:309–21, WLCL).

40 Wraxall, *Historical Memoirs*, 60; Gipson, *Triumphant Empire*, 23.

41 Gipson, *Great War for the Empire*, 310–11.

42 Rashed, *Peace of Paris*, 204.

43 Karl W. Schweizer, *Lord Bute: Essays in Re-enterpretation* (Leicester: Leicester University Press, 1988), 7.

44 Egremont to Grenville, February 12, 1763, in William James Smith, ed., *The Grenville Papers: Being the Correspondence of Richard Grenville, Earl Temple, and the Right Honorable George Grenville*, 2 vols. (London: John Murray, 1852), 2:29.

45 For correspondence regarding the treaty, see Egremont Papers, PRO 30/47/6; Richard Neville Neville to Bedford, February 16, 1763, in Russell, ed., *Bedford Correspondence*, 3:199–203.

46 Neville to Bedford, February 16, 1763, in Russell, ed., *Bedford Correspondence*, 3:199–203.

47 Grenville to Bedford, May 19, 1763, ibid., 230.

48 Rigby to Bedford, February 3, 1763, ibid., 185–88.

49 Rigby to Bedford, March 10, 1763, ibid., 218–20.

50 Bute to Bedford, April 2, 1763, ibid., 223–26.

51 Bedford to Bute, April 7, 1763, ibid., 227–30.

52 Grenville to Bute, March 25, 1763, in Smith, ed., *Grenville Papers*, 2:33.

53 Bute to Grenville, March 25, 1763, ibid., 32–33.

54 Memorandum by the King, [August 1765?], in Sir John Fortescue, ed., *The Correspondence of King George the Third*, 6 vols. (London: Macmillan, 1927), 1:162–66.

55 Ibid.

56 Hardwicke to Newcastle, May 13, 1763, Hardwicke to Lord Royston, August 5, 1763, in Yorke, ed., *Hardwicke Correspondence*, 3:495–96, 512–16.

57 Mr. Grenville's Diary, May 1763, in Smith, ed., *Grenville Papers*, 2:50.

58 Gipson, *Triumphant Empire*, 30.

59 Ibid., 31.

60 Ibid., 32.

61 J. Steven Watson, *The Reign of George III, 1760–1815* (Oxford: Clarendon Press, 1960), 98.

62 Jucker, ed. *Jenkinson Papers*, 192; Gipson, *Triumphant Empire*, 33.

63 Wilkes to Temple, August 29, 1763, in Smith, ed., *Grenville Papers*, 2:98.

64 Watson, *Reign of George III*, 93.

65 Egremont to Grenville, August 6, 1763, in Smith, ed., *Grenville Papers*, 2:88–89.

CHAPTER ELEVEN *The Transformation of British North America*

1 Henry Ellis to Egremont, December 15, 1762, Egremont Papers, PRO 30/47/14; an unattributed copy of Ellis's paper is in the Shelburne Papers, 60:131, WLCL, under title of "On the method to prevent giving any alarms to the Indians by taking possession of Florida and Louisiana."

2 Ellis to Egremont, December 15, 1762, Egremont Papers, PRO 30/47/14.

3 Egremont to Amherst, March 16, 1763, Amherst Papers, WLCL.

4 Alden, *John Stuart*, 135–36.

5 The governors' correspondence is printed in *Journal of the Congress of the Four Southern Governors and the Superintendent of That District, with the Five Nations of Indians at Augusta, 1763* (Charlestown: Peter Timothy, 1764), also in PRO, CO 5/65.

6 The Mortar's talk is in Georgia Council Minutes, July 14, 1763, *CRG* 9:70–77.

7 The Gun Merchant's talk is in ibid.

8   Stuart to Egremont, June 1, 1763, PRO, CO 5/65.

9   David Corkran identified the Upper Creek chief whose name was recorded as "Mustisikah" as Emistisiguo in *Creek Frontiers*, 240.

10 Talks by Stuart and Telletcher are in *Journal of the Congress*, PRO, CO 5/65, pt. 3.

11 McGillivray to Stuart, December 14, 1768, PRO, CO 5/70; *Georgia Gazette*, December 14, 1768; Georgia House Minutes, December 23, 1768, *CRG* 14:639.

12 Wright, Dobbs, Boone, Fauquier, and Stuart to Egremont, November 16, 1763, ms. CRG 37:62–65.

13 Stuart to Amherst, December 3, 1763, Amherst Papers, WLCL.

14 Emistisiguo's talk at Little Tallassee, April 10, 1764, in Wright to Gage, May 20, 1764, Gage Papers, American Series, WLCL.

15 Emistisiguo's talk at Okchoys, May 1, 1771, in K. G. Davies, ed., *Documents of the American Revolution, 1770–1783*, 21 vols. (Shannon: Irish University Press, 1972–81), 3:118–21.

16 Halifax to Wright, November 9, 1763, January 24, 1764, PRO, CO 324/40; Ellis to Knox, April 20, 30, 1762, Knox Papers, WLCL.

17 Wright to Egremont, April 20, May 6, 1763, Ms. CRG 37:36–45, 47–49.

18 Wright to Egremont, May 4, 1763, ibid., 7–11.

19 Boone to Amherst, December 6, 1763, Amherst Papers, WLCL; Gage to Halifax, August 10, 1764, PRO, CO 5/83.

20 "Hints relative to the settling of our newly acquired Territories in America," Egremont Papers, PRO 30/47/22.

21 Ibid.

22 Gipson, *Triumphant Empire*, 240–42.

23 "Plan of Forts and Establishments . . . ," Egremont Papers, PRO 30/47/22.

24 I am indebted to Professor Louis De Vorsey for the information that the map in question was an English copy of an original by the French cartographer D'Anville, published in 1752.

25 "Plan of Forts and Establishments."

26 Ibid.

27 Ibid.

28 Spaniards were, in Ellis's words, "more eligible neighbors" than the French (Ellis to Pitt, April 16, 1760, *CRG* 28, pt. 1:247–48).

29 "Plan of Forts and Establishments."

30 Clarence W. Alvord and Clarence E. Carter, eds., *The Critical Period, 1763–1765* (Springfield: Illinois State Historical Society, 1915), 11.

31 Robin F. A. Fabel, *Bombast and Broadsides: The Lives of George Johnstone* (Tuscaloosa: University of Alabama Press, 1987), 43.

32 Alvord and Carter, eds., *Critical Period*, 10.

33 The collection of papers on Canada is in PRO, CO 323/16.

34 Fabel, *Bombast and Broadsides*, 43.

35 Gage to Halifax, May 21, 1764, PRO, CO 5/83/34.

36 Fabel, *Bombast and Broadsides*, 26.

37 Donna T. McCaffrey, "Charles Townshend and Plans for British East Florida," *Florida Historical Quarterly* 68 (January 1990): 324–40.

38 Ibid., 326.

39 Egremont to Board of Trade, May 5, 1763, Shelburne Papers 64/505, WLCL; also in Adam Shortt and Arthur G. Doughty, eds., *Documents Relating to the Constitutional History of Canada, 1759–1791*, (Ottawa: King's Printer, 1918), 93–94.

40 "Remarks on Lord Barrington's plan for the settlement of the conquered countries in America," Shelburne Papers 60/143, WLCL.

41 The collection is now in the Shelburne Papers, WLCL.

42 Verner Crane, "Notes and Documents," *Mississippi Valley Historical Review* 8 (1922): 367–73, in a footnote signed C.W.A. (Clarence W. Alvord) the document is attributed to Ellis; R. A. Humphreys, "Lord Shelburne and the Proclamation of 1763," *English Historical Review* 49 (April 1934): 241–58; Gipson, *Triumphant Empire*, 44.

43 "Hints Relative to the Division and Government of the Conquered and Newly Acquired Countries in America," Shelburne Papers, 48/543; also in PRO, CO 323/16.

44 Ibid.

45 Humphreys, "Lord Shelburne," 246.

46 Shortt and Doughty, eds., *Documents*, 97–107; the report is printed as an appendix to Humphrey, "Lord Shelburne," 258–64.

47 "Particulars wherein the Report of the Board of Trade differs from the paper entitled 'Hints relative to the division and government of our new acquisitions in America,'" Egremont Papers, PRO 30/47/22.

48 Egremont to Board of Trade on settling the Governments of Canada, East and West Florida, July 14, 1763, Shelburne Papers, 64/515, WLCL. Egremont referred to James Grant, the new governor of East Florida, as "Francis" Grant and omitted George Johnstone's first name and misspelled his second.

49 Ellis's appointment, dated April 30, 1763, is in PRO, CO 323/16.

50 Lords of Trade to Egremont, August 5, 1763, in Shortt and Doughty, eds., *Documents*, 110–12.

51 Egremont to Grenville, August 6, 1763, in Smith, ed., *Grenville Papers*, 2:88–89.

52 Ibid., 50, 88–89.

53 Grenville's diary, August 20, 21, 1763, ibid., 193–94; Dudley Cosby to Edward Weston, August 22, 1763, HMC, vol. 10, *Reports on the Manuscripts of the Earl of Eglinton* (London: Eyre and Spottiswoode, 1885), 358–59.

54 Halifax to Weston, August 22, 1763, in HMC, *Reports*, 359.

55 Grenville's diary, August 23, 1763, in Smith, ed., *Grenville Papers*, 2:194.

56 Halifax to Weston, August 28, 1763, HMC, *Reports*, 359.

57 Bedford to Neville, September 5, 1763, in Russell, ed., *Bedford Correspondence*, 2:240–42.

58 Grenville Diary, August 28, 1763, in Smith, ed., *Grenville Papers*, 2:198–200.

59 Grenville Diary, September 2, 1763, ibid., 203.

60 "Anecdotes and Characteristics, Lord Lansdowne," July 6, 1785, Knox Papers, WLCL.

61 Grenville Diary, December 6, 7, 1763, in Smith, ed., *Grenville Papers*, 2:204.

62 "Anecdotes and Characteristics, Lord Lansdowne," Knox Papers, WLCL.

63 Grenville Diary, October 11, 1763, in Smith, ed., *Grenville Papers*, 2:211.

64   Joseph Read to Mr. Pettit, June 11, 1764, Read Papers, New York Historical Society.

65   Halifax to Board of Trade, September 19, 1763, in Shortt and Doughty, eds., *Documents*, 5.

66   Francis Maseres to Fowler Walker, November 19, 1767, in W. Stewart Wallace, ed., *The Maseres Letters, 1766–1768* (Toronto: Oxford University Press, 1910), 62–63.

67   Humphreys, "Lord Shelburne," 254.

68   Wright to Shelburne, November 18, 1766, Ms. CRG 37, pt. 1:141–44.

69   The date of appointment is given variously as April 3, 14, and 30, PRO CO 324/42 and 324/49.

70   *Journal of the Commissioners for Trade and Plantations*, 11:346.

71   Joseph Read to Mr. Pettit, June 11, 1764, Read Papers, New York Historical Society.

CHAPTER TWELVE   *Echoes of the Proclamation*

1   Gipson, *Triumphant Empire*, 276.

2   Halifax to John Stuart, July 10, 1764, PRO, CO 394/17.

3   Egremont to Amherst, December 12, 1761, Egremont Papers, Petworth House Archives.

4   Ellis's will is in PRO, PROB. II, 1450, Public Record Office; Maseres to Fowler Walker, November 19, 1767, in Wallace, ed., *Maseres Letters*, 62–63.

5   Johnstone to Egremont, July 13 [1763], Egremont Papers, PRO 37/40/15.

6   Ibid.

7   Ibid. There was another Ellis in public office. Welbore Ellis was secretary at war from 1763 to 1765. The context of Johnstone's letter indicates that he had Henry Ellis in mind, not Welbore. For one thing, the birthplace of Welbore Ellis, Lord Mendip, was well-known.

8   The date of Goldfrap's appointment is given in Shortt and Doughty, eds., *Documents*, 195; Hilda Neatby, *Quebec: The Revolutionary Age, 1760–1791* (Toronto: McClelland and Stewart, 1966), 51.

9   Neatby, *Quebec*, 37.

10   George Allsopp, William Mackenzie, Alex Mackenzie, Petition of Quebec Traders, n.d., in Shortt and Doughty, eds., *Documents*, 168–69.

11   Murray to Lords of Trade, October 29, 1764, ibid., 167–68, 172–73.

12   Minutes, July 29, 1766, *Journal of Commissioners for Trade and Plantations*, 12:312; George Allsopp to Lords of Treasury, Dartmouth Papers, Ms. 23, National Archives of Canada.

13   Murray to Board of Trade, April 14, 1766, PRO, CO 42/86.

14   Neatby, *Quebec*, 88.

15   "Papers delivered by Mr. Ellis relative to His Deputy in his Offices in Quebec," PRO 42/86; date of recall in Shortt and Doughty, eds., *Documents*, 192.

16   "An Account of the State of Canada from its Conquest to May 1766," Shelburne Papers, 64:525, WLCL.

17   Ibid.

18 Ibid.

19 Minutes, January 21, 1768, *Journal of the Commissioners for Trade and Plantations*, 12:5–6.

20 Gipson, *Triumphant Empire*, 175.

21 Neatby, *Quebec*, 93.

22 "Anecdotes and Characteristics, Lord Lansdowne," July 6, 1785, Knox Papers, WLCL.

23 Neatby, *Quebec*, 101.

24 Maurice Morgann to Dartmouth, May 12, 1773, Dartmouth Papers, M.G. 23, National Archives of Canada.

25 Carleton to Shelburne, December 24, 1767, in Shortt and Doughty, eds., *Documents*, 201–3.

26 Carleton to Shelburne, January 20, 1768, ibid., 205–6.

27 Hillsborough to Carleton, March 6, 1768, ibid., 207–8.

28 Ellis to Knox, December 27, 1767, Knox Papers, WLCL.

29 Ellis to Knox, August 7, 1770, ibid.

30 Ellis to Board of Trade, June 14, 1768, PRO, CO 324/42.

31 Henry Ellis to John Ellis, August 5 (n.d.), John Ellis Papers, Linnean Society Library.

32 Thomas Fleming, *The Man Who Dared the Lightning* (New York: William Morrow, 1971), 189–91. William Knox explained Hillsborough's resignation in a memorandum dated August 15, 1772, Knox Papers, WLCL.

33 Franklin's pamphlet was titled *Rules by which a great empire may be reduced to a small one*" (Fleming, *The Man Who Dared the Lightning*, 190, 217, 229); Ellis to Knox, October 17, 1772, Knox Papers, WLCL.

34 Pownall to Knox, December 3, 1773, Knox Papers, WLCL.

35 Neatby, *Quebec*, 127; Fleming, *The Man Who Dared the Lightning*, 255.

36 Ellis to Knox, December 8, 1773, Knox Papers, WLCL.

37 "An Act for Making More Effectual Provision for the Government of the Province of Quebec in North America," Dartmouth Papers, M.G. 23, National Archives of Canada.

38 Knox to Dartmouth, n.d., ibid.

39 Dartmouth to Hillsborough, May 1, 1774, ibid.

40 Bernard Donoughue, *British Politics and the American Revolution: The Path to War, 1773–1775* (London: Macmillan, 1964), 120–25.

41 Ibid., 106.

42 Ellis to Knox, July 15, 1774, Knox Papers, WLCL.

43 John Stuart to Dartmouth, December 15, 1774; Dartmouth to Stuart, February 1, 1775, PRO, CO 5/76.

CHAPTER THIRTEEN *The Inevitable Separation*

1 John Shy, *A People Numerous and Armed: Reflections on the Military Struggle for American Independence* (New York: Oxford University Press, 1976), 39, 72.

2 Wickwire points out that subministers were responsible for the Proclamation of

1763, Sugar and Stamp Acts, Townshend Duties, Quebec Act, and Boston Port Bill. See Franklin B. Wickwire, *British Subministers and Colonial America, 1763–1783* (Princeton: Princeton University Press, 1966), 182–84.

3   Jack M. Sosin, *Whitehall and the Wilderness: The Middle West in British Colonial Policy, 1760–1775* (Lincoln: University of Nebraska Press, 1961), 51–53.

4   Ellis to Pitt, August 14, 1790, Whewell Papers, Trinity College. Whewell is pronounced "Yule."

5   Ellis to Mr. Chambers, April 22, 1796, ibid.

6   Draft of newspaper article by Ellis, August 25, 1790, ibid.

7   Robert Alan Blackey, "The Political Career of George Montagu Dunk, 2nd Earl of Halifax, 1748–1771: A Study of an Eighteenth Century English Minister" (Ph.D. dissertation, New York University, 1968), 177.

8   For the Plan of 1764, PRO, CO 5/65.

9   Gage to Shelburne, February 22, 1767, in Clarence Edwin Carter, ed., *The Correspondence of General Thomas Gage with the Secretaries of State*, 2 vols. (New Haven: Yale University Press, 1931), 1:121–24.

10   Shelburne to Gage, December 11, 1766, ibid., 2:47–51.

11   Gage to Shelburne, August 20, 1767, ibid., 1:144–45.

12   Halifax to Gage, January 14, 1764, ibid., 2:9–10.

13   Jack M. Sosin, *Agents and Merchants: British Colonial Policy and the Origins of the American Revolution, 1763–1775* (Lincoln: University of Nebraska Press, 1965), 28. Halifax was indirectly connected with the Stamp Act in that Henry McCulloch submitted to him his "proposals with respect to a Stamp Duty on America" in 1755. See Smith, ed., *Grenville Papers*, 2:373–74.

14   William Knox, *The Claim of the Colonies to an Exemption from Internal Taxes Imposed by Authority of Parliament Examined* (London: W. Johnston, 1765), 15.

15   Habersham to Knox, October 28, 1765, *Georgia Historical Society Collections*, 6:44–46.

16   Ibid.

17   Blackey, "Political Career," 185.

18   Townshend to Temple, August 14, 1764, in Smith, ed., *Grenville Papers*, 2:426.

19   Grenville's Diary, March 19, 1764, ibid., 497.

20   Bedford to Marlborough, May 19, 1765, in Russell, ed., *Bedford Correspondence*, 3:278–81.

21   Rigby to Bedford, May 20, 1765, ibid., 281–82.

22   Grenville's Diary, January 6, March 14, September 22, 1764, in Smith, ed., *Grenville Papers*, 2:481, 496, 514.

23   Bushy House, built for Halifax when he was ranger of Bushy Park by George II, is now the residence of the director of the National Physical Laboratory. Hampton Court House, built by Halifax in 1757, is now a home for elderly ladies. Its music room, built later, is now the Hampton Court theater. When I visited Hampton in December 1991, the fog was so thick that I could barely make out the upper features of the house while standing in front of it. An eerie walk across Bushy Park ended in frustration; it was impossible to see Bushy House over the fence that surrounded it. Lord Halifax rented the house on Great George Street, possibly

the one eighteenth-century house on the street today. It adjoins No. 12, a building occupied by the Royal Institution of Chartered Surveyors. Earlier London residences of his were No. 75 South Audley Street in Mayfair from 1738 to 1746, No. 47 Grosvenor Square from 1747 to 1757, and briefly, No. 45 Brook Street in 1755 (information provided by Hermione Hobhouse, Survey of London, Newlands House, London).

24 Richard Cumberland, *Memoirs, Written by Himself, Containing an Account of His Life and Writings. . . .* (New York: Brisban and Brannan, 1806), 123–24.

25 Ellis to Knox, October 17, 1772, March 22, 1774, Knox Papers, WLCL.

26 Savage, ed., *Calendar of the Ellis Manuscripts*, 35.

27 William Knox, *The Controversy Between Great Britain and Her Colonies Reviewed* (London: J. Almon, 1769).

28 William Knox, *The Interests of the Merchants and Manufacturers of Great Britain in the Present Contest with the Colonies* (London: T. Cadell, 1774); Knox's *The Present State of the Nation Particularly with Respect to Its Trade, Finances, Etc. Addressed to the King and Both Houses of Parliament* (London: J. Almon, 1768) brought a blistering rebuttal from Edmund Burke, who construed it as an attack on William Pitt's opposition to the peace. Knox called Burke a "party man" in his reply, *An Appendix to the Present State of the Nation Containing a Reply to the Observation on That Pamphlet* (London: J. Almon, 1769).

29 Grenville to Knox, June 27, July 15, August 15, September 11, 1768, Knox Papers, WLCL.

30 Ellis to Knox, May 18, 1796, Whewell Papers, Trinity College.

31 Jack Greene, "William Knox's Explanation for the American Revolution," *William and Mary Quarterly* 3d. ser., 30(1973).

32 Ellis to Knox, March 22, June 27, 1774, Knox Papers, WLCL.

33 Ellis to Knox, January 22, March 10, 1783, ibid.

34 William Knox, "Anecdotes and Characteristics, Lord Lansdowne," Knox Papers, WLCL.

35 Drafts of articles by Ellis, August 25, 26, 1790, Whewell Papers, Trinity College.

CHAPTER FOURTEEN *The Empire Secured*

1 Ellis to Knox, October 17, 1772, Knox Papers, WLCL; Burke, *Genealogical and Heraldic History of the Landed Gentry of Ireland*, 205.

2 Ellis to Sargeant Marshall, February 25, 1796, Whewell Papers, Trinity College.

3 Francis Ellis to Henry Ellis, August 3, 1797, ibid.

4 Cradock, *Literary and Miscellaneous Memoirs*, 1:252–54.

5 Ibid., 227–28. There are several letters from the Twining brothers to Ellis in the Whewell Papers. Ellis frequented their quaint shop in the Strand, which stands today where it has since 1749, in the Strand across from the Inns of Court. The Twinings still own the business.

6 Cradock, *Literary and Miscellaneous Memoirs*, 2:179–80.

7 Ellis to Wilson, June 6, 1796, Whewell Papers, Trinity College.

8   Philip Thicknesse, *Sketches and Characters of the Most Eminent and Most Singular Persons Now Living*, 2 vols. (Bristol: John Wheble, 1770), 1:46.

9   Gardenstone cited in John Nichols, *Literary Anecdotes . . .* , 9 vols. (London, 1812–15), 9:533–34.

10   Bertrand to Ellis, April 24, 1785, Whewell Papers, Trinity College.

11   Philip Thicknesse, *A Year's Journey Through the Pais Bas or Austrian Netherlands* (London: J. Debrett, 1776), 102–12; Spa was in the then Austrian Netherlands.

12   Ellis to Knox, September 4, 1777, Knox Papers, WLCL.

13   Ellis to Knox, August 20, 1780, June 17, 1781, ibid.

14   The Benjamin Franklin Papers at the American Philosophical Society Library in Philadelphia list Henry Ellis as author of letters to Franklin dated December 8 and 28, 1773, regarding a new book about mocha coffee. The author of the letter almost certainly is John Ellis, the naturalist and friend of Henry Ellis.

15   Knox to Herschel, October 9, 1809, Herschel to Knox, October 13, 1809, Knox Papers, WLCL.

16   Weld, *History of the Royal Society*, 2:150–61.

17   Ellis to Sir Joseph Banks, March 6, 1789, delivered July 30, 1789, Archives of the Royal Society, Carleton House Terrace, London.

18   Undated, unsigned note, ibid.

19   Ellis to Banks, July 31, 1789, Banks to Ellis, August 1, 1789, ibid. The correspondence between Ellis and Banks is also available on Ga. reel 152/80, Georgia Department of Archives and History, Atlanta.

20   Ellis to Knox, June 17, 1781, Knox Papers, WLCL.

21   Abbé Guillaume Thomas François Raynal, *A Philosophical and Political History of the Settlements and Trade of the Europeans in the East and West Indies*, 10 vols. (1798. Reprint. 6 vols. New York: Negro Universities Press, 1969), 5:306–19.

22   Ellis to Thompson, April 22, 1796, Whewell Papers, Trinity College.

23   Ellis to Knox, November 10, 1773, Knox Papers, WLCL; Ellis to James Ellis, June 11, 1774, Whewell Papers, Trinity College.

24   Ellis to Knox, November 10, 1773, Knox Papers, WLCL.

25   Deed, Francis Lucas of Castleshane and Henry Ellis of Monaghan, September 13, 14, 1773, Ledger 298/376–7, National Registry of Deeds, Dublin. The Irish are casual about the use of their documents. Researchers are left alone in an upper chamber where huge handwritten ledgers line the shelves. Removing them to the high desks of the type associated with Ebenezer Scrooge is to risk back injury. Unfortunately, three centuries of use has blurred some of the entries.

26   Sir Charles Coote, *Statistical Survey of the County of Monaghan with Observations on the Means of Improvement* (Dublin: Graisberry and Campbell, 1801), xx, National Library, Dublin.

27   Deed, Alexander Montgomery and Henry Ellis of City of London, November 13, 1773, Ledger 229/236–7, National Registry of Deeds, Dublin.

28   Deed, John Harrison and Henry Ellis of London, August 17, 18, 1778, Ledger 321/549; Deed, Alexander Montgomery and Henry Ellis of London, January 20, 1781, Ledger 338/139–40; Deed, Thomas Tarrison and Henry Ellis of London, August 15, 1783, Ledger 351/568–69; Deed, John Ker, Cornet, Eighth Regiment,

and Henry Ellis of London, January 24, 1783, Ledger 348/459; Deed, Andrew Thomas Lord Baron Blayney and Henry Ellis of London, July 13, 1792, Ledger 452/134, ibid.

29   Ellis to Knox, November 10, 1773, Knox Papers, WLCL.

30   Livingstone, *Monaghan Story*, 161–65.

31   Ibid., 167–75.

32   John Thompson to Henry Ellis, August 29, 1798, Whewell Papers, Trinity College.

33   Coote, *Statistical Survey*, 169, 176.

34   Ellis to John Joyner Ellis, April 22, 1796, Whewell Papers, Trinity College.

35   Charlotte Collins to Ellis, May 1, 1804, ibid.

36   John Joyner to parents, December 2, 1762, ibid.

37   Gage to Barrington, May 6, 1771, in Carter, ed., *Correspondence of General Thomas Gage*, 2:575–76. The movements of the Royal Irish (Eighteenth) Regiment can be traced in Gage's correspondence.

38   Ellis to Haldimand, August 25, 1774, Liverpool Manuscripts, British Library. Charles Jenkinson, later Lord Liverpool, was secretary of war in 1774. Ellis's letter to Haldimand found its way to his office.

39   Richard Cannon, *Historical Record of the Eighteenth or the Royal Irish Regiment of Foot* (London: Parker, Furnwall, and Parker, 1848), 47.

40   A List of the Officers of the Army, War Office, April 28, 1783, 82, National Army Museum Archives, London.

41   Jenkinson to Ellis, March 30, 1780, Liverpool Manuscripts, British Library.

42   War Office Lists, 1785, 1786, 1787, National Army Museum Archives, London.

43   D. A. N. Lomax, *History of the Services of the 41st (the Welch) Regiment from Its Formation in 1719 to 1895* (Devonport: Hiorns and Miller, 1899), 30–36.

44   A. D. L. Cary and Stouppe McCance, eds., *Regimental Records of the Royal Welch Fusiliers (Late the 23rd Foot)*, 4 vols. (London: Forster Groom, 1921), 1:193–95.

45   Henry Ellis to John Joyner Ellis, April 22, 1796, Whewell Papers, Trinity College.

46   Cary and McCance, eds., *Royal Welch Fusiliers*, 1:273–74.

47   Ibid., 223.

48   Henry Walton Ellis is listed in Nova Scotia Headquarters Papers, Book O; his land transactions are in Halifax County Deeds, 39:114 and 40:394, Public Record Office of Nova Scotia, Halifax.

49   Cary and McCance, eds., *Royal Welch Fusiliers*, 1:240–41, 248–49, 253.

50   Ibid., 261–62, 272.

51   Ibid., 273–74.

52   Ibid., 283–85.

53   Ibid., 2:33. This writer inspected the memorial in a visit to Worcester in September 1992.

54   A biographical sketch of Henry Walton Ellis is in *Dictionary of National Biography*.

55   Jack Russell, *Nelson and the Hamiltons* (New York: Simon and Schuster, 1969), 22. Many of the details that follow are from this source.

56   Ibid., 85.

57   Ibid., 82.

58   Abraham Gibbs to Ellis, February 14, 1800, Whewell Papers, Trinity College.

59   Russell, *Nelson and the Hamiltons*, 106. Emma Hamilton proudly related her story about singing over the Bay of Naples to a Lady Morgan; see Constance H. D. Giglioli, *Naples in 1799: An Account of the Revolution of 1799 and of the Rise and Fall of the Parthenopean Republic* (London: John Murray, 1903), 339. Giglioli's account is very unflattering to Nelson, whom she regards as treacherous, and to Lady Hamilton, who was vulgar as well as treacherous.

60   Russell, *Nelson and the Hamiltons*, 135.

61   Abraham Gibbs to Ellis, February 14, 1800, Whewell Papers, Trinity College.

62   Emma Scott to Ellis, January 8, 1800, ibid.

63   Cary and McCance, eds., *Royal Welch Fusiliers*, 1:283–85.

64   Ellis to Hugh Elliot, June ?, 1803, Minto Papers, National Library of Scotland, Edinburgh.

65   Russell, *Nelson and the Hamiltons*, 359.

66   Ellis to Hugh Elliot, October 18, 1804, Minto Papers.

67   Ellis to Elliot, 1805, ibid.

68   Ellis to Knox, September 18, 1805, July 1804, Knox Papers, WLCL.

69   William Henry Flayhart III, *Counterpoint to Trafalgar: The Anglo-Russian Invasion of Naples, 1805–1806* (Columbia: University of South Carolina Press, 1992), 111–12. Flayhart's thesis is that the Anglo-Russian invasion made the British victory at Trafalgar possible.

70   Nelson to Gibbs, September 28, 1805, quoted in Russell, *Nelson and the Hamiltons*, 400. Nelson's reason for writing was to say, "Dear Lady Hamilton is as beautiful and as good as ever."

71   Ellis, *Voyage to Hudson's Bay*, dedication.

72   Thomas J. Stikeman to Knox, January 28, 1806, Knox Papers, WLCL.

Epilogue

1   Ellis's will is filed in Public Record Office, PROB. II, 1450.

2   See introduction to Whewell Papers, Trinity College.

3   The exception was Jimmy Carter, governor of Georgia from 1971 to 1975, who went on to the presidency of the United States, 1977 to 1981.

4   Jack P. Greene, *Imperatives, Behaviors, and Identities: Essays in Early American Cultural History* (Charlottesville: University Press of Virginia, 1992), 307.

Bibliography

PRIMARY SOURCES

Manuscript Collections

American Philosophical Society Library, Philadelphia
    Benjamin Franklin Papers
British Library, London
    Liverpool Manuscripts
Clones (Ireland) Public Library
    Griffith, Richard. *General Valuation of Rateable Property in Ireland.* Dublin: Alexander Thom and Sons, 1861.
Georgia Department of Archives and History, Atlanta
    Colonial Conveyances
    Creek Letters: Talks and Treaties (typescript)
    Letters of Governor John Reynolds and Henry Ellis from the Huntington Library, Microfilm Reel 230/39
    Letters of Henry Ellis in the Royal Society, Microfilm Reel 152/80
Georgia Historical Society, Savannah
    Antonio Waring Papers
Hagley Hall, Stourbridge, England
    Lyttelton Papers
Huntington Library, San Marino, California
    General James Abercromby Papers
    Earl of Loudoun Papers
Library of Congress, Washington, D.C.
    Amherst Papers (microfilm)
    Egremont Papers (microfilm)
Linnean Society Library, Burlington House, London
    John Ellis Papers
National Archives of Canada, Ottawa
    Chatham Papers
    Colonial Office Q Series
    Dartmouth Papers

National Army Museum Archives, London
    Regimental Histories
    War Office Lists of Officers of the Army, 1768–1800
National Library of Ireland, Dublin
    List of Historical Buildings . . . in the Town of Monaghan
    Newspapers and Maps
National Library of Scotland, Edinburgh
    Minto Papers
National Registry of Deeds, Dublin
    Eighteenth-century land sales
    Will of Thomas Ellis
New-York Historical Society, New York City
    Joseph Read Papers
Petworth House Archives, West Sussex, England
    Egremont Papers
Private Collection of Theo McMahon, Monaghan, Ireland
    Estate maps of Monaghan, 1791
    Index to Wills of Diocese of Clogher
    Tithe Applotment Book for Monaghan Parish, 1826
Public Record Office of Nova Scotia, Halifax
    Old Deed books 5 and 6
    Halifax County Deeds, 39 and 40
    Headquarters Papers, Book O
    Francis J. Audet. "Governors, Lieutenant-governors and Administrators of Nova
        Scotia, 1604–1932" (typescript)
Public Record Office, Chancery Lane, London
    Egremont Papers
    Will of Henry Ellis
Public Record Office, Kew, England
    Admiralty Office
    Colonial Office
    Treasury Office
    War Office
Royal Society Library, London
Royal Society of Arts Library, London
    Guard Books
South Carolina Department of Archives and History, Columbia
    South Carolina Records in the British Public Record Office (microfilm)
South Caroliniana Library, Columbia, South Carolina
    Dalhousie Muniments, including James Glen Correspondence (microfilm)
Staffordshire Record Office, Stafford, England
    Dartmouth Papers
Trinity College, Wren Library, Cambridge, England
    William Whewell Papers
University of Georgia Libraries, Athens
    Kenneth Coleman Photocopies

Telamon Cuyler Collection
DeRenne Collection
Henry Ellis Papers
Keith Read Collection
William L. Clements Library, Ann Arbor, Michigan
Lord Jeffrey Amherst Papers
Thomas Gage Papers
William Knox Papers
William Henry Lyttelton Papers
William Petty, Lord Shelburne Papers
Charles Townshend Papers
Worcestershire Public Record Office, Worcester, England
County Records

Published Collections and Contemporary Sources

Alvord, Clarence W., and Clarence E. Carter, eds. *The Critical Period, 1763–1765*. Collections of the Illinois Historical Society, British Series, Vol. 1. Springfield: Illinois State Historical Society, 1915.

Atkin, Edmond. *Historical Account of the Revolt of the Choctaw Indians in the Late War from the French to the British Alliance and of Their Return Since to That of the French.* London, 1753.

Baine, Rodney, and Phinizy Spalding, eds. *Some Account of the Design of the Trustees for Establishing Colonys in America by James Edward Oglethorpe.* Athens: University of Georgia Press, 1990.

Barrington, Shute. *The Political Life of William Wildman Viscount Barrington Compiled from Original Papers by His Brother Shute, Bishop of Durham.* London: W. Bulmer and Co., 1814.

Barrow, John, ed. *The Geography of Hudson's Bay: Being the Remarks of Captain W. Coats in Many Voyages to That Locality Between the Years 1727 and 1757.* London: Hakluyt Society, 1852.

Cannon, Richard. *Historical Record of the Eighteenth or the Royal Irish Regiment of Foot.* London: Parker, Furnwall, and Parker, 1848.

Carter, Clarence Edwin, ed. *The Correspondence of General Thomas Gage with the Secretaries of State.* 2 vols. New Haven: Yale University Press, 1931.

Cary, A. D. L., and Stouppe McCance, eds. *Regimental Records of the Royal Welch Fusiliers (Late the 23rd Foot).* 4 vols. London: Forster Groom, 1921.

Channing, Edward, and Archibald C. Coolidge, eds. *The Barrington-Bernard Correspondence and Illustrative Matter, 1760–1770.* Cambridge, Mass.: Harvard University Press, 1912.

Cook, Captain James, and Captain James King. *A Voyage to the Pacific Ocean Undertaken by Command of His Majesty for Making Discoveries in the Northern Hemisphere.* 4 vols. London: John Stockdale, 1784.

Coote, Sir Charles. *Statistical Survey of the County of Monaghan with Observations on the Means of Improvement.* Dublin: Graisberry and Campbell, 1801.

Corey, Albert B., and Milton W. Hamilton, eds. *The Papers of Sir William Johnson.* Vol. 10. Albany: University of the State of New York, 1951.

Cowley, Malcolm, ed. *Adventures of an African Slaver, Being a True Account of the Life of Captain Theodore Canot, Trader in Gold, Ivory and Slaves on the Coast of Guinea.* Garden City, N.Y.: Garden City Publishing Co., 1928.

Cradock, Joseph. *Literary and Miscellaneous Memoirs.* 4 vols. London: J. B. Nichols, 1828.

Cumberland, Richard. *Memoirs, Written by Himself, Containing an Account of His Life and Writings. . . .* New York: Brisban and Brannan, 1806.

Davies, K. G., ed. *Documents of the American Revolution, 1770–1783.* 21 vols. Shannon: Irish University Press, 1972–81.

De Vorsey, Louis, Jr., ed. *De Brahm's Report of the General Survey in the Southern District of North America.* Columbia: University of South Carolina Press, 1971.

Dobree, Bonamy, ed. *The Letters of Philip Dormer Stanhope, Fourth Earl of Chesterfield.* 6 vols. London: Eyre and Spottiswoode, 1932.

Ellis, Henry. "An Account of the History of the Weather in Georgia." *London Magazine,* July 1759, pp. 371–72.

———. *Considerations on the Great Advantages Which Would Arise from the Discovery of the North West Passage and a Clear Account of the Most Practicable Method for Attempting That Discovery.* London, 1750.

———. *A Voyage to Hudson's Bay by the Dobbs Galley and California in the Years 1746 and 1747 for Discovering a North West Passage with an Accurate Survey of the Coast and a Short Natural History of the Country.* London: H. Whitridge, 1748.

Ellis, William Smith. *Notices of the Ellises of England, Scotland and Ireland from the Conquest to the Present Times. . . .* 4 supplements. London: Privately printed, 1857–66.

Flick, Alexander C., ed. *The Papers of Sir William Johnson.* Vols. 4, 9. Albany: University of the State of New York, 1925, 1939.

Fortescue, Sir John, ed. *The Correspondence of King George the Third.* 6 vols. London: Macmillan, 1927.

Garden, Francis, Lord Gardenstone. *Travelling Memorandums Made in a Tour upon the Continent of Europe in the Years 1786, 1787 and 1788.* 2 vols. Edinburgh: Bell and Bradfute, 1792.

Geikie, Sir Archibald. *The Record of the Royal Society of London.* London: Royal Society, 1912.

Georgia Historical Society Collections. Vol. 8: *Letter Book of Thomas Rasberry, 1758–1761.* 21 vols. Savannah: Published by the Society, 1840–1989.

———. Vol. 6: *The Letters of Hon. James Habersham, 1756–1775.*

Hawes, Lilla M., ed. "Letters to the Georgia Colonial Agent, July 1762 to January 1771." *GHQ* 36 (September 1952): 250–86.

Historical Manuscripts Commission. Vol. 10. *Reports on the Manuscripts of the Earl of Eglinton.* London: Eyre and Spottiswoode, 1885.

———. Vol. 6. *Reports on Manuscripts in Various Collections.* Dublin: John Falconer, 1909. Reprinted as *The Manuscripts of Captain Howard Vincente Knox.* Boston: Gregg Press, 1972.

The Importance of Effectually Supporting the Royal African Company of England. London: M. Cooper, 1744.

Jacobs, Wilbur R., ed. *Indians of the Southern Colonial Frontier: The Edmond Atkin Report and Plan of 1755.* Columbia: University of South Carolina Press, 1954.

Journal of the Commissioners for Trade and Plantations. Vols. 11, 12, 13. London: His Majesty's Stationery Office, 1935.

Journal of the Congress of the Four Southern Governors and the Superintendent of That District, with the Five Nations of Indians at Augusta, 1763. Charlestown: Peter Timothy, 1764.

Jucker, Ninetta S., ed. *The Jenkinson Papers, 1760–1766.* London: Macmillan, 1949.

Juricek, John T. *Georgia Treaties, 1733–1763.* Frederick, Md.: University Publications of America, 1989. Vol. 11 in Alden T. Vaughan, ed., *Early American Indian Documents: Treaties and Laws, 1607–1789.* 11 vols. Frederick, Md.: University Publications of America, 1979–89.

Knox, William. *An Appendix to the Present State of the Nation Containing a Reply to the Observations on That Pamphlet.* London: J. Almon, 1769.

——. *The Claim of the Colonies to an Exemption from Internal Taxes Imposed by Authority of Parliament Examined.* London: W. Johnston, 1765.

——. *The Controversy Between Great Britain and Her Colonies Reviewed.* London: J. Almon, 1769.

——. *The Interests of the Merchants and Manufacturers of Great Britain in the Present Contest with the Colonies.* London: T. Cadell, 1774.

——. *The Present State of the Nation Particularly with Respect to Its Trade, Finances, etc. Addressed to the King and Both Houses of Parliament.* London: J. Almon, 1768.

——. *Three Tracts Respecting the Conversion and Instruction of the Free Indians and Negroe Slaves in the Colonies Addressed to the Venerable Society for the Propagation of the Gospel in Foreign Parts.* London: J. Debrett, 1768.

Labaree, Leonard W., Whitfield J. Bell, Helen C. Boatfield, and Helene H. Fineman, eds. *The Papers of Benjamin Franklin.* Vol. 4. New Haven: Yale University Press, 1961.

Lewis, W. S., ed. *A Selection of the Letters of Horace Walpole.* 2 vols. New York: Harper and Brothers, 1926.

Lomax, D. A. N. *History of the Services of the 41st (the Welch) Regiment from Its Formation in 1719 to 1895.* Devonport: Hiorns and Miller, 1899.

Lynam, Robert, ed. *The Complete Works of the Late Rev. Philip Skelton.* 6 vols. London: Richard Baynes, 1824.

McDowell, William L., Jr., ed. *Colonial Records of South Carolina: Documents Relating to Indian Affairs, May 2, 1750–August 7, 1754.* Columbia: South Carolina Archives Department, 1958.

——. *Documents Relating to Indian Affairs, 1754–1765: Colonial Records of South Carolina.* Columbia: University of South Carolina Press, 1970.

McPherson, Robert G., ed. *The Journal of the Earl of Egmont.* Athens: University of Georgia Press, 1962.

Martin, Eveline, ed. *Nicholas Owen, Journal of a Slave-Dealer: "A View of Some Remarkable Axcedents in the Life of Nics. Owen on the Coast of Africa and America from the Year 1746 to the Year 1757."* New York: Houghton Mifflin, 1930.

Miller, Christy. *The Voyages of Captain Luke Foxe of Hull and Captain Thomas James of*

Bristol in Search of a North-West Passage in 1631–32. New York: Burt, Franklin, 1893.

Minto, Countess of, ed. *Life and Letters of Sir Gilbert Elliot, First Earl of Minto, from 1751 to 1806.* 3 vols. London: Longmans, Green, 1874.

Murdoch, Beamish. *A History of Nova-Scotia or Acadie.* 2 vols. Halifax: James Barnes, 1866.

Nichols, John. *Illustrations of the Literary History of the Eighteenth Century Consisting of Authentic Memoirs and Original Letters of Eminent Persons and Intended as a Sequel to the Literary Anecdotes.* London: Printed for the author, 1817.

———. *Literary Anecdotes. . . .* 9 vols. London: Printed for the author, 1812–15.

Rich, E. E., ed. *James Isham's Observations on Hudson's Bay, 1743.* Toronto: Champlain Society, 1949.

Rowland, Dunbar, A. G. Sanders, and Patricia Kay Galloway. *Mississippi Provincial Archives: French Dominion, 1749–1763.* 5 vols. Baton Rouge: Louisiana State University Press, 1932–84.

Royal Society. *Philosophical Transactions.* Vols. 47, 48, 49, 50, 51.

Russell, Lord John, ed. *Correspondence of John, Fourth Duke of Bedford.* 3 vols. London: Longman, Brown, Green and Longmans, 1846.

Savage, Spencer, ed. *Catalogue of the Manuscripts in the Library of the Linnean Society of London, Part IV, Calendar of the Ellis Manuscripts.* London: Printed for the Linnean Society, 1948.

Shortt, Adam, and Arthur G. Doughty, eds. *Documents Relating to the Constitutional History of Canada, 1759–1791.* Ottawa: King's Printer, 1918.

Smith, William James, ed. *The Grenville Papers: Being the Correspondence of Richard Grenville, Earl Temple, and the Right Hon. George Grenville.* 2 vols. London: John Murray, 1852.

Stevens, S. K., Donald Kent, and Autumn L. Leonard, eds. *The Papers of Henry Bouquet.* 2 vols. Harrisburg: Pennsylvania Historical and Museum Commission, 1972.

Sullivan, James, ed. *The Papers of Sir William Johnson.* Vol. 3. Albany: University of the State of New York, 1921.

Swaine, Charles. *An Account of a Voyage for the Discovery of a North-West Passage by Hudson's Streights to the Western and Southern Ocean of America Performed in the Years 1746 and 1747 in the Ship California Francis Smith Commander.* 2 vols. London: Jolliffe, Corbett and Clarke, 1748.

Thicknesse, Philip. *Sketches and Characters of the Most Eminent and Most Singular Persons Now Living.* 2 vols. Briston: John Wheble, 1770.

———. *A Year's Journey Through the Pais Bas or Austrian Netherlands.* London: J. Debrett, 1776.

Timberlake, Henry. *Memoirs of Lieut. Henry Timberlake.* 1927. Reprint. New York: Arno Press, 1971.

Wallace, W. Stewart, ed. *The Maseres Letters, 1766–1768.* Toronto: Oxford University Press, 1910.

Weld, Charles Richard. *A History of the Royal Society with Memoirs of the Presidents.* 2 vols. London: John W. Parker, 1848.

Williams, Samuel Cole, ed. *Adair's History of the American Indian.* New York: Promontory Press, 1974.

Wraxall, Nathaniel William. *Historical Memoirs of My Own Time*. 1815. Reprint. London: Kegan, Paul, Trench, Trubner, 1904.

Wyndham, Henry Penruddocke, ed. *The Diary of the Late George Bubb Dodington Baron of Melcombe Regis, from March 8, 1749, to February 6, 1761*. Salisbury: E. Easton, 1784.

Yorke, Philip C., ed. *The Life and Correspondence of Philip Yorke, Earl of Hardwicke, Lord High Chancellor of Great Britain*. 3 vols. 1913. Reprint. New York: Octagon Books, 1977.

SECONDARY WORKS

Books

Abbot, William Wright. *The Royal Governors of Georgia, 1754–1775*. Chapel Hill: University of North Carolina Press, 1959.

Alden, John R. *John Stuart and the Southern Colonial Frontier: A Study of Indian Relations, War, Trade, and Land Problems in the Southern Wilderness, 1754–1775*. New York: Gordian Press, 1966.

Basye, Arthur Herbert. *The Lords Commissioners of Trade and Plantations Commonly Known as the Board of Trade, 1748–1782*. New Haven: Yale University Press, 1925.

Billington, Ray Allen. *Westward Expansion: A History of the American Frontier*. New York: Collier-Macmillan, 1967.

Brebner, John Bartlett. *The Neutral Yankees of Nova Scotia: A Marginal Colony During the Revolutionary Years*. New York: Columbia University Press, 1937.

Browning, Reed. *The Duke of Newcastle*. New Haven: Yale University Press, 1975.

Bull, Kinloch, Jr. *The Oligarchs in Colonial and Revolutionary Charleston: Lieutenant Governor William Bull II and His Family*. Columbia: University of South Carolina Press, 1991.

Burke, Sir Bernard. *A Genealogical and Heraldic History of the Landed Gentry of Ireland*. London: Harrison and Sons, 1912.

Butterfield, Herbert. *George III and the Historians*. New York: Macmillan, 1959.

Cashin, Edward J., ed. *Colonial Augusta: "Key of the Indian Countrey."* Macon: Mercer University Press, 1986.

Clarke, Desmond. *Arthur Dobbs, Esquire, 1689–1765, Surveyor-General of Ireland, Prospector and Governor of North Carolina*. Chapel Hill: University of North Carolina Press, 1957.

Coleman, Kenneth. *Colonial Georgia: A History*. New York: Charles Scribner's Sons, 1976.

Coleman, Kenneth, and Charles Stephen Gurr, eds. *Dictionary of Georgia Biography*. 2 vols. Athens: University of Georgia Press, 1983.

Corkran, David H. *The Creek Frontier, 1540–1783*. Norman: University of Oklahoma Press, 1967.

Crane, Verner W. *The Southern Frontier*. 1929. Reprint. Ann Arbor: University of Michigan Press, 1959.

Crouse, Nellis M. *The Search for the Northwest Passage*. New York: Columbia University Press, 1934.

Curtin, Philip D. *The Tropical Atlantic in the Age of the Slave Trade.* Washington, D.C.: American Historical Association, 1991.

Davis, Harold. *The Fledgling Province: Social and Cultural Life in Colonial Georgia, 1733–1776.* Chapel Hill: University of North Carolina Press, 1976.

Davis, Rose Mary. *The Good Lord Lyttelton: A Study in Eighteenth Century Politics and Culture.* Bethlehem, Pa.: Times Publishing Company, 1939.

Donoughue, Bernard. *British Politics and the American Revolution: The Path to War, 1773–1775.* London: Macmillan, 1964.

Fabel, Robin F. A. *Bombast and Broadsides: The Lives of George Johnstone.* Tuscaloosa: University of Alabama Press, 1987.

Fedden, Robin. *Petworth.* London: Curwen Press, 1973.

Flayhart, William Henry II. *Counterpoint to Trafalgar: The Anglo-Russian Invasion of Naples, 1805–1806.* Columbia: University of South Carolina Press, 1992.

Fleming, Thomas. *The Man Who Dared the Lightning.* New York: William Morrow, 1971.

Gallay, Alan. *The Formation of a Planter Elite: Jonathan Bryan and the Southern Colonial Frontier.* Athens: University of Georgia Press, 1989.

Garlick, Kenneth. *Sir Thomas Lawrence: A Complete Catalogue of the Oil Paintings.* New York: New York University Press, 1989.

Gayarré, Charles. *History of Louisiana.* 2 vols. New Orleans: James A. Gresham, 1879.

Giglioli, Constance H. D. *Naples in 1799: An Account of the Revolution of 1799 and of the Rise and Fall of the Parthenopean Republic.* London: John Murray, 1903.

Gipson, Lawrence Henry. *The British Isles and the American Colonies: Great Britain and Ireland, 1748–1754.* New York: Knopf, 1958.

———. *The British Isles and the American Colonies: The Northern Plantations.* New York: Knopf, 1960.

———. *The Great War for the Empire: The Culmination, 1760–1763.* New York: Knopf, 1953.

———. *The Triumphant Empire: New Responsibilities Within the Enlarged Empire, 1763–1766.* New York: Knopf, 1956.

Greene, Jack P. *Imperatives, Behaviors, and Identities: Essays in Early American Cultural History.* Charlottesville: University Press of Virginia, 1992.

Harlow, Vincent T. *The Founding of the Second British Empire, 1763–1793.* 2 vols. New York: Longmans, Green, 1952.

Herbin, John Frederic. *The History of Grand-Pre.* St. John, New Brunswick: Barnes and Company, n.d.

Ivers, Larry E. *Drums on the Southern Frontier: Military Colonization of Georgia, 1733–1749.* Chapel Hill: University of North Carolina Press, 1979.

Jackson, Harvey H., and Phinizy Spalding. *Forty Years of Diversity: Essays on Colonial Georgia.* Athens: University of Georgia Press, 1984.

Kenlon, John. *Fourteen Years a Sailor.* New York: George H. Doran, 1923.

Lanctot, Gustave. *A History of Canada: From the Treaty of Utrecht to the Treaty of Paris, 1713–1763.* Cambridge, Mass.: Harvard University Press, 1965.

Livingstone, Peadar. *The Monaghan Story: A Documented History of the County Monaghan from the Earliest Times to 1976.* Enniskillen: Clogher Historical Society, 1980.

Long, J. C. *George III: The Story of a Complex Man.* Boston: Little, Brown, 1961.

MacNutt, W. S. *The Atlantic Provinces: The Emergence of Colonial Society, 1712–1857.* Toronto: McClelland and Stewart, 1968.

Maxwell, Constantia. *Country and Town in Ireland Under the Georges.* Dundalk: Dundalgan Press, 1949.

M'Call, Hugh. *The House of Downshire: A Sketch of Its History from 1600 to 1868.* Belfast: Archer and Sons, 1881.

McCracken, David. *Junius and Philip Francis.* Boston: Twayne, 1979.

McKelvey, James Lee. *George III and Lord Bute.* Durham: Duke University Press, 1973.

Murphy, Jeannette. *To the Arctic!* 1934. Reprint. Chicago: University of Chicago Press, 1970.

Namier, Sir Lewis. *Crossroads of Power.* New York: Macmillan, 1962.

——. *England in the Age of the American Revolution.* London: Macmillan, 1963.

Neatby, Hilda. *Quebec: The Revolutionary Age, 1760–1791.* Toronto: McClelland and Stewart, 1966.

Neatby, Leslie H. *In Quest of the North West Passage.* New York: Thomas Y. Crowell, 1958.

Pares, Richard. *King George III and the Politicians.* London: Oxford University Press, 1953.

Porter, Dale H. *The Abolition of the Slave Trade in England, 1784–1807.* Archon Books, 1970.

Rashed, Zenab Esmat. *The Peace of Paris, 1763.* Liverpool: Liverpool University Press, 1951.

Rawlyk, George A. *Nova Scotia's Massachusetts: A Study of Massachusetts–Nova Scotia Relations, 1630 to 1784.* Montreal: McGill-Queen's University Press, 1973.

Raynal, Abbé Guillaume Thomas François. *A Philosophical and Political History of the Settlements and Trade of the Europeans in the East and West Indies.* 1798. Reprint. 6 vols. New York: Negro Universities Press, 1969.

Rea, Robert R. *Major Robert Farmar of Mobile.* Tuscaloosa: University of Alabama Press, 1990.

Reese, Trevor Richard. *Colonial Georgia: A Study in British Imperial Policy in the Eighteenth Century.* Athens: University of Georgia Press, 1963.

Rude, George. *Wilkes and Liberty: A Social Study of 1763 to 1774.* London: Oxford University Press, 1962.

Rushe, Denis Carolan. *History of Monaghan for Two Hundred Years, 1660–1860.* Dundalk: Wm. Tempest, 1921.

——. *Monaghan in the Eighteenth Century.* Dublin: M. H. Gill and Son, 1916.

Russell, Jack. *Nelson and the Hamiltons.* New York: Simon and Schuster, 1969.

Schweizer, Karl W. *Lord Bute: Essays in Re-interpretation.* Leicester: Leicester University Press, 1988.

Scott, H. M. *British Foreign Policy in the Age of the American Revolution.* Oxford: Clarendon Press, 1990.

Sherrard, O. A. *Freedom from Fear.* New York: St. Martin's Press, 1959.

Shy, John. *A People Numerous and Armed: Reflections on the Military Struggle for American Independence.* New York: Oxford University Press, 1976.

Sosin, Jack M. *Agents and Merchants: British Colonial Policy and the Origins of the American Revolution, 1763–1775.* Lincoln: University of Nebraska Press, 1965.

——. *Whitehall and the Wilderness: The Middle West in British Colonial Policy 1760–1775.* Lincoln: University of Nebraska Press, 1961.

Spalding, Phinizy. *Oglethorpe in America.* 1977. Reprint. Athens: University of Georgia Press, 1984.

Spalding, Phinizy, and Harvey H. Jackson, eds. *Oglethorpe in Perspective: Georgia's Founder After Two Hundred Years.* Tuscaloosa: University of Alabama Press, 1989.

Stevens, William Bacon. *A History of Georgia from Its First Discovery by Europeans to the Adoption of the Present Constitution in MDCCXCVIII.* 2 vols. 1847. Reprint. Savannah: Beehive Press, 1972.

TePaske, John Jay. *The Governorship of Spanish Florida, 1700–1763.* Durham: Duke University Press, 1964.

Thomson, Mark A. *The Secretaries of State, 1681–1782.* Oxford: Clarendon Press, 1932.

The Town of Stewiacke, Nova Scotia. Stewiacke: Centennial Project, 1967.

Twining, Sam. *Tea and Twinings: A History of the Famous Tea Company.* London: R. Twining and Company, 1988.

Valentine, Alan. *The British Establishment: An Eighteenth-Century Biographical Dictionary, 1760–1784.* 2 vols. Norman: University of Oklahoma Press, 1970.

——. *Lord North.* 2 vols. Norman: University of Oklahoma Press, 1967.

Van Every, Dale. *Forth to the Wilderness: The First American Frontier, 1754–1774.* New York: William Morrow, 1961.

Watson, J. Steven. *The Reign of George III, 1760–1815.* Oxford: Clarendon Press, 1960.

Winzerling, Oscar William. *Acadian Odyssey.* Baton Rouge: Louisiana State University Press, 1955.

Wickwire, Franklin B. *British Subministers and Colonial America, 1763–1783.* Princeton: Princeton University Press, 1966.

Wilkes, John W. *A Whig in Power: The Political Career of Henry Pelham.* Evanston: Northwestern University Press, 1964.

Wood, Betty. *Slavery in Colonial Georgia, 1730–1775.* Athens: University of Georgia Press, 1984.

Wyndham, Hugh Archibald. *A Family History, 1688–1837: The Wyndhams of Somerset, Sussex and Wiltshire.* London: Oxford University Press, 1850.

Journal Articles

Anderson, J. Randolph. "The Spanish Era in Georgia History." *GHQ* 20 (September 1936): 210–38.

Baine, Rodney. "James Oglethorpe and the Parliamentary Election of 1754." *GHQ* 71 (Fall 1987): 451–60.

——. "Myths of Mary Musgrove." *GHQ* 76 (Summer 1992): 428–35.

Coulter, E. Merton. "The Acadians in Georgia." *GHQ* 47 (March 1963): 68–75.

Crane, Verner. "Notes and Documents." *Mississippi Valley Historical Review* 8 (1922): 367–73.

Greene, Jack P. "William Knox's Explanation for the American Revolution." *William and Mary Quarterly*, 3d ser., 30 (1973): 293–306.

Groner, Julius, and Robert R. Rea. "John Ellis, King's Agent, and West Florida." *Florida Historical Quarterly* 66 (April 1988): 385–98.

Hackmann, W. Kent. "George Grenville and English Politics in 1763." *Yale University Library Gazette*, April 1990, pp. 158–66.

Humphreys, R. A. "Lord Shelburne and the Proclamation of 1763." *English Historical Review* 49 (April 1934): 241–58.

McArthur, Duncan. "The British Board of Trade and Canada, 1760–1774." *Annual Report*. Ottawa: Canadian Historical Association, 1932, pp. 97–113.

McCaffrey, Donna T. "Charles Townshend and Plans for British East Florida." *Florida Historical Quarterly* 68 (January 1990): 324–40.

Stearns, Raymond Phineas. "Colonial Fellows of the Royal Society of London, 1661–1788." *William and Mary Quarterly* 3d ser., 3 (April 1946): 208–68.

Tabor, Paul. "Bermuda Grass: A Georgia Name?" *GHQ* 52 (June 1968): 199–202.

Waller, Tom. "Henry Ellis, Enlightenment Gentleman." *GHQ* 64 (Fall 1979): 364–76.

Dissertations and Theses

Attig, Clarence John. "William Henry Lyttelton: A Study in Colonial Administration." Ph.D. dissertation, University of Nebraska, 1958.

Blackey, Robert Alan. "The Political Career of George Montagu Dunk, 2nd Earl of Halifax, 1748–1771: A Study of an Eighteenth Century English Minister." Ph.D. dissertation, New York University, 1968.

Cook, James F. "William Knox, Georgia Official and Pamphleteer for George Grenville." M.A. thesis, Emory University, 1962.

Groner, Julius. "Some Aspects of the Life and Work of John Ellis, King's Agent for West Florida, 1763 to 1776." Ph.D. dissertation, Loyola University of Chicago, 1987.

Newspapers

Georgia Gazette, Savannah, Georgia.
Irish Times, Dublin, Ireland.
London Chronicle, London, England.
South Carolina Gazette, Charlestown, South Carolina.

Index